The Art of Public Speaking

2023 RELEASE

Stephen E. Lucas
University of Wisconsin—Madison

Paul Stob
Vanderbilt University

Mc
Graw
Hill

THE ART OF PUBLIC SPEAKING: 2023 RELEASE

Published by McGraw Hill LLC, 1325 Avenue of the Americas, New York, NY 10019. Copyright ©2024 by Stephen E. Lucas. All rights reserved. Printed in the United States of America. Previous editions ©2020, 2015, and 2012. No part of this publication may be reproduced or distributed in any form or by any means, or stored in a database or retrieval system, without the prior written consent of McGraw Hill LLC, including, but not limited to, in any network or other electronic storage or transmission, or broadcast for distance learning.

Some ancillaries, including electronic and print components, may not be available to customers outside the United States.

This book is printed on acid-free paper.

1 2 3 4 5 6 7 8 9 LWI 28 27 26 25 24 23

ISBN 978-1-265-45564-4 (bound edition)
MHID 1-265-45564-3 (bound edition)
ISBN 978-1-265-45708-2 (loose-leaf edition)
MHID 1-265-45708-5 (loose-leaf edition)
ISBN 978-1-265-45666-5 (instructor's edition)
MHID 1-265-45666-6 (instructor's edition)

Executive Portfolio Manager: *Sarah Remington*
Lead Product Developer: *Betty Chen*
Marketing Manager: *Natalie Graner*
Associate Program Manager: *Danielle Clement*
Content Project Manager: *Vanessa McClune*
Manufacturing Project Manager: *Laura Fuller*
Content Licensing Specialist: *Sarah Flynn*
Cover Image: *©skyboysv/Shutterstock*
Compositor: *Aptara®, Inc.*

All credits appearing on page or at the end of the book are considered to be an extension of the copyright page.

Library of Congress Cataloging-in-Publication Data

Names: Lucas, Stephen, 1946- author. | Stob, Paul, author.
Title: The art of public speaking / Stephen E. Lucas, University of
  Wisconsin, Madison, Paul Stob, Vanderbilt University.
Description: 2023 release. | New York, NY : McGraw Hill LLC, [2024] |
  Includes index.
Identifiers: LCCN 2022029544 (print) | LCCN 2022029545 (ebook) | ISBN
  9781265455644 (bound edition) | ISBN 9781265457082 (loose-leaf edition)
  | ISBN 9781260095470 (ebook) | ISBN 9781265461331 (ebook other)
Classification: LCC PN4129.15 .L83 2024 (print) | LCC PN4129.15 (ebook) |
  DDC 808.5/1—dc23
LC record available at https://lccn.loc.gov/2022029544
LC ebook record available at https://lccn.loc.gov/2022029545

The Internet addresses listed in the text were accurate at the time of publication. The inclusion of a website does not indicate an endorsement by the authors or McGraw Hill LLC, and McGraw Hill LLC does not guarantee the accuracy of the information presented at these sites.

mheducation.com/highered

About the Authors

Stephen E. Lucas is Professor Emeritus in the Department of Communication Arts at the University of Wisconsin. His major books include *Portents of Rebellion: Rhetoric and Revolution in Philadelphia, 1765–1776; Words of a Century: The Top 100 American Speeches, 1900–1999;* and *Rhetoric, Independence, and Nationhood, 1760–1800.* A Distinguished Scholar of the National Communication Association, he has received the association's Golden Anniversary Book Award and Golden Anniversary Monograph Award.

He has also received a number of teaching awards, including the Chancellor's Award for Excellence in Teaching at the University of Wisconsin and the National Communication Association's Donald H. Ecroyd Award for Outstanding Teaching in Higher Education. His many pedagogical innovations have had a profound influence in the United States and beyond, and *The Art of Public Speaking* has been translated into multiple languages, including Chinese, Portuguese, Korean, Romanian, and Japanese.

Professor Lucas and his wife, Patty, split their time between Madison, Wisconsin, and Naples, Florida. They have two sons and four granddaughters.

Stephen E. Lucas

Paul Stob is Professor of Communication Studies at Vanderbilt University. A scholar of rhetorical criticism and American public address, his books include *William James and the Art of Popular Statement* and *Intellectual Populism: Democracy, Inquiry, and the People,* which received the James A. Winans-Herbert A. Wichelns Memorial Award for Distinguished Scholarship in Rhetoric and Public Address from the National Communication Association.

An accomplished teacher, Professor Stob teaches courses on public speaking, social movements, and American public address. He has received Vanderbilt's Jeffrey Nordhaus Award for Excellence in Undergraduate Teaching and the Faculty Advisor Award in the Humanities. This is his first edition as co-author of *The Art of Public Speaking.*

Paul Stob lives in Nashville, Tennessee, with his wife, Sarah. They have one son, Elliott, and two dogs, Missy and Reggie.

Vanderbilt University

Brief Contents

Contents

Mannic Media

Rawpixel/Shutterstock

Tom Cooper/Getty Images

Stefan Puchner/picture alliance/Getty Images

Randy Shropshire/Getty Images

Andrea Domeniconi/Alamy Stock Photo

SDI Productions/Getty Images

SPEECHES BY GENRE

INTRODUCTORY SPEECHES

INFORMATIVE SPEECHES

PERSUASIVE SPEECHES

SPEECHES OF PRESENTATION

SPEECHES OF ACCEPTANCE

COMMEMORATIVE SPEECHES

ONLINE SPEECHES

A Note from the Authors

When the first edition of *The Art of Public Speaking* was published in 1983, no one could have anticipated the extraordinary response it would receive. We are deeply appreciative of the students and teachers who have made it the leading work on its subject at colleges and universities across the United States and around the world.

In preparing this update, we have retained what readers have identified as the main strengths of the book. It is informed by classical and contemporary theories of rhetoric, but it does not present theory for its own sake. Keeping a steady eye on the practical skills of public speaking, it offers full coverage of all major aspects of speech preparation and presentation.

It also follows David Hume's advice that one "who would teach eloquence must do it chiefly by examples." Whenever possible, we have tried to show the principles of public speaking in action in addition to describing them. Thus you will find in the book a large number of narratives, speech excerpts, and full sample speeches that illustrate the principles of effective public speaking.

Because the immediate task facing students is to present speeches in the classroom, we rely heavily on examples that relate directly to students' classroom needs and experiences. The speech classroom, however, is a training ground where students develop skills that will serve them throughout life. Therefore, we also include a large number of illustrations drawn from the kinds of speaking experiences students will face after they graduate from college.

Because speeches are performative acts, students need to be able to view speakers in action as well as to read their words on the printed page. *The Art of Public Speaking* has an extensive video program that is available on Connect, McGraw Hill's online learning platform. The video program includes 53 full student speeches, plus more than 80 speech excerpts. Nine of the full speeches and 19 of the excerpts are new to this update.

Connect also provides a wide range of teaching and learning resources in addition to the speech videos. These resources include SmartBook, Video Capture powered by GoReact, hands-on study tools, critical-thinking exercises, speech-analysis questions, worksheets, assessment forms, and more. Taken together, *The Art of Public Speaking* and the digital resources available on Connect provide a time-tested interactive public speaking program that meets the needs of students and teachers alike.

The Art of Public Speaking has changed over the years in response to changes in technology, student demographics, and instructional needs. But it has never lost sight of the fact that the most important part of speaking is thinking. The ability to think critically is vital to a world in which personality and image too often substitute for thought and substance. While helping students become capable, responsible speakers, *The Art of Public Speaking* also aims to help them become capable, responsible thinkers who value the role of civil discourse in a democratic society.

Highlights of the 2023 Release of
The Art of Public Speaking

The award-winning *Art of Public Speaking* offers a time-tested approach that has made it the most widely used college textbook on its subject in the world. Seamlessly coordinated with Connect, McGraw Hill's pathbreaking online program, it supplies a proven set of teaching and learning tools that is without parallel among public speaking books.

For experienced instructors, *The Art of Public Speaking* presents a solid, fully customizable foundation and an abundance of teaching aids from which to choose, allowing for complete flexibility in the course. For novice instructors, its wisdom, steady hand, and unmatched ancillary package instill confidence and build success in the classroom from day one.

- **Expanded chapter on presenting online speeches.** Building on the innovative coverage of online speaking in the previous edition, this fully updated chapter gives students the guidance they need to make effective online presentations. Distinguishing between recorded and real-time online speeches, it explains the unique features of each and how students can adapt to those features when preparing, rehearsing, and delivering their speeches. Practical guidelines help students control the visual environment, create a suitable relationship with the online audience, and use online presentation software skillfully and professionally. The chapter also contains a new section devoted to optimizing visual aids in online speeches. Three full sample speeches with commentary—one in this chapter, one in Chapter 4, and one in Chapter 15—illustrate the principles of effective online speaking in action. Videos of the speeches are available on Connect in both final and needs improvement versions.

- **New full student speeches.** *The Art of Public Speaking* video program is designed to bridge the gap between the written page and the spoken word. Toward this end, the 2023 Release has nine new full speeches for analysis and discussion, all of which are available in both print and digital formats. They include three new introductory speeches, a new informative speech, and two new persuasive speeches—plus three new needs improvement speeches. Two of the new speeches also provide models of online public speaking.

- **Other video resources.** *The Art of Public Speaking*'s video program also includes more than 80 speech excerpts that are fully integrated into the eBook. Students can access these excerpts—along with full speeches—as they read the book to see the principles of public speaking in action. Whether a full speech or an excerpt, each video illustrates specific skills and concepts from the text.

- **Fresh real-world examples.** Every chapter of *The Art of Public Speaking* opens with an engaging and relevant example, and dozens of additional examples appear throughout the chapters, each demonstrating the importance—and art—of public speaking in school, business, and social settings. As in every edition, examples have been updated for currency, relevance, and interest.

- **Updated MLA and APA citation models.** Chapter 7, on gathering materials, presents all-new sample bibliography entries, reflecting the latest MLA and APA citation formats to help students correctly cite academic, digital, and other sources. As in each edition, the chapter as a whole has been revised to reflect technological changes.

- **Enhanced discussion of presentation technology.** Guidance on the use of visual aids and presentation technology has been updated in accord with current developments. This guidance can be found both in the chapter on visual aids and in the chapter on presenting speeches online. Best practices are illustrated by abundant examples in the book and in speech videos.

Resources for Instructors

- **Annotated Instructor's Edition.** The Annotated Instructor's Edition provides a wealth of teaching aids for each chapter in the book. It is also cross-referenced with Connect, the *Instructor's Manual,* and other supplements that accompany *The Art of Public Speaking.*

- **Instructor's Manual.** This comprehensive guide to teaching from *The Art of Public Speaking* contains suggested course outlines and speaking assignments; chapter outlines; supplementary exercises and classroom activities; and teaching tips for all exercises and activities.

- **Test Bank.** The Test Bank furnishes close to 3,000 exam questions based on *The Art of Public Speaking.*

- **PowerPoint Slides with Video Clips.** The PowerPoint presentations for *The Art of Public Speaking* provide chapter highlights that help instructors create focused, individualized lesson plans utilizing high-quality slides developed specifically for this update.

- **Digital Instructional Materials.** McGraw Hill's Connect provides access to a host of digital resources, including the *Instructor's Manual,* Test Bank, PowerPoint Slides, *Teaching Public Speaking Online, Selections from the Communication Teacher,* and the *Handbook for Teachers of Non-Native Speakers of English.*

- **Speeches for Analysis and Discussion.** Available through Connect, this invaluable resource presents 53 full-length student speeches, 9 of which are new to this updated edition. Included are 12 sets of paired needs improvement and final version presentations. In each set, the needs improvement version illustrates a work-in-progress that can be compared with the final version to help students understand the differences between an ordinary speech and a superior one.

- **Video Capture Powered by GoReact.** Designed for use in face-to-face, real-time classrooms, as well as in online courses, Video Capture allows instructors to evaluate their students' speeches using fully customizable rubrics. Instructors can also create and manage peer review assignments and upload videos on behalf of students for optimal flexibility.

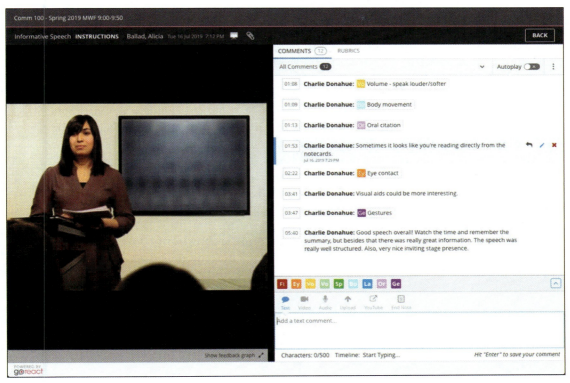

lucadp/Shutterstock

Acknowledgments

"'Tis the good reader," said Ralph Waldo Emerson, "that makes the good book." We have been fortunate to have very good readers indeed, and we would like to thank the reviewers and other contributors for their expertise and recommendations.

In addition, we would like to express our gratitude to Ananda Deacon, Casey Kaplan, Terrie Sanchez, and other students at the University of Wisconsin whose speeches provided the material for many of the examples in the book. We are grateful as well to the teaching staff of Communication Arts 100 and to Sarah Jedd, assistant course director, for her splendid work in that capacity and for her insights about the book and its pedagogy.

Thanks go to Ann Weaver for her work on the *Instructor's Manual* and the Test Bank; to Jennifer Cochrane for her generous advice about the online speaking chapter; to Jeffrey Fox for his insights about online public speaking and visual aids in the online environment; and to Juliana Urtubey for permission to print her speech accepting the National Teacher of the Year Award, which appears in Chapter 18.

We have been fortunate to work with many talented people at McGraw Hill, including Katie Stevens, Sarah Remington, Betty Chen, Dawn Groundwater, Natalie Graner, Danielle Clement, Vanessa McClune, Sarah Flynn, Susan Gall, and Ira Chawala.

Our biggest debt goes to Patty Lucas and Sarah Stob, whose love and support have sustained us and made this update possible. There might be an *Art of Public Speaking* without them, but it would be poorer indeed.

Stephen E. Lucas
Madison, Wisconsin

Paul Stob
Nashville, Tennessee

Reviewers; Contributors; Symposium, Focus Group, and Survey Participants

Raymond Bell, *Calhoun Community College*

Mardia Bishop, *University of Illinois Urbana-Champaign*

Ferald Bryan, *Northern Illinois University*

Leah Bryant, *DePaul University*

Shaunté Caraballo, *California State University—Dominguez Hills*

Keri Carroll, *Crowder College*

Lisa Coleman, *Southwest Tennessee Community College—Macon Campus*

Jean DeHart, *Appalachian State University*

Jennifer Foster, *University of Central Oklahoma*

Jeffrey Fox, *Northern Kentucky University*

Mark Frederick, *Tidewater Community College—Norfolk Campus*

Tammy French, *University of Wisconsin—Whitewater*

David Gaer, *Lone Star College—University Park*

Jessica Graves-Rack, *University of Cincinnati*

Carla Harrell, *Old Dominion University*

Kate Hooper, *University of Mississippi*

Zachary Jackson, *Guilford Technical Community College*

Lakesha Jefferson, *South Suburban College*

Susan Kilgard, *Anne Arundel Community College*

David Lee, *NY City College of Technology*

William Maze, *Northwest Mississippi Community College*

Anne Mcintosh, *Central Piedmont Community College*

David McKinney, *Jefferson State Community College*

Laurie Metcalf, *Blinn College—Bryan*

Jason Moldoff, *Durham Tech Community College*

Yolanda Monroe-Robinson, *Gadsden State Community College*

Stevie Munz, *Utah Valley University*

John Nash, *Moraine Valley Community College*

Amanda Pettigrew, *Moraine Valley Community College*

Kristen Ruppert-Leach, *Southwestern Illinois College*

Julie Snyder-Yuly, *Marshall University*

Sherry Todd, *Moberly Area Community College*

Dana Trunnell, *Prairie State College*

Stephen Underhill, *Marshall University*

Jeff Van Overbeke, *Southeast Tech Center*

Karin Wilking, *Northwest Vista College*

Josie Wood, *Chemeketa Community College*

Instructors
Student Success Starts with You

Tools to enhance your unique voice

Want to build your own course? No problem. Prefer to use an OLC-aligned, prebuilt course? Easy. Want to make changes throughout the semester? Sure. And you'll save time with Connect's auto-grading, too.

65%
Less Time Grading

Laptop: Getty Images; Woman/dog: George Doyle/Getty Images

A unique path for each student

In Connect, instructors can assign an adaptive reading experience with SmartBook® 2.0. Rooted in advanced learning science principles, SmartBook 2.0 delivers each student a personalized experience, focusing students on their learning gaps, ensuring that the time they spend studying is time well-spent. **mheducation.com/highered/connect/smartbook**

Affordable solutions, added value

Make technology work for you with LMS integration for single sign-on access, mobile access to the digital textbook, and reports to quickly show you how each of your students is doing. And with our Inclusive Access program, you can provide all these tools at the lowest available market price to your students. Ask your McGraw Hill representative for more information.

Solutions for your challenges

A product isn't a solution. Real solutions are affordable, reliable, and come with training and ongoing support when you need it and how you want it. Visit **supportateverystep.com** for videos and resources both you and your students can use throughout the term.

SUPPORT AT
every step

Students
Get Learning that Fits You

Effective tools for efficient studying

Connect is designed to help you be more productive with simple, flexible, intuitive tools that maximize your study time and meet your individual learning needs. Get learning that works for you with Connect.

Study anytime, anywhere

Download the free ReadAnywhere® app and access your online eBook, SmartBook® 2.0, or Adaptive Learning Assignments when it's convenient, even if you're offline. And since the app automatically syncs with your Connect account, all of your work is available every time you open it. Find out more at **mheducation.com/readanywhere**

"I really liked this app—it made it easy to study when you don't have your text-book in front of you."

- Jordan Cunningham, Eastern Washington University

iPhone: Getty Images

Everything you need in one place

Your Connect course has everything you need—whether reading your digital eBook or completing assignments for class, Connect makes it easy to get your work done.

Learning for everyone

McGraw Hill works directly with Accessibility Services Departments and faculty to meet the learning needs of all students. Please contact your Accessibility Services Office and ask them to email accessibility@mheducation.com, or visit **mheducation.com/about/accessibility** for more information.

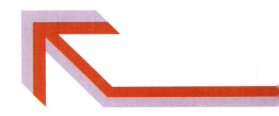

The Art of
Public Speaking

1

Speaking in Public

The Power of Public Speaking

The Tradition of Public Speaking

Public Speaking and Conversation

Developing Confidence: Your Speech Class

Public Speaking and Critical Thinking

The Speech Communication Process

Public Speaking in a Culturally Diverse World

A pathbreaking medical doctor, Nadine Burke Harris is also a world-class public speaker—an unusual combination, but one that has changed her life and improved medical care for millions of children.

Growing up in the San Francisco Bay area, Nadine dreamed of becoming a doctor, a dream she realized when she finished her studies and joined the California Pacific Medical Center in 2005. Specializing in pediatrics, she devoted herself to helping children in disadvantaged communities. In 2012 she founded the Center for Youth Wellness to provide an innovative approach to pediatric care. Today the center and Dr. Burke Harris are recognized around the world for their pioneering work on how childhood trauma and chronic stress can affect lifelong health conditions.

To accomplish all of this, Dr. Burke Harris needed more than medical expertise. She needed to be a public speaker who could advocate for her cause. She needed to persuade community partners and the city of San Francisco to back the Center for Youth Wellness. She needed to convince her colleagues in public health that her approach to treating childhood trauma would work. And she needed to raise money to keep the center productive once it was up and running.

All of this required her to communicate with people through public speaking—and communicate she did. She's been called a "brilliant speaker and advocate" who can engage "a room of a thousand people in a way that makes you feel like you're having a one-on-one conversation with her." As Dr. Burke Harris herself explains, "I see myself as a professional athlete, but my sport is public speaking."

If you had asked Dr. Burke Harris when she was in medical school, "Do you see yourself becoming an important public speaker?" she would have laughed at the idea. Yet today, she has spoken at the White House, testified before Congress, presented at public health conferences in the United States and abroad, and lectured at Harvard, Columbia, Stanford, and many other universities. Her TED Talk, titled "How Childhood Trauma Affects Health Across a Lifetime," has been viewed more than nine million times.

The Power of Public Speaking

Throughout history people have used public speaking as a vital means of communication. What the Greek leader Pericles said more than 2,500 years ago is still true today: "One who forms a judgment on any point but cannot explain" it clearly "might as well never have thought at all on the subject."[1] Public speaking, as its name implies, is a way of making your ideas public—of sharing them with other people and of influencing other people.

During modern times, many women and men around the globe have spread their ideas and influence through public speaking. In the United States, the list includes Franklin Roosevelt, Billy Graham, Cesar Chavez, Barbara Jordan, Martin Luther King, Ronald Reagan, Hillary Clinton, and Barack Obama. In other countries, we have seen the power of public speaking employed by people such as Margaret Thatcher, Nelson Mandela, and Malala Yousafzai.

As you read these names, you may think to yourself, "That's fine. Good for them. But what does that have to do with me? I don't plan to be a president or a preacher or a crusader for any cause." Nevertheless, the need for public speaking will almost certainly touch you sometime in your life—maybe tomorrow, maybe not for five years. Can you imagine yourself in any of these situations?

You are one of seven management trainees in a large corporation with offices across the globe. One of you will get the lower-management job that has just opened. At a large staff meeting held on Zoom, you and the other trainees will each discuss the project you have been developing. One by one your colleagues make their presentations. They lack experience with public speaking and are intimidated by the higher-ranking managers present. Their speeches are stumbling and awkward. You, however, call upon the skills you learned in your public speaking course. You deliver an informative talk that is clear, well reasoned, and articulate. You get the job.

One of your children has a learning disability. You hear that your local school board has decided, for budget reasons, to eliminate the special teacher who has been helping your child. At an open meeting of the school board, you stand up and deliver a thoughtful, compelling speech on the necessity for keeping the special teacher. The school board changes its mind.

You are the assistant regional director of a major nonprofit organization. Your immediate superior is about to retire, and there will be a retirement dinner. Everyone on the board of directors will attend, and you are asked to give a farewell toast. You prepare and deliver a speech that is both witty and moving—a perfect tribute to your boss. After the speech, everyone applauds enthusiastically. The following week you are named the new regional director.

Fantasies? Not really. Any of these situations could occur. In a recent survey of more than 550 corporate recruiters, 80 percent cited skills such as public speaking as the most important factor for success after graduation. In another survey, 1,200 job recruiters reported that one skill was more important and harder to find than any other. That skill? Effective communication.[2]

The importance of such skills is true across the board—for accountants and architects, teachers and technicians, scientists and stockbrokers. Even in highly specialized fields such as civil and mechanical engineering, employers consistently rank the ability to communicate above technical knowledge when deciding whom to hire and whom to promote.

Businesses are also asking people to give more speeches in the early stages of their careers, and many young professionals are using public speaking as a way to stand out in today's highly competitive job market.[3] In fact, the ability to speak effectively is so prized that college graduates are increasingly being asked to give a presentation as part of their job interview.

Nor has the growth of the internet and other new technologies reduced the need for public speaking. In this age of TikTok and Twitter, businesses are concerned that college graduates are losing the ability to talk in a professional way. As career expert Lindsey Pollak states, "It's so rare to find somebody who has that combination of really good technical skills and really good verbal communication skills. You will be head and shoulders above your colleagues if you can combine those two."[4]

The same is true in community life. Public speaking is a vital means of civic engagement. It is a way to express your ideas and to have an impact on issues that matter in society. As a form of empowerment, it can—and often does—make a difference in things people care about very much. The key phrase here is "make a difference." This is what most of us want to do in life—to make a difference, to change the world in some small way. Public speaking offers you an opportunity to make a difference in something you care about very much.

The Tradition of Public Speaking

Given the importance of public speaking, it's not surprising that it has been taught and studied around the globe for thousands of years. Almost all cultures have an equivalent of the English word "orator" to designate someone with special skills in public speaking. The oldest known handbook on effective speech was written on papyrus in Egypt some 4,500 years ago. Eloquence was highly prized in ancient India, Africa, and China, as well as among the Aztecs and other pre-European cultures of North and South America.[5]

In classical Greece and Rome, public speaking played a central role in education and civic life. It was also studied extensively. Aristotle's *Rhetoric,* composed during the third century B.C., is still considered the most important work on its subject, and many of its principles are followed by speakers (and writers) today. The great Roman leader Cicero used his speeches to defend liberty and wrote several works about oratory in general.

Over the centuries, many other notable thinkers have dealt with issues of rhetoric, speech, and language—including the Roman educator Quintilian, the

Christian preacher St. Augustine, the medieval writer Christine de Pizan, the British philosopher Francis Bacon, and the poet activist Audre Lorde. In recent years, communication researchers have provided an increasingly scientific basis for understanding the methods and strategies of effective speech.

Your immediate objective is to apply those methods and strategies in your classroom speeches. What you learn, however, will be applicable long after you leave college. The principles of public speaking are derived from a long tradition and have been confirmed by a substantial body of research. The more you know about those principles, the more effective you will be in your own speeches—and the more effective you will be in listening to the speeches of other people.

Public Speaking and Conversation

The average adult spends about 30 percent of his or her waking hours in conversation. By the time you read this book, you will have spent many hours perfecting the art of conversation. If you communicate well in daily talk, you can learn to communicate well in public speaking.

SIMILARITIES BETWEEN PUBLIC SPEAKING AND CONVERSATION

You may not realize it, but public speaking requires many of the same skills used in ordinary conversation. These skills include:

1. *Organizing your thoughts logically.* Suppose you are giving someone directions to your apartment. You don't convey the directions in random order. Instead, you take your listener systematically, step by step, from his or her apartment to your apartment. You organize your message.

2. *Tailoring your message to the audience.* Imagine that you are a biology major. Two people ask you how pearls are formed. One is your uncle, who majored in science as a college student. The other is your nine-year-old niece. You answer as follows:

   > To your uncle: "When any irritant, say a grain of sand, gets inside the oyster's shell, the oyster automatically secretes a substance called nacre, which is mostly calcium carbonate. The nacre accumulates around the irritant core to form the pearl."

   > To your niece: "Imagine you're an oyster on the ocean floor. A grain of sand gets inside your shell and makes you uncomfortable. So you decide to cover it up. The covering builds up around the grain of sand to make a pearl."

3. *Telling a story for maximum impact.* Suppose you are telling a friend about a funny incident at last week's track meet. You don't begin with the punch line ("Dani fell out of the stands right onto the track. Here's how it started. . . ."). Instead, you carefully build up your story, adjusting your words and tone of voice to get the best effect.

4. *Adapting to listener feedback.* Whenever you talk with someone, you are aware of that person's verbal, facial, and physical reactions. For example, when you tell your boyfriend or girlfriend that you need to study instead of going to a movie

Many skills used in conversation also apply in public speaking. As you learn to speak more effectively, you may also learn to communicate more effectively in other situations.
Tyler Olson/Shutterstock

on Saturday night, you notice an unmistakable look of unhappiness on their face. So you say, "Okay, let's go to the early show; then I can study later."

Each day, in casual conversation, you do all these things many times without thinking about them. You already possess these communication skills, all of which are among the most important skills you will need for public speaking.

DIFFERENCES BETWEEN PUBLIC SPEAKING AND CONVERSATION

Despite their similarities, public speaking and everyday conversation are not identical. Imagine you are telling a story to a friend. Then imagine yourself telling the story to a group of seven or eight friends. Now imagine telling the same story to 20 or 30 people. As the size of your audience grows, you will find yourself adapting to three major differences between conversation and public speaking:

1. *Public speaking is more highly structured.* It usually imposes strict time limitations on the speaker. In most cases, the situation does not allow listeners to interrupt with questions or commentary. The speaker must accomplish her or his purpose in the speech itself. When preparing the speech, the speaker must anticipate questions that might arise in the minds of listeners and answer them. Consequently, public speaking demands much more detailed planning and preparation than ordinary conversation.

2. *Public speaking requires more formal language.* Slang, jargon, and bad grammar have little place in public speeches. Even as dress codes and social mores have become more informal, listeners usually react negatively to speakers who do not elevate and polish their language when addressing an audience. A speech should be "special."

3. *Public speaking requires a different method of delivery.* When conversing informally, most people talk quietly, interject stock phrases such as "well" and "you

know," adopt a casual posture, and use what are called vocalized pauses ("uh," "er," "um"). Effective public speakers, however, adjust their voices to be heard clearly throughout the audience. They assume a more erect posture. They avoid distracting mannerisms and verbal habits.

With study and practice, you will master these differences and expand your conversational skills into speechmaking. Your speech class will provide the opportunity for this study and practice.

Developing Confidence: Your Speech Class

One of the major concerns of students in any speech class is stage fright. We may as well face the issue squarely. Stage fright is a universal phenomenon that cuts across language, culture, and national borders. Comedian Jerry Seinfeld once famously said, "Given a choice at a funeral, most of us would rather be the one in the coffin than the one giving the eulogy."

Seinfeld was speaking in jest. Yet many people who converse easily in all kinds of everyday situations become terrified at the prospect of standing in front of an audience to give a speech. In one survey of more than 1,000 undergraduate students, 64 percent reported being fearful of public speaking, while 89 percent believed their school should provide public speaking instruction.[6]

In a different study, researchers concentrated on social situations and asked respondents to list their greatest fears. Here is the ranking of their answers:[7]

Greatest Fear

Public speaking

Speaking up in a meeting or class

Meeting new people

Talking to people in authority

Important examination or interview

Going to parties

Talking with strangers

Not only did public speaking top the list, but it was joined by other forms of communication anxiety.

NERVOUSNESS IS NORMAL

If you feel nervous about giving a speech, you are in very good company. Some of the greatest public speakers in history have suffered from stage fright, including Abraham Lincoln, Margaret Sanger, and Winston Churchill. The famous Roman orator Cicero said, "I turn pale at the outset of a speech and quake in every limb and in my soul."[8]

Jennifer Lawrence, Harrison Ford, and Naomi Osaka all report being anxious about speaking in public. Early in his career, Leonardo DiCaprio was so nervous about giving an acceptance speech that he hoped he would not win the Academy Award for which he had been nominated. Eighty-one percent of business executives say public speaking is the most nerve-wracking experience they face.[9]

Actually, most people tend to be anxious before doing something important in public. Actors are nervous before a play, politicians are nervous before a campaign speech, athletes are nervous before a big game. The ones who succeed have learned to use their nervousness to their advantage.

Listen to U.S. gymnastics star Suni Lee at the 2021 Summer Olympics, held in Tokyo, Japan. "I'm really nervous," she said before the competition, which she described as "very hard and stressful. . . . But I just had to go out there and have the best competition of my life." Putting her butterflies to good use, Lee did exactly that, winning the women's all-around gold medal at the biggest sporting event in the world.

Much the same thing happens in speechmaking. Most experienced speakers have stage fright before taking the floor, but their nervousness is a healthy sign that they are getting "psyched up" for a good effort. Novelist and lecturer I. A. R. Wylie once said: "I rarely rise to my feet without a throat constricted with terror and a furiously thumping heart. When, for some reason, I *am* cool and self-assured, the speech is always a failure."

In other words, it is perfectly normal—even desirable—to be nervous at the start of a speech. Your body is responding as it would to any stressful situation—by producing extra adrenaline.

This sudden shot of adrenaline is what makes your heart race, your hands shake, your knees knock, and your skin perspire. Every public speaker experiences all these reactions to some extent. The question is: How can you control your nervousness and make it work for you rather than against you?

adrenaline
A hormone released into the bloodstream in response to physical or mental stress.

DEALING WITH NERVOUSNESS

Rather than trying to eliminate every trace of stage fright, you should aim at transforming it from a negative force into what one expert calls positive nervousness—"a zesty, enthusiastic, lively feeling with a slight edge to it. . . . It's still nervousness, but it feels different. You're no longer victimized by it; instead, you're vitalized by it. You're in control of it."[10]

positive nervousness
Controlled nervousness that helps energize a speaker for her or his presentation.

Don't think of yourself as having stage fright. Instead, think of it as "stage excitement" or "stage enthusiasm."[11] It can help you get focused and energized in the same way as it helps athletes, musicians, and others get primed for a game or a concert. Jane Lynch, talking about her gig hosting *Saturday Night Live,* said that she got through it with "that perfect cocktail of nervousness and excitement." Think of that cocktail as a normal part of giving a successful speech.

Here are six time-tested ways you can turn your nervousness from a negative force into a positive one.

Acquire Speaking Experience

You have already taken the first step. You are enrolled in a public speaking course, where you will learn about speechmaking and gain speaking experience. Think back to your first day in kindergarten, your first date, your first day at a new job. You were probably nervous in each situation because you were facing something new and unknown. Once you became accustomed to the situation, it was no longer threatening. So it is with public speaking. For most students, the biggest part of stage fright is fear of the unknown. The more you learn about public speaking and the more speeches you give, the less threatening speechmaking will become.

Of course, the road to confidence will sometimes be bumpy. Learning to give a speech is not much different from learning any other skill—it proceeds by trial and error.

The need for public speaking arises in many situations. Here pop singer Olivia Rodrigo speaks at a White House press conference on vaccines and public health.

Oliver Contreras/Bloomberg/Getty Images

The purpose of your speech class is to shorten the process, to minimize the errors, to give you a nonthreatening arena—a sort of laboratory—in which to undertake the "trial."

Your instructor recognizes that you are a novice and is trained to give the kind of guidance you need to get started. In your fellow students you have a highly sympathetic audience who will provide valuable feedback to help you improve your speaking skills. As the class goes on, your fears about public speaking will gradually recede until they are replaced by only a healthy nervousness before you rise to speak.[12]

Prepare, Prepare, Prepare

Another key to gaining confidence is to pick speech topics you truly care about—and then to prepare your speeches so thoroughly that you cannot help but be successful. Here's how one student combined enthusiasm for his topic with thorough preparation to score a triumph in speech class:

> Jesse Young was concerned about taking a speech class. Not having any experience as a public speaker, he got butterflies in his stomach just thinking about talking in front of an audience. But when the time came for Jesse's first speech, he was determined to make it a success.
>
> Jesse chose Habitat for Humanity as the topic for his speech. He had been a volunteer for three years, and he believed deeply in the organization and its mission. The purpose of his speech was to explain the origins, philosophy, and activities of Habitat for Humanity.
>
> As Jesse spoke, it became clear that he was enthusiastic about his subject and genuinely wanted his classmates to share his enthusiasm. Because he was intent on communicating with his audience, he forgot to be nervous. He spoke clearly, fluently, and dynamically. Soon the entire class was engrossed in his speech.
>
> Afterward, Jesse admitted that he had surprised even himself. "It was amazing," he said. "Once I passed the first minute or so, all I thought about were those people out there listening. I could tell that I was really getting through to them."

How much time should you devote to preparing your speeches? A standard rule of thumb is that each minute of speaking time requires one to two hours of preparation time—perhaps more, depending on the amount of research needed for the speech. This may seem like a lot of time, but the rewards are well worth it. One professional speech consultant estimates that proper preparation can reduce stage fright by up to 75 percent.[13]

If you follow the techniques suggested by your instructor and in the rest of this book, you will stand up for every speech fully prepared. Imagine that the day for your first speech has arrived. You have studied your audience and selected a topic you know will interest them. You have researched the topic thoroughly and practiced the speech several times until it feels absolutely comfortable. You have even tried it out before two or three trusted friends. How can you help but be confident of success?

Think Positively

Confidence is mostly the well-known power of positive thinking. If you think you can do it, you usually can. On the other hand, if you predict disaster and doom, that is almost always what you will get. This is especially true when it comes to public speaking. Speakers who think negatively about themselves and the speech experience are much more likely to be overcome by stage fright than are speakers who think positively. Here are some ways you can transform negative thoughts into positive ones as you work on your speeches:

Negative Thought	Positive Thought
I wish I didn't have to give this speech.	This speech is a chance for me to share my ideas and gain experience as a speaker.
I'm not a great public speaker.	No one's perfect, but I'm getting better with each speech I give.
I'm always nervous when I give a speech.	Everyone's nervous. If other people can handle it, I can, too.
No one will be interested in what I have to say.	I have a good topic and I'm fully prepared. Of course they'll be interested.

Many psychologists believe that the ratio of positive to negative thoughts in regard to stressful activities such as speechmaking should be at least five to one. That is, for each negative thought, you should counter with a minimum of five positive ones. Doing so will not make your nerves go away completely, but it will help keep them under control so you can concentrate on communicating your ideas rather than on brooding about your fears and anxieties.

Use the Power of Visualization

Visualization is closely related to positive thinking. It is used by athletes, musicians, actors, speakers, and others to enhance their performance in stressful situations. How does it work? Listen to NBA legend Chris Bosh, who described the importance of visualization in his 2021 book *Letters to a Young Athlete*:

> Usually after a workout, I'd sit there and visualize myself being successful. Using those moves we had been working on all summer in the game

visualization
Mental imaging in which speakers vividly picture themselves giving a successful presentation.

when the season started. Seeing myself knocking down that crucial free throw at the line. Visualizing myself lifting the trophy. Doing the work allows you to go through all of these emotions and actions in your mind before you go through them on the court.

Of course, visualization doesn't mean that Bosh won every game he played. But research has shown that the kind of mental imaging he describes can significantly increase athletic performance.[14] It has also shown that visualization can help speakers control their stage fright.[15]

The key to visualization is creating a vivid mental blueprint in which you see yourself succeeding in your speech. Picture yourself in your classroom rising to speak. See yourself at the lectern, poised and self-assured, making eye contact with your audience and delivering your introduction in a firm, clear voice. Feel your confidence growing as your listeners get more and more caught up in what you are saying. Imagine your sense of achievement as you conclude the speech knowing you have done your very best.

As you create these images in your mind's eye, be realistic but stay focused on the positive aspects of your speech. Don't allow negative images to eclipse the positive ones. Acknowledge your nervousness, but picture yourself overcoming it to give a vibrant, articulate presentation. If one part of the speech always seems to give you trouble, visualize yourself getting through it without any hitches. And be specific. The more lucid your mental pictures, the more successful you are likely to be.

As with your physical rehearsal of the speech, this kind of mental rehearsal should be repeated several times in the days before you speak. It doesn't guarantee that every speech will turn out exactly the way you envision it—and it certainly is no substitute for thorough preparation. But used in conjunction with the other methods of combating stage fright, it is a proven way to help control your nerves and to craft a successful presentation.

Know That Most Nervousness Isn't Visible

Many novice speakers are worried about appearing nervous to the audience. It's hard to speak with poise and assurance if you think you look tense and insecure. One of the most valuable lessons you will learn as your speech class proceeds is that only a fraction of the turmoil you feel inside is visible on the outside. "Your nervous system may be giving you a thousand shocks," says one experienced speaker, "but the viewer can see only a few of them."[16]

Even though your palms are sweating and your heart is pounding, your listeners probably won't realize how tense you are—especially if you do your best to act cool and confident on the outside. Most of the time when students confess after a speech, "I was so nervous I thought I was going to die," their classmates are surprised. To them the speaker looked calm and assured.

Knowing this should make it easier for you to face your listeners with confidence. As one student stated after watching a video of her first classroom speech, "I was amazed at how calm I looked. I assumed everyone would be able to see how scared I was, but now that I know they can't, I won't be nearly so nervous in the future. It really helps to know that you look in control even though you may not feel that way."

Don't Expect Perfection

It may also help to know that there is no such thing as a perfect speech. At some point in every presentation, every speaker says or does something that does not come across exactly as planned. Fortunately, such moments are usually not evident to the audience. Why? Because the audience doesn't know what the speaker *plans* to say. It hears only what the speaker *does* say. If you momentarily lose your place, reverse the order of a couple of statements, or forget to pause at a certain spot, no one need be the wiser. When such moments occur, just proceed as if nothing happened.

Even if you do make an obvious mistake during a speech, that is no catastrophe. If you have ever listened to Martin Luther King's "I Have a Dream," you may recall that he stumbles twice during the speech. Most likely, however, you don't remember. Why? Because you were focusing on King's message rather than on the fine points of his delivery.

One of the biggest reasons people are concerned about making a mistake in a speech is that they view speechmaking as a performance rather than an act of communication. They feel the audience is judging them against a scale of absolute perfection in which every misstated word or awkward gesture will count against them. But speech audiences are not like judges in a violin recital or an ice-skating contest. They are not looking for a virtuoso performance, but for a well-thought-out address that communicates the speaker's ideas clearly and directly. Sometimes a small error or two can enhance a speaker's appeal by making the speaker seem more human.

As you work on your speeches, make sure you prepare thoroughly and do all you can to get your message across to your listeners. But don't panic about being perfect or about what will happen if you make a mistake. Once you free your mind of these burdens, you will find it much easier to approach your speeches with confidence and even with enthusiasm.[17]

Additional Tips

Besides stressing the six points just discussed, your instructor will probably give you several tips for dealing with nervousness in your first speeches. They may include:

- Be at your best physically and mentally. It's not a good idea to stay up until 3:00 A.M. partying with friends or cramming for an exam the night before your speech. A good night's sleep will serve you better.

- As you are waiting to speak, quietly tighten and relax your leg muscles, or squeeze your hands together and then release them. Such actions help reduce tension by providing an outlet for your extra adrenaline.

- Take a couple slow, deep breaths before you start to speak. When they are tense, most people take short, shallow breaths, which only reinforces their anxiety. Deep breathing breaks this cycle of tension and helps calm your nerves.

- Work especially hard on your introduction. Research has shown that a speaker's anxiety level begins to drop significantly after the first 30 to 60 seconds of a presentation.[18] Once you get through the introduction, you should find smoother sailing the rest of the way.

- Make eye contact with members of your audience. Remember that they are individual people, not a blur of faces. And they are your friends.
- Concentrate on communicating with your audience rather than on worrying about your stage fright. If you get caught up in your speech, your audience will, too.
- Use visual aids. They create interest, draw attention away from you, and make you feel less self-conscious.

If you are like most students, you will find your speech class to be a very positive experience. As one student wrote on her course evaluation at the end of the term:

> I was really dreading this class. The idea of giving all those speeches scared me half to death. But I'm glad now that I stuck with it. It's a small class, and I got to know a lot of the students. Besides, this is one class in which I got to express *my* ideas, instead of spending the whole time listening to the teacher talk. I even came to enjoy giving the speeches. I could tell at times that the audience was really with me, and that's a great feeling.

Over the years, thousands of students have developed confidence in their speech-making abilities. As your confidence grows, you will be better able to stand before other people and tell them what you think and feel and know—and to make them think and feel and know those same things. The best part about confidence is that it nurtures itself. After you score your first triumph, you will be that much more confident the next time. And as you become a more confident public speaker, you will likely become more confident in other areas of your life as well.

 checklist

Speaking with Confidence

YES	NO	
☐	☐	1. Am I enthusiastic about my speech topic?
☐	☐	2. Have I thoroughly developed the content of my speech?
☐	☐	3. Have I worked on the introduction so my speech will get off to a good start?
☐	☐	4. Have I worked on the conclusion so my speech will end on a strong note?
☐	☐	5. Have I rehearsed my speech orally until I am confident about its delivery?
☐	☐	6. Have I worked on turning negative thoughts about my speech into positive ones?
☐	☐	7. Do I realize that nervousness is normal, even among experienced speakers?
☐	☐	8. Do I understand that most nervousness is not visible to the audience?
☐	☐	9. Am I focused on communicating with my audience, rather than on worrying about my nerves?
☐	☐	10. Have I visualized myself speaking confidently and getting a positive response from the audience?

Terrified early in his career by the prospect of giving a public speech, today Leonardo DiCaprio is an accomplished speaker who confidently addresses audiences around the globe.

Michael Tran/FilmMagic/Getty Images

Public Speaking and Critical Thinking

That guy at the party last night really owned me when we were talking about the economy. I know my information is right, and I'm sure his argument didn't make sense, but I can't put my finger on the problem.

I worked really hard on my term paper, but it's just not right. It doesn't seem to hang together, and I can't figure out what's wrong.

Political speeches are so one-sided. The candidates sound good, but they all talk in slogans and generalities. It's really hard to decide who has the best stand on the issues.

Have you ever found yourself in similar situations? If so, you may find help in your speech class. Besides building confidence, a course in public speaking can develop your skills as a critical thinker. Those skills can make the difference between the articulate debater and the pushover, the A student and the C student, the thoughtful voter and the coin tosser.

What is critical thinking? To some extent, it's a matter of logic—of being able to spot weaknesses in other people's arguments and to avoid them in your own. It also involves related skills such as distinguishing fact from opinion, judging the credibility of statements, and assessing the soundness of evidence. In the broadest sense, critical thinking is focused, organized thinking—the ability to see clearly the relationships among ideas.[19]

If you are wondering what this has to do with your public speaking class, the answer is, quite a lot. As the class proceeds, you will probably spend a good deal of time organizing your speeches. While this may seem like a purely mechanical exercise, it is closely interwoven with critical thinking. If the structure of your speech is disjointed and confused, odds are that your thinking is also disjointed and confused. If, on the other hand, the structure is clear and cohesive, there is a good chance your

critical thinking
Focused, organized thinking about such things as the logical relationships among ideas, the soundness of evidence, and the differences between fact and opinion.

It's been three years since you graduated from college, and one year since you joined a start-up that builds air purifiers for people in developing countries. The purifiers are innovative and promising, but bringing them to market has been a major challenge. Now you and your team are convinced that you need more financial backing to move things forward. Next week, you will pitch the project to various humanitarian investors.

Although you have given a few brief talks since your speech class in college, this will be your first major online presentation to people in different cities and time zones. The closer you get to the day of the speech, the harder it is to control the butterflies in your stomach. More than 75 people will be watching you on Zoom. It's important that you come across as confident and well informed, but you're afraid your stage fright will send the opposite message. What strategies will you use to control your nerves and make them work for you?

Nick David/Getty Images

thinking is, too. Organizing a speech is not just a matter of arranging the ideas you already have. Rather, it is an important part of shaping the ideas themselves.

What is true of organization is true of many aspects of public speaking. The skills you learn in your speech class can help you become a more effective thinker in a number of ways. As you work on expressing your ideas in clear, accurate language, you will enhance your ability to think clearly and accurately. As you study the role of evidence and reasoning in speechmaking, you will see how they can be used in other forms of communication as well. As you learn to listen critically to speeches in class, you will be better able to assess the ideas of speakers (and writers) in a variety of situations.

To return to the examples at the beginning of this section:

The guy at the party last night—would well-honed critical thinking skills help you find the holes in his argument?

The term paper—would better organization and a clear outline help pull it together?

Political speeches—once you get past the slogans, are the candidates drawing valid conclusions from sound evidence?

If you take full advantage of your speech class, you will be able to enhance your skills as a critical thinker in many circumstances. This is one reason public speaking has been regarded as a vital part of education since the days of ancient Greece.[20]

The Speech Communication Process

As you begin your first speeches, you may find it helpful to understand what goes on when one person talks to another. Regardless of the kind of speech communication involved, there are seven elements—speaker, message, channel, listener, feedback, interference, and situation. Here we focus on how these elements interact when a public speaker addresses an audience.

SPEAKER

Speech communication begins with a speaker. Your success as a speaker depends on *you*—your personal credibility, your knowledge of the subject, your preparation of the speech, your manner of speaking, your sensitivity to the audience and the occasion. But successful speaking also requires enthusiasm. You can't expect people to be interested in what you say unless you are interested yourself.

You can learn all the techniques of effective speechmaking, but before they can be of much use, you must first have something to say—something that sparks your own enthusiasm.

speaker
The person who is presenting an oral message to a listener

MESSAGE

The message is whatever a speaker communicates to someone else. Your goal in public speaking is to have your *intended* message be the message that is *actually* communicated. Achieving this depends both on what you say (the verbal message) and on how you say it (the nonverbal message).

Getting the verbal message just right requires work. You must narrow your topic down to something you can discuss adequately in the time allowed for the speech. You must do research and choose supporting details to make your ideas clear and convincing. You must organize your ideas so listeners can follow them without getting lost. And you must express your message in words that are accurate, clear, vivid, and appropriate.

Besides the message you send with words, you send a message with your tone of voice, appearance, gestures, facial expression, and eye contact. Imagine that one of your classmates gets up to speak about student loans. Throughout her speech she slumps behind the lectern, takes long pauses to remember what she wants to say, stares at the ceiling, and fumbles with her visual aids.

Her intended message is "We must make more money available for student loans." But the message she actually communicates is "I haven't prepared very well for this speech." One of your jobs as a speaker is to make sure your nonverbal message does not distract from your verbal message.

message
Whatever a speaker communicates to someone else.

CHANNEL

The channel is the means by which a message is communicated. Public speakers may use one or more of several channels, each of which will affect the message received by the audience.

Consider a speech to the United Nations by the President of the United States. The speech is carried to many parts of the globe by the channels of radio, television, and the internet. For the radio audience, the message is conveyed entirely by the president's voice. For the television or internet audience, the message is conveyed by both the president's voice and the broadcast image. The people at the UN have a more direct channel. They not only hear the president's voice as amplified through a microphone, but they also see him and the setting firsthand.

channel
The means by which a message is communicated.

LISTENER

The listener is the person who receives the communicated message. Without a listener, there is no communication. When you talk to a friend on the phone, you have one listener. In public speaking you will have many listeners.

listener
The person who receives the speaker's message.

The powers of critical thinking you develop in researching and organizing your speeches can be applied in many forms of communication, including meetings and group projects.

Gpointstudio/123RF

Everything a speaker says is filtered through a listener's frame of reference—the total of his or her knowledge, experience, goals, values, and attitudes. Because a speaker and a listener are different people, they can never have exactly the same frame of reference. And because a listener's frame of reference can never be exactly the same as a speaker's, the meaning of a message will never be exactly the same to a listener as to a speaker.

frame of reference

The sum of a person's knowledge, experience, goals, values, and attitudes. No two people can have exactly the same frame of reference.

You can easily test the impact of different frames of reference. Ask each of your classmates to describe a chair. If you have 20 classmates, you'll probably get 20 different descriptions. One student might picture a large, overstuffed easy chair, another an elegant straight-backed chair, yet another an office chair, a fourth a rocking chair, and so on. And "chair" is a fairly simple concept. What about "patriotism" or "freedom"?

To be an effective public speaker, you need to take account of your listeners' frames of reference. You must be *audience-centered*. You will quickly lose your listeners' attention if your presentation is either too basic or too sophisticated. You will also lose your audience if you do not relate to their experiences, interests, knowledge, and values. When you make a speech that causes listeners to say "That is important to *me*," you will almost always be successful.

FEEDBACK

feedback

The messages, usually nonverbal, sent from a listener to a speaker.

Feedback refers to the messages—usually nonverbal—that are sent from a listener to a speaker. Do listeners lean forward in their seats, as if paying close attention? Do they applaud in approval? Do they laugh at your jokes? Do they have quizzical looks on their faces? Do they shuffle their feet and gaze at the clock?

The message sent by these reactions could be "I am fascinated," "I am bored," "I agree with you," "I don't agree with you," or any number of others. As a speaker, you need to be alert to these reactions and adjust your message accordingly.

Like any kind of communication, feedback is affected by one's frame of reference. How would you feel if, immediately after your speech, all your classmates started to rap their knuckles on the desks? Would you run out of the room in despair? Not if you were in a European university. In many parts of Europe, students rap their knuckles on their desks to show admiration for a classroom lecture. You must understand the feedback to be able to deal with it.

INTERFERENCE

Interference is anything that impedes the communication of a message. In public speaking there are two kinds of interference. One is *external* to the audience—traffic outside the building, people conversing in the hall, a room that is stifling hot or freezing cold. Any of these can distract listeners from what a speaker is saying.

interference
Anything that impedes the communication of a message. Interference can be external or internal to listeners.

A second kind of interference is *internal* and comes from within the audience. Perhaps one of your listeners has a toothache. She may be so distracted by the pain that she doesn't pay attention to your speech. Another listener could be worrying about a test in the next class period. Yet another could be brooding about an argument with his girlfriend.

As a speaker, you must try to hold your listeners' attention despite these kinds of interference. In the chapters that follow, you will find many ways to do this.

SITUATION

The situation is the time and place in which speech communication occurs. Certain situations—funerals, weddings, graduation ceremonies—require certain kinds of speeches. Physical setting is also important. It makes a great deal of difference whether a speech is presented indoors or out, to a densely packed crowd or to a handful of scattered souls. When you adjust to the situation of a public speech, you are only doing on a larger scale what you do every day in conversation.

situation
The time and place in which speech communication occurs.

A complete model of the speech communication process is shown in Figure 1.1.

FIGURE 1.1

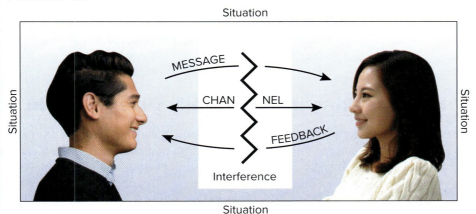

(male) Ranta Images/Shutterstock;
(female) Lan Images/Shutterstock

THE SPEECH COMMUNICATION PROCESS: EXAMPLE WITH COMMENTARY

The following example shows how the various components of the speech communication process interact:

Situation	It was 5:15 P.M., and the Midwest Food Festival and Expo had been going on all day. Gourmet food vendors from across the Great Lakes region were presenting their products to distributors and restaurant owners, but the presentations had taken much longer than expected.
Speaker	Jason Cruz, owner and operator of a gourmet salsa company, was worried. As the last speaker of the day, he knew he faced a tough situation. He had been allotted 30 minutes, but the festival was scheduled to end in 15 minutes, and the success of his products depended in large part on his presentation.
Channel	Jason stepped to the microphone and began to speak. He could see members of the audience looking at their watches, and he knew they were eager to get to dinner after a long day of meetings.
Adapting to Interference	"Good afternoon," Jason said, "and thanks for your attention. I know everyone is ready to relax after a long day—I certainly am. I was given 30 minutes to tell you about my salsa, but I'll do my best to finish in 15. I think you'll find the time well worth your while, because your customers are going to love my products." Jason was relieved to see people smiling as they settled back in their seats.
Message	Now that he had the audience's attention, Jason presented each of his products as briefly as he could. He streamlined his planned remarks to emphasize the salsas that would be most appealing to grocery shoppers and restaurant diners. He ended by handing out samples of two new salsas that had won awards in recent food shows.
Feedback	As promised, Jason finished in 15 minutes. "So, that's it!" he concluded. "Thanks for your attention after such a long day." The festival organizer came up to Jason after his presentation. "Great stuff—both the talk and the salsa," she said. "Next year I think we'll try to make all the presentations as concise and efficient as yours."

Public Speaking in a Culturally Diverse World

The United States has always been a diverse society. By the middle of the 19th century, it contained so many people from so many lands that novelist Herman Melville exclaimed, "You cannot spill a drop of American blood without spilling the blood of the whole world."[21]

One can only imagine what Melville would say today! The United States is the most diverse society on earth. That diversity can be seen in cities and towns, schools and businesses, community groups and houses of worship all across the land.

Public speaking is a vital mode of communication in cultures around the world. Here Spanish prime minister Pedro Sanchez speaks at a press conference about his country's stance on the Russian invasion of Ukraine.

Toms Norde/AFP/Getty Images

Globally, we live in an age of international multiculturalism. Despite political, social, and religious differences, all nations are part of a vast communication network.

- There are more than 100,000 transnational corporations around the world, and they account for half of all global trade.

- TikTok has 1 billion active users every month, spread across 155 countries and speaking 75 different languages.

- Apple sells close to 70 percent of its iPhones abroad; there are twice as many KFC restaurants in China than in the United States.

CULTURAL DIVERSITY AND PUBLIC SPEAKING

Speechmaking becomes more complex as cultural diversity increases. Many stories have been told about the fate of public speakers who fail to take into account cultural differences between themselves and their audiences. Consider the following scenario:[22]

> The sales manager of a U.S. electronics firm is in Brazil to negotiate a large purchase of computers by a South American corporation. After three days of negotiations, the sales manager holds a gala reception for all the major executives to build goodwill between the companies.
>
> As is the custom on such occasions, time is set aside during the reception for an exchange of toasts. When it is the sales manager's turn to speak, he praises the Brazilian firm for its many achievements and talks eloquently of his respect for its president and other executives. The words are perfect, and the sales manager can see his audience smiling in approval.
>
> And then—disaster. As the sales manager closes his speech, he raises his hand and flashes the classic U.S. "OK" sign to signal his pleasure at the progress of the negotiations. Instantly the festive mood is replaced with stony silence; smiles turn to icy stares. The sales manager has given his

Brazilian audience a gesture with roughly the same meaning as an extended middle finger in the United States.

The next day, the Brazilian firm announces that it will buy its computers from another company.

As this story illustrates, public speakers can ill afford to overlook their listeners' cultural values and customs. The methods of effective speech explained throughout this book will be helpful to you when addressing culturally diverse audiences. Here we need to stress the importance of avoiding the ethnocentrism that often blocks communication between speakers and listeners of different cultural backgrounds.

AVOIDING ETHNOCENTRISM

ethnocentrism

The belief that one's own group or culture is superior to all other groups or cultures.

Ethnocentrism is the belief that our own group or culture—whatever it may be—is superior to all other groups or cultures. Because of ethnocentrism, we identify with our group or culture and see its values, beliefs, and customs as "right" or "natural"—in comparison to the values, beliefs, and customs of other groups or cultures, which we tend to think of as "wrong" or "unnatural."[23]

Ethnocentrism is part of every culture, and it can play a positive role in creating group pride and loyalty. But it can also lead to prejudice and hostility toward different racial, ethnic, religious, or cultural groups. To be an effective public speaker in a multicultural world, you need to keep in mind that all people have their special beliefs and customs.

When you work on your speeches, be alert to how cultural factors might affect how listeners respond. Try to put yourself in their place and to hear your message through their ears. If there is a language difference, avoid words or phrases that might cause misunderstanding. When researching the speech, keep an eye out for visual aids and other materials that will relate to a wide range of listeners. When delivering the speech, be alert to feedback that might indicate the audience is having trouble grasping your ideas.

It is also important to avoid ethnocentrism when listening to speeches. When you listen to a speaker from a different cultural background, be on guard against the temptation to judge the speaker on the basis of his or her appearance or manner of delivery. No matter what the cultural background of the speaker, you should listen to her or him as attentively as you would want your audience to listen to you.[24]

Summary

Public speaking has been a vital means of personal empowerment and civic engagement throughout history. The need for effective public speaking will almost certainly touch you sometime in your life. Your speech class will give you training in researching topics, organizing your ideas, and presenting yourself skillfully. This training is invaluable for every type of communication.

There are many similarities between public speaking and daily conversation, but public speaking is also different from conversation. First, it usually imposes strict time limitations and requires more detailed preparation than ordinary conversation. Second, it requires more formal language. Listeners react negatively to speeches loaded with slang, jargon, and bad grammar. Third, public speaking demands a different method of delivery. Effective speakers adjust their voices to the larger audience and work at avoiding distracting physical mannerisms and verbal habits.

One of the major concerns of students in any speech class is stage fright. Your class will give you an opportunity to gain confidence and make your nervousness work for you rather than against you. You will take a big step toward overcoming stage fright if you think positively, prepare thoroughly, visualize yourself giving a successful speech, keep in mind that most nervousness is not visible to the audience, and think of your speech as communication rather than as a performance in which you must do everything perfectly.

A course in public speaking can also help develop your skills as a critical thinker. Critical thinking helps you organize your ideas, spot weaknesses in other people's reasoning, and avoid them in your own.

The speech communication process includes seven elements—speaker, message, channel, listener, feedback, interference, and situation. The speaker is the person who initiates a speech transaction. Whatever the speaker communicates is the message, which is sent by means of a particular channel. The listener receives the communicated message and provides feedback to the speaker. Interference is anything that impedes the communication of a message, and the situation is the time and place in which speech communication occurs. The interaction of these seven elements determines the outcome in any instance of speech communication.

Because of the diversity of modern life, many of the audiences you address will include people of different cultural backgrounds. When you work on your speeches, be alert to how such factors might affect the responses of your listeners and adapt your message accordingly. Above all, avoid the ethnocentric belief that your own culture or group is superior to all others. Also keep in mind the importance of avoiding ethnocentrism when listening to speeches. Accord every speaker the same courtesy and attentiveness you would want from your listeners.

Key Terms

stage fright (8)
adrenaline (9)
positive nervousness (9)
visualization (11)
critical thinking (15)
speaker (17)
message (17)

channel (17)
listener (17)
frame of reference (18)
feedback (18)
interference (19)
situation (19)
ethnocentrism (22)

Review Questions

After reading this chapter, you should be able to answer the following questions:

1. In what ways is public speaking likely to make a difference in your life?
2. How is public speaking similar to everyday conversation?
3. How is public speaking different from everyday conversation?
4. Why is it normal—even desirable—to be nervous at the start of a speech?
5. How can you control your nervousness and make it work for you in your speeches?

6. What are the seven elements of the speech communication process? How do they interact to determine the success or failure of a speech?

7. What is ethnocentrism? Why do public speakers need to avoid ethnocentrism when addressing audiences with diverse cultural, racial, or ethnic backgrounds?

Exercises for Critical Thinking

1. Divide a sheet of paper into two columns. Label one column "Characteristics of an Effective Public Speaker." Label the other column "Characteristics of an Ineffective Public Speaker." In the columns, list and briefly explain what you believe to be the five most important characteristics of effective and ineffective speakers. Be prepared to discuss your ideas in class.

2. On the basis of the lists you developed for Exercise 2, candidly evaluate your own strengths and weaknesses as a speaker. Identify the three primary aspects of speechmaking you most want to improve.

3. Think of a situation in which you sought to understand the message of, or to convey your own message to, someone from a different culture. The situation might have involved either public speaking or everyday conversation. What did the situation—and its outcome—reveal about the process of communicating cross-culturally? If you could approach the same situation again, what changes would you make to communicate more effectively?

End Notes

[1]Pericles, quoted in Richard Whately, *Elements of Rhetoric,* 7th ed. (London: John W. Parker, 1846), p. 10.

[2]"Corporate Recruiters Survey," *Graduate Management Admission Council,* June 2021 (https://www.gmac.com/market-intelligence-and-research/market-research/corporate-recruiters-survey); Francesca Levy and Christopher Cannon, "The Bloomberg Job Skills Report 2016: What Recruiters Want," February 9, 2016 (https://www.bloomberg.com/graphics/2016-job-skills-report/).

[3]Dave McGinn, "Me? Public Speaking?" *Globe and Mail,* December 1, 2009, p. L1.

[4]Quoted in Emily Driscoll, "Um, Like, Whatever: College Grads Lack Verbal Skills," Foxbusiness.com, March 4, 2011.

[5]George A. Kennedy, *Comparative Rhetoric: An Historical and Cross-Cultural Introduction* (New York: Oxford University Press, 1998).

[6]Anna Carolina Ferreira Marinho, Adriane Mesquita de Medeiros, Ana Cristina Côrtes Gama, and Letícia Caldas Teixeira, "Fear of Public Speaking: Perception of College Students and Correlates," *Journal of Voice,* 31 (2017), pp. E7–E11.

[7]A. M. Ruscio, T. A. Brown, W. T. Chiu, J. Sareen, M. B. Steain, and R. C. Kessler, "Social Fears and Social Phobia in the USA: Results from the National Comorbidity Survey Replication," *Psychological Medicine* (January 2008), pp. 15–28.

[8]Cicero, *De Oratore,* trans. E. W. Sutton (Cambridge, MA: Harvard University Press, 1942), p. xxvi.

[9]Digby Jones, "Public Speaking Tests the Nerves of Most Directors," *Birmingham Post,* August 25, 2003.

[10]Elayne Synder, *Speak for Yourself—With Confidence* (New York: New American Library, 1983), p. 113.

[11]Sharon Aschaiek, "Conquer Your Fear of Public Speaking," *Toronto Sun,* March 16, 2005.

[12]A number of studies have shown that taking a public speaking course is effective in reducing stage fright. For an excellent review of the research, consult Graham D. Bodie, "A Racing Heart, Rattling Knees, and Ruminative Thoughts: Defining, Explaining, and Treating Public Speaking Anxiety," *Communication Education,* 59 (2010), pp. 70–105.

[13]Lilly Walters, *Secrets of Successful Speakers* (New York: McGraw-Hill, 1993), pp. 32–36.

[14]See Steven Ungerleider, *Mental Training for Peak Performance,* rev. ed. (Emmaus, PA: Rodale Books, 2005).

[15]Joe Ayres, Tim Hopf, Michael T. Hazel, Debbie M. A. Sonandre, and Tanichya K. Wongprasert, "Visualization and Performance Visualization: Applications, Evidence, and Speculation," in John A. Daly et al. (eds.), *Avoiding Communication: Shyness, Reticence, and Communication Apprehension,* 3rd ed. (Cresskill, NJ: Hampton Press, 2009), pp. 375–394.

[16]Dick Cavett, quoted in Steve Allen, *How to Make a Speech* (New York: McGraw-Hill, 1986), p. 10.

[17]There are many books on stage fright and performance anxiety in general. Three of the most systematic are Michael T. Motley, *Overcoming Your Fear of Public Speaking: A Proven Method* (Boston: Houghton Mifflin, 1998); Janet E. Esposito, *In the Spotlight: Overcome Your Fear of Public Speaking and Performing* (Bridgewater, CT: In the Spotlight LLC, 2000); and Burton Jay Rubin, *Stagefright Solved* (Burton Jay Rubin, 2013).

[18]Chris R. Sawyer and Ralph R. Behnke, "Reduction in Public Speaking State Anxiety During Performance as a Function of Sensitization Processes," *Communication Quarterly,* 50 (2002), pp. 110–121.

[19]For more detail on the dimensions of critical thinking, see M. Neil Browne and Stuart M. Keeley, *Asking the Right Questions: A Guide to Critical Thinking,* 12th ed. (Boston: Pearson, 2018).

[20]Michael Kallet, *Think Smarter: Critical Thinking to Improve Problem-Solving and Decision-Making Skills* (New York: Wiley, 2014) shows how critical thinking can be applied in a wide range of business and other professional activities.

[21]Herman Melville, *Redburn: His First Voyage* (New York: Harper and Brothers, 1850), p. 214.

[22]Adapted from Roger E. Axtell (ed.), *Do's and Taboos Around the World,* 3rd ed. (New York: Wiley, 1993), p. 41.

[23]Myron W. Lustig, Jolene Koester, and Rona Halualani, *Intercultural Competence: Interpersonal Communication Across Cultures,* 8th ed. (New York: Pearson, 2018), p. 99.

[24]For a useful guide to these and other strategies of intercultural communication, see Paula Caligiuri, *Build Your Cultural Agility: The Nine Competencies of Successful Global Professionals* (New York: Kogan Page Limited, 2021).

2

Ethics and Public Speaking

When *The Wall Street Journal* first broke the story that Theranos was misleading investors and patients about its medical diagnostic technology, the company's founder, Elizabeth Holmes, fired back in a series of media appearances. One week after the original article, she spoke at *The Wall Street Journal*'s global technology conference. "We don't do what's in that article," she declared. "We know the facts, we know the integrity of what we've done."

For a time, it looked as though Holmes and Theranos were going to survive the storm. But as investors and regulators looked more deeply, they discovered that the lies and cover-ups were much worse than originally reported. Holmes had falsified financial documents, destroyed data, changed lab results, and lied about Theranos's technology, putting patients in jeopardy. All of this while she spoke stridently about the integrity of the company.

Once the full scope of Holmes's deception came to light, Theranos's valuation went from $9 billion to practically nothing. Then the U.S. government charged Holmes with fraud and conspiracy.

After a lengthy trial, she was convicted of lying to cover up her company's failures. As Assistant U.S. Attorney Jeffrey Schenk summarized the case, Holmes "chose to be dishonest with her investors and patients. That choice was not only callous, it was criminal."

This is not a happy story, but it shows why public speaking needs to be guided by a strong sense of ethical integrity. Elizabeth Holmes was charming and persuasive when speaking about Theranos, but she was unethical in lying to cover up her illegal activities. As a result, she did great harm to patients and investors and destroyed her reputation.

The goal of public speaking is to gain a desired response from listeners—but not at any cost. Speechmaking is a form of power and therefore carries with it heavy ethical responsibilities. As the Roman rhetorician Quintilian stated 2,000 years ago, the ideal of speechmaking is the good person speaking well. In this chapter, we explore that ideal by looking at the importance of ethics in public speaking, the ethical obligations of speakers and listeners, and the practical problem of plagiarism and how to avoid it.

The Importance of Ethics

ethics
The branch of philosophy that deals with issues of right and wrong in human affairs.

Ethics is the branch of philosophy that deals with issues of right and wrong in human affairs. Questions of ethics arise whenever we ask whether a course of action is moral or immoral, fair or unfair, just or unjust, honest or dishonest.

We face such questions daily in almost every part of our lives. The parent must decide how to deal with a child who has been sent home from school for unruly behavior. The researcher must decide whether to shade her data "just a bit" to gain credit for an important scientific breakthrough. The shopper must decide what to do with the $5 extra change mistakenly given by the clerk at the grocery store. The student must decide whether to say anything about a friend he has seen cheating on a final exam.

Questions of ethics also come into play whenever a public speaker faces an audience. In an ideal world, as the Greek philosopher Plato noted, all public speakers would be truthful and devoted to the good of society. Yet history tells us that the power of speech is often abused—sometimes with disastrous results. Adolf Hitler was unquestionably a persuasive speaker. His oratory galvanized the German people, but his aims were horrifying and his tactics despicable. He remains to this day the ultimate example of why the power of the spoken word needs to be guided by a strong sense of ethical integrity.

As a public speaker, you will face ethical issues at every stage of the speechmaking process—from the initial decision to speak through the final presentation of the message. And the answers will not always be easy. Consider the following example:

> Felicia Robinson is running for school board in a large eastern city. Her opponent is conducting what Felicia regards as a highly unethical campaign. In addition to twisting the facts about school taxes, the opponent is pandering to racial prejudice by raising resentment against African Americans and recently arrived immigrants.
>
> Five days before the election, Felicia, who is slightly behind in the polls, learns that the district attorney is preparing to indict her opponent for shady business practices. But the indictment will not be formally issued until after the election. Nor can it be taken as evidence that her opponent is guilty—like all citizens, he has the right to be presumed innocent until proven otherwise.
>
> Still, news of the indictment could be enough to throw the election Felicia's way, and her advisers urge her to make it an issue in her remaining campaign speeches. Should Felicia follow their advice?

There are creditable arguments to be made on both sides of the ethical dilemma faced by Felicia Robinson. She has tried to run an honest campaign, and she is troubled by the possibility of unfairly attacking her opponent—despite the fact that he has shown no such scruples himself. Yet she knows that the impending indictment may be her last chance to win the election, and she is convinced that a victory for her opponent will spell disaster for the city's school system. Torn between her commitment to fair play, her desire to be elected, and her concern for the good of the community, she faces the age-old ethical dilemma of whether the ends justify the means.

"So," you may be asking yourself, "what is the answer to Felicia Robinson's dilemma?" In complex cases such as hers there are no cut-and-dried answers. As the leading book on communication ethics states, "We should formulate meaningful ethical guidelines, not inflexible rules."[1] Your ethical decisions will be guided by your values, your conscience, and your sense of right and wrong.

But this does not mean such decisions are simply a matter of personal whim or fancy. Sound ethical decisions involve weighing a potential course of action against a set of ethical standards or guidelines. Just as there are guidelines for ethical behavior in other areas of life, so there are guidelines for ethical conduct in public speaking. These guidelines will not automatically solve every ethical quandary you face as a speaker, but knowing them will provide a reliable compass to help you find your way.

Guidelines for Ethical Speaking

MAKE SURE YOUR GOALS ARE ETHICALLY SOUND

Several years ago, a former student—we'll call her Melissa—turned down a job in the public relations department of the American Tobacco Institute. Why? Because the job would have required her to lobby on behalf of the cigarette industry. Melissa did not believe she could ethically promote a product that she saw as responsible for thousands of deaths and illnesses each year.

Given Melissa's view of the dangers of cigarette smoking, there can be no doubt that she made an ethically informed decision. On the other side of the coin, someone with a different view of cigarette smoking could make an ethically informed decision to *take* the job. The point of this example is not to judge the rightness or wrongness of Melissa's decision (or of cigarette smoking), but to illustrate how ethical considerations can affect a speaker's choice of goals.

Your first responsibility as a speaker is to ask whether your goals are ethically sound. During World War II, Hitler stirred the German people to condone war, invasion, and genocide. More recently, we have seen politicians who betray the public trust for personal gain, business leaders who defraud investors of millions of dollars, preachers who lead lavish lifestyles at the expense of their religious duties. There can be no doubt that these are not worthy goals.

But think back for a moment to the examples of speechmaking given in Chapter 1. What do the speakers hope to accomplish? Improve children's health. Pay tribute to a fellow worker. Support Habitat for Humanity. Few people would question that these goals are ethically sound.

As with other ethical issues, there can be gray areas when it comes to assessing a speaker's goals—areas in which reasonable people with well-defined standards of right and wrong can legitimately disagree. But this is not a reason to avoid asking ethical questions. If you are to be a responsible public speaker, you cannot escape assessing the ethical soundness of your goals.

BE FULLY PREPARED FOR EACH SPEECH

"A speech," as Jenkin Lloyd Jones stated, "is a solemn responsibility." You have an obligation—to yourself and to your listeners—to prepare fully every time you stand in front of an audience. The obligation to yourself is obvious: The better you prepare, the better your speech will be. But the obligation to your listeners is no less important. Think of it this way: The person who makes a bad 30-minute speech to an audience of 200 people wastes only a half hour of her or his own time. But that same speaker wastes 100 hours of the audience's time—more than four full days. This, Jones exclaimed, "should be a hanging offense!"

At this stage of your speaking career, of course, you will probably not be facing many audiences of 200 people. And you will probably not be giving many speeches in which the audience has come for the sole purpose of listening to you. But neither the size nor the composition of your audience changes your ethical responsibility to be fully prepared. Your speech classmates are as worthy of your best effort as if you were addressing a jury or a business meeting, a union conference or a church congregation, the local city council or even the United States Senate.

Being prepared for a speech involves everything from analyzing your audience to creating visual aids, from organizing your ideas to rehearsing your delivery. Most crucial from an ethical standpoint, though, is being fully informed about your subject. Why is this so important? Consider the following story:

> Victoria Nuñez, a student at a large state university, gave a classroom speech on suicide prevention. Victoria had learned about the topic from her mother, a volunteer on a suicide-prevention hotline, but she also consulted her psychology textbook, read several articles on the warning signs of suicide, and interviewed a crisis-intervention counselor at the campus health service.
>
> In addition to her research, Victoria gave a lot of thought to planning and delivering her speech. She created a handout for the class listing signs that a person might attempt suicide and providing contact information for local mental-health resources. On the day of her speech, Victoria was thoroughly prepared—and she gave an excellent presentation.
>
> Only a few days later, one of Victoria's classmates, Paul Nichols, had a conversation with his roommate that raised a warning flag about whether the roommate might be depressed and in danger of suicide. Based on the information in Victoria's speech, Paul spoke to his roommate, got him to talk about his worries, and convinced him to seek counseling. Paul might have saved his roommate's life, thanks to Victoria's speech.

This is an especially dramatic case, but it demonstrates how your speeches can have a genuine impact on your listeners. As a speaker, you have an ethical responsibility to consider that impact and to make sure you prepare fully so as not to communicate erroneous information or misleading advice. If Victoria had not done such a thorough job researching her speech, she might have given her classmates faulty information—information that might have had tragic results.

No matter what the topic, no matter who the audience, you need to explore your speech topic as thoroughly as possible. Investigate the whole story; learn about all sides of an issue; seek out competing viewpoints; get the facts right. Not only will you give a better speech, you will also fulfill one of your major ethical obligations.

BE HONEST IN WHAT YOU SAY

Nothing is more important to ethical speechmaking than honesty. Public speaking rests on the unspoken assumption that "words can be trusted and people will be

Questions of ethics arise whenever a speaker faces an audience. Here Nobel laureate Malala Yousafzi addresses listeners at the Massachusetts Conference for Women.

Marla Aufmuth/Getty Images

truthful."[2] Without this assumption, there is no basis for communication, no reason for one person to believe anything that another person says.

Does this mean *every* speaker must *always* tell "the truth, the whole truth, and nothing but the truth"? We can all think of situations in which this is impossible (because we do not know the whole truth) or inadvisable (because it would be tactless or imprudent). Consider a parent who tells his two-year-old daughter that her screeching violin solo is "beautiful." Or a speaker who tells a falsehood in circumstances when disclosing the truth might touch off mob violence. Few people would find these actions unethical.[3]

In contrast, think back to the case of Elizabeth Holmes at the start of this chapter. She knew she had defrauded investors and misled patients. Yet she repeatedly lied by denying that she had done so. There is no way to excuse her behavior.

Such blatant contempt for the truth is one kind of dishonesty in public speaking. But more subtle forms of dishonesty are just as unethical. They include juggling statistics, quoting out of context, misrepresenting sources, painting tentative findings as firm conclusions, citing unusual cases as typical examples, and substituting innuendo and half-truths for evidence and proof. All of these violate the speaker's duty to be accurate and fair in presenting information.

While on the subject of honesty in speechmaking, we should also note that ethically responsible speakers do not present other people's words as their own. They do not plagiarize their speeches. This subject is so important that we devote a separate section to it later in this chapter.

AVOID NAME-CALLING AND OTHER FORMS OF ABUSIVE LANGUAGE

"Sticks and stones can break my bones, but words can never hurt me." This popular children's chant could not be more wrong. Words may not literally break people's bones, but they can leave psychological scars as surely as sticks and stones can leave

As stated by the Roman rhetorician Quintilian, the ideal of speechmaking is the good person speaking well. Of all the ethical obligations facing a speaker, none is more important than honesty in order to maintain the bond of trust with listeners.

Steve Debenport/Getty Images

name-calling
The use of language to defame, demean, or degrade individuals or groups.

Bill of Rights
The first 10 amendments to the United States Constitution.

physical scars. As one writer explains, "Our identities, who and what we are, how others see us, are greatly affected by the names we are called and the words with which we are labeled."[4] This is why communication ethicists warn public speakers to avoid name-calling and other forms of abusive language.

Name-calling is the use of language to defame, demean, or degrade individuals or groups. This includes using epithets and labels based on people's race, national origin, sexual orientation, gender identity, religious beliefs, or ethnic background. Such terms are ethically suspect because they stereotype and devalue the people in question.

Name-calling is also a destructive social force. When used repeatedly and systematically over time, it helps reinforce attitudes that encourage prejudice, hate crimes, and civil rights violations. The issue is not one of political correctness, but of respecting the dignity of diverse groups in contemporary society.

In addition, name-calling and abusive language pose ethical problems in public speaking when they are used to silence opposing voices. A democratic society depends upon the free and open expression of ideas. In the United States, all citizens have the right to join in the never-ending dialogue of democracy. As a public speaker, you have an ethical obligation to help preserve that right.

Like other ethical questions in public speaking, name-calling raises some thorny issues. Although name-calling can be hazardous to free speech, it is still protected under the free-speech clause of the Bill of Rights. This is why broadly worded codes against hate speech on college campuses—and in society at large—have not survived legal challenges.[5]

But regardless of the legal issues, they do not alter the ethical responsibility of public speakers to avoid name-calling and abusive language. Legality and ethics, though related, are not identical. There is nothing illegal about falsifying statistics in a speech, but there is no doubt that it is unethical. The same is true of name-calling. It may not be illegal to cast racial, sexual, or religious slurs at people in a speech, but it is still unethical. Not only does it demean the dignity of the groups or individuals being attacked, but it undermines the right of all groups in the United States to be fairly heard.[6]

PUT ETHICAL PRINCIPLES INTO PRACTICE

It is easy to pay lip service to the importance of ethics. It is much harder to act ethically. Yet that is just what a responsible public speaker must do. As one popular book on ethics states, "Being ethical means behaving ethically *all the time*—not only when it's convenient."[7]

As you work on your speeches, you will ask yourself such questions as "Is my choice of topic suitable for the audience?" "Are my supporting materials clear and

 **checklist**

Ethical Public Speaking

YES	NO	
☐	☐	1. Have I examined my goals to make sure they are ethically sound?
		a. Can I defend my goals on ethical grounds if they are questioned or challenged?
		b. Would I want other people to know my true motives in presenting this speech?
☐	☐	2. Have I fulfilled my ethical obligation to prepare fully for the speech?
		a. Have I done a thorough job of studying and researching the topic?
		b. Have I prepared diligently so as not to communicate erroneous or misleading information to my listeners?
☐	☐	3. Is the speech free of plagiarism?
		a. Can I vouch that the speech represents my own work, my own thinking, my own language?
		b. Do I cite the sources of all quotations and paraphrases?
☐	☐	4. Am I honest in what I say in the speech?
		a. Is the speech free of any false or deliberately deceptive statements?
		b. Does the speech present statistics, testimony, and other kinds of evidence fairly and accurately?
		c. Does the speech contain valid reasoning?
		d. If the speech includes visual aids, do they present facts honestly and reliably?
☐	☐	5. Do I use the power of language ethically?
		a. Do I avoid name-calling and other forms of abusive language?
		b. Does my language show respect for the right of free speech and expression?
☐	☐	6. All in all, have I made a conscious effort to put ethical principles into practice in preparing my speech?

convincing?" "How can I phrase my ideas to give them more punch?" These are *strategic* questions. As you answer them, you will try to make your speech as informative, as persuasive, or as entertaining as possible.

But you will also face moments of *ethical* decision—similar, perhaps, to those faced by Elizabeth Holmes, Felicia Robinson, and other speakers in this chapter. When those moments arrive, don't simply brush them aside and go on your way. Keep in mind the guidelines for ethical speechmaking we have discussed and do your best to follow them through thick and thin. Make sure you can answer yes to all the questions on the Checklist for Ethical Public Speaking.

Plagiarism

plagiarism

Presenting another person's language or ideas as one's own.

Plagiarism comes from *plagiarius,* the Latin word for kidnapper. To plagiarize means to present another person's language or ideas as your own—to give the impression you have written or thought something yourself when you have actually taken it from someone else.[8] We often think of plagiarism as an ethical issue in the classroom, but it can have repercussions in other situations:

> With a 43-year military career that culminated in leading the U.S. Military Academy at West Point, Robert Caslen was already an experienced public speaker. Then he became president of the University of South Carolina, a position that gave him many more occasions to address large crowds.
>
> Caslen addressed one such crowd during a commencement ceremony in 2021. Speaking to the graduates before him, Caslen talked about the importance of character and resilience. But some listeners thought the words sounded familiar.
>
> After a little online sleuthing, they discovered a YouTube video of a commencement address at the University of Texas by Navy Admiral William McRaven. It turned out that Caslen had lifted the conclusion of his speech directly from McRaven's. Word of Caslen's plagiarism spread quickly online and made national headlines.
>
> Facing widespread pressure to step down, including from many at the University of South Carolina, Caslen submitted his resignation less than a week later. "I sincerely apologize," he said, "to Admiral McRaven, someone I know and respect, our graduates, their families and the entire university community for not leading by example."

As this story shows, plagiarism is a serious matter. If you are caught plagiarizing a speech in class, the punishment can range from a failing grade to expulsion from school. If you are caught plagiarizing outside the classroom, you stand to forfeit your good name, to damage your career, or, if you are sued, to lose a large amount of money. It is worth your while, then, to make sure you know what plagiarism is and how to avoid it.

GLOBAL PLAGIARISM

Global plagiarism is stealing your speech entirely from another source and passing it off as your own. The most blatant—and unforgivable—kind of plagiarism, it is grossly unethical.

Global plagiarism in a college classroom usually occurs because a student puts off the assignment until the last minute. Then, in an act of desperation, the student downloads a speech from the Internet or gets one written by a friend and delivers it as his or her own.

The best way to avoid this, of course, is not to leave your speech until the last minute. Most instructors explain speech assignments far enough in advance that you should have no trouble getting an early start. By starting early, you will give yourself plenty of time to prepare a first-rate speech—a speech of your own.

If, for some reason, you fail to get your speech ready on time, do not succumb to the lure of plagiarism. Whatever penalty you suffer from being late will pale in comparison with the consequences if you are caught plagiarizing.

PATCHWORK PLAGIARISM

Unlike global plagiarism, in which a speaker pirates an entire speech from a single source, patchwork plagiarism occurs when a speaker pilfers from two or three sources. Here's an example:

> Lexi Nau chose "The Benefits and Drawbacks of Autonomous Vehicles" as the topic for her informative speech. In her research, Lexi found three especially helpful sources. The first was a recent article in the journal *Science* on the ethical challenges of programming autonomous vehicles. The second was Wikipedia, and the third was the website of the Stanford University Center for Automotive Research.
>
> Unfortunately, instead of using these materials creatively to write a speech in her own words, Lexi lifted long passages from the article, from Wikipedia, and from the university website and patched them together with a few transitions. When she was finished, she had a speech that was composed almost entirely of other people's words.
>
> When Lexi's teacher read her speech outline, it did not sound authentic to him. So he plugged several phrases from the outline into Google. In less than a minute, he had found both the Wikipedia article and the Stanford University website. After searching on Google Scholar, he also found the journal article. Lexi was caught red-handed.

This story illustrates an important point about plagiarism. Lexi did not take her speech from a single source. She even did a little research. But copying from a few sources is no less plagiarism than copying from a single source. When you give a speech, you declare that it is your work—the product of your thinking, your beliefs, your language. Lexi's speech did not contain any of these. Instead, it was cut and pasted wholly from other people's words.

As with global plagiarism, one key to averting patchwork plagiarism is to start working on your speech as soon as possible. The longer you work on it, the more apt you are to come up with your own slant on the topic. It is also vital to consult a large number of sources in your research. If you have only two or three sources, you are far more likely to fall into the trap of patchwork plagiarism than if you consult a wide range of research materials.

INCREMENTAL PLAGIARISM

In global plagiarism and patchwork plagiarism, the entire speech is cribbed more or less verbatim from a single source or a few sources. But plagiarism can exist even

Speakers who begin work on their speeches early and consult a wide range of sources are less likely to fall into the trap of plagiarism than are speakers who procrastinate and rely on a limited number of sources.

Dotshock/Shutterstock

when the speech as a whole is not pirated. This is called incremental plagiarism. It occurs when the speaker fails to give credit for particular parts—increments—of the speech that are borrowed from other people. The most important of these increments are quotations and paraphrases.

Quotations

Whenever you quote someone directly, you must attribute the words to that person. Suppose you are giving a speech on Malcolm X, the famous African American leader of the 1960s. While doing your research, you run across the following passage from Bruce Perry's biography, *Malcolm: The Life of the Man Who Changed Black America:*

> Malcolm X fathered no legislation. He engineered no stunning Supreme Court victories or political campaigns. He scored no major electoral triumphs. Yet because of the way he articulated his followers' grievances and anger, the impact he had upon the body politic was enormous.[9]

This is a fine quotation that summarizes the nature and importance of Malcolm's impact on American politics. It would make a strong addition to your speech—as long as you acknowledge Perry as the author. The way to avoid plagiarism in this instance is to introduce Perry's statement by saying something like:

> In *Malcolm: The Life of the Man Who Changed Black America,* historian Bruce Perry says the following about Malcolm's impact on American politics: . . .

Or,

> According to historian Bruce Perry in his book *Malcolm: The Life of the Man Who Changed Black America,* . . .

Now you have clearly identified Perry and given him credit for his words rather than presenting them as your own.

Paraphrases

When you paraphrase an author, you restate or summarize her or his ideas in your own words. Suppose, once again, that your topic is Malcolm X. But this time you decide to paraphrase the statement from Bruce Perry's biography rather than quoting it. You might say:

> Malcolm X was not a politician. He did not pass any laws, or win any Supreme Court victories, or get elected to any office. But he stated the grievances and anger of his followers so powerfully that the whole nation took notice.

paraphrase

To restate or summarize an author's ideas in one's own words.

Even though you do not quote Perry directly, you still appropriate the structure of his ideas and a fair amount of his language. Thus you still need to give him credit—just as if you were repeating his words verbatim.

It is especially important in this case to acknowledge Perry because you are borrowing his opinion—his judgment—about Malcolm X. If you simply recount basic facts about Malcolm's life, you do not have to report the source of your information. These facts are well known and can be found in any standard reference work.

On the other hand, there is still considerable debate about Malcolm's views of other African American leaders and what he might have done had he lived. If you were to cite Perry's views on either of these matters—regardless of whether you quoted or paraphrased—you would need to acknowledge him as your source.

As more than one speaker (and writer) has discovered, it is possible to commit incremental plagiarism quite by accident. This is less offensive than deliberate plagiarism, but it is plagiarism nonetheless. There are two ways to guard against incremental plagiarism. The first is to be careful when taking research notes to distinguish among direct quotations, paraphrased material, and your own comments. (See Chapter 7 for a full discussion of research methods.) The second way to avoid incremental plagiarism is to err on the side of caution. In other words, when in doubt, cite your source.

PLAGIARISM AND THE INTERNET

When it comes to plagiarism, no subject poses more confusion—or more temptation—than the Internet. Because it's so easy to copy information from the web, many people are not aware of the need to cite sources when they use Internet materials in their speeches. If you don't cite Internet sources, you are just as guilty of plagiarism as if you take information from print sources without proper citation.

One way to avoid patchwork plagiarism or incremental plagiarism when working with the Internet is to take careful research notes. Make sure you keep a record of the following: (1) the title of the Internet document, (2) the author or organization responsible for the document, (3) the date on which the document was last updated, and (4) the date on which you accessed the site. You will need all this information for your speech bibliography.

You will also need to identify your Internet sources when you present the speech. It's not enough to say "As I found on the web" or "According to the Internet." You

Having graduated with a degree in public administration and hoping to pursue a career in politics, you have been fortunate to receive a staff position with one of the leading senators in your state legislature. Since your arrival two months ago, you have answered phones, ordered lunch, made copies, stapled mailings, and stuffed envelopes. Finally you have been asked to look over a speech the senator will deliver at your alma mater. Surely, you think, this will be the first of many important assignments once your value is recognized.

After reading the speech, however, your enthusiasm is dampened. You agree wholeheartedly with its support of a bill to fund scholarships for low-income students, but you're dismayed by its attack on opponents of the bill as "elitist bigots who would deny a college education to those who need it most." You haven't been asked to comment on the ethics of the speech, and you certainly don't want to jeopardize your position on the senator's staff. At the same time, you think his use of name-calling may actually arouse sympathy for the opposition. The senator would like your comments in two hours. What will you tell him?

Peshkova/Shutterstock

need to specify the author and the website. In Chapter 8, we'll look more closely at how to cite Internet documents. For now, keep in mind that providing such citations is one of your ethical responsibilities as a public speaker.

Another problem with regard to the Internet is the large number of websites that sell entire speeches or papers. In addition to being highly unethical, using material from one of these sites is extremely risky. The same technology that makes it easy to plagiarize from the web makes it easy for instructors to locate material that has been plagiarized and the exact source from which it has been taken.

You should also know that almost all the speeches (and papers) offered for sale on the web are of very low quality. If you are ever tempted to purchase one, keep in mind there is a good chance you will waste your money and get caught in the process. Here, as in other aspects of life, honesty is the best policy.

Guidelines for Ethical Listening

So far in this chapter we have focused on the ethical duties of public speakers. But speechmaking is not a one-way street. Listeners also have ethical obligations. They are (1) to listen courteously and attentively, (2) to avoid prejudging the speaker, and (3) to maintain the free and open expression of ideas. Let us look at each.

BE COURTEOUS AND ATTENTIVE

Imagine that you are giving your first classroom speech. You have put a great deal of time into writing the speech, and you have practiced your delivery until you are confident you can do well—especially once you get over the initial rush of stage fright.

You have worked hard on your introduction, and your speech gets off to a fine start. Most of your classmates are paying close attention, but some are not. One appears to be doing homework for another class. Another keeps sneaking glances at his cell phone. Two or three are gazing out the window, and one is leaning back in his chair with his eyes shut!

You try to block them out of your mind—especially since the rest of the class seems interested in what you are saying—but the longer you speak, the more concerned you become. "What am I doing wrong?" you wonder to yourself. "How can I get these people to pay attention?" The more you think about this, the more your confidence and concentration waver.

When you momentarily lose your place halfway through the speech, you start to panic. Your nerves, which you have held in check so far, take the upper hand. Your major thought now becomes, "How can I get this over as fast as possible?" Flustered and distracted, you rush through the rest of your speech and sit down.

Just as public speakers have an ethical obligation to prepare fully for each speech, so listeners have a responsibility to be courteous and attentive during the speech. This responsibility—which is a matter of civility in any circumstance—is especially important in speech class. You and your classmates are in a learning situation in which you need to support one another.

When you listen to speeches in class, give your fellow students the same courtesy and attention you want from them. Come to class prepared to listen to—and to learn from—your classmates' speeches. As you listen, be conscious of the feedback you are sending the speaker. Sit up in your chair rather than slouching; maintain eye contact with the speaker; show support and encouragement in your facial expressions. Keep in mind the power you have as a listener over the speaker's confidence and composure, and exercise that power with a strong sense of ethical responsibility.

AVOID PREJUDGING THE SPEAKER

We have all heard that you can't judge a book by its cover. The same is true of speeches. You can't judge a speech by the name, race, lifestyle, appearance, or reputation of the speaker. As the National Communication Association states in its Credo for Ethical Communication, listeners should "strive to understand and respect" speakers "before evaluating and responding to their messages."[10]

This does not mean you must agree with every speaker you hear. Your aim is to listen carefully to the speaker's ideas, to assess the evidence and reasoning offered in support of those ideas, and to reach an intelligent judgment about the speech. In Chapter 3, we will discuss specific steps you can take to improve your listening skills. For now, it is enough to know that if you prejudge a speaker—either positively or negatively—you will fail in one of your ethical responsibilities as a listener.

MAINTAIN THE FREE AND OPEN EXPRESSION OF IDEAS

As we saw earlier in this chapter, a democratic society depends on the free and open expression of ideas. The right of free expression is so important that it is protected

It is vital for a democratic society to maintain the free and open expression of ideas. Here Nobel Peace Prize recipient Maria Ressa speaks at the International Press Freedom Awards in New York City.

Dia Dipasupil/Getty Images

by the First Amendment to the U.S. Constitution, which declares, in part, that "Congress shall make no law . . . abridging the freedom of speech." Just as public speakers need to avoid name-calling and other tactics that can undermine free speech, so listeners have an obligation to maintain the right of speakers to be heard.

As with other ethical issues, the extent of this obligation is open to debate. Disputes over the meaning and scope of the First Amendment arise almost daily in connection with issues such as terrorism, surveillance, bullying, and hate speech. The question underlying such disputes is whether *all* speakers have a right to be heard.

There are some kinds of speech that are not protected under the First Amendment—including defamatory falsehoods that destroy a person's reputation, threats against the life of the President, and inciting an audience to illegal action in circumstances where the audience is likely to carry out the action. Otherwise, the Supreme Court has held—and most experts in communication ethics have agreed—that public speakers have an almost unlimited right of free expression.

In contrast to this view, it has been argued that some ideas are so dangerous, so misguided, or so offensive that society has a duty to suppress them. Yet free-speech advocates would ask: Who is to determine which ideas are too dangerous, misguided, or offensive to be uttered? Who is to decide which speakers are to be heard and which are to be silenced?

It is important to keep in mind that ensuring the freedom of people to express their ideas does not imply agreement with those ideas. You can disagree entirely with the message but still support the speaker's right to express it. As the National Communication Association states in its Credo for Ethical Communication, "freedom of expression, diversity of perspective, and tolerance of dissent" are vital to "the informed decision making fundamental to a civil society."[11]

Summary

Because public speaking is a form of power, it carries with it heavy ethical responsibilities. Today, as for the past 2,000 years, the good person speaking well remains the ideal of commendable speechmaking.

There are five basic guidelines for ethical public speaking. The first is to make sure your goals are ethically sound—that they are consistent with the welfare of society and your audience. The second is to be fully prepared for each speech. The third is to be honest in what you say. The fourth is to avoid name-calling and other forms of abusive language. The final guideline is to put ethical principles into practice at all times.

Of all the ethical lapses a speaker can commit, few are more serious than plagiarism. Global plagiarism is lifting a speech entirely from a single source. Patchwork plagiarism involves stitching a speech together by copying from a few sources. Incremental plagiarism occurs when a speaker fails to give credit for specific quotations and paraphrases that are borrowed from other people.

In addition to your ethical responsibilities as a speaker, you have ethical obligations as a listener. The first is to listen courteously and attentively. The second is to avoid prejudging the speaker. The third is to support the free and open expression of ideas. In all these ways, your speech class will offer a good testing ground for questions of ethical responsibility.

Key Terms

ethics (28)

ethical decisions (29)

name-calling (32)

Bill of Rights (32)

plagiarism (34)

global plagiarism (35)

patchwork plagiarism (35)

incremental plagiarism (35)

paraphrase (37)

Review Questions

After reading this chapter, you should be able to answer the following questions:

1. What is ethics? Why is a strong sense of ethical responsibility vital for public speakers?

2. What are the five guidelines for ethical speechmaking discussed in this chapter?

3. What is the difference between global plagiarism and patchwork plagiarism? What are the best ways to avoid these two kinds of plagiarism?

4. What is incremental plagiarism? How can you steer clear of it when dealing with quotations and paraphrases?

5. What are the three guidelines for ethical listening discussed in this chapter?

Exercises for Critical Thinking

1. Look back at the story of Felicia Robinson on pages 28–29. Evaluate her dilemma in light of the guidelines for ethical speechmaking presented in this chapter. Explain what you believe would be the most ethical course of action in her case.

2. The issue of insulting and abusive speech—especially slurs directed against people on the basis of race, religion, gender identity, or sexual orientation—is extremely controversial. Do you believe society should punish such speech with criminal penalties? To what degree are colleges and universities justified in trying to discipline students who engage in such speech? Do you feel it is proper to place any boundaries on free expression to prohibit insulting and abusive speech? Why or why not? Be prepared to explain your ideas in class.

3. All of the following situations could arise in your speech class. Identify the ethical issues in each and explain what, as a responsible speaker or listener, your course of action would be.

   a. You are speaking on the topic of prison reform. In your research, you run across two public opinion polls. One of them, an independent survey by the Gallup Organization, shows that a majority of people in your state oppose your position. The other poll, suspect in its methods and conducted by a partisan organization, says a majority of people in your state support your position. Which poll do you cite in your speech? If you cite the second poll, do you point out its shortcomings?

   b. When listening to an informative speech by one of your classmates, you realize that much of it is plagiarized from a website you visited a couple of weeks earlier. What do you do? Do you say something when your instructor asks for comments about the speech? Do you mention your concern to the instructor after class? Do you talk with the speaker? Do you remain silent?

   c. While researching your persuasive speech, you find a quotation from an article by a highly respected expert that will nail down one of your most important points. But as you read the rest of the article, you realize that the author does not in fact support the policy you are advocating. Do you still include the quotation in your speech? Why or why not?

End Notes

[1] Richard L. Johannesen, Kathleen S. Valde, and Karen E. Whedbee, *Ethics in Human Communication,* 6th ed. (Prospect Heights, IL: Waveland Press, 2008), p. 14.

[2] Johannesen, Valde, and Whedbee, *Ethics in Human Communication,* p. 13.

[3] See, for example, Vincent Ryan Ruggiero, *Thinking Critically About Ethical Issues,* 10th ed. (New York: McGraw Hill, 2020).

[4] Haig A. Bosmajian, *The Language of Oppression* (Lanham, MD: University Press of America, 1983), p. 5.

[5] Thomas L. Tedford and Dale A. Herbeck, *Freedom of Speech in the United States,* 8th ed. (State College, PA: Strata Publishing, 2017), pp. 202–210.

[6] Hate speech on campus has been a subject of considerable debate in recent years. Thoughtful discussions can be found in Michael S. Roth, *Safe Enough Spaces: A Pragmatist's Approach to Inclusion, Free Speech, and Political Correctness on College Campuses* (New Haven, CT: Yale

University Press, 2019), and Erwin Chemerinsky and Howard Gilman, *Free Speech on Campus* (New Haven, CT: Yale University Press, 2017).

[7]Kenneth Blanchard and Norman Vincent Peale, *The Power of Ethical Management* (New York: Ballantine Books, 1988), p. 64.

[8]*MLA Handbook,* 9th ed. (New York: Modern Language Association of America, 2021), p. 96.

[9]Bruce Perry, *Malcolm: The Life of the Man Who Changed Black America* (Tarrytown, NY: Station Hill, 1991), p. 380.

[10]The credo can be accessed at https://www.natcom.org/sites/default/files/pages/1999_Public_ Statements_NCA_Credo_for_Ethical_Communication_November.pdf.

[11]See https://www.natcom.org/sites/default/files/pages/1999_Public_Statements_NCA_Credo_ for_Ethical_Communication_November.pdf.

3 Listening

Rose Finnegan burst through the front door of her condo ready to share the good news: She had just been promoted to operations manager at the FedEx distribution center where she works. Bubbling with excitement, she found her husband on the couch staring into his laptop. "Guess what?" she asked.

"What?" he replied, his eyes never leaving the computer screen.

"I got the promotion at work!"

"That's great," he murmured.

"Let's go out to dinner to celebrate," she said, heading into the bedroom to change clothes.

Fifteen minutes later, Rose emerged from the bedroom and saw her husband in the same position on the couch, his eyes still glued to the screen. Finally looking up, he noticed his wife's clothes. "You look nice!" he exclaimed. "Where are you going?"

This story illustrates what one research study after another has revealed—most people are shockingly poor listeners. We fake paying attention. We can look right at someone, appear interested in what that person says, even nod our head or smile at the appropriate moments—all without really listening.

hearing
The vibration of sound waves on the eardrums and the firing of electrochemical impulses in the brain.

Not listening doesn't mean we don't hear. *Hearing* is a physiological process, involving the vibration of sound waves on our eardrums and the firing of electrochemical impulses from the inner ear to the central auditory system of the brain. But *listening* involves paying close attention to, and making sense of, what we hear. Even when we think we are listening carefully, we usually grasp only 50 percent of what we hear. After 24 hours we can remember only 10 percent of the original message.[1] It's little wonder that listening has been called a lost art.[2]

Listening Is Important

Although most people listen poorly, there are exceptions. Top-flight business executives, successful politicians, brilliant teachers—nearly all are excellent listeners.[3] So much of what they do depends on absorbing information that is given verbally—and absorbing it quickly and accurately. If you had an interview with the president of a major corporation, you might be shocked (and flattered) to see how closely that person listened to your words.

In our communication-oriented age, listening is more important than ever. According to one study, more than 60 percent of errors made in business come from poor listening.[4] When business managers are asked to rank-order the communication skills most crucial to their jobs, they usually rank listening number one.[5]

Even if you don't plan to be a corporate executive, the art of listening can be helpful in almost every part of your life. This is not surprising when you realize that people spend more time listening than in any other communicative activity—more than reading, more than writing, more even than speaking.[6]

Think for a moment about your own life as a college student. Most class time in U.S. colleges and universities is spent listening to discussions and lectures. A number of studies have shown a strong correlation between listening and academic success. Students with the highest grades are usually those with the strongest listening skills. The reverse is also true—students with the lowest grades are usually those with the weakest listening skills.[7]

Listening is also important to you as a speaker. It is probably the way you get most of your ideas and information—from television, YouTube, conversation, and lectures. If you do not listen well, you will not understand what you hear and may pass along your misunderstanding to others.

Besides, in class—as in life—you will listen to many more speeches than you give. It is only fair to pay close attention to your classmates' speeches; after all, you want them to listen carefully to *your* speeches. An excellent way to improve your own speeches is to listen attentively to the speeches of other people. Over and over, instructors find that the best speakers are usually the best listeners.

A side benefit of your speech class is that it offers an ideal opportunity to work on the art of listening. During the 95 percent of the time when you are not speaking, you have nothing else to do but listen and learn. You can sit there like a stone—or you can use the time profitably to master a skill that will serve you in a thousand ways.[8]

Listening and Critical Thinking

One of the ways listening can serve you is by enhancing your skills as a critical thinker. We can identify four kinds of listening:[9]

- *Appreciative listening*—listening for pleasure or enjoyment, as when we listen to music, to a comedy routine, or to an entertaining speech.
- *Empathic listening*—listening to provide emotional support for the speaker, as when a psychiatrist listens to a patient or when we lend a sympathetic ear to a friend in distress.
- *Comprehensive listening*—listening to understand the message of a speaker, as when we attend a classroom lecture or listen to directions for finding a friend's house.

listening
Paying close attention to, and making sense of, what we hear.

appreciative listening
Listening for pleasure or enjoyment.

empathic listening
Listening to provide emotional support for a speaker.

comprehensive listening
Listening to understand the message of a speaker.

- *Critical listening*—listening to evaluate a message for purposes of accepting or rejecting it, as when we listen to the sales pitch of a car salesperson or the campaign speech of a political candidate.

Although all four kinds of listening are important, this chapter deals primarily with comprehensive listening and critical listening. They are the kinds of listening you will use most often when listening to speeches in class, when taking lecture notes in other courses, when communicating at work, and when responding to the barrage of commercials, political messages, and other persuasive appeals you face every day. They are also the kinds of listening that are most closely tied to critical thinking.

As we saw in Chapter 1, critical thinking involves a number of skills. Some of those skills—summarizing information, recalling facts, distinguishing main points from minor points—are central to comprehensive listening. Other skills of critical thinking—separating fact from opinion, spotting weaknesses in reasoning, judging the soundness of evidence—are especially important in critical listening.

When you engage in comprehensive listening or critical listening, you must use your mind as well as your ears. When your mind is not actively involved, you may be hearing, but you are not *listening*. In fact, listening and critical thinking are so closely allied that training in listening is also training in how to think.

At the end of this chapter, we'll discuss steps you can take to improve your skills in comprehensive and critical listening. If you follow these steps, you may also become a better critical thinker.

Four Causes of Poor Listening

NOT CONCENTRATING

The brain is incredibly efficient. Although we talk at a rate of 120 to 180 words a minute, the brain can process 400 to 500 words a minute.[10] This would seem to make listening very easy, but actually it has the opposite effect. Because we can process a speaker's words and still have plenty of spare "brain time," we are tempted to interrupt our listening by thinking about other things. Here's what happens:

> A senior majoring in kinesiology, Jessica Chen is excited to be wrapping up her course work. She is particularly eager to finish her class on exercise and mental health, which meets at 3 P.M. on Fridays. Her professor is great—this is her second class with him—but keeping focused on Friday afternoon can be a challenge.
>
> On this particular Friday in April, Jessica's professor is lecturing on the relationship between body temperature and anxiety. "This calming effect," he explains, "often stems from a person's increased temperature. . . ."
>
> "Temperature," thinks Jessica, her eyes drifting out the window next to her. "I bet it's almost 75 degrees. Beach weather. I can't wait for Newport in July. . . ."
>
> Sternly, Jessica pulls her attention back to the lecture. Her professor is now reviewing research on regular exercise and the immune system, which Jessica heard about last semester. As a result, her attention wanders once more.
>
> "I haven't been to the gym in five days," she thinks. "But the student gym is always so busy. Maybe I should get a membership at the health club. I wonder how much that would cost?"

People spend more time listening than in any other communicative activity. One benefit of your speech class is that it can improve your listening skills in a variety of situations.

Maskot/Getty Images

". . . a topic that Jessica encountered during her internship last summer," the professor is saying. Uh oh! What topic does the professor mean? Everyone looks at Jessica, as she frantically tries to recall the connection between exercise, the immune system, and her internship.

It's not that Jessica *meant* to lose track of the discussion. But there comes a point at which it's so easy to let your thoughts wander rather than to concentrate on what is being said. After all, concentrating is hard work. Louis Nizer, the famous trial lawyer, once said: "So complete is this concentration that at the end of a court day in which I have only listened, I find myself wringing wet despite a calm and casual manner."[11]

Later in this chapter, we'll look at some things you can do to concentrate better on what you hear.

LISTENING TOO HARD

Until now we have been talking about not paying close attention to what we hear. But sometimes we listen *too* hard. We turn into human sponges, soaking up a speaker's every word as if every word were equally important. We try to remember all the names, all the dates, all the places. In the process we often miss the speaker's main point. What is worse, we may end up confusing the facts as well.

Shortly after graduating from college, Carlos Molina landed an excellent job as an app developer. Knowing he had never been good at budgeting his money, he signed up for a financial planning workshop.

The first session was about retirement planning. Simone Fisher, who was conducting the workshop, explained that 7 in 10 Americans between the ages of 22 and 35 do not have a monthly budget or a savings plan. Carlos wrote down every number Simone mentioned.

"To have a retirement income equal to 75 percent of your current salary," Simone continued, "you will need to invest at least 6 percent of your present earnings. You also need to account for inflation over time. This afternoon, we will meet with each of you personally to calculate your individual savings needs. In the meantime, I want to stress that the most important thing is to start saving now."

Carlos zealously typed each statistic into his laptop. When Simone opened the floor for questions, Carlos raised his hand and said, "I have two questions. When should I start saving for retirement? And how do I figure out how to account for future inflation?"

This is a typical example of losing the speaker's point by concentrating on details. Carlos had fixed his mind on remembering all the statistics in Simone's presentation, but he blocked out the main message—that it is best to start saving now and that he would get help developing an individual plan.

Rather than trying to remember everything a speaker says, efficient listeners usually concentrate on main points and evidence. We'll discuss these things more thoroughly later in the chapter.

JUMPING TO CONCLUSIONS

Alyssa Shields, a recent college graduate, took a job as a staff writer for a local entertainment and fashion blog. Shortly after Alyssa arrived, the blog's editor left the magazine for another job. For the next two months, Alyssa struggled to handle the former editor's blog posts by herself. She often felt in over her head, but she knew this was a good opportunity to learn, and she hated to give up her new responsibilities.

One day Michael Perkins, publisher of the blog, calls Alyssa to talk. The following conversation takes place:

Michael: You've done a great job these last two months, Alyssa. But you know we really need a new editor. So we've decided to make some changes.

Alyssa: I'm not surprised; I know this is an important site.

Michael: Yes, it is. And it's not an easy job. We really need an editor and a staff writer or two to handle all the work. That's why I wanted to tell you . . .

Alyssa: I understand. I knew all along that I was just filling in.

Michael: Alyssa, you're not listening.

Alyssa: Yes, I am. You're trying to be nice, but you're going to tell me that you've hired a new editor and I'll be going back to my old job.

Michael: No, that's not it at all. I think you've done a fine job under difficult circumstances. You've proved yourself, and I intend to make you the editor. We're also going to hire two new writers to work under you.

Why is there so much confusion here? Clearly, Alyssa is unsure about her future at the blog. So when Michael starts to talk about making some changes, Alyssa jumps to a conclusion and assumes the worst. The misunderstanding could have been avoided if, when Michael had said, "We've decided to make some changes," Alyssa had asked, "What changes?"—and then *listened*.

This is one form of jumping to conclusions—putting words into a speaker's mouth. It is one reason why we sometimes communicate so poorly with people we are closest to. Because we're so sure we know what they mean, we don't listen to what they actually say.

Another way of jumping to conclusions is prematurely rejecting a speaker's ideas as boring or misguided. That would be a mistake. Let's say the announced topic is "Architecture and History." It sounds dull. So you tune out—and miss a fascinating discussion filled with human-interest stories about buildings and other structures from the ancient pyramids to the latest skyscrapers.

Nearly every speech has something to offer you—whether it be information, point of view, or technique. You are cheating yourself if you prejudge and choose not to listen.

FOCUSING ON DELIVERY AND PERSONAL APPEARANCE

As new parents interested in finding a good day care for their young daughter, Abby and Noah were excited to attend an information session at a school close to their apartment. At 10:00 A.M. Saturday morning, they gathered in a classroom with 20 other parents to hear from the school's director.

When the director entered the room in a wheelchair, Noah glanced quizzically at Abby. For the next 20 minutes, they listened as the director discussed the school's curriculum, activities, and opportunities for young children. "It sounds like a great school," Abby said when they got back to the car. But Noah seemed concerned. "What's wrong?" Abby asked.

"I know you're going to think this is stupid," Noah began, "but I never pictured the director in a wheelchair. Now I can't get the idea out of my head. Would she really be able to handle a school full of energetic little kids?"

This story illustrates a common problem. Sometimes we judge people by the way they look or speak and don't listen to what they say. It's easy to become distracted by a speaker's accent, personal appearance, or vocal mannerisms and lose sight of the message. Focusing on a speaker's delivery or personal appearance is one of the major sources of interference in the speech communication process, and it is something we always need to guard against.

How to Become a Better Listener

TAKE LISTENING SERIOUSLY

The first step toward becoming a better listener is to accord listening the seriousness it deserves. Good listeners are not born that way. They have *worked* at learning how to listen effectively. Good listening does not go hand in hand with intelligence, education, or social standing. Like any other skill, it comes from practice and self-discipline. Check your current skills as a listener by completing the Listening Self-Evaluation Worksheet on page 51.[12] Once you have identified your shortcomings as a listener, make a serious effort to overcome them.

BE AN ACTIVE LISTENER

So many aspects of modern life encourage us to listen passively. We listen to Spotify while studying. Parents listen to their children while fixing dinner. Television reporters listen to a politician's speech while walking around the auditorium looking for their next interview.

LISTENING SELF-EVALUATION

How often do you indulge in the following bad listening habits? Check yourself carefully in each one.

HABIT	Almost Always	Usually	Sometimes	Seldom	Almost Never	SCORE
1. Giving in to mental distractions	_____	_____	_____	_____	_____	_____
2. Giving in to physical distractions	_____	_____	_____	_____	_____	_____
3. Trying to recall everything a speaker says	_____	_____	_____	_____	_____	_____
4. Rejecting a topic as uninteresting before hearing the speaker	_____	_____	_____	_____	_____	_____
5. Faking paying attention	_____	_____	_____	_____	_____	_____
6. Jumping to conclusions about a speaker's meaning	_____	_____	_____	_____	_____	_____
7. Deciding a speaker is wrong before hearing everything she or he has to say	_____	_____	_____	_____	_____	_____
8. Judging a speaker on personal appearance	_____	_____	_____	_____	_____	_____
9. Not paying attention to a speaker's evidence	_____	_____	_____	_____	_____	_____
10. Focusing on delivery rather than on what the speaker says	_____	_____	_____	_____	_____	_____
					TOTAL	_____

How to score:

For every "almost always" checked, give yourself a score of	2
For every "usually" checked, give yourself a score of	4
For every "sometimes" checked, give yourself a score of	6
For every "seldom" checked, give yourself a score of	8
For every "almost never" checked, give yourself a score of	10

Total score interpretation:

0 to 70	You need lots of training in listening.
71 to 89	You listen well.
90 to 100	You listen exceptionally well.

Effective listeners take their task seriously. If you approach listening as an active process, you will significantly sharpen your powers of concentration and comprehension.

ESB Professional/Shutterstock

active listening
Giving undivided attention to a speaker in a genuine effort to understand the speaker's point of view.

This type of passive listening is a habit—but so is active listening. Active listeners give their undivided attention to the speaker in a genuine effort to understand his or her point of view. In conversation, they do not interrupt the speaker or finish his or her sentences. When listening to a speech, they do not allow themselves to be distracted by internal or external interference, and they do not prejudge the speaker. They take listening seriously and do the best they can to stay focused on the speaker and his or her message.[13]

There are a number of steps you can take to improve your skills of active listening. They include resisting distractions, not allowing yourself to be diverted by a speaker's appearance or delivery, suspending judgment until you have heard the speaker out, focusing your listening, and developing note-taking skills. We'll discuss each of these in turn.

RESIST DISTRACTIONS

In an ideal world, we could eliminate all physical and mental distractions. In the real world, however, we cannot. Because we think so much faster than a speaker can talk, it's easy to let our attention wander. Sometimes it's very easy—when the room is too hot, when construction machinery is operating right outside the window, when the speaker is tedious. But our attention can stray even in the best of circumstances—if for no other reason than a failure to stay alert and make ourselves concentrate.

Then there's the biggest distraction of all—your smartphone. We all know how tempting it is to peek at it for new messages, breaking news, sports scores, and social media likes. Surely you can quickly check your phone and then return to what the speaker is saying. Right?

Not so fast. Even though most of us think we're good at multitasking, the human brain just isn't wired for it. Researchers have repeatedly found that multitasking comes with considerable "switch costs," which reduce memory, cognition, productivity, and creativity.[14] This is especially true of the "media multitasking" we do with our phones.[15]

In fact, smartphones are so deadly to effective listening that most instructors require that they be turned off in class whenever students are presenting speeches. This is good advice whether you are in class or out. Don't just silence your phone or put it in do-not-disturb mode; turn it off completely and put it away so you're not tempted to glance at it.

The same is true when you're listening to online presentations. In addition to turning off your phone, you must also resist the temptation to multitask on your computer screen. Many people think they can easily listen to a speech via Zoom while also responding to email, keeping an eye on the news, and perusing some shopping sites. But again, your brain isn't wired to do that. Close the unnecessary windows and focus on what the speaker is saying.

DON'T BE DIVERTED BY APPEARANCE OR DELIVERY

If you had attended Abraham Lincoln's momentous Cooper Union speech of 1860, this is what you would have seen:

> The long, ungainly figure upon which hung clothes that, while new for this trip, were evidently the work of an unskilled tailor; the large feet and clumsy hands, of which, at the outset, at least, the orator seemed to be unduly conscious; the long, gaunt head, capped by a shock of hair that seemed not to have been thoroughly brushed out, made a picture which did not fit in with New York's conception of a finished statesman.[16]

Although he seemed awkward and uncultivated, Lincoln had a powerful message about the moral evils of slavery. Fortunately, the audience at Cooper Union did not let his appearance stand in the way of his words.

Similarly, you must be willing to set aside preconceived judgments based on a person's looks or manner of speech. Gandhi was an unimpressive-looking man who often spoke dressed in a simple white cotton cloth. Renowned physicist Stephen Hawking was severely disabled and could speak only with the aid of a voice synthesizer. Yet imagine how much poorer the world would be if no one had listened to them. Even though it may tax your tolerance, patience, and concentration, don't let negative feelings about a speaker's appearance or delivery keep you from listening to the message.

On the other hand, try not to be misled if the speaker has an unusually attractive appearance. It's all too easy to assume that because someone is good-looking and has a polished delivery, he or she is speaking eloquently. Some of the most unscrupulous speakers in history have been handsome people with hypnotic delivery skills. Again, be sure you respond to the message, not to the package it comes in.

SUSPEND JUDGMENT

Unless we listen only to people who think exactly as we do, we are going to hear things with which we disagree. When this happens, our natural inclination is to argue mentally with the speaker or to dismiss everything she or he says. But neither response is fair, and in both cases we blot out any chance of learning or being persuaded.

Does this mean you must agree with everything you hear? Not at all. It means you should hear people out *before* reaching a final judgment. Try to understand their point of view. Listen to their ideas, examine their evidence, assess their reasoning. *Then* make up your mind. The aim of active listening is to set aside "one's own prejudices, frames of reference, and desires so as to experience as far as possible the speaker's world from the inside."[17] It has been said more than once that a closed mind is an empty mind.

FOCUS YOUR LISTENING

As we have seen, skilled listeners do not try to absorb a speaker's every word. Rather, they focus on specific things in a speech. Here are three suggestions to help you focus your listening.

Listen for Main Points

Most speeches contain from two to four main points. Here, for example, are the main points of a speech by Glenn Gerstell, general counsel for the U.S. National Security Agency:[18]

1. Cyber vulnerability is one of the biggest threats to the United States.
2. The nation is ill equipped to deal with this threat because responsibility for cyber protection is scattered across the federal government.
3. The federal government should centralize responsibility for cyber protection by creating a new department of cyber security.

These three main points are the heart of Gerstell's message. As with any speech, they are the most important things to listen for.

Unless a speaker is terribly scatterbrained, you should be able to detect his or her main points with little difficulty. Often a speaker will give some idea at the outset of the main points to be discussed in the speech. For example, at the end of his introduction, Gerstell said he was going to explain "the current scope of the threat, how we are currently postured to address that threat, and . . . some thoughts on how our federal government should organize itself to address" the threat.

As the speech progressed, Gerstell moved from point to point with signposts such as "In short, we can all agree that glaring gaps remain in our nation's cyber security posture" and "So let's turn to what should be done." After this, only the most inattentive of listeners could have missed his main points.

Listen for Evidence

Identifying a speaker's main points, however, is not enough. You must also listen for supporting evidence. By themselves, Gerstell's main points are only assertions. You may be inclined to believe them just because they come from an important national security official. Yet a careful listener will be concerned about evidence no matter who is speaking. Had you been listening to Gerstell's speech, you would have heard him support his claims with a mass of verifiable evidence. Here is an excerpt:

> There are 23 victims of malicious cyber activity per second, according to a 2016 report from Norton. The Center for Strategic and International Studies recently estimated that such activity costs our national economy $140 billion each year. By comparison, the Institute for Economics and Peace, which publishes a yearly Global Terrorism Index, estimated that the global economic impact of terrorism was about $90 billion in 2015. . . .
>
> The Chair of the SEC last year said that the gravest threat to the American financial system was cyber. The threat is so grave, in fact, that former CIA director and Secretary of Defense Leon Panetta described our nation's cyber security weaknesses as amounting to a pre-9/11 moment.

There are four basic questions to ask about a speaker's evidence:

Is it *accurate*?

Is it taken from *objective* sources?

Is it *relevant* to the speaker's claims?

Is it *sufficient* to support the speaker's point?

In Gerstell's case, the answer to each question is yes. His figures about cyber security threats are well established in research studies and can be verified by independent sources. The figures are clearly relevant to Gerstell's claim that cyber vulnerability is a serious threat to the United States, and they are sufficient to support that claim. If Gerstell's evidence were inaccurate, biased, irrelevant, or insufficient, you should be wary of accepting his claim.

We shall discuss these—and other—tests of evidence in detail in Chapters 8 and 17. For now, it's enough to know that you should be on guard against unfounded assertions and sweeping generalizations. Keep an eye out for the speaker's evidence and for its accuracy, objectivity, relevance, and sufficiency.

Listen for Technique

We said earlier that you should not let a speaker's delivery distract you from the message, and this is true. However, if you want to become an effective speaker, you should study the methods other people use to speak effectively.

Analyze the introduction: What methods does the speaker use to gain attention, to relate to the audience, to establish credibility and goodwill? Assess the organization of the speech: Is it clear and easy to follow? Can you pick out the speaker's main points? Can you follow when the speaker moves from one point to another?

Study the speaker's language: Is it accurate, clear, vivid, appropriate? Does the speaker adapt well to the audience and occasion? Finally, diagnose the speaker's delivery: Is it fluent, dynamic, convincing? Does it strengthen or weaken the impact of the speaker's ideas? How well does the speaker use eye contact, gestures, and visual aids?

As you listen, focus on the speaker's strengths and weaknesses. If the speaker is not effective, try to determine why. If he or she is effective, try to pick out techniques you can use in your own speeches. If you listen in this way, you will be surprised by how much you can learn about successful speaking.

DEVELOP NOTE-TAKING SKILLS

Speech students are often amazed at how easily their instructor can pick out a speaker's main points, evidence, and techniques. Of course, the instructor knows what to listen for and has had plenty of practice. But the next time you get an opportunity, watch your instructor during a speech. Chances are she or he will be listening with a laptop or pen and paper. When note taking is done properly, it is a surefire way to improve your concentration and keep track of a speaker's ideas.

The key words here are *when done properly*. Unfortunately, many people don't take notes effectively. Some try to take down everything a speaker says. They view the enterprise as a race that pits their note-taking speed against the speaker's rate of speech. As the speaker starts to talk, the note taker starts to write or type. But soon

Research confirms that listening carefully and taking effective notes are vital skills for success in college. They will also benefit you in countless situations throughout life.

Paul Bradbury/Getty Images

the speaker is winning the race. In a desperate effort to keep up, the note taker tries to go faster and faster. But even this is not enough. The speaker pulls so far ahead that the note taker can never catch up.[19]

Some people go to the opposite extreme. They arrive armed with pen, laptop, and the best of intentions. They know they can't write down everything, so they wait for the speaker to say something that grabs their attention. Every once in a while the speaker rewards them with a joke, a dramatic story, or a startling fact. Then the note taker records a few words and leans back to await the next fascinating tidbit. By the end of the lecture, the note taker has a set of tidbits—and little or no record of the speaker's important ideas.

As these examples illustrate, most inefficient note takers suffer from one or both of two problems: They don't know *what* to listen for, and they don't know *how* to record what they do listen for.[20] The solution to the first problem is to focus on a speaker's main points and evidence. But once you know what to listen for, you still need a sound method of note taking.

Although there are a number of systems, most students find the *key-word outline* best for listening to classroom lectures and formal speeches. As its name suggests, this method briefly notes a speaker's main points and supporting evidence in rough outline form. Suppose a speaker says:

key-word outline
An outline that briefly notes a speaker's main points and supporting evidence in rough outline form.

> The global shark population is in drastic decline. According to the journal *Marine Policy*, 100 million sharks die from human activity every year—the equivalent of 11,000 sharks per hour. Today, almost 30 percent of all shark species are at risk of going extinct. A recent report on National Public Radio states that sharks "are among the most endangered animals in the world."
>
> There are three main causes for the decline in shark populations. The first cause is illegal fishing; humans are killing sharks in unprecedented numbers. A second cause is the slow growth and reproduction rate of

sharks; we're wiping out sharks much faster than they can reproduce. The third cause is pollution and habitat destruction, which are disrupting the entire marine ecosystem.

A key-word note taker would record something like this:

Shark population in decline
    100 million die each year
    30 percent at risk of extinction
    Among most endangered in world

Three major causes
    Illegal fishing
    Slow reproduction rate
    Pollution & habitat destruction

Notice how brief the notes are. Yet they accurately summarize the speaker's ideas. They are also very clear. By separating main points from subpoints and evidence, the outline format shows the relationships among the speaker's ideas.

Perfecting this—or any other—system of note taking requires practice. But with a little effort you should see results soon. As you become a better note taker, you will become a better listener. There is also a good chance you will become a better student. Research confirms that students who take effective notes usually receive higher grades than those who do not.[21]

Summary

Most people are poor listeners. Even when we think we are listening carefully, we usually grasp only half of what we hear, and we retain even less. Improving your listening skills can be helpful in every part of your life, including speechmaking.

The most important cause of poor listening is giving in to distractions and letting our thoughts wander. Sometimes, however, we listen too hard. We try to remember every word a speaker says, and we lose the main message by concentrating on details. In other situations, we may jump to conclusions and prejudge a speaker without hearing out the message. Finally, we often judge people by their appearance or speaking manner instead of listening to what they say.

You can overcome these poor listening habits by taking several steps. First, take listening seriously and commit yourself to becoming a better listener. Second, work at being an active listener. Give your undivided attention to the speaker in a genuine effort to understand her or his ideas. Third, resist distractions. Make a conscious effort to keep your mind on what the speaker is saying. Fourth, try not to be diverted by appearance or delivery. Set aside preconceived judgments based on a person's looks or manner of speech. Fifth, suspend judgment until you have heard the speaker's entire message. Sixth, focus your listening by paying attention to main points, to evidence, and to the speaker's techniques. Finally, develop your note-taking skills. When done properly, note taking is an excellent way to improve your concentration and to keep track of a speaker's ideas.

Key Terms

hearing (44)

listening (46)

appreciative listening (46)

empathic listening (46)

comprehensive listening (46)

critical listening (47)

spare "brain time" (47)

active listening (52)

key-word outline (56)

Review Questions

After reading this chapter, you should be able to answer the following questions:

1. What is the difference between hearing and listening?
2. How is listening connected with critical thinking?
3. Why is it important to develop strong listening skills?
4. What are the four main causes of poor listening?
5. What are seven ways to become a better listener?

Exercises for Critical Thinking

1. Which of the four causes of poor listening discussed in this chapter do you consider the most important? Choose a specific case of poor listening in which you were involved. Explain what went wrong.

2. Using the Listening Self-Evaluation Worksheet on page 51, undertake a candid evaluation of your major strengths and weaknesses as a listener. Explain what steps you need to take to become a better listener.

3. Listen to a recent episode of an information-driven podcast series, such as *Freakonomics, Radiolab,* or *Hidden Brain*. Using the key-word outline method of note taking, record the main ideas of the story.

4. Choose a lecture in one of your other classes. Analyze what the lecturer does most effectively. Identify three things the lecturer could do better to help students keep track of the lecture.

End Notes

[1]Larry Barker and Kittie Watson, *Listen Up: What You've Never Heard About the Other Half of Every Conversation* (New York: St. Martin's, 2001), p. 5.

[2]Michael P. Nichols and Martha B. Straus, *The Lost Art of Listening: How Learning to Listen Can Improve Relationships,* 3rd ed. (New York: Guilford Press, 2021).

[3]See Lyman K. Steil and Richard K. Bommelje, *Listening Leaders: The Ten Golden Rules to Listen, Lead, and Succeed* (Edina, MN: Beaver's Pond Press, 2004).

[4]Judi Brownell, *Listening: Attitudes, Principles, and Skills,* 6th ed. (New York: Routledge, 2018), p. 10.

[5]Kyle E. Brink and Robert D. Costigan, "Oral Communication Skills: Are the Priorities of the Workplace and AACSB-Accredited Business Programs Aligned?" *Academy of Management Learning and Education,* 14 (2015), pp. 205–221.

[6]Debra L. Worthington and Margaret E. Fitch-Hauser, *Listening: Processes, Functions, and Competency,* 2nd ed. (New York: Routledge, 2018), pp. 5–7.

[7]See, for example, Melissa L. Beall, Jennifer Gill-Rosier, Jeanine Tate, and Amy Matten, "State of the Context: Listening in Education," *International Journal of Listening,* 22 (2008), pp. 123–132; Graham D. Bodie and Margaret Fitch-Hauser, "Quantitative Research in Listening: Explication and Overview," in Andrew D. Wolvin (ed.), *Listening and Human Communication in the 21st Century* (Malden, MA: Wiley-Blackwell, 2010), pp. 46–93.

[8]Listening, as one author aptly states, "can transform your understanding of the people and the world around you, which inevitably enriches and elevates your experience and existence. It is how you develop wisdom and form meaningful relationships." See Kate Murphy, *You're Not Listening: What You're Missing and Why It Matters* (New York: Celadon Books, 2019).

[9]Andrew W. Wolvin and Carolyn Gwynn Coakley, *Listening,* 5th ed. (Dubuque, IA: Brown and Benchmark, 1995), pp. 223–396.

[10]Brownell, *Listening: Attitudes, Principles, and Skills,* pp. 89–90.

[11]Louis Nizer, *My Life in Court,* reprint ed. (Whitefish, MT: 2010), pp. 297–298.

[12]Adapted from Lyman K. Steil, Larry L. Barker, and Kittie W. Watson, *Effective Listening* (Reading, MA: Addison-Wesley, 1983).

[13]Two excellent guides to the premises and methods of active listening are Bernard T. Ferrari, *Power Listening: Mastering the Most Critical Business Skill of All* (New York: Penguin, 2012); and Tim Hast, *Powerful Listening. Powerful Influence* (North Charleston, NC: CreateSpace Independent Publishing, 2013).

[14]See Worthington and Fitch-Hauser, *Listening,* p. 108.

[15]Kevin P. Madore and Anthony D. Wagner, "Multicosts of Multitasking," *Cerebrum* (Mar-Apr 2019) (https://www.ncbi.nlm.nih.gov/pmc/articles/PMC7075496/).

[16]George H. Putnam, *Abraham Lincoln* (New York: Putnam, 1909), pp. 44–45.

[17]M. Scott Peck, *The Road Less Traveled: A New Psychology of Love, Traditional Values, and Spiritual Growth,* 25th anniversary ed. (New York: Touchstone Books, 2003), p. 127.

[18]Glenn Gerstell, "Confronting the Cybersecurity Challenge," February 25, 2017 (https://www.nsa.gov/news-features/speeches-testimonies/speeches/20170225-gerstell-duke-keynote.shtml).

[19]See Ralph G. Nichols and Leonard A. Stevens, *Are You Listening?* (New York: McGraw-Hill, 1957), pp. 113–114. This classic work still has much of value to say about its subject.

[20]On some of the other challenges involved in note taking, see Deborah K. Reed, Hillary Rimel, and Abigail Hallett, "Note-Taking Interventions for College Students: A Synthesis and Meta-Analysis of the Literature," *Journal of Research on Educational Effectiveness,* 9 (2016), pp. 307–333.

[21]See, for example, Tamas Makany, Jonathan Kemp, and Itiel E. Dror, "Optimizing the Use of Note-Taking as an External Cognitive Aid for Increasing Learning," *British Journal of Educational Technology,* 40 (2009), pp. 619–635.

Giving Your First Speech

You may be surprised to learn that one of the first assignments in your class is to give a speech. You say to yourself, "What am I going to do? I have barely started this course, yet I'm supposed to stand up in front of everyone and give a speech! I've only read a few pages in the textbook, and I don't know much about public speaking. Where do I begin?"

If these are your thoughts, you aren't alone. Most beginning speech students have a similar reaction. Fortunately, giving your first speech sounds a lot harder than it is. The purpose of this chapter is to help you get started on preparing and delivering your speech. Later chapters will expand on the subjects discussed here and will apply them to different kinds of speeches.

Preparing Your Speech

ice breaker speech
A speech early in the term designed to get students speaking in front of the class as soon as possible.

Usually a brief, simple presentation, the first assignment is often called an ice breaker speech because it is designed to "break the ice" by getting students up in front of the class as soon as possible. This is an important step because much of the anxiety associated with public speaking comes from lack of experience giving speeches. Once you have broken the ice by giving a speech, you will feel less anxious and will have taken the first step on the road to confidence.

DEVELOPING THE SPEECH

There are a number of possible assignments for the first speech. One is a speech of self-introduction that provides insight into the speaker's background, personality, beliefs, or goals. In other cases, students are asked to introduce a classmate, rather than themselves. Some instructors require yet a different kind of speech. Make sure you understand exactly what your instructor requires.

Focusing Your Topic

No matter what kind of introductory speech you are assigned, be sure to focus your presentation sharply so it conforms to the assigned time limit. One of the most common mistakes students make on their first speech is trying to cover too much.

It would be impossible, for example, to tell your audience everything about your life in a two- or three-minute speech. A better approach would be to focus on one or two events that have helped define who you are—competing in the state track meet, tutoring disadvantaged children, getting your first job, and the like. This allows you to make a few well-developed points about a clearly defined subject.

On the other hand, avoid the temptation to narrow the focus of your topic too much. Few listeners would be pleased to hear a two- or three-minute discussion of advanced trumpet-playing techniques. Such a speech would be too specialized for most classroom audiences.

Developing Your Topic

Once you have a topic for your speech, be creative in developing it. Think of ways to structure the speech so it will be interesting and meaningful to your audience.

Look, for example, at the sample speeches with commentary at the end of this chapter. The first speaker explains aspects of her identity by referring to her middle name, which she shares with several family members. The second speaker uses the color purple to introduce one of his classmates. The third speaker discusses the twists and turns in her life that took her back to college as a returning student. In each case, the speaker finds a creative way to frame their information.

Another possibility is to think of ways you can make your presentation mysterious or suspenseful. Suppose you are telling the audience about meeting a celebrity, visiting a famous place, or participating in a newsworthy event. Rather than identifying the celebrity at the outset, you might save his or her name for the end of your speech. As your story unfolds, tantalize your classmates with clues about your celebrity's gender, physical characteristics, special talents, and the like, but keep the name secret until the last moment.

Audiences are also interested in dangerous situations, adventure, and drama. If your task is to introduce a fellow student, find out if she or he has ever been in danger. Suppose your classmate was caught in a flood or spent a year in Africa with the Peace Corps. The details would make excellent material for a speech.

You can also make your speech interesting by using colorful, descriptive language. One speaker used this technique when introducing a fellow student, named Alexa, to the class. The speaker began by saying:

> The spotlight shines. The music blares. The crowd cheers. The colors, bright and vibrant, bleed together as Alexa and her partner sail around the dance floor. Her partner touches her hand and her waist, but only briefly. He then spins her away, and she glides across the floor in what seems like a single motion. Alexa has worked many weeks for this moment. Alexa, you see, is a championship ballroom dancer.

The speaker could have said, "Alexa is a terrific ballroom dancer and finds it quite thrilling." Instead, the speaker painted a word picture so listeners could visualize the dance floor, the brilliant colors of the costumes, and the excitement of the competition as Alexa and her partner perform in perfect symmetry. Colorful and concrete illustrations like this are always more interesting than dull language and abstract generalizations.

connect

View the introduction from "Gotta Dance" in the online Media Library for this chapter (Video 4.1).

When working on your first speech, ask friends or family members for feedback and suggestions. In addition to helping you improve the speech, they can provide valuable personal support.
asiseeit/Getty Images

You might wonder whether you should use humor to make your first speech entertaining. Audiences love witty remarks, jokes, and funny situations, but like anything else, humor is effective only when done well. It should flow naturally out of the speech content rather than being contrived. If you are not normally a funny person, you are better off giving a sincere, enthusiastic speech and leaving out the jokes. In no case should you include humor that involves obscenity, embarrasses individuals, or negatively stereotypes groups of people. The best kind of humor gently pokes fun at ourselves or at universal human foibles.

ORGANIZING THE SPEECH

Regardless of your topic, a speech usually has three main parts—an introduction, a body, and a conclusion. In Chapter 10, we will discuss each of these parts in detail. Here we focus on what you need to know about them as you prepare your introductory speech.

introduction
The opening section of a speech.

Introduction

Your first job in the introduction is to get the attention and interest of the audience. You can do this by posing a question, telling a story, making a startling statement, or opening with a quotation. The purpose of all these methods is to create a dramatic, colorful opening that will make your audience want to hear more.

For an example, look at the speech excerpt on Video 4.2. The speaker's assignment was to present a narrative about a significant experience in her life. This is how she began:

connect
View the beginning of "The Rapids" in the online Media Library for this chapter (Video 4.2).

> It happened in an instant. The raft flipped end over end, and before I knew it, I was underwater, with no idea which way was up. That was the first time my raft flipped over on the Ocoee River in the Great Smoky Mountains, but it was certainly not the last. You see, this past summer I worked as a rafting guide on powerful class III and IV rapids, which reminded me, day after day, about the power of nature.

After this introduction, the audience was eager to hear more about the speaker's experience.

In addition to gaining attention and interest, the introduction should orient your listeners toward the subject matter of your speech. In the longer speeches you will give later in the term, you will usually need to provide an explicit preview statement that identifies the main points to be discussed in the body of your speech.

Because your introductory speech is so short, you may not need a detailed preview statement. But you still need to give your audience a clear sense of your topic and purpose. (Be sure to check with your instructor to see what kind of preview statement he or she prefers for the introductory speech.)

Body

body
The main section of a speech.

After getting the audience's attention and revealing your topic, you are ready to move into the body of your speech. In some speeches, the body seems to organize itself. If you are telling a story about a significant experience in your life, you will relate the events chronologically, in the order they occurred.

But not all speeches follow such a format. Suppose you have been asked to give a presentation introducing a classmate. You could organize the most important biographical facts about your subject in chronological order, but this might result in a dull, superficial speech: "Maria was born in Miami in 2005, attended elementary school from 2011 to 2017, and graduated from high school in 2023."

chronological order
A method of speech organization in which the main points follow a time pattern.

A better way of structuring your remarks might be to discuss three of the most important aspects of Maria's life, such as hobbies, career goals, and family. This is called the topical method of organization, which subdivides the speech topic into its natural, logical, or conventional parts. Although there are many other ways to organize a speech, your first presentation will probably use either chronological or topical order.

topical order
A method of speech organization in which the main points divide the topic into logical and consistent subtopics.

Regardless of the method of organization you use, remember to limit the number of main points in the body of your speech. In a two-minute presentation, you won't have time to develop more than two or three main points.

Once you have selected those points, make sure each one focuses on a single aspect of the topic. For example, if your first point concerns your classmate's hometown, don't introduce irrelevant information about her job or favorite music. Save this material for a separate point, or cut it.

main points
The major points developed in the body of a speech.

Try to make your main points stand out by introducing each with a transition statement. In a speech about a classmate, you might begin the first main point by saying:

> Jasmine has been interested in drawing as long as she can remember.

When you reach the second point, you might introduce it like this:

> Jasmine's passion for drawing helps explain her desire to major in architecture.

transition
A word or phrase that indicates when a speaker has finished one thought and is moving on to another.

You have now let your audience know that the first main point is over and that you are starting the second one. The third main point might begin as follows:

> As much as Jasmine hopes to have a career as an architect, she also wants to keep time for friends and family.

Transitions such as these will help your audience keep track of your main points.

Your first speech provides a foundation for speeches you will give later. As you develop your skills of extemporaneous speaking, you will find yourself able to speak confidently and with strong eye contact in class and out.

Tunart/Getty Images

Conclusion

When you finish discussing your final point, you will be ready to move into your conclusion. You need to accomplish two tasks in this part of the speech: let the audience know you are about to finish and reinforce your central idea.

If possible, end on a dramatic, clever, or thought-provoking note. For example, when talking about her experience as a rafting guide in the speech mentioned earlier, the student devoted the body of her presentation to her adventures on the river. Then, in her conclusion, she wrapped up by saying:

> I'm delighted to say that no one in my tour group was seriously injured. But all of us learned the strength of the river and our weakness at the hands of mother nature. To get to the end of our journey, we had to let the rapids move us instead of fighting against them. That's a lesson for us all: the more we work with our environment, the more likely we'll be to arrive at our destination.

The final lines end the speech on a strong note and underscore why the speaker's time as a rafting guide was so important.

conclusion
The final section of a speech.

connect
View the ending of "The Rapids" in the online Media Library for this chapter (Video 4.3).

Delivering Your Speech

Once you have selected a subject and organized the content into a clear structure, it's time to work on the delivery of your speech. Your delivery will depend partly on whether you'll be speaking to an in-person audience or addressing your classmates online. This section will give you pointers for both.

Regardless of whether you speak in-person or online, you should know that no one expects you to give a perfectly polished presentation in your first speech of the term. Your aim is to do as well as possible while laying a foundation you can build upon in later speeches. With this in mind, we'll look briefly at the extemporaneous method of delivery, the importance of rehearsing your speech, and some of the major factors to consider when speech day arrives.

SPEAKING EXTEMPORANEOUSLY

You might be inclined, as are many beginning speakers, to write out your speech like an essay and read it word for word to your listeners. The other extreme is to prepare very little for the speech—to wing it by trusting your wits and the inspiration of the moment. Neither approach is appropriate.

Most experts recommend speaking extemporaneously, which combines the careful preparation and structure of a manuscript presentation with the spontaneity and enthusiasm of an unrehearsed talk. Your aim in an extemporaneous speech is to plan your major points and supporting material without trying to memorize the precise language you will use on the day of the speech.

The extemporaneous method requires you to know the content of your speech quite well. In fact, when you use this method properly, you become so familiar with the substance of your talk that you need only a few notes to remind you of the points you intend to cover. The notes should consist of key words or phrases, rather than complete sentences and paragraphs. This way, when you are in front of the audience, you will tell them what you know about the topic in your own words.

Prepare your notes by writing or printing key terms and phrases on index cards or sheets of paper. Whichever you use, your notes should be large enough to read clearly at arm's length. Many experienced speakers double-space their notes because this makes them easier to see at a glance. Write or print on only one side of the index card or paper, and use the fewest notes you can manage and still present the speech fluently and confidently.

You can see an example of extemporaneous delivery on Video 4.4. The speaker is giving an online speech of self-introduction. As a returning student, she explains the twists and turns her life has taken during the years since she originally enrolled in college. As you view this excerpt, notice that even though the speaker's points are well planned, she is not tied to her notes. She speaks personally and makes strong eye contact with her listeners.

At first, it may seem demanding to deliver a speech extemporaneously. In fact, though, you use the extemporaneous method in everyday conversation. Do you read from a manuscript when you tell your friends an amusing story? Of course not. You recall the essential details of your story and tell the tale to different friends, on different occasions, using somewhat different language each time. You feel relaxed and confident with your friends, so you just tell them what is on your mind in a conversational tone. Try to do the same thing in your speech.

REHEARSING THE SPEECH

When you watch a truly effective extemporaneous speaker, the speech comes out so smoothly that it seems almost effortless. In fact, that smooth delivery is the result of a great deal of practice. As your speech course progresses, you will gain more experience and will become more comfortable delivering your speeches extemporaneously.

The first time you rehearse your introductory speech, however, you will probably struggle. Words may not come easily, and you may forget some things you planned to say. Don't become discouraged. Keep going and complete the speech as well as you can. Concentrate on gaining control of the ideas rather than on trying to learn the speech word for word. You will improve every time you practice.

extemporaneous speech
A carefully prepared and rehearsed speech that is presented from a brief set of notes.

connect
View an excerpt from "Twists and Turns" in the online Media Library for this chapter (Video 4.4).

For this approach to work, you must rehearse the speech aloud. Looking silently over your notes is not enough. Speaking the words aloud will help you master the content of your talk. Once you have a fairly good grasp of the speech, ask friends or family members to listen and to give constructive feedback. Don't be shy about asking. Most people love to give their opinion about something, and it's crucial that you rehearse with a live audience before presenting the speech in class.

As you practice, time your speech to make sure it is neither too long nor too short. Because of nerves, most people talk faster during their first speech than when they practice it. When you rehearse at home, make certain your speech runs slightly longer than the minimum time limit. That way, if your speaking rate increases when you get in front of your classmates, your speech won't end up being too short.

PRESENTING THE SPEECH

Delivering your first speech can be nerve-wracking. As your class proceeds and you gain more experience, your confidence (and skill) will grow by leaps and bounds. We will take a detailed look at speech delivery in Chapter 13, but here are a few things to concentrate on in your first presentation.

Starting Your Speech

If you're presenting your speech in class, move to the front of the room and face the audience. Assume a relaxed but upright posture. Plant your feet a bit less than shoulder-width apart, and allow your arms to hang loosely by your side. Arrange your notes before you start to speak. Then take a moment to look over your audience and to smile. This will help you establish rapport from the start.

When you're talking online, choose an uncluttered location that is well-lighted and properly framed, so it draws attention to you rather than your surroundings. If you're addressing a small audience assembled specifically for your speech, which is being recorded for viewing later by your instructor, proceed as you would in the classroom.

If you do not have an in-person audience, look into the webcam, smile, and begin your speech. As you proceed, remember that the webcam is "the eye of the audience." Just like a television newscaster, you must speak to the camera to stay connected with your remote audience.

Gestures

Once you are into the speech, feel free to use your hands to gesture, but don't try to plan all your gestures ahead of time. If you don't normally use your hands expressively during informal conversation, you shouldn't feel compelled to gesture a lot during your speech. Whatever gestures you do use should flow naturally from your feelings.

gestures
Motions of a speaker's hands or arms during a speech.

Above all, don't let your gestures or bodily actions distract listeners from your message. Do your best to avoid nervous mannerisms such as twisting your hair, wringing your hands, shifting your weight from one foot to the other, or jingling the keys in your pocket. No matter how nervous you feel, try to appear calm and relaxed.

Eye Contact

One of the major reasons for speaking extemporaneously is to maintain eye contact with your audience. In your own experience, you know how much more impressive a speaker is when she or he looks at the audience while speaking. If you have practiced the extemporaneous method of delivery and prepared your notes properly, you should be able to keep eye contact with your audience most of the time.

eye contact
Direct visual contact with the eyes of another person.

For an in-person speech, look to the left and right of the room, as well as to the center, and avoid the temptation to speak exclusively to one or two sympathetic individuals. If you are too nervous to look your classmates directly in the eye, try looking just to the side of each person. In this way, you will convey a sense of eye contact while easing your nerves.

For an online speech, you will make eye contact through the webcam, which is located on the top frame of your computer screen. If you look at the screen itself, it will appear to your audience that you are looking down rather than directly at them.

Voice

connect
View excerpts from "The Courtyard" and "Fearless" in the online Media Library for this chapter (Video 4.5).

Try to use your voice as expressively as you would in normal conversation. Whether you are speaking online or in person, concentrate on projecting your voice so it can be heard clearly and, despite your nerves, fight the temptation to race through your speech. If you make a conscious decision to speak up, slow down, and communicate in a lively manner, you will be on the right track.

Look, for example, at Video 4.5, which presents excerpts from two ice breaker speeches. Neither speaker had taken a public speaking class before, yet both rose to the occasion by focusing on the basic elements of delivery we have just discussed. As you watch the video, notice how both convey a sense of poise and confidence, establish strong eye contact with their classmates, and use the extemporaneous method of delivery. Work on doing the same in your first speech.

Dealing with Nerves

As we saw in Chapter 1, it's normal to be nervous before delivering a speech of any kind. By applying the tips presented in that chapter for managing stage fright, you can stand up for your speech primed for success.

If you have butterflies in your stomach while you wait to speak, sit quietly and take several slow, deep breaths. You can also help reduce your tension by tightening and relaxing your leg muscles, or by squeezing your hands together and then releasing them. Keep in mind that while you may be anxious about giving your speech, usually your nervousness will not be visible to your audience.

All the topics discussed in this chapter are developed in much more detail in the rest of this book. For now, keep your introductory assignment in perspective. Remember that neither your audience nor your instructor expects perfection. You are not a professional speaker, and this is the first speech of the class. Do your best on the assignment and have fun with it. Plan what you want to say, organize the material clearly, practice thoroughly, and use the extemporaneous method of delivery. You may be surprised by how much you enjoy giving your first speech.

Sample Speeches with Commentary

connect
View "The Inevitability of Evette," "The Color Purple," and "Twists and Turns" in the online Media Library for this chapter (Videos 4.6, 4.7, and 4.8).

The following speeches were prepared by students at the University of Wisconsin. The first two were delivered in class—one is a speech of self-introduction, the other is a speech introducing a classmate. The third is an online speech of self-introduction that was uploaded for viewing by the class and instructor.

As you read the speeches, notice how clearly they are organized and how creatively they are developed. You can view the delivery of all three on Videos 4.6–4.8.

The Inevitability of Evette

COMMENTARY	**SPEECH**
The speaker begins by arousing curiosity about her middle name, Evette, which she found unusual when she was a child.	Most of you know me by my first name, Ananda. But you probably don't know my middle name, Evette, spelled "E-V-E-T-T-E." When I was younger, I thought it sounded like an old-time Hollywood starlet, who definitely would not have looked like me.
Today she takes pride in having the same middle name as her mother, sister, and niece. Her introduction ends by previewing the main points she will discuss in the body.	But in fact, I'm not the only Evette in my family. My mom, my sister, and my niece all share the same middle name. The name connects me with my mom and her resilience, with my sister and her intelligence, and with my niece and her curiosity.
The first main point deals with the speaker's mother. Well-chosen supporting materials convey the speaker's love and respect for her mom's accomplishments and her resilience in the face of adversity.	My mom is the resilient Evette. She was forced to grow up quickly after the birth of my brother. With little help from others, she put herself through college, cared for her son between classes, and earned a degree in nursing. For decades now she's been a registered nurse and has raised four children. Her resilience has taught me that when I'm faced with adversity, I need to meet it head on, as so many Black women before me have done.
The second main point deals with the speaker's younger sister. As you can see from Video 4.6, the speaker has strong eye contact, natural gestures, and an expressive voice.	I like to call my sister the intelligent Evette. She's as smart as me, if not smarter. At ten years old, she has the vocabulary and the reading level of a ninth grader. Sometimes I look up to my little sister, which is a little strange, given how much shorter she is than me. But her intelligence has taught me that being smart is always something to be proud of.
The third main point deals with the speaker's niece. Vivid, descriptive language captures her niece's curiosity and energetic personality. Echoing a pattern from the first two main points, this one ends by stating a vital lesson the speaker has learned from her niece.	Then there's my niece, the curious Evette. She's only three years old—or really, three and a half, and she will correct you on that if you ask. She investigates the world with big brown eyes, soaking up everything around her and always wanting to know more. Her curiosity has taught me how important it is to treasure the joy of discovery.
In her conclusion, the speaker summarizes her main points, reinforces her central idea, and ends on a touching note.	No matter what I thought of my middle name when I was young, today I cherish how it links me with my mom, my sister, and my niece. I'm proud to let people know that I, too, am an Evette—one of many.

The Color Purple

The speaker's use of the color purple provides a creative theme that runs throughout his remarks.

> The color purple. It's the title of a famous book and movie. It's also the favorite color of our classmate Liana, which is fitting, because it's a color that represents her.

An excellent preview statement ends the introduction with a bridge to the body of the speech.

> Purple is created by combining two primary colors—red and blue. These colors signify many positive characteristics, two of which—determination and wisdom—come together to form Liana.

Organized in topical order, the body contains two main points. The first deals with Liana's determination, which the speaker correlates with the red component of purple.

> Red is a color of fierce energy that represents determination. A big moment in Liana's life came when she had to tackle her fear of heights. The thought of climbing a 50-foot rock wall was downright terrifying. But determined to conquer her fear, Liana climbed the wall anyway, one hand-hold at a time.

When used well, as in this speech, stories are a fine way to make ideas concrete and to keep listeners interested.

> As she climbed, "I can't" became "I can" and "I'm scared" became "I'm brave." Before she knew it, Liana was at the top, and she happily glided down the zipline. It takes a fighter to overcome a fear of heights, and Liana is that fighter. That is the fiery red of determination inside her.

The second main point deals with Liana's wisdom, which the speaker correlates with the blue component of purple.

> Then there's blue—a color of calm stability that represents wisdom. Liana is as wise as she is determined, and her friends have known that about her for a long time. They often turn to her for guidance on important decisions.

As can be seen from Video 4.7, the speaker presents his ideas extemporaneously. He has superb eye contact, impressive vocal variety, and a confident, poised delivery—all of which reflect his thorough preparation and rehearsal.

> In high school, for instance, even as she was making her own college choice, she helped her friends make their choices. So far, they're happy and thriving at their new schools, just as Liana is happy and thriving here. The ability to weigh pros and cons in the face of a tough decision—that's the wisdom of the color blue inside of Liana.

The speaker concludes by returning to his theme of the color purple. The final sentence reiterates his central idea and unifies the entire speech.

> Which brings us back to purple—the result of red and blue mixed together. It isn't just Liana's favorite color; it's central to her character. Just as the determination of red mixes together with the wisdom of blue to form the color purple, so they come together to make Liana the person she is today.

The Color Purple

 COMMENTARY

 SPEECH

The speaker's use of the color purple provides a creative theme that runs throughout his remarks.

The color purple. It's the title of a famous book and movie. It's also the favorite color of our classmate Liana, which is fitting, because it's a color that represents her.

An excellent preview statement ends the introduction with a bridge to the body of the speech.

Purple is created by combining two primary colors—red and blue. These colors signify many positive characteristics, two of which—determination and wisdom—come together to form Liana.

Organized in topical order, the body contains two main points. The first deals with Liana's determination, which the speaker correlates with the red component of purple.

Red is a color of fierce energy that represents determination. A big moment in Liana's life came when she had to tackle her fear of heights. The thought of climbing a 50-foot rock wall was downright terrifying. But determined to conquer her fear, Liana climbed the wall anyway, one hand-hold at a time.

When used well, as in this speech, stories are a fine way to make ideas concrete and to keep listeners interested.

As she climbed, "I can't" became "I can" and "I'm scared" became "I'm brave." Before she knew it, Liana was at the top, and she happily glided down the zipline. It takes a fighter to overcome a fear of heights, and Liana is that fighter. That is the fiery red of determination inside her.

The second main point deals with Liana's wisdom, which the speaker correlates with the blue component of purple.

Then there's blue—a color of calm stability that represents wisdom. Liana is as wise as she is determined, and her friends have known that about her for a long time. They often turn to her for guidance on important decisions.

As can be seen from Video 4.7, the speaker presents his ideas extemporaneously. He has superb eye contact, impressive vocal variety, and a confident, poised delivery—all of which reflect his thorough preparation and rehearsal.

In high school, for instance, even as she was making her own college choice, she helped her friends make their choices. So far, they're happy and thriving at their new schools, just as Liana is happy and thriving here. The ability to weigh pros and cons in the face of a tough decision—that's the wisdom of the color blue inside of Liana.

The speaker concludes by returning to his theme of the color purple. The final sentence reiterates his central idea and unifies the entire speech.

Which brings us back to purple—the result of red and blue mixed together. It isn't just Liana's favorite color; it's central to her character. Just as the determination of red mixes together with the wisdom of blue to form the color purple, so they come together to make Liana the person she is today.

The Inevitability of Evette

COMMENTARY	SPEECH

The speaker begins by arousing curiosity about her middle name, Evette, which she found unusual when she was a child.

Most of you know me by my first name, Ananda. But you probably don't know my middle name, Evette, spelled "E-V-E-T-T-E." When I was younger, I thought it sounded like an old-time Hollywood starlet, who definitely would not have looked like me.

Today she takes pride in having the same middle name as her mother, sister, and niece. Her introduction ends by previewing the main points she will discuss in the body.

But in fact, I'm not the only Evette in my family. My mom, my sister, and my niece all share the same middle name. The name connects me with my mom and her resilience, with my sister and her intelligence, and with my niece and her curiosity.

The first main point deals with the speaker's mother. Well-chosen supporting materials convey the speaker's love and respect for her mom's accomplishments and her resilience in the face of adversity.

My mom is the resilient Evette. She was forced to grow up quickly after the birth of my brother. With little help from others, she put herself through college, cared for her son between classes, and earned a degree in nursing. For decades now she's been a registered nurse and has raised four children. Her resilience has taught me that when I'm faced with adversity, I need to meet it head on, as so many Black women before me have done.

The second main point deals with the speaker's younger sister. As you can see from Video 4.6, the speaker has strong eye contact, natural gestures, and an expressive voice.

I like to call my sister the intelligent Evette. She's as smart as me, if not smarter. At ten years old, she has the vocabulary and the reading level of a ninth grader. Sometimes I look up to my little sister, which is a little strange, given how much shorter she is than me. But her intelligence has taught me that being smart is always something to be proud of.

The third main point deals with the speaker's niece. Vivid, descriptive language captures her niece's curiosity and energetic personality. Echoing a pattern from the first two main points, this one ends by stating a vital lesson the speaker has learned from her niece.

Then there's my niece, the curious Evette. She's only three years old—or really, three and a half, and she will correct you on that if you ask. She investigates the world with big brown eyes, soaking up everything around her and always wanting to know more. Her curiosity has taught me how important it is to treasure the joy of discovery.

In her conclusion, the speaker summarizes her main points, reinforces her central idea, and ends on a touching note.

No matter what I thought of my middle name when I was young, today I cherish how it links me with my mom, my sister, and my niece. I'm proud to let people know that I, too, am an Evette—one of many.

Twists and Turns

COMMENTARY

Unlike the previous two speeches, which were presented in a classroom, this one was delivered online. A speech of self-introduction, it was recorded by the speaker at home and was then uploaded for viewing by the rest of the class.

The opening paragraphs gain attention and arouse curiosity about the speaker's previous experiences as a college student.

This paragraph completes the introduction by previewing the main points of the body.

Each main point is developed in a separate paragraph. The first deals with the speaker's husband, the second with her children, and the third with the spirit of adventure that brought the family back to Wisconsin.

The speaker's delivery enhances the impact of her ideas. She communicates engagingly, with natural gestures and pleasing vocal variety. These elements are as important in online speeches as they are in speeches presented to in-person audiences.

As you can see from Video 4.8, the speaker chose an uncluttered, well-lighted setting that does not distract from her message. She looks directly into the webcam and maintains eye contact throughout.

The conclusion ties everything together and ends on a thought-provoking note that unifies the rest of the speech.

SPEECH

Today, I'm a college student, but not for the first time. I've actually attended college twice before. The first time was twenty years ago when I came here to the University of Wisconsin all the way from my hometown of San Antonio, Texas. But after one semester, I realized that high school had not prepared me well for college, so I went back home.

The second time was when I enrolled at a community college in San Antonio to study social work. I was excited at first, but then I lost interest and went to work instead of staying in school.

So how did I wind up back here in Wisconsin again so many years later? It all comes down to one man, two kids, and the spirit of adventure.

The man I'm referring to is Carlos, my husband. When I first moved back to San Antonio, Carlos and I became friends, then we dated off and on for a few years before finally getting married. He's always believed in me and knows how to make me laugh. He's also encouraged me to pursue my dreams, which meant giving school another try.

But giving school another try didn't happen right away because Carlos and I welcomed two kids into the world. The moment I discovered I was pregnant, my life took on new meaning. Having kids fills you with a strange mixture of joy and dread, love and anxiety. Carlos and I want nothing more than to teach our kids right from wrong and to help them succeed. Our dreams are now intermingled with those of our kids, and that makes education all the more important.

That's where the spirit of adventure came in. After Carlos received his degree in architecture, I knew it was time for me to go back to school—and to return to Wisconsin. So this spring we sold our furniture, packed our car, and drove 1,200 miles here to Madison. It was a long trip, but I'm thrilled to be back in school, and our family has been loving our time here.

In conclusion, life is an adventure, especially with a spouse and two kids. But I wouldn't change my journey for anything. After all, it's the twists and turns that make us who we are.

Summary

The purpose of this chapter is to help you get ready for your ice breaker speech. Later chapters will look more closely at all the aspects of speech preparation and delivery discussed here.

Once you know the exact assignment for your ice breaker speech, you can start working out your ideas. Focus on a limited number of main points and develop them creatively. Your speech will have three parts—introduction, body, and conclusion. Use transition statements to help the audience keep track of your points as the speech progresses.

Your teacher will probably ask you to deliver the speech extemporaneously. This means that the speech is carefully prepared in advance, but the exact language is chosen at the moment of delivery. To be successful, you will need to rehearse the speech multiple times to make sure you have full command of it.

When speech day comes, you will almost surely have butterflies in your stomach. Remember that nervousness is normal. Concentrate on communicating with your audience, rather than on worrying about your nerves. Try to appear calm and relaxed on the outside, no matter how you feel on the inside. Establish eye contact with the audience, use your voice expressively, and make sure your gestures and mannerisms do not distract from your message.

Key Terms

ice breaker speech (60)

introduction (63)

body (64)

chronological order (64)

topical order (64)

main points (64)

transition (64)

conclusion (65)

extemporaneous speech (66)

gestures (67)

eye contact (67)

Review Questions

After reading this chapter, you should be able to answer the following questions:

1. What two major steps are discussed in this chapter for developing your introductory speech?
2. When organizing your introductory speech, you should divide it into what three sections?
3. What method of delivery does this chapter recommend for your introductory speech?
4. What steps should you take when rehearsing your first speech?
5. What five elements of speech delivery are discussed in this chapter with regard to presenting your first speech?

Exercises for Critical Thinking

1. Examine the three sample speeches included in this chapter. Choose one, and answer the following questions about it.

   a. How do the opening paragraphs gain the attention of the audience, introduce the subject of the speech, and preview the main points to be discussed in the body?

   b. How clearly is the body of the speech organized? What does the speaker do to help listeners follow the progression of ideas?

   c. How does the speaker conclude? Does the conclusion reinforce the central theme of the speech?

2. Are there occasions outside the classroom on which you might give a speech of self-introduction? Identify such an occasion and explain how you might apply the principles of introductory speeches discussed in this chapter.

5 Selecting a Topic and a Purpose

As you read through this book, you will find examples of hundreds of speeches that were delivered in classrooms, in the political arena, in community and business situations. Here is a very small sample of the topics they cover:

artificial intelligence	Native American art
blockchain	opioid addiction
dog breeds	paragliding
eSports	Ramadan
first responders	sustainable fashion
Grand Canyon	tropical fish
hurricanes	volleyball
identity theft	wildfires
jazz	x-rays
kayaking	Yom Kippur
Martin Luther King	zoos

Undoubtedly you noticed that the list runs from A to Z. This array of topics wasn't planned. It happened naturally in the course of presenting many different kinds of speeches. The list is given here to show you that there are literally endless possibilities for speech topics—from A to Z.

Daniel Milchev/Getty Images

Choosing a Topic

topic
The subject of a speech.

The first step in speechmaking is choosing a topic. For speeches outside the classroom this is seldom a problem. Usually the speech topic is determined by the occasion, the audience, and the speaker's qualifications. When Barack Obama lectures at a college campus, he often speaks about political leadership. Rachel Maddow will discuss current events. Spike Lee might share his views on new developments in film. The same is true of ordinary citizens. The doctor is asked to inform high-school athletes and their parents about sports injuries, the head of a neighborhood coalition speaks about zoning regulations, the florist discusses how to grow thriving houseplants.

In a public speaking class, the situation is different. Students generally have great leeway in selecting topics. This would appear to be an advantage, since it allows you to talk about matters of personal interest. Yet there may be no facet of speech preparation that causes more gnashing of teeth than selecting a topic.

It is a constant source of amazement to teachers that students who regularly chat with their friends about almost any subject under the sun become mentally paralyzed when faced with the task of deciding what to talk about in their speech class. Fortunately, once you get over this initial paralysis, you should have little trouble choosing a good topic.

There are two broad categories of potential topics for your classroom speeches: (1) subjects you know a lot about and (2) subjects you want to know more about. Let's start with the first.

TOPICS YOU KNOW A LOT ABOUT

Most people speak best about subjects with which they are most familiar. When thinking about a topic, draw on your own knowledge and experience. Everyone knows things or has done things that can be used in a speech.

Think for a moment about unusual experiences you may have had or special expertise you may have acquired. One student, who grew up in Turkey, presented a fascinating speech about daily life in that country. Another used her knowledge as a jewelry store salesperson to prepare a speech on how to judge the value of cut diamonds. A third student, who had lived through a tornado, gave a gripping speech about that terrifying experience.

Too dramatic? Nothing in your life is as interesting? Yet another student, who described herself as "just a housewife who is returning to school to finish the education she started 20 years ago," delivered a witty speech on the adjustments she had to make in coming back to college—sitting in class with students young enough to be her children, balancing her academic work against her family commitments, and the satisfaction of completing the education she had begun years earlier.

Here are a few more examples of speech topics based largely on the students' personal knowledge and experience:

Knitting for Fun and Profit

Behind the Scenes at Disney World

Communicating with Sign Language

The Basics of Rugby

When you think of a speech topic, keep in mind special interests you have or sports, hobbies, travel, and other personal experiences that would make for an interesting presentation.

Traumlichtfabrik/Getty Images

TOPICS YOU WANT TO KNOW MORE ABOUT

On the other hand, you may decide to make your speech a learning experience for yourself as well as for your audience. You may choose a subject about which you already have some knowledge or expertise but not enough to prepare a speech without doing additional research. You may even select a topic that you want to explore for the first time. Say, for example, you've always been interested in Stonehenge but never knew much about it. This would be a perfect opportunity to research a fascinating subject and turn it into a fascinating speech.

Or suppose you run across a subject in one of your other classes that catches your fancy. Why not investigate it further for your speech class? One student used this approach to develop a speech on the subject of neuromarketing, which uses recent advancements in neuroscience to study the way people respond to products and promotions. After hearing about the subject in her marketing class, the student researched the topic further. In the process, she learned that neuromarketing is currently being used by some of the biggest corporations in the world. Using what she learned in her research, she put together a captivating speech that kept everyone's attention from beginning to end.

Still another possibility—especially for persuasive speeches—is to think of subjects about which you hold strong opinions and beliefs. They may include national or international concerns such as school safety or environmental protection. Or perhaps you are closely involved in a local issue such as a school board election or a proposal to build a new student center. Not all such topics must be "political." They can deal with anything from graduation requirements to helping people with physical disabilities, from dormitory regulations to building a church recreation center.

connect

View an excerpt from "Neuromarketing: Whispers of the Brain" in the online Media Library for this chapter (Video 5.1).

BRAINSTORMING FOR TOPICS

After all this, you may still be thinking, "I *don't* care about neuromarketing. I've *never* been to Turkey. I'm *not* active in politics. WHAT am I going to talk about?" If you are having trouble selecting a topic, there are a number of brainstorming procedures you can follow to get started.

brainstorming
A method of generating ideas by free association of words and thoughts.

Personal Inventory

First, make a quick inventory of your experiences, interests, hobbies, skills, beliefs, and so forth. Jot down anything that comes to mind, no matter how silly or irrelevant it may seem. From this list may come a general subject area out of which you can fashion a specific topic. This method has worked for many students.

Clustering

If the first method doesn't work, try a technique called clustering. Take a sheet of paper and divide it into nine columns as follows: People, Places, Things, Events, Processes, Concepts, Natural Phenomena, Problems, and Plans and Policies. Then list in each column the first four or five items that come to mind. The result might look like this:

People	Places	Things
first responders	Jerusalem	vaccines
Viola Davis	Mars	TikTok
MrBeast	national parks	movies
my family	my hometown	Statue of Liberty

Events	Processes
Olympics	writing a job resumé
graduation	starting an online business
Juneteenth	applying a tourniquet
family celebrations	cooking Ethiopian food

Concepts	Natural Phenomena
conservatism	wildfires
bioethics	earthquakes
critical race theory	glaciers
freeganism	lightning

Problems	Plans and Policies
ransomware	affordable housing
campus crime	reducing plastics
murder hornets	immigration policy
online misinformation	digital security

Very likely, several items on your lists will strike you as potential topics. If not, take the items you find most intriguing and compose sublists for each. Try to free-associate. Write down a word or idea. What does that trigger in your mind? Whatever it is, write that down next, and keep going until you have four or five ideas on your list. For example, working from the previous lists, one student composed sublists for movies, campus crime, and lightning:

Movies	Campus Crime	Lightning
Academy Awards	police	thunder
prizes	fingerprints	noise
lotteries	hands	traffic
gambling	gloves	air pollution

Can you follow her trail of association? In the first column, movies made her think of the Academy Awards. The Academy Awards are prizes. Prizes reminded her of lotteries. Lotteries are a form of gambling. Suddenly, this student remembered an article she had read on the problem of gambling addiction in America. The idea clicked in her mind. After considerable research, she developed an excellent speech titled "Gambling Addiction: Why You Can't Beat the Odds."

That's a far cry from movies! If you started out free-associating from movies, you would doubtless end up somewhere completely different. This is what clustering is all about.

Internet Search

By clustering, most people come up with a topic rather quickly. But if you are still stymied, try an Internet search. Browse through a subject-based website, an online encyclopedia, or some other reference portal until you come across what might be a good topic. As an experiment, one student scanned the *Merriam-Webster Online Dictionary,* limiting herself to the letter *s*. Within 10 minutes, she had come up with these potential topics:

salaries	sleepwalking	sushi	safecracking
sink holes	stars	Sphinx	scuba diving
states' rights	Singapore	Sabbath	smuggling
spiders	stock market	sugar	science fiction

Whatever the means you use for selecting a topic, *start early*. Pay attention to interesting subjects in conversation, on television and the Internet, in newspapers and magazines. Jot down ideas for topics as they occur to you. Having an inventory of possible topics to choose from is much better than having to rack your brain for one at the last minute. If you get an early start on choosing a topic, you will have plenty of time to pick just the right one and prepare a first-rate speech.

Determining the General Purpose

Along with choosing a topic, you need to determine the general purpose of your speech. Usually it will fall into one of two overlapping categories—to inform or to persuade.

When your general purpose is to inform, you act as a teacher or lecturer. Your goal is to convey information clearly, accurately, and interestingly. If you describe how to lift weights, narrate the major events of the latest Middle East crisis, or report on your sorority's financial position, you are speaking to inform. Your aim is to enhance the knowledge and understanding of your listeners—to give them information they did not have before.

When your general purpose is to persuade, you act as an advocate or a partisan. You go beyond giving information to espousing a cause. You want to change or structure the attitudes or actions of your audience. If you try to convince your listeners that they should start a regular program of weight lifting, that the United States should modify its policy in the Middle East, or that your sorority should start a fund-raising drive to balance its budget, then you are speaking to persuade. In doing so, you cannot help but give information, but your primary goal is to win over your listeners to your point of view—to get them to believe something or do something as a result of your speech.

In speech classes, the general purpose is usually specified as part of the speech assignment. For speeches outside the classroom, however, you have to make sure of your general purpose yourself. Usually this is easy to do. Are you going to explain, report, or demonstrate something? Then your general purpose is to inform. Are you going to sell, advocate, or defend something? Then your general purpose is to persuade. But no matter what the situation, you must be certain of exactly what you hope to achieve by speaking.

Determining the Specific Purpose

Once you have chosen a topic and a general purpose, you must narrow your choices to determine the specific purpose of your speech. The specific purpose should focus on one aspect of a topic. You should be able to state your specific purpose in a single infinitive phrase ("to inform my audience about . . ."; "to persuade my audience to . . .") that indicates *precisely* what you hope to accomplish with your speech.

For example, Laleh Amiri, a student at a large state university, decided to give her first classroom speech on a topic from her personal experience. For the past two years, she had volunteered her time to perform music for patients in mental hospitals, nursing homes, and residences for adults with disabilities. She had seen how enthusiastically the patients responded to music, even when they remained unmoved by other kinds of stimuli. Laleh's experience had given her a better understanding of the benefits of music therapy, and she wanted to share this understanding with her classmates. This gave her a topic and a general purpose, which she stated like this:

Topic: Music therapy

General Purpose: To inform

So far, so good. But what aspect of her topic would Laleh discuss? The kinds of facilities in which she had worked? Her specific role as a performer? The evidence that music therapy can improve patients' mental health? The needs of patients with different kinds of illnesses? She had to choose something interesting that she could cover in a six-minute speech. Finally, she settled on describing her most memorable experiences with patients to show how music therapy affected them. She stated her specific purpose this way:

Specific Purpose: To inform my audience about the benefits of music therapy for people with psychological or cognitive disabilities.

This turned out to be an excellent choice, and Laleh's speech was among the best in the class.

Notice how clear the specific purpose statement is. Notice also how it relates the topic directly to the audience. That is, it states not only what the *speaker* wants to *say* but also what the speaker wants the *audience* to *know* as a result of the speech. This is very important, for it helps keep the audience at the center of your attention as you prepare your speech.

Look what happens when the specific purpose statement does not include the audience.

Specific Purpose: To explain the benefits of music therapy for people with psychological or cognitive disabilities.

Explain to whom? To musicians? To medical students? To social workers? Those would be three different speeches. The musicians would want to know about the kinds of music Laleh played. The medical students would want to hear about research on the benefits of music therapy. The social workers would want to learn how to implement a music program. Communicating effectively with each group would require preparing a different speech.

Using public speaking in your CAREER

Your communication degree has helped you land a job as spokesperson for the mayor of a medium-sized city on the West Coast. A year after starting the job, you are selected to organize an information campaign explaining the benefits of a new youth center proposed by the mayor.

To launch this campaign, you've decided to hold a news briefing at the end of the week. To open the briefing, you will present a short set of comments on the mayor's initiative. You decide to focus on four benefits of the youth center: (1) It will offer a range of activities—from sports to the arts—in a safe environment. (2) It will provide social networks for youths from all walks of life. (3) It will operate most hours of the day and night. (4) It will be free and open to everyone.

Following the format used in this chapter, state the general purpose, specific purpose, central idea, and main points of your comments.

Steve Debenport/Getty Images

When the audience slips out of the specific purpose, it may slip out of the speaker's consciousness. You may begin to think that your task is the general one of preparing "an informative speech," when in fact your task is the specific one of informing a particular group of people. As we shall see in the next chapter, it is almost impossible to prepare a good speech without keeping constantly in mind the *people* for whom it is intended.

TIPS FOR FORMULATING THE SPECIFIC PURPOSE STATEMENT

Formulating a specific purpose is the most important early step in developing a successful speech. When writing your purpose statement, follow the general principles outlined next.

Write the Purpose Statement as a Full Infinitive Phrase, Not as a Fragment

Ineffective: Avalanches

More Effective: To inform my audience about the three major kinds of avalanches.

The ineffective statement is adequate as an announcement of the speech topic, but it is not thought out fully enough to indicate the specific purpose.

Express Your Purpose as a Statement, Not as a Question

Ineffective: What is Día de los Muertos?

More Effective: To inform my audience about the history of Mexico's Día de los Muertos celebration.

The question might arouse the curiosity of an audience, but it is not effective as a specific purpose statement. It gives no indication about what direction the speech will take or what the speaker hopes to accomplish.

Avoid Figurative Language in Your Purpose Statement

Ineffective: To persuade my audience that the campus policy on student parking really stinks.

More Effective: To persuade my audience that the campus policy on student parking should be revised to provide more spaces for students before 5 P.M.

Although the ineffective statement indicates something of the speaker's viewpoint, it does not state concisely what he or she hopes to achieve. Figurative language can reinforce ideas within a speech, but it is too ambiguous for a specific purpose statement.

Limit Your Purpose Statement to One Distinct Idea

Ineffective: To persuade my audience to become literacy tutors and to donate time to Meals on Wheels.

Think of opinions you hold when looking for speech topics. One student spoke on the specific purpose "To persuade my audience that stronger measures should be taken to prevent the extinction of elephants."

Claudia Paulussen/Shutterstock

This purpose statement expresses two unrelated ideas, either of which could be the subject of a speech. The easiest remedy is to select one or the other as a focus for your presentation.

More Effective: To persuade my audience to become literacy tutors.

Or:

More Effective: To persuade my audience to donate time to Meals on Wheels.

Does this mean that you can never use the word "and" in your specific purpose statement? Not at all. Suppose your specific purpose is: "To inform my audience about the causes and effects of epilepsy." In this case, "and" is appropriate because it connects two related parts of a unified topic. What you need to avoid is not simply the word "and" but a specific purpose statement that contains two unrelated ideas, either of which could be developed into a speech in its own right.

Make Sure Your Specific Purpose Is Not Too Vague or General

Ineffective: To persuade my audience that something should be done about gerrymandering.

More Effective: To persuade my audience that each state should create a nonpartisan commission to establish criteria for congressional redistricting.

The ineffective purpose statement falls into one of the most common traps—it is too broad and ill-defined. It gives no clues about what the speaker believes should be done about gerrymandering. The more effective purpose statement is sharp and concise. It reveals clearly what the speaker plans to discuss.

The more precise your specific purpose, the easier it will be to prepare your speech. Consider this topic and specific purpose:

Topic: Hot-air balloons

Specific Purpose: To inform my audience about hot-air balloons.

With such a hazy purpose, you have no systematic way of limiting your research or of deciding what to include in the speech and what to exclude. The origins of hot-air balloons, how they work, their current popularity—all could be equally relevant to a speech designed "to inform my audience about hot-air balloons."

In contrast, look at this topic and specific purpose:

Topic: Hot-air balloons

Specific Purpose: To inform my audience about the scientific uses of hot-air balloons.

Now it is easy to decide what is germane and what is not. The origins of hot-air balloons, how they work, their popularity for recreation—all are interesting, but none is essential to the specific purpose of explaining "the scientific uses of hot-air balloons." Thus you need not worry about researching these matters or about explaining them in your speech. You can spend your preparation time efficiently.

QUESTIONS TO ASK ABOUT YOUR SPECIFIC PURPOSE

Sometimes you will arrive at your specific purpose almost immediately after choosing your topic. At other times you may do quite a bit of research before deciding on a specific purpose. Much will depend on how familiar you are with the topic, as well as on any special demands imposed by the assignment, the audience, or the occasion. But whenever you settle on your specific purpose, ask yourself the following questions about it.

Does My Purpose Meet the Assignment?

Students occasionally stumble over this question. Be sure you understand your assignment and shape your specific purpose to meet it. If you have questions, check with your instructor.

Can I Accomplish My Purpose in the Time Allotted?

Most classroom speeches are quite short, ranging from 4 to 10 minutes. That may seem like a lot of time, but you will quickly find what generations of students have discovered—time flies when you are giving a speech!

Most people speak at an average rate of 120 to 180 words a minute. This means that a six-minute speech will consist of roughly 720 to 1,000 words. That is not long enough to develop a highly complex topic. Here are some specific purpose statements that would defy being handled well in the time normally allotted for class-room speeches:

> To inform my audience about the rise and fall of Mayan civilization.
>
> To inform my audience about the role of technology in human history.
>
> To persuade my audience to convert to Buddhism.

You are much better off with a limited purpose that you have some reasonable hope of achieving in the short span of 4 to 10 minutes.

Is the Purpose Relevant to My Audience?

The price of retirement homes in Palm Springs might be an engrossing topic for older citizens who are in the market for such dwellings. And the quality of hot lunches in the elementary schools is of great concern to the students who eat them and the parents who pay for them. But neither subject has much relevance for an audience of college students. No matter how well you construct your speeches, they are likely to fall flat unless you speak about matters of interest to your listeners.

This is not to say you must select only topics that pertain directly to the college student's daily experience. Most students have wide-ranging backgrounds, interests,

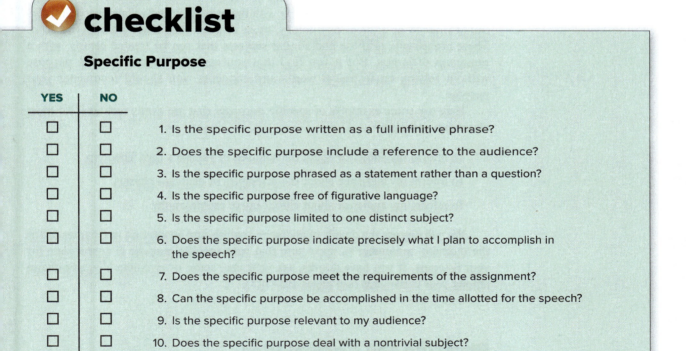

✔ checklist

Specific Purpose

YES	NO	
☐	☐	1. Is the specific purpose written as a full infinitive phrase?
☐	☐	2. Does the specific purpose include a reference to the audience?
☐	☐	3. Is the specific purpose phrased as a statement rather than a question?
☐	☐	4. Is the specific purpose free of figurative language?
☐	☐	5. Is the specific purpose limited to one distinct subject?
☐	☐	6. Does the specific purpose indicate precisely what I plan to accomplish in the speech?
☐	☐	7. Does the specific purpose meet the requirements of the assignment?
☐	☐	8. Can the specific purpose be accomplished in the time allotted for the speech?
☐	☐	9. Is the specific purpose relevant to my audience?
☐	☐	10. Does the specific purpose deal with a nontrivial subject?
☐	☐	11. Is the specific purpose suitable for a nontechnical audience?

ideas, and values. And most of them are intellectually curious. They can get involved in an astonishing variety of subjects. Follow your common sense and make sure *you* are truly interested in the topic. Also, when speaking on a subject that is not obviously relevant to your listeners, find a way to tie it in with their goals, values, interests, and well-being. We'll discuss how to do this in the next chapter.

Is the Purpose Too Trivial for My Audience?

Just as you need to avoid speech topics that are too broad or complicated, so you need to steer clear of topics that are too superficial. How to tie a perfect square knot might absorb a group of Cub Scouts, but your classmates would probably consider it frivolous. Unfortunately, there is no absolute rule for determining what is trivial to an audience and what is not. Here are some examples of specific purposes that most people would find too trivial for classroom speeches:

> To inform my audience about the parts of a backpack.
>
> To inform my audience how to do laundry.
>
> To persuade my audience that espresso is better than cappuccino.

Is the Purpose Too Technical for My Audience?

Nothing puts an audience to sleep faster than a dry and technical speech. Beware of topics that are inherently technical and of treating ordinary subjects in a technical fashion. Although you may be familiar with the principles and vocabulary of international finance or clinical psychology, most of your classmates probably are not. There are aspects of these and similar subjects that can be treated clearly, with a minimum of jargon. But if you find that you can't fulfill your specific purpose without relying on technical words and concepts, you should reconsider your purpose.

Here are some examples of specific purposes that are overly technical for most classroom speeches:

> To inform my audience about the solution to Fermat's Last Theorem.
>
> To inform my audience about the principles of neutrino physics.
>
> To inform my audience about elliptic-curve cryptography.

We will discuss the details of audience analysis and adaptation in Chapter 6. For the moment, remember to make sure that your specific purpose is appropriate for your listeners. If you have doubts, ask your instructor, or circulate a questionnaire among your classmates (see pages 105–107).

Phrasing the Central Idea

WHAT IS THE CENTRAL IDEA?

The specific purpose of a speech is what you hope to accomplish. The central idea is a concise statement of what you *expect to say*. Sometimes it is called the thesis statement, the subject sentence, or the major thought. Whatever the term, the central idea is usually expressed as a simple, declarative sentence that refines and sharpens the specific purpose statement.

Imagine that you run into a friend on your way to speech class. She says, "I have to dash to my psych lecture, but I hear you're giving a speech today. Can you tell me the gist of it in one sentence?" "Sure," you reply. "America's prison system suffers from three major problems—overcrowding of inmates, lack of effective rehabilitation programs, and persistent racial disparities."

Your answer is the central idea of your speech. It is more precise than your topic (America's prison system) or your specific purpose statement ("To inform my audience of three major problems facing America's prison system"). By stating exactly what the three major problems are, the central idea sums up your speech in a single sentence.

Another way to think of the central idea is as your residual message—what you want your audience to remember after they have forgotten everything else in the speech. Most of the time the central idea will encapsulate the main points to be developed in the body of the speech. To show how this works, let's take a few of the examples we saw earlier in this chapter and develop them from the topic, general purpose, and specific purpose to the central idea.

We can start with the speech about music therapy.

Topic:	Music therapy
General Purpose:	To inform
Specific Purpose:	To inform my audience about the benefits of music therapy for people with psychological or cognitive disabilities.
Central Idea:	Music therapy developed as a formal mode of treatment during the 20th century, utilizes a number of methods, and is explained by several theories that account for its success.

Look carefully at this example. It shows how the speaker might start with a broad subject (music therapy) that becomes narrower and narrower as the speaker moves from the general purpose to the specific purpose to the central idea. Notice also how much more the central idea suggests about the content of the speech. From it we can expect the speaker to address three main points—the first summarizing the development of music therapy, the second looking at methods of music therapy, and the third exploring theories that account for the success of music therapy.

This sharpening of focus as one proceeds to the central idea is crucial. Here is another example:

Topic:	Día de los Muertos
General Purpose:	To inform
Specific Purpose:	To inform my audience about the history of Mexico's Día de los Muertos celebration.
Central Idea:	Día de los Muertos can be traced to the Aztecs, was moved from summer to fall by Spanish priests, and today is celebrated in a number of ways in different regions of Mexico.

central idea
A one-sentence statement that sums up or encapsulates the major ideas of a speech.

residual message
What a speaker wants the audience to remember after they have forgotten everything else in a speech.

connect
View the introduction from "The Benefits of Music Therapy" in the online Media Library for this chapter (Video 5.2).

This central idea is especially well worded. We can assume from it that the body of the speech will contain three main points: (1) on the Aztec origins of Día de los Muertos, (2) on how it was changed by the Spanish, and (3) on the ways it is celebrated today.

Notice in each of these examples how much more the central idea reveals about the content of the speech than does the specific purpose. This is not accidental. Often you can settle on a specific purpose statement early in preparing your speech. The central idea, however, usually emerges later—after you have done your research and have decided on the main points of the speech. The process may work like this:

> As an aerospace engineering major, James Curry had learned about challenges facing the airline industry, including a shortfall in the number of qualified pilots. He decided this would make a good topic for his informative speech. Tentatively, he adopted the following specific purpose statement: "To inform my audience about the growing shortage of commercial airline pilots." Then James started his research.
>
> He found a report on the website of the Federal Aviation Administration explaining that the time required for airline pilot certification has grown from 250 hours to 1,500 hours. This has greatly increased the time a new pilot must train to be eligible to fly a commercial airplane.
>
> Next James located an article on CNN stating that 42 percent of current U.S. airline pilots will reach the mandatory retirement age of 65 during the next decade. That alone will create a need for 27,000 new pilots at the biggest American carriers.
>
> Then James hit upon the idea of interviewing one of his aerospace professors. In addition to confirming James's other research, the professor mentioned the rapidly expanding international demand for air travel. Worldwide, some 637,000 new airline pilots will be needed by 2040 to meet passenger demand. That is equivalent to producing 87 fully trained pilots every day—or 1 every 17 minutes.
>
> James digested all this information. Now he was ready to formulate his central idea: "Changes in certification requirements, an increase in retirements, and ever-growing demand for air travel are creating a serious shortage of pilots in the United States and around the world."

GUIDELINES FOR THE CENTRAL IDEA

What makes a well-worded central idea? Essentially the same things that make a well-worded specific purpose statement. The central idea (1) should be expressed in a full sentence, (2) should not be in the form of a question, (3) should avoid figurative language, and (4) should not be vague or overly general.

Here, for example, are four poorly written central ideas. See if you can identify the problem with each and figure out how each might be phrased more effectively:

Ineffective: Studying abroad while in college is a good idea.

Ineffective: Benefits of parkour.

Unlike the specific purpose, which you need to settle on early in the speech preparation process, the central idea usually takes shape later, as a result of your research and analysis of the topic.

fizkes/Shutterstock

Ineffective: What are nanorobots?

Ineffective: Costa Rica is an awesome place for a vacation.

The first is too general. To say that studying abroad while in college is a "good idea" does not convey the speaker's viewpoint sharply and clearly. What does the speaker mean by a "good idea"? A revised central idea for this speech might be:

More Effective: Studying abroad helps students expand their cultural horizons, develop their language skills, and enhance their employability.

The second ineffective central idea is also too general, but it suffers further from not being written as a complete sentence. "Benefits of parkour" does not reveal enough about the content of the speech to serve as the central idea. It should be rewritten as a full sentence that identifies the benefits of parkour to be discussed in the speech:

More Effective: The benefits of parkour include working all muscle groups, developing cardiovascular endurance, and boosting self-confidence.

The third poorly written central idea is phrased as a question rather than as a full declarative sentence. Asking "What are nanorobots?" might be a good way to catch the attention of listeners, but it does not encapsulate the main points to be developed in the speech. A more effective central idea would be:

More Effective: Microscopic in size, nanorobots continue to be refined for use in medicine, weaponry, and daily life.

checklist

Central Idea

YES	NO	
☐	☐	1. Is the central idea written as a complete sentence?
☐	☐	2. Is the central idea phrased as a statement rather than a question?
☐	☐	3. Is the central idea free of figurative language?
☐	☐	4. Does the central idea clearly encapsulate the main points to be discussed in the body of the speech?
☐	☐	5. Can the central idea be adequately discussed in the time allotted for the speech?
☐	☐	6. Is the central idea relevant to the audience?
☐	☐	7. Is the central idea appropriate for a nontechnical audience?

The final ineffective central idea is flawed by its use of figurative language. To say that Costa Rica is an "awesome" place for a vacation does not indicate what characteristics of Costa Rica the speaker intends to discuss. A better central idea might be:

More Effective: Costa Rica has many attractions for vacationers, including spectacular beaches, lush rainforests, and stunning mountains.

Notice that in all these examples the more effective central idea sums up the main points of the speech in a single sentence. If you are having trouble phrasing your central idea, the reason may be that you do not yet have a firm grasp on the main points of your speech.

Don't worry too much about your central idea until after you have developed the body of your speech (see Chapter 9). If, at that point, you still can't come up with a clear, concise central idea, your speech itself may not be clear or concise. Keep working on the speech until you can compose a central idea that fits the criteria just discussed. The result will be a sharper central idea and a tighter, more coherent speech.

Summary

The first step in speechmaking is choosing a topic. For classroom speeches, you can choose a subject you know well or one you research especially for the speech. If you have trouble picking a topic, you can use one of three brainstorming procedures. First, make an inventory of your hobbies, interests, skills, beliefs, and so forth. Second, use clustering to list the first topics that come to mind in several categories. Third, use an Internet subject directory, encyclopedia, or similar reference site to help you scan possible topics.

The general purpose of your speech will usually be to inform or to persuade. When your general purpose is to inform, your goal is to communicate information clearly, accurately, and interestingly. When your general purpose is to persuade, your goal is to win listeners over to your point of view.

Once you know your topic and general purpose, you must focus on a specific purpose statement that indicates precisely what your speech seeks to achieve. The specific purpose statement should (1) be a full infinitive phrase; (2) be worded as a statement, not a question; (3) avoid figurative language; (4) concentrate on one distinct idea; and (5) not be vague or general.

Keep several questions in mind as you formulate your specific purpose statement: Does my purpose meet the assignment? Can I accomplish my purpose in the time allotted? Is the purpose relevant to my audience? Is the purpose too trivial or too technical for my audience?

The central idea refines and sharpens your specific purpose. It is a concise statement of what you will say in your speech, and it usually crystallizes in your thinking after you have done your research and have decided on the main points of your speech. The central idea usually encapsulates the main points to be developed in the body of your speech.

Key Terms

topic (76)
brainstorming (78)
general purpose (80)

specific purpose (80)
central idea (87)
residual message (87)

Review Questions

After reading this chapter, you should be able to answer the following questions:

1. What three brainstorming methods can you follow if you are having trouble choosing a topic for your speech?

2. What are the two general purposes of most classroom speeches? How do they differ?

3. Why is determining the specific purpose such an important early step in speech preparation? Why is it important to include the audience in the specific purpose statement?

4. What are five tips for formulating your specific purpose?

5. What are five questions to ask about your specific purpose?

6. What is the difference between the specific purpose and the central idea of a speech? What are four guidelines for an effective central idea?

Exercises for Critical Thinking

1. Using one of the brainstorming methods described in this chapter, come up with three topics you might like to deal with in your next classroom speech. For each topic, devise a specific purpose statement suitable for the speech assignment. Make sure your specific purpose statements fit the guidelines discussed in the chapter.

2. Here are several specific purpose statements for classroom speeches. Identify the problem (or problems) with each.

   To inform my audience about Vietnam.

   To persuade my audience that something has to be done about the problem of ransomware attacks.

   Start an exercise program.

   To inform my audience why arbitrage pricing theory is superior to the capital asset model for pricing assets in financial markets.

   To persuade my audience that the U.S. government should eliminate the Department of Education and send an astronaut to Mars by 2030.

   What is biophilic design?

   To inform my audience how to register for classes.

3. Following are three sets of main points for speeches. For each set, supply the general purpose, specific purpose, and central idea.

   General Purpose:

   Specific Purpose:

   Central Idea:

   Main Points: I. You should support free community college for all Americans because it will send more people to college.

                   II. You should support free community college for all Americans because it will benefit low-income students.

             III. You should support free community college for all Americans because it will improve people's job skills.

   General Purpose:

   Specific Purpose:

   Central Idea:

   Main Points: I. The first event in a triathlon is swimming.

             II. The second event in a triathlon is cycling.

          III. The third event in a triathlon is running.

General Purpose:

Specific Purpose:

Central Idea:

Main Points: I. As a boxer, Muhammad Ali won an Olympic gold medal and the world heavyweight championship.

    II. As an activist, Muhammad Ali supported civil rights and opposed the war in Vietnam.

    III. As a humanitarian, Muhammad Ali devoted his life after boxing to charitable causes.

6 Analyzing the Audience

Audience-Centeredness

Your Classmates as an Audience

The Psychology of Audiences

Demographic Audience Analysis

Situational Audience Analysis

Getting Information About the Audience

Adapting to the Audience

When Oprah Winfrey stepped to the microphone, few could have anticipated the response her speech would receive. She was onstage at the 2018 Golden Globes ceremony accepting the Cecil B. DeMille lifetime achievement award—the first Black woman to receive the honor.

But surrounding the ceremony was a scandal that had sent shockwaves through Hollywood. For months accusations of sexual harassment had been ending the careers of powerful figures in the entertainment industry. Facing a room of people fed up with business as usual in Hollywood, Winfrey knew she had to reach multiple audiences, including people affected by the scandal, people watching at home, and people who looked to her for leadership and inspiration.

Winfrey spent the first part of her speech juxtaposing her humble upbringing in Milwaukee to the place of honor she now occupied. Turning to the sexual-harassment scandal, she praised the women who "felt strong enough and empowered enough to speak up and share their personal stories." She ended by focusing on what united the audience—"hope for a brighter morning, even during our darkest nights."

The speech garnered almost universal praise. Columnist David Zurawik called it "a moving jolt of moral authority." Others described it as "powerful," "mesmerizing," "pitch-perfect," and "public speaking at its finest." Sheryl Sandberg's Facebook post captured what many people were thinking: "Leave it to Oprah to speak to this moment with such brilliance—and hope."

Audience-Centeredness

This story points to an important fact: Good public speakers are audience-centered. They know the primary purpose of speechmaking is not to browbeat the audience or to blow off steam. Rather, it is to gain a *desired response* from listeners.

Being audience-centered does not involve compromising your beliefs to get a favorable response. Nor does it mean using devious, unethical tactics to achieve your goal. You can remain true to yourself and speak ethically while adapting your message to the goals, values, and attitudes of your audience.

To be audience-centered, you need to keep several questions in mind when you work on your speeches:

To whom am I speaking?

What do I want them to know, believe, or do as a result of my speech?

What is the most effective way of composing and presenting my speech to accomplish that aim?

The answers to these questions will influence every decision you make along the way—selecting a topic, determining a specific purpose, settling on your main points and supporting materials, organizing the message, and, finally, delivering the speech.

In many ways, adapting to an audience during a public speech is not much different from what you do in your daily social contacts. Few people would walk into a party and announce, "You know those people protesting at the administration building are way over the edge!"

People usually prefer to open controversial topics with a fairly noncommittal position. You might say, "What's going on at the administration building?" Then when you have heard and processed your companion's response, you can present your position accordingly. (You don't have to *agree* with a viewpoint different from your own, but neither do you have to hit your listeners over the head with your own opinion.)

When you make a speech, either in class or in some other forum, keep in mind the need to be audience-centered. Think in advance about your listeners' background and interests, about their level of knowledge regarding the speech topic, and about their attitudes regarding your stance on the topic. As you develop the speech, work on explaining your ideas so they will be clear, interesting, and persuasive to the audience.

At this point, you may be nodding your head and saying, "Of course, everyone knows that. It's only common sense." But knowing a precept and putting it into practice are two different matters. The aim of this chapter is to introduce the basic principles of audience analysis and adaption. Chapters 15 and 16 will deal with those features of audience analysis unique to informative and persuasive speaking.

Your Classmates as an Audience

There is a tendency—among students and teachers alike—to view the classroom as an artificial speaking situation. In a way, it is. Your speech class is a testing ground where you can develop your communication skills before applying them outside the classroom. The most serious measure of success or failure is your grade, and that is determined ultimately by your instructor.

Because of this, it is easy to lose sight of your fellow students as an authentic audience. But each of your classmates is a real person with real ideas, attitudes, and

audience-centeredness
Keeping the audience foremost in mind at every step of speech preparation and presentation.

feelings. Your speech class offers an enormous opportunity to inform and persuade other people. As one student wrote on her evaluation form at the end of her speech class, "I thought the speeches would all be phony, but they weren't. I've not only learned a lot about speaking—I've learned a lot about other things from listening to the speeches in class."

The best classroom speeches are those that take the classroom audience as seriously as a lawyer, a politician, a minister, or an advertiser takes an audience. You should consider every audience—inside the classroom and out—as worthy of your best efforts to communicate your knowledge or convictions. At the least you show respect for your listeners. At the most you could make a real difference in their lives. The following story demonstrates the latter:

> Etta Green gave an informative speech on the subject of test anxiety and the campus resources available to students who experience it. Part of her speech went like this:
>
> "You've had it on your calendar since the start of the semester. Now it's only one week away—that dreaded midterm worth 40 percent of your final grade. You find yourself thinking about it every hour, even as you're struggling to fall asleep. You do your best to study, but the pressure is overwhelming. Finally, you throw your hands up, take the exam, and get one of the lowest grades you've received in college. Too bad. There's nothing you could have done about it, right? Wrong! You could have taken advantage of the campus counseling resources available to students who suffer from test anxiety."
>
> Leonard Christiansen, one of Etta's classmates, paid close attention. He had a midterm coming up next month, and the thought of it was starting to consume him. He hadn't known there was help available for students who were worried about something as ordinary as taking a test. But now, having listened to Etta's speech, Leonard decided he would take advantage of what the school had to offer. He went to the counseling center, got help with his exam anxiety, and did much better on his midterm than he had expected—thanks in part to his classmate's speech!

Most of your classroom speeches won't have this much immediate impact. Nevertheless, any topic that you handle conscientiously can influence your listeners—can enrich their experience, broaden their knowledge, perhaps change their views about something important.[1]

The Psychology of Audiences

What do you do when you listen to a speech? Sometimes you pay close attention; other times you let your thoughts wander. People may be compelled to attend a speech, but no one can make them listen. The speaker must make the audience *choose* to pay attention.

Even when people do pay attention, they don't process a speaker's message exactly as the speaker intends. Auditory perception is always selective. Every speech contains two messages—the one sent by the speaker and the one received by the listener.

As we saw in Chapter 1, what a speaker says is filtered through a listener's frame of reference—the sum of her or his needs, interests, expectations, knowledge, and experience. As a result, we listen and respond to speeches not as they are, but as we are. Or, to borrow from Paul Simon's classic song "The Boxer," people hear what they want to hear and disregard the rest.

What do people want to hear? Very simply, they usually want to hear about things that are meaningful to them. People are *egocentric*. They pay closest attention to messages that affect their own values, beliefs, and well-being. Listeners approach speeches with one question uppermost in mind: "Why is this important to *me*?" As Harry Emerson Fosdick, the great preacher, once said: "There is nothing that people are so interested in as themselves, their own problems, and the way to solve them. That fact is . . . the primary starting point of all successful public speaking."

egocentrism

The tendency of people to be concerned above all with their own values, beliefs, and well-being.

What do these psychological principles mean to you as a speaker? First, they mean your listeners will hear and judge what you say on the basis of what they already know and believe. Second, they mean you must relate your message to your listeners—show how it pertains to them, explain why they should care about it as much as you do. Here's an example:

> Marcos Torres is a 20-year veteran of the local fire department, specializing in fire prevention. He frequently gives presentations to groups of schoolchildren, to their parents, to neighborhood associations, and at city council meetings. Although his basic message—a little preparation can go a long way in preventing fires—never varies, he has learned how important it is to tailor the message to his specific audience.
>
> When Marcos speaks to children, his presentations involve humor, colorful stories from his experiences, and plenty of visual aids. Kids love to see a real firefighter's outfit. Sometimes he even lets them try on his helmet.
>
> When his audience consists of parents of schoolchildren, Marcos focuses on simple steps they can take to protect their homes. For neighborhood associations, he emphasizes how the fire department partners with neighborhoods across the city on prevention strategies. When speaking to city council meetings, Marcos uses statistics about the most common kinds of fires and how city leaders can spread the message of fire safety.

As Marcos's experience shows, you need some grasp of what your listeners know, believe, and care about. Saul Alinsky, the noted community organizer, advises, "People only understand things in terms of their experience," which means that to communicate with them, "you must get inside their experience."[2]

Of course, you can't actually get inside another person's experience. But you can learn enough about your audience to know what you should do to make your ideas clear and meaningful. How you can do this is our next topic.

Demographic Audience Analysis

demographic audience analysis

Audience analysis that focuses on demographic factors such as age; religion; racial, ethnic, and cultural background; gender identity and sexual orientation; group membership; and the like.

One of the ways speakers analyze audiences is by looking at demographic traits such as age; religion; racial, ethnic, and cultural background; gender identity and sexual orientation; group membership; and the like. This is called demographic audience analysis. It consists of two steps: (1) identifying the general demographic features of your audience, and (2) gauging the importance of those features to a particular speaking situation.

While demographic audience analysis can be a useful tool in understanding your audience, like all tools, it can be used improperly. When analyzing demographic information about your audience, it is essential that you avoid stereotyping.

Good speakers are audience-centered. Whether speaking formally or informally, they look for creative ways to communicate their ideas and keep their audience's attention.

Django/Getty Images

Stereotyping involves creating an oversimplified image of a particular group of people, usually by assuming that all members of the group are alike. Examples of stereotyping include the erroneous notions that all Blacks are athletic or that all Asians excel in science. Looking at demographic factors can provide important clues about your audience, but you must use those factors prudently and responsibly.

In addition, as we shall see later in this chapter, you should always combine your demographic audience analysis with situational audience analysis. The importance of any given demographic factor will vary from audience to audience depending on the occasion and the speech topic. If you keep this in mind, demographic analysis can be a valuable starting point in gauging your audience's background, interests, values, and beliefs. Here are a few of the major demographic factors you should consider.

stereotyping

Creating an oversimplified image of a particular group of people, usually by assuming that all members of the group are alike.

AGE

As Aristotle noted 2,300 years ago and as researchers have confirmed many times since, few things affect a person's outlook more than his or her age. Of course, no age group is monolithic. There is no generation in which everyone thinks alike, buys the same products, or votes for the same political candidates. Yet each generation has more or less common values and experiences that set it apart from other generations. Whatever your age, you are a product of your world.

You can see what this means for your speeches. Suppose you address an audience of older people. If you refer to 6LACK, Pia Mia, or Bad Bunny, your audience may have no idea who you mean. Similarly, if you speak to an audience of young adults and casually mention Watergate, they may not know what you are talking about. Even if younger listeners do recognize the name, it will not produce the same emotional associations as in people who lived through the Watergate break-in and the subsequent resignation of President Richard Nixon.

Depending on the composition of your speech class, you may face an audience that is mostly in their late teens and early twenties. If so, you can assume a common level of age experience. On the other hand, 40 percent of college students today are age 25 or older, and some classrooms include students in their thirties, forties, and beyond. You may then have to tackle two or three generations. This will give you good practice for speeches outside the classroom, where age is usually a major factor in audience analysis.

RELIGION

Current events around the world demonstrate that religious views are among the most emotionally charged and passionately defended of all human concerns. Even your small speech class might include a wide range of faiths, as well as atheists and agnostics. You cannot assume that your views on religion—whatever they may be—are shared by your listeners.

As the United States has become more diverse culturally, it has also become more diverse religiously. The traditional mix of Protestantism, Catholicism, and Judaism has been enriched by growing numbers of Buddhists, Muslims, Hindus, Sikhs, Russian Orthodox, and others. One leading scholar on the subject says the United States is "the most religiously diverse nation in the world."[3]

There is also great diversity within different faiths. You cannot assume that all Catholics support the official view of their church on birth control or women in the priesthood, that all Baptists are born-again, or that all Muslims favor a subservient status for women. In matters of religion, the United States is truly a nation of many faiths, many voices, many views.

Whenever you speak on a topic with religious dimensions, be sure to consider the religious orientations of your listeners. Doing so can help you avoid potentially embarrassing pitfalls. In some cases, it may make the difference between an unsuccessful speech and a successful one.

RACIAL, ETHNIC, AND CULTURAL BACKGROUND

The United States is a multiracial, multiethnic country of unmatched diversity. Notwithstanding political debates about nationalism, immigration, and the like, surveys show that a majority of Americans support the country's diversity as a positive development.[4] General attitudes about race and ethnicity are quite different from what they were even a few decades ago.

These new attitudes are especially evident among Americans born after 1996, often referred to as Gen Z. The most racially and ethnically diverse generation in U.S. history, it is also the most tolerant of racial and ethnic differences. Even as politicians argue over who belongs in the United States, members of Gen Z seem resolute in their commitment to diversity. A report from the Brookings Institute summarized the importance of diversity for Gen Z: "Diversity is not just their future—it is the nation's future."[5]

Yet even if you are speaking to an audience composed primarily of members of Gen Z, you must be sensitive to issues of race, ethnicity, and cultural background. Despite their similarities as Americans, Blacks, whites, Latinos, Asians, and many others have different customs and beliefs that will bear upon your speech topic.

Because we live in an age of globalization, you may also find yourself addressing listeners from countries other than your own. Not only does the United States contain a substantial percentage of people born in other lands, but more than 9 million Americans (not including those in military service) live abroad. If all these Americans were placed in one state, it would be the 11th largest state in the Union. This is one reason

Demographic audience analysis plays a role in every public speaking situation. Whenever you present a speech, be sure to consider factors such as the age, race, gender, and occupation of your listeners.

SDI Productions/Getty Images

why employers identify the ability to communicate effectively with people of different cultural backgrounds as one of the most desirable skills for college graduates.

Regardless of where you are speaking, be aware that some of your listeners may have racial, ethnic, or cultural perspectives that will affect their attitudes toward your speech topic. Try to gauge what those perspectives are and how they will be likely to affect the audience's response to your message. Adjust your remarks so they will be as clear, suitable, and convincing as possible.

GENDER IDENTITY AND SEXUAL ORIENTATION

Just as attitudes about race and ethnicity are different from what they were even a few decades ago, attitudes about gender identity and sexual orientation have also changed. A generation ago, standard advice for beginning public speakers was to be wary of pigeonholing listeners into stereotypical gender roles. That's still good advice. If you're delivering a speech about small businesses, for example, and you refer to business owners generically as "he," or to all shoppers as "she," your word choice will doubtless lead more than a few listeners to raise their eyebrows—or worse.

But the point goes further than that. Some scholars now argue that the binary of "he" and "she" does not reflect the full range of human experience.[6] And scholars are not alone. A recent Pew Research Center survey asked more than 10,000 Americans for their views on gender identity. Forty-one percent believed that "a person's gender can be different from the sex they were assigned at birth." In addition, more than 4 in 10 say they personally know someone who is transgender.[7]

What does this have to do with public speaking? Just as audiences often include people of varying occupations, ages, races, and religions, so too do they contain people of different sexual orientations and gender identities. When you work on your speeches, keep an eye out for language, examples, and other elements that may unintentionally exclude listeners with same-sex partners or listeners who identify with a gender other than the sex assigned at their birth. Effective public speakers take all demographic factors into account when preparing their remarks.

GROUP MEMBERSHIP

"Tell me thy company," says Don Quixote, "and I'll tell thee what thou art." For all our talk about rugged individualism, Americans are very group-oriented. Workers belong to unions, businesspeople to chambers of commerce. Hunters join the National Rifle Association, environmentalists the Sierra Club, feminists the National Organization for Women. Doctors enroll in the American Medical Association, lawyers in the American Bar Association. There are thousands of such voluntary organizations in the United States.

Similar groups abound on campus. Some of your classmates may belong to fraternities or sororities, some to InterVarsity, some to the Young Republicans, some to the film society, some to the ski club, and so forth. For speeches in the classroom, as well as for those outside the classroom, the group affiliations of your audience may provide excellent clues about your listeners' interests and attitudes.

Age; religion; racial, ethnic, and cultural background; gender identity and sexual orientation; group membership—these are just a few of the variables to consider in demographic audience analysis. Others include occupation, economic position, social standing, education, and place of residence. Indeed, *anything* characteristic of a given audience is potentially important to a speaker addressing that audience. For your classroom speeches, you may want to learn about your classmates' academic majors, years in school, extracurricular activities, living arrangements, and job aspirations.

Perhaps the most important thing to keep in mind about demographic audience analysis is that it is not an end in itself. Your aim is not just to list the major traits of your listeners, but to find in those traits clues about how your listeners will respond to your speech. Once you have done that, you are ready to move on to the next stage of audience analysis.

Situational Audience Analysis

Situational audience analysis usually builds on demographic analysis. It identifies traits of the audience unique to the speaking situation at hand. These traits include the size of the audience, the physical setting, and the disposition of the audience toward the topic, the speaker, and the occasion.

SIZE

Outside the classroom, the size of an audience can, with the aid of television and the Internet, range in the millions. Most speech classes, however, consist of between 20 and 30 people—a small- to medium-sized audience. This is a good size for beginning speakers, most of whom are terrified at the prospect of addressing a huge crowd. As you gain more experience, though, you may welcome the challenge of speaking to larger groups. Some speakers actually prefer a large audience to a small one.

No matter what size group you are addressing, bear in mind one basic principle: In most cases, the larger the audience, the more formal your presentation must be. Audience size may also affect your language, choice of appeals, and use of visual aids.

PHYSICAL SETTING

Which of the following would you rather address?

> An audience assembled immediately after lunch, crammed into an overheated room with inadequate seating

An audience assembled at 10:00 A.M., comfortably seated in an airy, well-lighted room

Undoubtedly you chose the second option. Any of the adverse conditions listed in the first could seriously impair your audience's willingness to accept your ideas or even listen to you at all.

When you face any speaking situation, it is important to know in advance if there will be any difficulties with the physical setting. For classroom speeches, of course, you already do know. But speeches outside the classroom can present unpleasant surprises unless you do your homework beforehand.

When you are invited to speak, don't be shy about asking questions of the person who arranged the speech. If possible, look over the room a few days in advance, or else arrive early on the day of your speech to inspect the room. If it is too warm or too cold, see about adjusting the thermostat. Check the seating arrangements and the location of the lectern to be sure your audience can see you. In short, do everything you can to control the influence of physical setting on your audience.

DISPOSITION TOWARD THE TOPIC

As we saw in Chapter 5, you should keep your audience in mind when choosing a topic. Ideally, you will pick a topic that suits them as well as it suits you. Once you have your topic, however, you must consider in more detail their interest in the topic, knowledge about it, and attitudes toward it.

Interest

People do not usually expend the time and effort to attend a speech unless they have some interest in the topic. Yet some listeners will inevitably have a higher interest level than will others. One of your tasks as a speaker is to assess their interest in advance and to adjust your speech accordingly.

Most important, if you think your topic is not likely to generate great interest, you must take special steps to get your listeners involved. In the chapters that follow, we'll look at ways you can develop interest in your topic—by an arresting introduction, provocative supporting materials, vivid language, dynamic delivery, and so forth.

Knowledge

There is often a strong correlation between interest in a topic and knowledge about it. People tend to be interested in what they know about. Likewise, they are inclined to learn about subjects that interest them. But there are exceptions. Few people know much about handwriting analysis, yet most would find it an interesting topic. On the other hand, almost everyone knows a lot about going to the supermarket, but few would find it a fascinating subject for a speech.

Why is it important to gauge your listeners' knowledge about your topic? Quite simply, because it will to a large extent determine what you can say in your speech. If your listeners know little about your topic—whether or not they find it interesting—you will have to talk at a more elementary level. If they are reasonably well informed, you can take a more technical and detailed approach.

Attitude

The attitude of your listeners toward your topic can be extremely important in determining how you handle the material. If you know in advance the prevailing attitude

attitude
A frame of mind in favor of or opposed to a person, policy, belief, institution, etc.

Adapting one's message to the occasion is a vital part of public speaking. Here Amal Clooney speaks at the Pennsylvania Conference for Women.

Marla Aufmuth/Getty Images

among members of your audience, you can adjust your speech to address their concerns or to answer their objections.

Consider the approach of one student who espoused a controversial viewpoint:

> Concerned about generations of economic disadvantage for Black Americans, Ananda decided to give a persuasive speech calling for the U.S. government to pay reparations to the descendants of enslaved people. After distributing an audience-analysis questionnaire among her classmates, she found that a number of them had questions about the practicality of her plan. They gave two major reasons. First, reparations would be expensive. Second, reparations might not accomplish what they set out to accomplish.
>
> Although Ananda disagreed with these beliefs, she realized she could neither ignore them nor insult her classmates for holding them. She knew she would have to discuss these points logically and with hard evidence if she were to have any chance of persuading her audience.

As it turned out, Ananda did convince some classmates to reconsider their beliefs. She could not have done so without first investigating what those beliefs were and then adapting her message to them.

connect

View an excerpt from "The Case for Reparations" in the online Media Library for this chapter (Video 6.1).

DISPOSITION TOWARD THE SPEAKER

An audience's response to a message is invariably influenced by their perception of the speaker. The more competent listeners believe a speaker to be, the more likely they are to accept what he or she says. Likewise, the more listeners believe that a speaker has their best interests at heart, the more likely they are to respond positively to the speaker's message.

We will come back to this subject in detail when we deal with strategies for persuasive speaking in Chapter 17. For now, keep in mind that your listeners will always have *some* set of attitudes toward you as a speaker. Estimating what those attitudes are and how they will affect your speech is a crucial part of situational audience analysis.

DISPOSITION TOWARD THE OCCASION

No matter what the occasion, listeners have fairly definite ideas about the speeches they consider appropriate. Speakers who seriously violate those expectations can almost always count on infuriating the audience.

Perhaps most important, the occasion will dictate how long a speech should be. When you are invited to speak, the chairperson will usually say how much time you have for your talk. If not, be sure to ask.

Once you know, pare down your speech so it fits easily within the allotted time. Do not exceed that time under any circumstances, for you are likely to see your audience dwindle as you drone on. (This is one reason why teachers insist that classroom speeches be kept within the designated time limit. It provides crucial training for speeches you will give outside the classroom.)

There are other audience expectations that apply to your classroom situation. One is that speeches will conform to the assignment. Another is that speakers will observe appropriate standards of taste and decorum. Failure to adhere to these expectations may disturb your classmates and will almost certainly damage your grade.

Getting Information About the Audience

Now that you know *what* to learn about an audience, the next question is, *how* do you learn it? A person running for political office can rely on hired professional pollsters. If, as is more likely, you are invited sometime to address a particular group, the person who invites you can usually provide a good sketch of the audience. Ask your contact where you can find out more about the group's history and mission. If you know someone who has spoken to the same group, be sure to sound out that person.

What about your classmates as an audience? You can learn a lot about them just by observation and conversation, but you may want to know more about their

Using public speaking in your CAREER

As a social media consultant for several local businesses, your work on marketing through social networks has attracted a lot of attention in your community. Now the local chamber of commerce has invited you to speak on the subject at next month's meeting.

Having taken a public speaking class in college, you know how important it is to analyze the audience you will be addressing. To prepare for your speech, you have arranged a phone interview with the chamber's president. List (1) the two most important questions you want to ask the president about the demographics of your audience, and (2) the two most important questions you want to ask about the situational traits of your audience. Be specific in your questions and be prepared, if necessary, to explain your choice of questions.

Antonio Guillem/123RF

knowledge and attitudes on specific speech topics. Some teachers require students to do a formal audience-analysis questionnaire for at least one of their speeches. In addition to providing information about your classroom audience, such a questionnaire gives you practice in developing the skills of audience analysis you will need for speeches after your class is over.

There are three major types of questions to choose from when developing an audience-analysis questionnaire: fixed-alternative questions, scale questions, and open-ended questions.

Fixed-alternative questions, as their name implies, offer a fixed choice between two or more responses. For example:

> Do you know what gerrymandering is in the U.S. political system?
>
> Yes _____
>
> No _____
>
> Not sure _____

By limiting the possible responses, such questions produce clear, unambiguous answers. They also tend to yield superficial answers. Other techniques are needed to get beneath the surface.

Scale questions resemble fixed-alternative questions, but they allow more leeway in responding. For example:

> How often do you believe state legislatures engage in gerrymandering?
>
> Very seldom ├──────┼──────┼──────┼──────┤ Very often

Questions like these are especially useful for getting at the strength of a respondent's attitudes.

Open-ended questions give maximum leeway in responding. For example:

> What is your opinion about gerrymandering in U.S. politics?
>
> Who do you think should set the boundaries of congressional districts—state legislatures, the courts, independent commissions, or some other option?

Although open-ended questions invite more detailed responses than the other two types of questions, they also increase the likelihood of getting answers that do not give the kind of information you need.

Because each type of question has its advantages and disadvantages, many questionnaires contain all three types. Figure 6.1 shows a questionnaire that was distributed before a classroom speech on volunteering. By using all three types of questions, the speaker did two things—elicited specific information about the audience and probed more deeply into their attitudes toward the speech topic.

When putting together your own questionnaire, keep the following principles in mind:

1. Plan the questionnaire carefully to elicit precisely the information you need.
2. Use all three types of questions—fixed-alternative, scale, and open-ended.
3. Make sure the questions are clear and unambiguous.
4. Keep the questionnaire relatively brief.

fixed-alternative questions
Questions that offer a fixed choice between two or more alternatives.

scale questions
Questions that require responses at fixed intervals along a scale of answers.

open-ended questions
Questions that allow respondents to answer however they want.

connect

View how the speaker in Video 6.1 used an audience-analysis questionnaire in her speech (Video 6.2).

FIGURE 6.1 Sample Questionnaire

Two fixed-alternative questions establish the listeners' level of knowledge about and degree of involvement with the topic.

1. Have you ever engaged in volunteer work for a community, religious, or charitable organization?

   Yes _____

   No _____

2. Have you or anyone close to you ever benefited from the volunteer work of a community, religious, or charitable organization?

   Yes _____

   No _____

   Not sure _____

This scale question is designed to show the attitudes of listeners who have participated in volunteer work.

3. If you have engaged in volunteer work, how would you rate the experience?

   ☐ Very rewarding
   ☐ Somewhat rewarding
   ☐ Neutral
   ☐ Somewhat unrewarding
   ☐ Very unrewarding

Another scale question gauges the listeners' sense of social obligation.

4. Do you agree or disagree with the following statement? To the extent possible, people have an obligation to help those in less fortunate circumstances.

   ☐ Strongly agree
   ☐ Mildly agree
   ☐ Undecided
   ☐ Mildly disagree
   ☐ Strongly disagree

Two open-ended questions help gauge the listeners' disposition toward volunteer work. The last question is especially important. It probes the specific issues the speaker needs to address for listeners who have not engaged in volunteer work.

5. If you have worked as a volunteer, do you plan to do so again? Why or why not?

6. If you have not worked as a volunteer, what is your major reason for not doing so? Please explain.

Adapting to the Audience

Once you have completed the audience analysis, you should have a pretty clear picture of your listeners. But this does not guarantee a successful speech. The key is how well you *use* what you know in preparing and presenting the speech.

AUDIENCE ADAPTATION BEFORE THE SPEECH

As we have seen, you must keep your audience in mind at every stage of speech preparation. This involves more than simply remembering who your listeners will be. Above all, it means two things: (1) assessing how your audience is likely to respond to what you say in your speech, and (2) adjusting what you say to make it as clear, appropriate, and convincing as possible.

You must submerge your own views so completely that you can adopt, temporarily, those of your listeners. When you do this, you will begin to hear your speech through the ears of your audience and to adjust it accordingly. Try to imagine what they will like, what they will dislike, where they will have doubts or questions, whether they will need more details here or fewer there, what will interest them and what will not. At every point you must *anticipate* how your audience will respond.

Here is how one student worked out his problems of audience adaptation:

> Having spent his past two summers working for a craft-beer company, Shaun Bakker decided to give his informative speech on the science of brewing beer. From his audience analysis, he learned that only a couple of his classmates knew much about beer making. Shaun realized he would have to present his speech at an elementary level and with a minimum of technical language.
>
> As he prepared the speech, Shaun kept asking himself: "How can I make this clear and meaningful to someone who knows nothing about the science behind craft beer?" Because he was speaking in Wisconsin, he decided to begin by noting that 5 of the 10 oldest American breweries started in Wisconsin. He also explained that every year Wisconsin breweries add $9 billion to the state economy and support more than 62,000 jobs. That, he figured, should get his classmates' attention.
>
> Throughout the body of his speech, Shaun focused on the basic processes of making craft beer. He avoided arcane details and steered away from technical terms such as "ethyl acetate," "humolone," and "biosynthesis." He also prepared PowerPoint slides to illustrate his points.
>
> To be absolutely safe, Shaun asked his roommate—who knew nothing about brewing beer—to listen to the speech. "Stop me," he said, "anytime I say something you don't understand." Shaun's roommate stopped him four times, and at each spot Shaun worked out a way to make his point more clearly. Finally, he had a speech that was interesting and perfectly understandable to his audience.

As you work on your speeches, try to keep your listeners constantly in mind. Anticipate how they will respond to your ideas. Be creative in thinking about ways to adapt your message to them. Like Shaun, you will give a much better speech.

AUDIENCE ADAPTATION DURING THE SPEECH

No matter how hard you prepare ahead of time, things may not go exactly as planned on the day of your speech. For speeches in the classroom, you may find that the projector for your visual aids is not available or that another student has the same topic as you. For speeches outside the classroom, you might learn that the audience will be much larger (or smaller) than you had anticipated, or that the amount of time available for your speech has been cut in half because a previous speaker has droned on for too long.

If something like this happens to you, don't panic. Find another way to present your visual aids. Modify your introduction to mention the other student's speech on your topic. Adjust your delivery to the changed audience size. If you find that you have less time than you had planned, condense your speech to its most essential points and present them in the time available. Your listeners will sympathize with your predicament and will appreciate your regard for their time. This will more than compensate for your lost speaking time.

In political campaigns, poll-taking helps the candidates keep track of public opinion. For classroom speeches, you can use an audience-analysis questionnaire to gauge the knowledge and opinions of your listeners.

Steve Debenport/Getty Images

Finally, be sure to keep an eye out during your speech for audience feedback. If you find your listeners frowning or responding with quizzical looks, you may need to back up and go over your point again, as in the following example:

> Saanvi Shah, an economics major, had worked diligently to make sure her speech on cryptocurrency was not too technical for her classmates. She explained everything from the ground up, prepared two excellent visual aids, and practiced giving the speech to her best friend, a music major and self-confessed "economics dummy."
>
> On the day of Saanvi's speech, everything went well until she got to her second main point, when she noticed that several of her classmates seemed puzzled by the process of "mining" in cryptocurrency. Knowing they would be lost for the rest of the speech if they didn't understand mining, Saanvi paused and said, "I can see some of you are confused by my explanation. Let me try it again from a different angle."
>
> As Saanvi went through the material again, she could see her classmates nodding their heads in understanding. She could now go on with the rest of her speech, confident that her audience was ready to go with her.

Adapting to your audience is one of the most important keys to successful public speaking. Like other aspects of speechmaking, it is sometimes easier said than done. But once you master it, you'll see that it pays dividends in more personal facets of your life—when you adapt to an audience of one.

Summary

Good speakers are audience-centered. They know that the aim of speechmaking is to gain a desired response from listeners. When working on your speeches, keep three questions in mind: To whom am I speaking? What do I want them to know, believe, or do as a result of my speech? What is the most effective way of composing and presenting my speech to accomplish that aim?

To be an effective speaker, you should know something about the psychology of audiences. People are egocentric. They typically approach speeches with one question uppermost in mind: "Why is this important to *me*?" Therefore, you need to study your audience and adapt your speech to their beliefs and interests.

The first stage in learning about your audience is to identify demographic traits such as age; religion; racial, ethnic, and cultural background; gender identity and sexual orientation; and group membership. The second stage is identifying traits of the audience unique to the speaking situation. These traits include the size of the audience, attitudes influenced by the physical setting, and your listeners' disposition toward the topic, toward you as a speaker, and toward the occasion.

For speeches outside the classroom, you can best get information about the audience by asking the person who invites you to speak. For classroom speeches, you can learn about your audience by observation and conversation. You also can circulate an audience-analysis questionnaire.

Once you complete the audience analysis, you must adapt your speech so it will be clear and convincing to your listeners. Put yourself in their place. Try to hear the speech as they will. Anticipate questions and objections, and try to answer them in advance. When you deliver your speech, keep an eye out for audience feedback and adjust your remarks in response.

Key Terms

audience-centeredness (96)

egocentrism (98)

demographic audience analysis (98)

stereotyping (99)

situational audience analysis (102)

attitude (103)

fixed-alternative questions (106)

scale questions (106)

open-ended questions (106)

Review Questions

After reading this chapter, you should be able to answer the following questions:

1. Why must a public speaker be audience-centered?

2. What does it mean to say that people are egocentric? What implications does the egocentrism of audiences hold for you as a public speaker?

3. What are the five demographic traits of audiences discussed in this chapter? Why is each important to audience analysis?

4. What is situational audience analysis? What factors do you need to consider in situational audience analysis?

5. How can you get information about an audience?

6. What are the three kinds of questions used in questionnaires? Why is it a good idea to use all three in audience analysis?

7. What methods can you use to adapt your speech to your audience before the speech? During the speech?

Exercises for Critical Thinking

1. Advertisers are usually very conscious of their audience. Visit a popular website such as *Instagram, ESPN, YouTube,* or the like. From that website select three advertisements to analyze. Try to determine the audience being appealed to in each and analyze the appeals (verbal and visual) used to persuade buyers. How might the appeals differ if the ads were designed to persuade a different audience?

2. Below are two general speech topics and, for each, two hypothetical audiences to which a speech might be delivered. For each topic, write a brief paragraph explaining how you might adjust your specific purpose and message according to the demographic characteristics of the audience.

   a. *Topic:* "Cryptography"

      Audience #1: 50% computer science majors, 30% physics majors, 20% fine arts majors

      Audience #2: 40% business majors, 40% history majors, 20% computer science majors

   b. *Topic:* "Sexual Assault: The Biggest Campus Crime"

      Audience #1: 80% female, 20% male

      Audience #2: 80% male, 20% female

3. For your next speech, design and circulate among your classmates an audience-analysis questionnaire like that discussed on pages 105–107. Use all three kinds of questions explained in the text: fixed-alternative, scale, and open-ended. After you have tabulated the results of the questionnaire, write an analysis explaining what the questionnaire reveals about your audience and what steps you must take to adapt your speech to the audience.

End Notes

[1] Seeing the speech classroom as a real audience is also important because it engages students in a form of rhetorical activity that is vital to participatory democracy. See Rosa A. Eberly, "Rhetoric and the Anti-Logos Doughball: Teaching Deliberating Bodies the Practices of Participatory Democracy," *Rhetoric and Public Affairs,* 5 (2002), p. 296.

[2] Saul Alinsky, *Rules for Radicals* (New York: Random House, 1971), p. 81.

[3] Diana L. Eck, *A New Religious America* (New York: HarperCollins, 2001), p. 4.

[4] See, for example, Abby Budiman, "Americans Are More Positive about the Long-term Rise in U.S. Racial and Ethnic Diversity Than in 2016," Pew Research Center, October 1, 2020 (https://www. pewresearch.org/fact-tank/2020/10/01/americans-are-more-positive-about-the-long-term-rise-in-u-s-racial-and-ethnic-diversity-than-in-2016/).

[5] William H. Frey, "The Nation's Racial Justice Protests Are a Pivotal Moment for Millennials and Gen Z," Brookings, June 9, 2020 (https://www. brookings.edu/blog/the-avenue/2020/06/20/the-nations-racial-justice-protests-are-a-pivotal-moment-for-millennials-and-gen-z/).

[6] See, for example, Natalie Fixmer-Oraiz and Julia T. Wood, *Gendered Lives: Communication, Gender, and Culture,* 13th ed. (Boston: Cengage Learning, 2018).

[7] Rachel Minkin and Anna Brown, "Rising Shares of U.S. Adults Know Someone Who is Transgender or Goes by Gender-Neutral Pronouns," Pew Research Center, July 27, 2021 (https://www.pewresearch.org/fact-tank/2021/07/27/rising-shares-of-u-s-adults-know-someone-who-is-transgender-or-goes-by-gender-neutral-pronouns/).

7 Gathering Materials

Using Your Own Knowledge and Experience

Doing Library Research

Searching the Internet

Interviewing

Tips for Doing Research

Suppose you are planning a trip to Amsterdam. You want to know the major sites so you can work out an itinerary. You also need to know what things will cost, where the hostels are located, and how the train and bus systems work. How do you go about gathering all this information?

You can talk to people who have been to Amsterdam and get ideas from them. You can consult guidebooks. You can search the Internet for information. If you have traveled to Europe before, you can draw on that experience. Since you want your trip to be a success, you gather as much information as you can before you leave.

Gathering materials for a speech is like gathering information for any project. There are many resources available if you take advantage of them. You can interview people with specialized knowledge. You can do research on the Internet or in the library. Sometimes you can use yourself as a resource—whenever you have personal experience or above-average knowledge about a subject. Let's turn first to the resource of your own experience.

Using Your Own Knowledge and Experience

Everybody is an expert on something, whether it is video games, child care, or backpacking. As we saw in Chapter 5, we often speak best about subjects with which we are familiar. This is why many teachers encourage students to capitalize on their own knowledge and experience in developing speech topics.

When you choose a topic from your own experience, you may be tempted to depersonalize it by relying solely on facts and figures from books and the Internet. Such outside information is almost always necessary. But supplementing it with the personal touch can really bring your speeches to life.

One student, passionate about protecting ocean life since she was a child, chose to speak on vulnerable marine animals along the California coast. She cited figures about dwindling animal populations, she explained how coastal animals influence the surrounding environment, and she discussed ongoing preservation efforts. Along the way, she illustrated her points by talking about her personal experiences. Here is part of what she said:

> Last summer I was able to participate in preservation efforts through an internship at the Marine Mammal Center in Monterey, California. Five days a week I traveled the area gathering data, surveying beaches, and assisting with rescues. When a sea lion was hurt, I was there. When a seal needed assistance, I was there, too.
>
> But of course I wasn't alone. I got to work alongside people who were just as passionate about protecting animals as I was. These included veterinarians, educators, and volunteers of all ages. Working with these people, I came away from my internship more hopeful about the future of our precious coasts and the animals they sustain.

This speech has color and human interest. By drawing on her personal experience, the speaker conveyed her points more meaningfully than she could have in any other way.

Like this speaker, you may be able to put your life stories to work for you. By thinking about your knowledge and experience—gathering material from yourself—you can find many supporting materials for your speeches.

Doing Library Research

Even in this age of the Internet, you will get some of the information for your speeches from the library. It contains many resources to help you find what you need, including librarians, the catalogue, reference works, and databases. We'll look at each in turn.

catalogue
A listing of all the books, periodicals, and other resources owned by a library.

LIBRARIANS

Too often students waste their time wandering aimlessly in the library because they are afraid to ask for assistance. They don't want to appear ignorant or to "bother" anyone. But would you be as sensitive about asking a doctor for help with a medical problem? Librarians are experts in their own field, trained in library use and research methods. If you have a question, don't hesitate to ask a librarian. He or she can help you find your way, locate sources, even track down a specific piece of information.

THE CATALOGUE

The catalogue lists all the books, periodicals, and other resources owned by the library. Although there are many different computer systems for library catalogues, most allow you to search for books by author, title, subject, or key word. The catalogue also tells you whether the book you want is available or is already checked out.

Figure 7.1 shows a sample catalogue entry for a book. The key to finding the book on the shelves is the *call number.* Once you have the call number, all you have to do is find the right section of the shelves (or stacks, as they are called in some libraries) and retrieve your book.

REFERENCE WORKS

Reference works are often kept in a part of the library called the reference section, though most are also available electronically. In either case, the right reference work can save you hours of time by putting at your fingertips a wealth of information that might be difficult to locate elsewhere. The major kinds of reference works you are likely to use for your speeches are encyclopedias, yearbooks, quotation books, and biographical aids.

Encyclopedias

We are all familiar with general encyclopedias such as the *Encyclopaedia Britannica.* But there are also special encyclopedias that cover their fields in more depth than do general encyclopedias. Some of the most frequently used special encyclopedias are the *African American Encyclopedia,* the *Encyclopedia of Religion,* and the *McGraw Hill Encyclopedia of Science and Technology.*

Yearbooks

As the name implies, yearbooks are published annually. They contain an amazing amount of current information that would otherwise be all but impossible to track down. Two of the most valuable yearbooks are *Facts on File* and *World Almanac and Book of Facts.*

call number
A number used in libraries to classify books and periodicals and to indicate where they can be found on the shelves.

reference work
A work that synthesizes a large amount of related information for easy access by researchers.

FIGURE 7.1   Sample Catalogue Entry for a Book

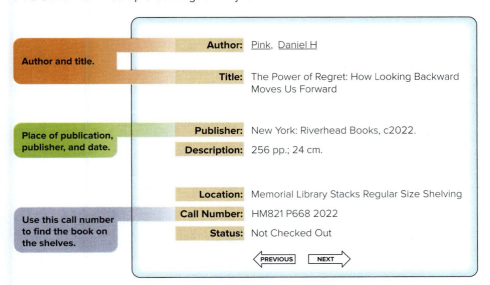

Author and title.

Author: Pink, Daniel H

Title: The Power of Regret: How Looking Backward Moves Us Forward

Place of publication, publisher, and date.

Publisher: New York: Riverhead Books, c2022.

Description: 256 pp.; 24 cm.

Location: Memorial Library Stacks Regular Size Shelving

Call Number: HM821 P668 2022

Use this call number to find the book on the shelves.

Status: Not Checked Out

PREVIOUS   NEXT

Library research is vital for most speeches. Knowing the resources available in your library and how to use them efficiently will make the research process much more productive.

Gorodenkoff/123RF

Quotation Books

The best-known collection of quotations is *Bartlett's Familiar Quotations.* With more than 25,000 quotations from historical and contemporary figures, it has long been regarded as an indispensable source for speakers and writers alike. Other excellent quotation books include the *Oxford Dictionary of Quotations, The New Quotable Woman,* and *Ancient Echoes: Native American Words of Wisdom.*

Biographical Aids

When you need information about people in the news, you can turn to one of the many reference works that contain brief life and career facts about contemporary men and women. The most popular biographical aids are published by Who's Who, which produces such titles as *International Who's Who* and *Who's Who in America.* More specialized biographical aids include *Contemporary Black Biography, Dictionary of Hispanic Biography,* and *Who's Who Among Asian Americans.*

NEWSPAPER AND PERIODICAL DATABASES

newspaper and periodical database
A research aid that catalogues articles from a large number of magazines, journals, and newspapers.

Newspaper and periodical databases allow you to locate articles in thousands of publications, including *Time, Atlantic,* the *New York Times,* and the *Wall Street Journal.* Type a subject in your database's search box, and citations for articles on your subject will appear on-screen.

In some cases, you may get an abstract of the article in addition to—or instead of—the full article. Keep in mind that the abstract is only a summary of the article. You should *never* cite an article in your speech on the basis of the abstract alone. Always consult the full article.

The exact databases you can use will depend on what is available through your library. Here are three major databases; odds are that your library will have at least one of them.

ProQuest. An excellent database that indexes thousands of periodicals and newspapers. Figure 7.2 shows a sample screen from ProQuest with a magazine citation and abstract.

Nexis Uni. Formerly *LexisNexis Academic,* this database provides full-text access to more than 15,000 information sources, including magazines, legal documents, and broadcast transcripts. *Nexis Uni* also furnishes articles from more than 1,000 newspapers worldwide.

abstract
A summary of a magazine or journal article, written by someone other than the original author.

World News Digest. Provides full-text access to news articles from 1940 to the present. Allows searching by topic, country, and decade.

ACADEMIC DATABASES

At colleges and universities around the world, experts are researching almost every aspect of the natural world and human society. Their work appears in respected, peer-reviewed journals. Academic databases make those journals available to you.

academic database
A database that catalogues articles from scholarly journals.

The best place to find scholarly research is in one of the following academic databases. Because each searches across different academic disciplines, you should be able to find what you need in one of the databases.

Academic OneFile. Provides access to millions of scholarly articles in areas from economics and sociology to science and medicine.

JSTOR. In addition to cataloguing more than 2,600 academic journals in various disciplines, JSTOR allows you to search images, letters, and other primary documents.

FIGURE 7.2   Sample Periodical Entry from ProQuest

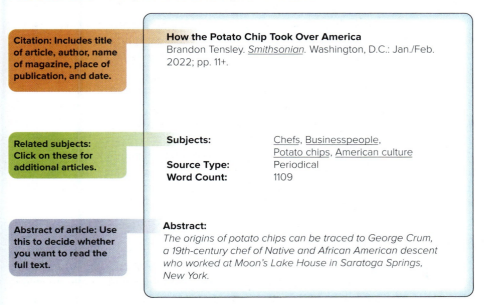

Citation: Includes title of article, author, name of magazine, place of publication, and date.

How the Potato Chip Took Over America
Brandon Tensley. *Smithsonian.* Washington, D.C.: Jan./Feb. 2022; pp. 11+.

Related subjects: Click on these for additional articles.

Subjects: Chefs, Businesspeople, Potato chips, American culture
Source Type: Periodical
Word Count: 1109

Abstract of article: Use this to decide whether you want to read the full text.

Abstract:
The origins of potato chips can be traced to George Crum, a 19th-century chef of Native and African American descent who worked at Moon's Lake House in Saratoga Springs, New York.

Google Scholar. A fast and easy way to search a broad range of scholarly literature. Advanced search tools let you narrow your search by author, publication, date, and subject matter.

Searching the Internet

The Internet has been called the world's biggest library. But unlike a library, the Internet has no central information desk, no librarians, no catalogue, and no reference section. Nor does it have a person or department in charge of determining whether materials are of high quality. You can unearth a great deal of information on the Internet, but you cannot always find the same range and depth as in a good library. This is why experts advise that you use the Internet to supplement, not to replace, library research.

In this section, we will look at ways you can go beyond browsing the web and turn it into a powerful research tool for your speeches. After discussing search engines and other resources for conducting efficient, focused inquiries, we'll explain how to evaluate the reliability and objectivity of the research materials you find online.

SEARCH ENGINES

Search engines are the key to finding materials on the Internet. There are numerous search engines, but the most widely used by far is Google, which provides access to billions of web pages.

The question is: How can you use Google and other search engines *systematically* to find what you need? The answer is: Develop a search strategy that will allow you to zero in precisely on the information required for your speech.

Suppose you are using Google to look for information on the riskiness of payday loans—short-term, high-interest loans that target people in already-difficult financial straits. If you simply search for *payday loans,* you will come up with hundreds of businesses offering to give you such a loan.

Instead, you should narrow your search by looking for *dangers of payday loans* or *hidden costs of payday loans.* Another option is to type a question into the search box: *What are the financial risks of taking out a payday loan?* or *What are the legalities of payday loans?*

Google also lets you focus your efforts by identifying the kind of research source that will serve you best. Once your terms are in the Google search box, you can click on *news* to explore recent news stories. You can also click on *images, videos,* and *books* to search those kinds of resources.

Of course, you will have to adjust your search terms depending on your subject and the kinds of materials you are looking for, but once you learn the basic principles for doing precise, pinpointed searches, you will greatly increase your odds of finding exactly what you need for your speeches.

SPECIALIZED RESEARCH RESOURCES

Search engines are extremely helpful, but they are not the only vehicles for finding information. The Internet also contains a wealth of specialized resources created to help you find useful information. From databases about health to reports on the

Research gives speakers facts and figures to back up their ideas. Whether researching online or in the library, you should use high-quality sources of information that will give your presentation strength and credibility.

Michael Candelori/NurPhoto/Getty Images

environment to archives of history and culture, chances are there exists a specially crafted site relating to your research area. Here are some specialized resources that are likely to be helpful as you work on your speeches.

Government Resources

One of the great strengths of the Internet as a research tool is the access it provides to government documents and publications. Whether you are looking for information from the federal government or from a state or local agency, chances are you can find it by starting your search at one of these websites:

USA.gov (www.usa.gov). One-stop shopping for all U.S. government information on the Internet. Provides links to web pages from federal, state, local, and tribal governments.

United States Census Bureau (www.census.gov). Contains a wealth of statistical information on social, political, and economic aspects of American life. Much of the data is organized in table form. Figure 7.3 shows some of the information available about population.

World Factbook (www.cia.gov/the-world-factbook). Published annually by the Central Intelligence Agency, the *World Factbook* is a rich compendium of information on every country in the world. Topics include people, government, economy, communication, transportation, and transnational issues.

Wikipedia

With more than 6.5 million articles in English alone, Wikipedia is the biggest encyclopedia in human history. Each month, the site serves over 20 billion pages, making it the fifth most visited website in the world.

FIGURE 7.3   Population Screen from U.S. Census Bureau

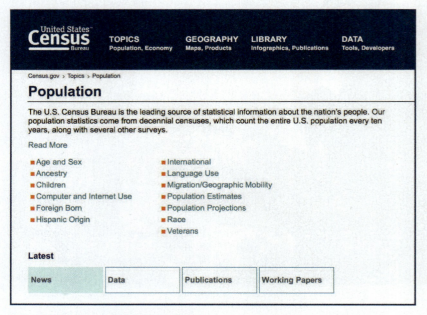

Source: https://www.census.gov/topics/population.html

But is Wikipedia a reliable source of information? Several years ago, it was not. Today, however, its reliability ratings compare favorably with those for print encyclopedias.[1] Major articles have been edited and refined over time to improve currency and accuracy. Articles still in development are flagged so readers know not to take their information at face value.

The most important thing to know about Wikipedia is that it can be a good place to *start* learning about a topic, but it is not a good place to end. Because of its convenience, Wikipedia is used by many people—including teachers and journalists—as a source of basic information. But experienced researchers know not to rely on it as their sole source of information.

One benefit of Wikipedia is that its major articles are followed by an extensive set of additional resources. Those resources include footnotes, a list of references, external links, and, in some cases, video and/or still images. If you take advantage of these resources, they will lead you to a vast amount of information beyond that in Wikipedia.

EVALUATING INTERNET DOCUMENTS

When you do research in a library, everything you find has been evaluated in one way or another before it gets to you. Books, magazines, and journals have editorial procedures to determine whether a given work should or should not be published. Once a work is published, it has to be approved by the acquisitions staff for inclusion in the library.

The Internet, of course, is a very different story. Anyone with a computer and access to the Internet can share his or her opinions on social media, publish an electronic newsletter, or create a personal web page. Never has the adage been more true than when applied to the Internet: "Don't believe everything you read."

checklist

Evaluating Internet Documents

YES	NO	
☐	☐	1. Is the author of the document clearly identified?
☐	☐	2. If the author is identified, is he or she an expert on the topic?
☐	☐	3. If the author is not an expert, can his or her opinions be accepted as objective and unbiased?
☐	☐	4. If the author is not identified, can the sponsoring organization be determined?
☐	☐	5. Does the sponsoring organization have a reputation for expertise and objectivity?
☐	☐	6. Does the document include a copyright date, publication date, or date of last revision?
☐	☐	7. If a date is included, is the document recent enough to cite in my speech?

In Chapter 8, we will discuss how to judge the soundness of supporting materials in general. Here we look at three criteria you can use to help distinguish between the jewels and the junk on the Internet.[2]

Authorship

Is the author of the web document you are assessing clearly identified? If so, what are his or her qualifications? Is the author an expert on the topic? Can her or his data and opinions be accepted as objective and unbiased? Just as you should not cite a book or magazine article without identifying the author and his or her credentials, so you should not cite an electronic work in the absence of this information.

In a book or magazine article, information about the author is usually fairly easy to find. Too often, this is not true on the Internet. If you can't find information about the author in the document itself, look for a link to the author's homepage or to another site that explains the author's credentials.

Often you can learn about an author by typing his or her name in the Google search box. If the author is an accepted authority on the subject, there's a good chance Google will turn up information about his or her credentials, publications, and affiliation.

Sponsorship

Many web documents are published by businesses, government agencies, public-interest groups, and the like rather than by individual authors. In such cases, you must judge whether the *sponsoring organization* is impartial enough to cite in your speech. Is the organization objective in its research and fair-minded in its statements? Is it economically unbiased with regard to the issue under discussion? Does it have a history of accuracy and nonpartisanship?

Over the years, some organizations have developed strong reputations for their expertise and objectivity. Many of these are public-interest groups such as Consumers Union, Common Cause, and the American Cancer Society. Others include the

sponsoring organization
An organization that, in the absence of a clearly identified author, is responsible for the content of a document on the Internet.

National Archives, Centers for Disease Control and Prevention, and similar government agencies. Private think tanks such as RAND, the Cato Institute, and the Brookings Institution often have definite political leanings but are usually well respected for the quality and substance of their research.

On the other hand, you need to be wary of groups that may sound respectable but in fact are not. Don't let a fancy-sounding name trick you into accepting a sponsoring organization's credibility at face value. One way to gauge the credibility of an organization is to type its name into Google. If commentators have raised serious questions about an organization, those questions will usually surface in the first few pages of search results. You can also check the *About* link on the organization's homepage. Often the resulting screen will identify the site's founders, purpose, and/or philosophy.

What if you can't verify the credentials of an author or identify a credible sponsoring organization for an Internet document? The answer is easy: Don't use the document in your speech!

Recency

One of the advantages of using the Internet for research is that it often has more recent information than you can find in print sources. But just because a document is on the Internet does not mean its facts and figures are up-to-the-minute.

The best way to determine the recency of an Internet document is to look for a copyright date, publication date, or date of last revision at the top or bottom of the document. If you are using a source located through a campus library, you can usually be confident of its currency, as well as its objectivity and reliability. News and government sites usually include the date on which a document was last updated.

Once you know the date of the document, you can determine whether it is current enough to use in your speech. This is especially important with regard to

Using public speaking in your CAREER

After receiving your master's degree in education administration, you took a job at the state department of education. At the request of the governor, your section of the department has developed a new early childhood intervention program for children from impoverished households.

Now you have been asked to help publicize the program and to build support for it. You will be speaking to church groups, teachers' associations, family advocacy groups, and others with an interest in children's welfare. You want to prepare a talk that makes good use of statistics and expert testimony to demonstrate the value of early childhood education programs, especially for poor children.

As part of your research, you decide to look on the web for supporting materials. List three reputable websites that provide useful statistics or testimony on the value of early childhood education. Explain why each website is reputable and list one statistic or expert quotation you obtain from each source.

Junjie/Shutterstock

statistics, which you should never cite from an undated source, whether in print or on the Internet.

Of course, the date of a web page is easy to change, so someone who wants to make information appear up-to-date can easily do so. But if you have already verified the credibility of the author and the sponsoring organization, you can usually assume that the date of the information is valid. If you can't find the date on which a web document was created or last modified, search for another work whose recency you can verify.

Interviewing

Most people think of interviewing in terms of job interviews or conversations with celebrities. But there is another kind of interview—the research (or investigative) interview. Among journalists, it is a time-honored way to collect information. It is also an excellent way to gather materials for speeches.

research interview
An interview conducted to gather information for a speech.

When done well, interviewing (like many things) looks deceptively easy. In practice, it is a complex and demanding art. The principles of effective interviewing fall into three groups—what to do before the interview, what to do during the interview, and what to do after the interview.

To illustrate, we'll follow the entire interview process for a hypothetical speech about current issues in college athletics.

BEFORE THE INTERVIEW

The outcome of most research interviews is decided by how well the interviewer prepares. Here are five steps you should take ahead of time to ensure a successful outcome.

Define the Purpose of the Interview

You have done Internet and library research about current issues in college athletics and have a good grasp of the major points of view. But you still have many questions about the situation at your school. You decide that the only way to get answers is to interview someone associated with the athletic program. In that decision you have begun to formulate a purpose for the interview.

Decide Whom to Interview

There are several possibilities, but you elect to start at the top—with the athletic director. That may seem a bit presumptuous, but in dealing with administrative organizations, it is usually best to go to the leaders first. They are likely to have a broad understanding of the issues. And if you need more specific information, they can get it for you or put you in touch with the right person.

Arrange the Interview

Because the athletic director is a busy person, you work out a plan for setting up the interview. Knowing that it's easier to brush off someone over email or the telephone than in person, you go to the athletic office to request the interview. The athletic director agrees, and you set up the interview for three days later.

Decide Whether to Record the Interview

The major advantage of recording an interview is that it gives you an exact record you can check later for direct quotes and important facts. Even if you record the interview, however, you should still take notes by hand in case of technical malfunctions.

If the athletic director does not want the interview recorded, you will need to rely solely on your handwritten notes. Whatever you do, *never* record a conversation without the knowledge or consent of the person being interviewed. Not only is it unethical to do so, but the interviewee is bound to find out and you will only cause yourself trouble.

Prepare Your Questions

You now face the most important of your preinterview tasks—working out the questions you will ask. You should devise questions that are sensible, intelligent, and meaningful. Here are some types of questions to *avoid:*

- Questions you can answer without the interview. (How many sports does your school offer? What is the size of its athletic budget?) Queries like these just waste the subject's time and make you look foolish. Research this information before the interview.

- Leading questions. (Opinion polls show that most Americans believe athletics today have little relation to the academic purposes of a college education. You *do* think it's a problem, too, *don't you*?)

- Hostile, loaded questions. (I think it's disgraceful that many schools spend gobs of money on salaries for football and basketball coaches. Don't you think good teachers for all students are more important than coaches for a few athletes? What do you say to *that,* hmmm?)

You need not shy away from tough questions; just phrase them as neutrally as possible and save them until near the end of the interview. That way, if your interviewee becomes irritated or uncooperative, you'll still get most of the information you want.

Although some experienced journalists conduct interviews with only a few keyword notes on the areas to be covered, you want to be sure not to forget anything during the interview. So you arrange your questions in the order you want to ask them and take the list with you to the interview.

DURING THE INTERVIEW

Every interview is unique. Because the session will seldom go exactly as you plan, you need to be alert and flexible. Here are several steps you can take to make things proceed smoothly.

Dress Appropriately and Be on Time

The athletic director has a busy schedule and is doing you a favor by agreeing to an interview, so you show up on time. Since the interview is a special occasion, you dress appropriately. This is one way of confirming that you regard the interview as serious business.

Repeat the Purpose of the Interview

The athletic director invites you into the office; you exchange a few introductory remarks. Now, before you plunge into your questions, you take a moment to restate

Interviewing people with expertise on your speech topic can provide valuable information. When conducting an interview, be sure to listen attentively and to take accurate notes.

Kate/Getty Images

the purpose of the interview. You are more likely to get clear, helpful answers if your subject knows why you are following a certain line of questioning.

Set Up the Recorder, If You Are Using One

If your subject has agreed to being recorded, keep one principle in mind: The recorder should be as casual and inconspicuous as possible. Most cell phones now offer applications for audio recording, giving you an easy way to capture the interview.

Keep the Interview on Track

Your goal in the interview is to get answers to the questions you have prepared. Suppose, however, that in answering one of your questions, the athletic director brings up an important point that is not covered on your list of questions. Rather than ignoring the point, you decide to pursue the new issue. You pose a couple of questions about it, get helpful answers, then return to your prepared questions.

Throughout the interview, you pursue new leads when they appear, improvise follow-up questions when called for, then move on again in an orderly fashion. When the interview is over, you have answers to all your prepared questions—and a lot more.

Listen Carefully

During the interview, you listen attentively to the athletic director's answers. When you don't understand something, you ask for clarification. Chances are the athletic director has been misquoted more than once in the press, so he or she will be happy to oblige.

Don't Overstay Your Welcome

Keep within the stipulated time period for the interview, unless your subject clearly wants to prolong the session. When the interview is over, you thank the athletic director for taking the time to talk with you.

AFTER THE INTERVIEW

Although the interview is over, the interviewing process is not. You must now review and transcribe your notes.

Review Your Notes as Soon as Possible

When you leave the athletic director's office, the interview is fresh in your mind. You know what the cryptic comments and scrawls in your notes mean. But as time passes, the details will become hazy. Don't let something like this true story happen to you:

> Years ago, a prominent woman—writer and diplomat—was being interviewed by a young reporter. Among other things, the reporter asked about hobbies and leisure activities. The woman replied that she enjoyed skeet shooting and raised Siamese cats. The reporter scribbled in her notes "shoots" and "cats"—but didn't bother to put a comma or a dash between the words. The interview was published. And ever since, that prominent woman found herself trying to live down the reputation that she "shoots cats."

In reviewing your notes, try to concentrate on two things—discovering the main points that emerged during the interview and pulling out specific information that might be useful in your speech.

Transcribe Your Notes

Once you settle on the most important ideas and information from the interview, you should transcribe that material so it is in the same format as the rest of your research notes (see pages 127–129). By putting all your research notes in a consistent format, you can arrange and rearrange them easily when you start to organize your speech.

Tips for Doing Research

Few people regard doing research as one of life's great joys. But there are ways to make it less tedious and more productive. Here are four ways that are guaranteed to help.

START EARLY

The biggest mistake students make when faced with a research project is waiting too long to begin. The longer you wait, the more problems you will encounter. You may find that a vital book has been checked out of the library or that you no longer have time to arrange a crucial interview. No matter what kind of research you do, you can be sure of one thing: It will *always* take longer than you expect.

Starting early also gives you plenty of time to think about what you find. In researching, you will collect much more material than you will actually use. Preparing a speech is a little like constructing a jigsaw puzzle. Once you gather the pieces, you have to decide how they fit together. The more time you give yourself, the more likely you are to get the pieces to fit just right.

MAKE A PRELIMINARY BIBLIOGRAPHY

In your research, you will run across the titles of books, magazine articles, Internet documents, and so on that look as if they might contain helpful information about your speech topic. Enter *each* item you find in your preliminary bibliography, even though you don't know whether you will use it in your speech. As a result, you may have 15 or 20 works in your preliminary bibliography. But remember that you have not yet examined all those works. Of the 15 or 20 preliminary sources, only 7 or 8 are likely to be of much use. Those final sources will be listed on the bibliography you turn in with your speech outline (see Chapter 11, page 197).

There are two major formats for citing documents in a bibliography. One comes from the Modern Language Association (MLA), the other from the American Psychological Association (APA). Both are widely used by communication scholars; ask your instructor which he or she prefers.

Whichever format you adopt, make sure your bibliography is clear, accurate, and consistent. Figure 7.4 (page 128) lists sample MLA and APA citations for 10 kinds of sources that are cited most frequently in student speeches.

preliminary bibliography
A list compiled early in the research process of works that look as if they might contain helpful information about a speech topic.

TAKE NOTES EFFICIENTLY

Asia Marshall started her speech preparation with the best of intentions. She was excited about her topic, "Great Women of Jazz," and she started research on the Internet the same day the assignment was announced. She found several interesting sources and took some notes about them. That evening, she checked out a fascinating book about Billie Holiday and read it straight through. She didn't bother taking notes because she was sure she'd remember it all. The next day, she looked through the *Encyclopedia of Jazz* and jotted a few notes on the back of her syllabus.

Then Asia remembered that she had a test in another class. Somewhat panicked, she put aside her speech research to study. When she got back to the speech, the deadline was only four days away. She dug out her notes, but what did they mean? One said, "Medford—*important!!!*" But who or what was Medford? Asia had thought she'd remember all about the Billie Holiday book, but without notes, it was mostly a blur by now. With a sense of doom, she faced up to the fact that she would have to start over—and finish in four days.

Sound familiar? This has happened to almost everyone at least once. But once is enough. There's a better way to take research notes. The following method has worked well for many students.

Take Plenty of Notes

Few things are more aggravating than trying to recall some bit of information you ran across in your research but neglected to record. The moral of Asia Marshall's story is clear: If there is even an outside chance that you may need a piece of information, make a note of it. This will take a little extra time in the short run, but in the long run it can save you much grief.

Record Notes in a Consistent Format

You should use the same format for all your research notes, whether they come from Internet sources, library documents, or personal interviews. In each case, record the note, the source of the note, and a heading indicating the subject of the note (see Figure 7.5, page 129).

The importance of the subject heading cannot be overemphasized. It is the first step to more efficient note taking. By telling you at a glance what each note is about, it will simplify the task of organizing your notes when you start to compose the speech. Once you start using subject headings, you'll see how helpful they can be.

FIGURE 7.4 Sample Bibliography Formats

Book

MLA: McGhee, Heather. *The Sum of Us: What Racism Costs Everyone and How We Can Prosper Together*. Random House, 2022.

APA: McGhee, H. (2022). *The sum of us: What racism costs everyone and how we can prosper together*. Random House.

Magazine article

MLA: Somers, James. "The Science of Mind Reading." *The New Yorker,* 29 Nov. 2021, www.newyorker.com/magazine/2021/the-science-of-mind-reading. Accessed 11 Sept. 2022.

APA: Somers, J. (2021, November 24). The science of mind reading. *The New Yorker*. Retrieved 11 September 2022, from https://www.newyorker.com/magazine/2021/the-science-of-mind-reading

Newspaper article

MLA: Alexander, Kurtis. "California Slips into Its Worst Mega-Drought in 1,200 Years." *San Francisco Chronicle*, 14 Feb. 2022, www.sfchronicle.com/bayarea/California-rest-of-the-West. Accessed 9 Oct. 2022.

APA: Alexander, K. (2022, February 14). California slips into its worst mega-drought in 1,200 years. *San Francisco Chronicle*. Retrieved 9 October 2022, from https://www.sfchronicle.com/bayarea/California-rest-of-the-West

Government publication

MLA: United States Department of Labor, Bureau of Labor Statistics. "Fastest Growing Occupations." *Occupational Outlook Handbook*, 15 May 2022, www.bls.gov/ooh/fastest-growing.htm

APA: United States Department of Labor, Bureau of Labor Statistics. (2022). *Fastest Growing Occupations*. https://www.bls.gov/ooh/fastest-growing.htm

Website

MLA: Troutner, Allison. "Cadmium: The Highly Toxic Metal That Powers the World." *HowStuffWorks*, 21 Jan. 2022, science.howstuffworks.com/cadmium.htm

APA: Troutner, A. (2022, January 21). *Cadmium: The highly toxic metal that powers the world*. HowStuffWorks. https://science.howstuffworks.com/cadmium.htm

Personal interview

MLA: Kahn, Farooq. Personal interview. 26 Jan. 2023.

APA: Kahn, F. (Personal communication, January 26, 2023).

Speech or lecture

MLA: Schuller, Kyla. "Counterhistories of Feminism." Humanities Center, Stanford University, 13 Jan. 2022. Lecture.

APA: Schuller, K. (2022, January 13). *Counterhistories of feminism* [Public lecture]. Humanities Center, Stanford University, Stanford, CA, United States.

Television program

MLA: "Riveted: The History of Jeans." *American Experience*, written and directed by Michael Bicks & Anna Lee Strachan, WGBH Educational Foundation, 2022.

APA: Bicks, M. & Strachan, A. L. (Writers & Directors). (2022, February 7). Riveted: The history of jeans. [TV series episode]. In Cameo George (Executive Producer), *American experience*. WGBH Educational Foundation.

Video

MLA: Olguin, Irma L. "How to Turn Around a City." *YouTube*, uploaded by TED, 7 Jan. 2022, www.youtube.com/watch?v=1TzIzuW1uGA

APA: Olguin, I. L. (2022, January 7). How to turn around a city [Video]. Youtube. https://www.youtube.com/watch?v=1TzIzuW1uGA

FIGURE 7.5 Sample Research Note

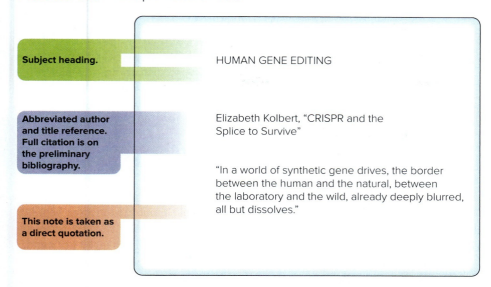

Subject heading.

HUMAN GENE EDITING

Abbreviated author and title reference. Full citation is on the preliminary bibliography.

Elizabeth Kolbert, "CRISPR and the Splice to Survive"

"In a world of synthetic gene drives, the border between the human and the natural, between the laboratory and the wild, already deeply blurred, all but dissolves."

This note is taken as a direct quotation.

Make a Separate Entry for Each Note

Many students try to record all the information from one source on a single note. This is not an effective procedure because it makes your notes almost impossible to review and organize. A better approach is to make a separate note for *each* quotation or piece of information you record. Although you may end up with several notes from the same document, you will find that this approach allows you to keep better track of your research.

Distinguish Among Direct Quotations, Paraphrases, and Your Own Ideas

As we saw in Chapter 2, it's easy to plagiarize accidentally by not taking careful research notes. As you do research for your speeches, be sure to use quotation marks when you copy the exact words of a source. If you paraphrase, rather than quote verbatim, be sure to include the source when you record the note.

By keeping track of quotations and paraphrases, you will be able to separate your own words and ideas from those of other people. This will help you avoid the trap of inadvertent plagiarism when you put your speech together.

THINK ABOUT YOUR MATERIALS AS YOU RESEARCH

Students often approach research as a mechanical routine that simply involves gathering the materials to be used in a speech or paper. But when done properly, research can be extremely creative.

If you *think about* what you are finding in your research, you will see your topic just a little bit differently with each note you take. You will find new relationships, develop new questions, explore new angles. You may even change your point of view, as did this student:

Francesca Lopez began her speech preparation with this central idea in mind: "Wild animals make more interesting pets than dogs and cats." She went about her research conscientiously, spending many hours online and in the library. In the process, she came upon some disturbing information about the capture of wild animals. She read that young chimpanzees and other apes were literally snatched out of their mothers' arms, and that the mothers were afterward heard to cry almost like humans. Back in her room that night, Francesca couldn't get her mind off the baby chimpanzees.

The next day, Francesca found some more disturbing material. One source told about the extraordinarily high death rate of wild animals during shipment to the United States. Again, that night Francesca brooded about the young animals dying of fear and cold in the cargo holds of airplanes.

By the time she finished her research, Francesca's central idea was completely different. When she spoke, her central idea was "The importation of wild animals for use as pets is inhumane."

This is an example of creative research—and of critical thinking. Francesca kept her mind open, read everything she could find about her topic, and thought seriously about what she found. Because of this thoughtful approach, she changed her mind.

Your own speech preparation may not cause you to reverse your position, but it should give you new insights into your topic. If you approach research in this way, you may find that the time you spend researching is the most productive of all the time you devote to preparing your speech.

Summary

There are many resources you can use when gathering information for a speech. If you have personal experience or above-average knowledge about a topic, you can use yourself as a resource. Most of the time, however, you will need outside information, which you can get in the library, on the Internet, or by interviewing people with specialized information.

Finding what you need in the library is largely a matter of knowing how to search for information. The catalogue lists all the books, periodicals, and other resources owned by the library. Databases help you find articles in magazines, newspapers, and journals. The reference section includes encyclopedias, yearbooks, biographical aids, and books of quotations. If you have trouble finding something, don't hesitate to ask a librarian.

When looking for information online, you require a search strategy that will help you find exactly what you need. Given the lack of editorial review for most documents on the web, it is especially important to evaluate the authorship, sponsoring organization, and recency of the research materials you find there.

You can also get information by conducting a personal interview. Before the interview, you should define its purpose, decide whom you are going to interview, and prepare the interview questions. Once the interview begins, be sure to listen attentively and take accurate notes. Afterward, review and transcribe your notes as soon as possible.

No matter what sources you draw on in gathering information, your research will be more effective if you start early and make a preliminary bibliography to keep track of all the books, articles, and Internet documents that look as if they might be helpful.

Key Terms

catalogue (114)

call number (115)

reference work (115)

newspaper and periodical
database (116)

abstract (117)

academic database (117)

sponsoring organization (121)

research interview (123)

preliminary bibliography (127)

Review Questions

After reading this chapter, you should be able to answer the following questions:

1. Why can it be valuable to draw on your own knowledge and experience in gathering materials for your speeches?

2. What are five resources for finding what you need in the library?

3. What are three criteria for evaluating the soundness of research materials that you find on the Internet?

4. What are the three stages of a research interview? What should you do in each stage to help ensure a successful interview?

5. Why is it important to start your speech research early?

6. What is a preliminary bibliography? Why is it helpful to you in researching a speech?

7. What four things should you do to take research notes efficiently?

Exercises for Critical Thinking

1. Using one of the periodical and newspaper databases discussed on page 117, find three magazine or newspaper articles on the topic of your next speech. Prepare a preliminary bibliography entry for each article. Read the full text of the articles and assess their value for your speech.

2. Using Google or another search engine, find three high-quality documents on the topic of your next speech. Prepare a preliminary bibliography entry for each document. Read the full text of the documents and assess them in light of the criteria for evaluating Internet documents discussed on pages 120–123.

3. Plan to conduct an interview for one of your classroom speeches. Be sure to follow the guidelines presented in this chapter for effective interviewing. Afterward, evaluate the interview. Did you prepare for it adequately? Did you get the information you needed? What would you do differently if you could conduct the interview again?

End Notes

[1]Matt Chase, "The Other Tech Giant: Wikipedia Is 20, and Its Reputation Has Never Been Higher," *The Economist,* January 9, 2021, pp. 56–57; Dariusz Jemielniak, "Wikipedia: Why Is the Common Knowledge Resource Still Neglected by Academics?" *Gigascience* 8 (2019), p. 139.

[2]These criteria are adapted from Sheridan Libraries, "Evaluating Internet Resources," *Johns Hopkins University.* Web. September 20, 2022.

Supporting Your Ideas

Examples

Statistics

Testimony

Citing Sources Orally

Good speeches are not composed of hot air and generalizations. They need strong supporting materials to answer the three questions listeners always ask of a speaker: "What do you mean?" "Why should I believe you?" "So what?" Consider, for example, the following statements:

General	Less General	Specific
Food waste is a serious problem.	In the United States, we waste perfectly good food at an alarming rate.	According to a report from the Environmental Protection Agency, 35 percent of the U.S. food supply is wasted every year. That's around 300 billion pounds of food, which could feed 150 million people.

supporting materials
The materials used to support a speaker's ideas. The three major kinds of supporting materials are examples, statistics, and testimony.

Which statement do you find most interesting? Most convincing? Chances are you prefer that in the right-hand column. It is sharp and specific, clear and credible—just what a speech needs to come alive.

The skillful use of supporting materials often makes the difference between a poor speech and a good one. In Chapters 15 and 17, we will look at special uses of supporting materials in informative and persuasive speeches. In this chapter, we focus on the basic kinds of supporting materials—examples, statistics, and testimony—and on general principles for using them effectively and responsibly.

CONFRONTING
HEALTH
MISINFORMATION

The U.S. Surgeon General's Advisory on
Building a Healthy Information Environment

Examples

example

A specific case used to illustrate or represent a group of people, ideas, conditions, experiences, or the like.

Research has shown that vivid, concrete examples have a strong impact on listeners' beliefs and actions. Without examples, ideas often seem vague, impersonal, and lifeless. With examples, ideas become specific, personal, and lively. One social psychologist has concluded that "most people are more deeply influenced by one clear, vivid, personal example than by an abundance of statistical data."[1] Examples are so important that many experienced speakers consider them "the very life of the speech."[2]

There are several kinds of examples you may want to try in your speeches.

BRIEF EXAMPLES

brief example

A specific case referred to in passing to illustrate a point.

Brief examples—also called specific instances—may be referred to in passing to illustrate a point. The following excerpt uses a brief example to illustrate advances in creating artificial limbs for animals, large and small:

> Meet Mosha, an Asian elephant who was seven months old when she lost her left foreleg after stepping on a landmine. Thanks to a series of artificial legs provided by Thailand's Foundation for the Asian Elephant, Mosha has been able to regain her mobility, even though she has to support her body weight of 4,400 pounds.

Another way to use brief examples is to pile them one upon the other until you create the desired impression. Here is how one speaker used this technique to reinforce the point that Mexican Americans have made many valuable contributions to U.S. life:

connect

View this excerpt from "Living in America" in the online Media Library for this chapter (Video 8.1).

> Many of us are familiar with prominent Chicanos and Chicanas such as actress Jessica Alba, boxer Oscar De La Hoya, and guitarist Carlos Santana. But you may be less familiar with other Americans of Mexican origin who have made important contributions to U.S. society. Nancy Lopez played a crucial role in popularizing women's professional golf and won 48 tour championships. Dr. Ellen Ochoa is a former astronaut who logged more than 480 hours in space and invented several optical methods that greatly aid space exploration. Dr. Mario Molina won the 1995 Nobel Prize in Chemistry for his research on the formation and decomposition of the ozone layer.

EXTENDED EXAMPLES

extended example

A story, narrative, or anecdote developed at some length to illustrate a point.

Extended examples are often called narratives, illustrations, or anecdotes. By telling a story vividly and dramatically, they pull listeners into the speech. Here is such an example from a student speech about health care for military veterans:

connect

View this excerpt from "Caring for America's Veterans" in the online Media Library for this chapter (Video 8.2).

> One friend called him "the funniest person I've ever known." Other friends called him a military hero. Everyone said that what happened to him was tragic.
>
> Curtis Gearhart was a lovable guy who grew up in Iowa and went to Des Moines Lincoln High School. Eager to serve his country, he enlisted in the military right after graduation and served two tours of duty in Iraq. But when he came home to Iowa, he knew things were different. He felt guilty that fellow soldiers were losing their lives overseas. And every day he suffered blinding, excruciating headaches. So he went to the nearby V.A. hospital for help. They told him he'd have to wait five to six weeks for treatment.

> The wait was too much. The headaches and heartaches were too much. So one Monday evening, Curtis took his own life. Tragically, he became one of the 20 American veterans who commit suicide every day.

This long example captures vividly the pain and frustration one veteran experienced in trying to seek help for his condition. The speaker could merely have said, "Military veterans often have a hard time getting the medical care they need," but the story makes the point far more poignantly.

HYPOTHETICAL EXAMPLES

All the examples presented up to now have been factual; the incidents they refer to really happened. Sometimes, however, speakers will use a hypothetical example—one that describes an imaginary situation. Usually such examples are brief stories that relate a general principle.

Here's how one student used a hypothetical example to illustrate the problem of eyewitness misidentification:

> Imagine you're an eyewitness to a violent crime. Because it's violent, the situation is tense and you're naturally scared. Even if you get a good look at the suspect, your brain and body are on edge. Then the police bring you to the station for a lineup. Could you accurately pinpoint the perpetrator?

This hypothetical example is especially effective. The speaker creates a realistic scenario, relates it directly to her listeners, and gets them involved in the speech.

TIPS FOR USING EXAMPLES

Use Examples to Personalize Your Ideas

People are interested in people. Whenever you talk to a general audience (such as your speech class), you can include examples that will add human interest to your speech.

That's what one student did in a speech titled "Changing Lives Through the Literacy Network." In addressing the problem of low adult literacy and how to alleviate it, the student cited figures from the U.S. Department of Education and the National Research Council. But she knew that figures alone wouldn't move her audience to action.

So she relayed the example of Dwayne MacNamara, a father of two daughters, who had struggled with reading and writing for years before turning to the Literacy Network for help. She talked about the problems Dwayne faced because of low literacy and of how the Literacy Network helped him acquire the skills he needed to succeed in life.

This example was effective because it put the issue in human terms that everyone could understand. Try using examples with human interest in your speeches. You'll discover that a well-placed example can personalize your topic in ways that other kinds of supporting materials cannot.

Reinforce Examples with Statistics or Testimony

Examples can bring an issue alive and dramatize it in personal terms. But listeners may still wonder how many people the issue actually affects. In such a situation, you should reinforce your examples with statistics or testimony. Research has shown that the impact of examples is enhanced when they are combined with other supporting materials that show the examples to be typical.[3]

hypothetical example
An example that describes an imaginary or fictitious situation.

connect
View this excerpt from "Eyewitness Misidentification" in the online Media Library for this chapter (Video 8.3).

connect
View this portion of "Changing Lives Through the Literacy Network" in the online Media Library for this chapter (Video 8.4).

No matter what the occasion, personal examples are an excellent way to clarify ideas and to build audience interest. To be most effective, they should be delivered sincerely and with strong eye contact.

Mannic Media

Consider the case of a speaker discussing how psychedelics have been shown to combat depression. The speaker could cite recent incidents of people working through their depression with psychedelic therapy. These examples help make the case persuasive, but a listener could dismiss them as sensational and atypical. To prevent this, the speaker might go on to say:

> According to a recent study published in the psychiatric journal of the American Medical Association, psychedelics were found to be four times more effective at treating depression than traditional antidepressants. As Jerrold Rosenbaum, a professor of psychiatry at Harvard Medical School, summarizes: "The effects of these drugs are pretty profound," and they will soon reveal "new approaches to brain disease."

With this backup material, not even a skeptical listener could reject the examples as atypical.

Make Your Examples Vivid and Richly Textured

The richly textured example supplies everyday details that help pull listeners into a speech. Recall the example on pages 134–135 of military veteran Curtis Gearhart. The speaker provides us with many details about Curtis's time in the Army, his health problems after returning home, and how hard it was for him to get medical care. Curtis feels guilty about leaving other soldiers behind to fight. Despite suffering excruciating headaches, he has to wait weeks for an appointment at the V.A. hospital. Finally he takes his own life.

How much less compelling the example would have been if the speaker had merely said:

> One veteran experienced severe problems after returning from combat, eventually committing suicide.

Instead, the details let us see Curtis as he confronts the challenges of returning from war. He is much more likely to stay in our minds than a veteran who "experienced severe problems." The more vivid your examples, the more impact they are likely to have on your audience.

Practice Delivery to Enhance Your Extended Examples

An extended example is just like a story or narrative. Its impact depends as much on delivery as on content. Many students have discovered this the hard way. After spending much time and energy developing a splendid example, they have seen it fall flat because they did not make it vivid and gripping for listeners.

Look again at the speaker in Video 8.2. Notice how she uses her voice to increase the impact of her story about Army veteran Curtis Gearhart. Like that speaker, you should think of yourself as a storyteller. Don't rush through your examples as though you were reading the newspaper. Use your voice to get listeners involved. Speak faster here to create a sense of action, slower there to build suspense. Raise your voice in some places; lower it in others. Pause occasionally for dramatic effect.

Most important, maintain eye contact with your audience. The easiest way to ruin a fine example is to read it from your notes. As you practice the speech, "talk through" your extended examples without relying on your notes. By the day of your speech, you should be able to deliver your extended examples as naturally as if you were telling a story to a group of friends.

Statistics

We live in an age of statistics. Day in and day out we are bombarded with a staggering array of numbers: Drake is the first musician to reach 50 billion streams on Spotify. One of every six U.S. children under the age of 18 has some type of mental

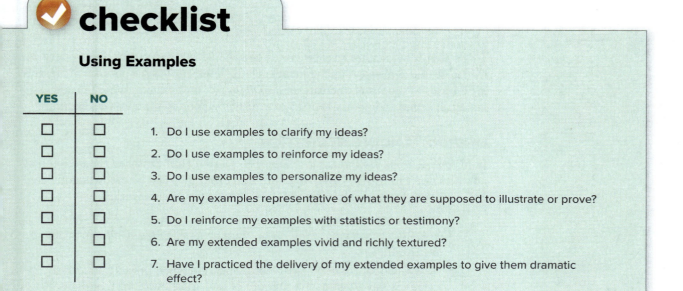

checklist

Using Examples

YES	NO	
☐	☐	1. Do I use examples to clarify my ideas?
☐	☐	2. Do I use examples to reinforce my ideas?
☐	☐	3. Do I use examples to personalize my ideas?
☐	☐	4. Are my examples representative of what they are supposed to illustrate or prove?
☐	☐	5. Do I reinforce my examples with statistics or testimony?
☐	☐	6. Are my extended examples vivid and richly textured?
☐	☐	7. Have I practiced the delivery of my extended examples to give them dramatic effect?

disorder. Americans drink 146 billion cups of coffee annually. Last year extreme weather cost the U.S. $152 billion.

What do all these numbers mean? Most of us would be hard-pressed to say. Yet we feel more secure in our knowledge when we can express it numerically. According to Lord Kelvin, the 19th-century physicist, "When you can measure what you are speaking about, and express it in numbers, you know something about it. But when you cannot measure it, when you cannot express it in numbers, your knowledge is . . . meager and unsatisfactory." It is this widely shared belief that makes statistics, when used properly, such an effective way to clarify and support ideas.[4]

Like brief examples, statistics are often cited in passing to clarify or strengthen a speaker's points. For instance:

> To document the importance of community colleges: "According to the Department of Education, there are more than 1,100 community colleges in the United States, and they enroll 45 percent of all undergraduates."

> To illustrate the dramatic increase in pay for professional athletes: ESPN reports that 30 years ago, the highest paid basketball player made less than $6 million. Today, the highest paid player makes almost $46 million a year.

Statistics can also be used in combination to show the magnitude or seriousness of an issue. We find a good instance of this technique in a student presentation about global air pollution. To demonstrate his point that poor air quality remains a massive problem for developed and developing countries alike, the speaker cited the following figures:

> According to the most recent issue of *National Geographic,* air pollution results in the deaths of 7 million people each year. That makes it five times as deadly as traffic accidents. In purely economic terms, air pollution costs the global economy over $5 trillion annually. Even here in the United States, 60,000 people die each year from this silent killer.

This is a well-supported argument. But suppose the speaker had merely said:

> Air pollution kills lots of people every year.

This statement is neither as clear nor as convincing as the one containing statistics. Of course, the audience didn't remember all the numbers, but the purpose of presenting a series of figures is to create an *overall* impact on listeners. What the audience did recall is that an impressive array of statistics supported the speaker's position.[5]

UNDERSTANDING STATISTICS

In his classic book *How to Lie with Statistics,* Darrell Huff exploded the notion that numbers don't lie. Strictly speaking, they don't. But they can be easily manipulated and distorted. For example, which of the following statements is true?

a. Enriched white bread is more nutritious than whole-wheat bread because it contains as much or more protein, calcium, niacin, thiamine, and riboflavin.

b. Whole-wheat bread is more nutritious than white bread because it contains seven times the amount of fiber, plus more iron, phosphorus, and potassium.

statistics
Numerical data.

connect
View this excerpt from "The Air We Breathe" in the online Media Library for this chapter (Video 8.5).

When used properly, statistics make us feel more secure in our knowledge. A speech that is supported by statistics is usually more persuasive than an undocumented presentation.

Rosdiana Ciaravolo/Getty Images

As you might expect, *both* statements are true. And you might hear either one of them, depending on who is trying to sell you the bread.

One can play with statistics in all kinds of areas. Which of these statements is true?

a. The cheetah, clocked at 70 miles per hour, is the fastest animal in the world.

b. The pronghorn antelope, clocked at 61 miles per hour, is the fastest animal in the world.

The cheetah, right? Not necessarily. The cheetah can go faster, but only for short sprints. The antelope can maintain its high speed over a much greater distance. So which is faster? It depends on what you're measuring. Put in terms of human races, the cheetah would win the 100-yard dash, but the antelope would win the marathon.

When you are dealing with money, statistics become even trickier. Consider the following facts:

a. In 1942, the U.S. president earned a salary of $75,000.

b. In 1982, the U.S. president earned a salary of $200,000.

c. In 2022, the U.S. president earned a salary of $400,000.

In what year did the president receive the highest salary? In purely mathematical terms, the answer is 2022. But a dollar does not buy nearly as much today as it did then. One measure of the inflation rate is the Consumer Price Index, which lets us gauge the value of the dollar in any given year against its purchasing power in 1982. If we apply the Consumer Price Index to presidential salaries, we can see how much each earned in 1982 dollars:

a. In 1942, the U.S. president earned a salary of $440,000.

b. In 1982, the U.S. president earned a salary of $200,000.

c. In 2022, the U.S. president earned a salary of $140,000.

In other words, although the president had the highest salary in 2022, the value of his $400,000 was less than one-fifth of the value of the president's $75,000 salary in 1942.

The point is that there is usually more to statistics than meets the eye.[6] When you track down statistics for your speeches, be sure to evaluate them in light of the following questions.

Are the Statistics Representative?

Say that on your way to class you choose 10 students at random and ask them whether they favor or oppose banning recreational vehicles on public lands. Say also that 6 students approve of such a ban and 4 students do not. Would you then be accurate in claiming that 60 percent of the students on your campus favor banning recreational vehicles from public lands?

Of course not. Ten students is not a big enough sample. But even if it were, other problems would arise. Do the 10 students interviewed accurately reflect your school's proportion of freshmen, sophomores, juniors, and seniors? Do they mirror the proportion of male and female students? Are the various majors accurately represented? What about part-time and full-time students? Students of different cultural and religious backgrounds?

In short, make sure your statistics are representative of what they claim to measure.

Are Statistical Measures Used Correctly?

Here are two groups of numbers:

Group A	Group B
7,500	5,400
6,300	5,400
5,000	5,000
4,400	2,300
4,400	1,700

mean
The average value of a group of numbers.

Let us apply to each group three basic statistical measures—the mean, the median, and the mode.

The *mean*—popularly called the average—is determined by summing all the items in a group and dividing by the number of items. The mean for group A is 5,520; for group B it is 3,960.

median
The middle number in a group of numbers arranged from highest to lowest.

The *median* is the middle figure in a group once the figures are put in order from highest to lowest. The median for both group A and group B is exactly the same—5,000.

The *mode* is the number that occurs most frequently in a group of numbers. The mode for group A is 4,400; for group B it is 5,400.

Notice the results:

	Group A	Group B
Mean	5,520	3,960
Median	5,000	5,000
Mode	4,400	5,400

mode
The number that occurs most frequently in a group of numbers.

All these measures have the same goal—to indicate what is typical or characteristic of a certain group of numbers. Yet see how different the results are, depending on which measure you use.

The differences among the various measures can be striking. For instance, the *mean* salary of local TV news anchorpersons is $94,300 a year. But the mean is inflated by the huge salaries (over $1 million a year) paid to a few star anchors in media centers such as New York, Los Angeles, and Chicago. In contrast, the *median* salary of local news anchors is $80,000—not a sum to scoff at, but still $14,000 less than the mean.[7]

How might a speaker use these different measures? The owner of a television station would probably cite the mean ($94,300) to show that local news anchors are handsomely compensated for their work. An organization of news anchors might emphasize the median ($80,000) to demonstrate that salaries are not nearly as high as the station owner makes them out to be. Both speakers would be telling the truth, but neither would be completely honest unless she or he made clear the meaning of the statistics.

Are the Statistics from a Reliable Source?

Which is the more reliable estimate of the environmental dangers of toxic waste in a landfill—one from the Sierra Club or one compiled by the company that owns the landfill? Easy—the estimate by the Sierra Club, which does not have a vested interest in what the figures look like. What about nutritional ratings for fast foods offered by Consumers Union (a highly respected nonprofit organization) or by Burger King? That's easy, too—Consumers Union.

But now things get tougher. What about the competing statistics offered by groups for and against charter schools? Or the conflicting numbers tossed out by Republican and Democratic presidential candidates? In these cases, the answer is not so clear, since both sides would present the facts according to their own partisan motives.

As a speaker, you must be aware of possible bias in the use of numbers. Because statistics can be interpreted so many ways and put to so many uses, you should seek figures gathered by objective, nonpartisan sources.

TIPS FOR USING STATISTICS

The main value of statistics is to give your ideas numerical precision. This can be especially important when you are trying to document the existence of a problem. Examples can bring the problem alive and dramatize it in personal terms, but your listeners may still wonder how many people the problem actually affects. In such a situation, you should turn to statistics.

Here are some tips for using statistics effectively.

Use Statistics Strategically

As helpful as statistics can be, nothing puts an audience to sleep faster than a speech cluttered with numbers from beginning to end. Insert statistics only when they are needed, and then make sure they are easy to grasp. Even the most attentive listener would have trouble sorting out this barrage of figures:

> According to the *World Factbook,* life expectancy in the United States ranks 46th in the world. The United States ranks 52nd in the world in infant mortality. Iceland ranks 3rd. Americans spend more each year on health care than any other nation—$3.2 trillion, or 17.8 percent of the gross domestic product—yet Bloomberg ranks the U.S. health care system 50th in the world in overall efficiency.

Instead of drowning your audience in a sea of statistics, use only those that are most important. For example:

> According to the *World Factbook*, the United States has one of the lowest life expectancies among industrialized nations—plus one of the highest rates of infant mortality. Even though we spend more on health care than any other nation, Bloomberg ranks 49 nations ahead of us on the overall performance of our health care system.

This second statement makes the same point as the first statement, but now the ideas are not lost in a torrent of numbers.

Identify the Sources of Your Statistics

As we have seen, figures are easy to manipulate. This is why careful listeners keep an ear out for the sources of a speaker's statistics. One student learned this by experience. In a speech titled "Family Life in America," she claimed that 23 percent of American children live in a single-parent household, the highest rate in the world and three times the global average. These are startling figures. But because the student did not say where she got them, her classmates were sure she must be wrong.

As it turned out, the numbers were reliable. They had come from a 2019 study by the highly respected Pew Research Center and cited in the *New York Times*. If the speaker had mentioned the source in her speech, she would have been more successful.[8]

Explain Your Statistics

Statistics don't speak for themselves. They need to be interpreted and related to your listeners. Notice how effectively one student did this in a speech about increasingly destructive natural disasters:

> When Hurricane Harvey pounded the Gulf Coast of Texas, it created a major disaster. According to a report by Ann Simmons in the *Los Angeles Times*, the storm flooded 28,000 square miles around Houston. That's roughly the size of a massive body of water I'm sure you all know—Lake Michigan.

Explaining what statistics mean is particularly important when you deal with large numbers, since they are hard to visualize. How, for example, can we comprehend the size of the U.S. national debt, which is more than $30 trillion? We could explain that a trillion is a thousand billion and a billion is a thousand million. But millions and billions are almost as hard to visualize as trillions. Suppose, instead, we translate the huge numbers into terms a listener can relate to. Here is one speaker's solution:

> How much money is a trillion dollars? Think of it this way. If you had $1 million and spent it at the rate of $1,000 a day, you would run out of money in less than three years. If you had $1 billion and spent it at the rate of $1,000 a day, you would not run out of money for almost 3,000 years. And if you had $1 trillion and spent it at the rate of $1,000 a day, you wouldn't run out of money for nearly 3 million years!

Instead of drowning your audience in a sea of statistics, use only those that are most important. For example:

> According to the *World Factbook*, the United States has one of the lowest life expectancies among industrialized nations—plus one of the highest rates of infant mortality. Even though we spend more on health care than any other nation, Bloomberg ranks 49 nations ahead of us on the overall performance of our health care system.

This second statement makes the same point as the first statement, but now the ideas are not lost in a torrent of numbers.

Identify the Sources of Your Statistics

As we have seen, figures are easy to manipulate. This is why careful listeners keep an ear out for the sources of a speaker's statistics. One student learned this by experience. In a speech titled "Family Life in America," she claimed that 23 percent of American children live in a single-parent household, the highest rate in the world and three times the global average. These are startling figures. But because the student did not say where she got them, her classmates were sure she must be wrong.

As it turned out, the numbers were reliable. They had come from a 2019 study by the highly respected Pew Research Center and cited in the *New York Times*. If the speaker had mentioned the source in her speech, she would have been more successful.[8]

Explain Your Statistics

Statistics don't speak for themselves. They need to be interpreted and related to your listeners. Notice how effectively one student did this in a speech about increasingly destructive natural disasters:

> When Hurricane Harvey pounded the Gulf Coast of Texas, it created a major disaster. According to a report by Ann Simmons in the *Los Angeles Times*, the storm flooded 28,000 square miles around Houston. That's roughly the size of a massive body of water I'm sure you all know—Lake Michigan.

Explaining what statistics mean is particularly important when you deal with large numbers, since they are hard to visualize. How, for example, can we comprehend the size of the U.S. national debt, which is more than $30 trillion? We could explain that a trillion is a thousand billion and a billion is a thousand million. But millions and billions are almost as hard to visualize as trillions. Suppose, instead, we translate the huge numbers into terms a listener can relate to. Here is one speaker's solution:

> How much money is a trillion dollars? Think of it this way. If you had $1 million and spent it at the rate of $1,000 a day, you would run out of money in less than three years. If you had $1 billion and spent it at the rate of $1,000 a day, you would not run out of money for almost 3,000 years. And if you had $1 trillion and spent it at the rate of $1,000 a day, you wouldn't run out of money for nearly 3 million years!

Whenever you use statistics in your speeches, think of how you can make them meaningful to your audience. Rather than simply reciting figures about, say, the world refugee crisis, find a way to bring those figures home to your audience. You might say, as did one speaker:

> The global refugee crisis is now larger than at any time since World War II. According to data from the United Nations, every day 28,000 people are forced to flee their homes because of conflict and persecution. In total, there are 22.5 million refugees around the world. How many people is that? It's more than the population of America's five biggest cities combined. Now...

connect

View this excerpt from "The Refugee Crisis" in the online Media Library for this chapter (Video 8.0).

Be creative in thinking of ways to relate your statistics to your audience. This is

10%

1923   1943   1963   1983   2003   2023

start by explaining that 100 years ago, only 12 percent of Americans belonged to a union. In 1945, union membership reached its peak, with 33 percent of Americans belonging to one. Membership began to slide in the 1960s and declined rapidly after 1980. Today, the percentage of Americans in a union has fallen back to where it was

These are interesting statistics, and you could build a good speech around them. But strung together in a few sentences they are hard to digest. Figure 8.1 shows how much more clearly the points can be made with a simple graph. We shall discuss

high; the world land speed record is 763 miles per hour; the population of Germany is more than 84 million; and the moon is 239,000 miles from Earth.

visual aids in detail in Chapter 14. For the moment, keep in mind that they can be helpful in presenting statistical information.

Use Visual Aids to Clarify Statistical Trends

Visual aids can save you a lot of time, as well as make your statistics easier to comprehend. Suppose you're discussing the decline in U.S. union membership. You could

✔ checklist

Using Statistics

YES	NO	
☐	☐	1. Do I use statistics to quantify my ideas?
☐	☐	2. Are my statistics representative of what they purport to measure?
☐	☐	3. Are my statistics from reliable sources?
☐	☐	4. Do I cite the sources of my statistics?
☐	☐	5. Do I use statistical measures (mean, median, mode) correctly?
☐	☐	6. Do I round off complicated statistics?
☐	☐	7. Do I use visual aids to clarify statistical trends?
☐	☐	8. Do I explain my statistics and relate them to the audience?

just mouthing your own opinions, but that your position is supported by people who are knowledgeable about the topic.

Expert testimony is even more important when a topic is controversial or when the audience is skeptical about a speaker's point of view. The following story explains how one student enlisted expert testimony for a speech on the problem of lead pollution in America's drinking water:

expert testimony
Testimony from people who are recognized experts in their fields.

> As Nathan Richter researched the topic of lead in the U.S. water supply, he became convinced that the problem affected millions of Americans and required urgent action by municipalities, states, and the federal government. Yet Nathan was not an expert. How could he convince his classmates to share his concern?
>
> Statistics helped, and so did examples. But on such an important topic, that was not enough. So, to reinforce his credibility, Nathan cited a wide range of experts who agreed with him—including the Environmental Protection Agency, Northwestern University professor Joseph Ferrie, and the American Public Health Association. By citing the views of these and other experts, Nathan made his speech much more persuasive.

connect
View an excerpt from "Getting the Lead Out" in the online Media Library for this chapter (Video 8.7).

PEER TESTIMONY

Another type of testimony often used in speeches is peer testimony—opinions of people like ourselves; not prominent figures, but ordinary citizens who have first-hand experience on the topic. This kind of testimony is especially valuable because it gives a more personal viewpoint on issues than can be gained from expert testimony.

peer testimony
Testimony from ordinary people with firsthand experience or insight on a topic.

For example, if you were speaking about the barriers faced by people with physical disabilities, you would surely include testimony from doctors and other medical authorities. But in this case, the expert testimony would be limited because it cannot communicate what it really means to have a physical disability. To communicate that, you need a statement from someone who can speak with the voice of genuine experience—as in the following case:

> Itzhak Perlman, the world-renowned violinist whose legs are paralyzed, once said: "When you are in a wheelchair, people don't talk to you. Perhaps they think it is contagious, or perhaps they think crippled legs mean a crippled mind. But whatever the reason, they treat you like a thing."

There is no way expert testimony could express these ideas with the same authenticity and emotional impact.

QUOTING VERSUS PARAPHRASING

The statement from Itzhak Perlman is presented as a direct quotation. Testimony can also be presented by paraphrasing. Rather than quoting someone verbatim, you present the gist of that person's ideas in your own words—as one student did in her speech about the insecurity of America's electrical grid:

direct quotation
Testimony that is presented word for word.

> In an article on *Wired.com*, Eric Chien, an analyst for the security firm Symantec, says we have irrefutable evidence of foreign hackers trying to take over our electrical grid. Without major security fixes, he says, there's little to stop someone who is determined to cut off our power.

When should you use a direct quotation as opposed to paraphrasing? The standard rule is that quotations are most effective when they are brief, when they convey your meaning better than you can, and when they are particularly eloquent, witty, or compelling. If you find a quotation that fits these criteria, then recite the quotation word for word.

Paraphrasing is better than direct quotation in two situations: (1) when the wording of a quotation is obscure or cumbersome, and (2) when a quotation is longer than two or three sentences. Audiences often tune out partway through lengthy quotations, which tend to interrupt the flow of a speaker's ideas. Since the rest of the speech is in your own words, you should put longer quotations in your own words as well.

TIPS FOR USING TESTIMONY

Quote or Paraphrase Accurately

Accurate quotation involves three things: (1) making sure you do not misquote someone, (2) making sure you do not violate the meaning of statements you paraphrase, and (3) making sure you do not quote out of context.

Of these, the last is the most subtle—and the most dangerous. By quoting out of context, you can twist someone's remarks so as to prove almost anything. Take movie advertisements. A critic pans a movie with these words:

> This movie is a colossal bore. From beginning to end it is a disaster. What is meant to be brilliant dialogue is about as fascinating as the stuff you clean out of your kitchen drain.

But when the movie is advertised in the newspapers, what appears in huge letters over the critic's name? "COLOSSAL! FROM BEGINNING TO END—BRILLIANT! FASCINATING!"

This is so flagrant as to be humorous. But quoting out of context can have serious consequences. Consider the following statement by a political candidate:

> Creating a national sales tax would provide needed revenue for programs such as education, health care, and national defense. Several

paraphrase
To restate or summarize an author's ideas in one's own words.

quoting out of context
Quoting a statement in such a way as to distort its meaning by removing the statement from the words and phrases surrounding it.

✔ checklist

Using Testimony

YES	NO	
☐	☐	1. Do I use testimony to support my ideas?
☐	☐	2. Do I use testimony from qualified sources?
☐	☐	3. Do I use testimony from unbiased sources?
☐	☐	4. Do I distinguish between expert testimony and peer testimony?
☐	☐	5. Do I identify the sources of all testimony?
☐	☐	6. Do I quote and paraphrase all sources of testimony with complete accuracy?

Citing expert testimony is an excellent way for student speakers to lend credibility to their presentations. Finding strong testimony requires time and effort, but the results are well worth it.

Orathaimukky/123RF

European countries have such a tax, and it could work here. However, I do not support such a tax here—in fact, I don't support new taxes of any kind.

Now look what happens when the first part of that statement is quoted out of context by a competing candidate:

Americans already pay too much in taxes. Yet my opponent in this election has stated—and I quote: "Creating a national sales tax would provide needed revenue for programs such as education, health care, and national defense. Several European countries have such a tax, and it could work here." Well, my opponent may think new taxes are good for Europe, but they're the last thing we need in the United States.

By quoting the original statement out of context, the competing candidate has created a false impression. Such behavior is highly unethical. Be sure, when you quote or paraphrase someone, that you represent his or her words and ideas with complete accuracy.

Use Testimony from Qualified Sources

We have all become accustomed to the celebrity testimonial in television and magazine advertising. The professional basketball player endorses a brand of athletic shoes. The movie star praises a hair spray or shampoo. So far, so good. These are the tools of the trade for the people who endorse them.

But what happens when an Academy Award winner endorses a cell phone company? A tennis player represents a line of watches? Do they know more about these products than you or I? Probably not.

Being a celebrity or an authority in one area does not make someone competent in other areas. Listeners will find your speeches much more credible if you use testimony from sources qualified *on the subject at hand*. As we have seen, this may include either recognized experts or ordinary citizens with special experience on the speech topic.

Use Testimony from Unbiased Sources

In a speech about the use of stun guns by police officers to subdue unruly students in public schools, a student said:

> Steve Tuttle, a spokesman for Taser International, said in a statement that "the Taser device has been shown to be medically safe when used on children" and that there is no reason to prohibit its use when necessary to maintain security in the public schools.

As you might expect, the students' classmates were not persuaded. After all, what would you expect someone at Taser International, the leading manufacturer of stun guns, to say—that its product is unsafe and should be banned?

Careful listeners are suspicious of testimony from biased or self-interested sources. Be sure to use testimony from credible, objective authorities.

Identify the People You Quote or Paraphrase

The usual way to identify your source is to name the person and sketch his or her qualifications before presenting the testimony. The following excerpt is from a speech arguing that excessive time spent at work is harming the quality of education for many American high-school students:

> In their book, *When Children Work,* psychology professors Ellen Greenberger of the University of California and Lawrence Steinberg of Temple University note that intensive levels of work among youth tend to produce higher truancy and lower grades. According to Greenberger and Steinberg, one study after another has found that working more than a few hours a week has a negative impact on teenagers' academic performance.

Had the speaker not identified Greenberger and Steinberg, listeners would not have had the foggiest idea who they are or why their opinion should be heeded.

As we saw in Chapter 2, identifying the source of testimony is also an important ethical responsibility. If you use another person's words or ideas without giving credit to that person, you will be guilty of plagiarism. This is true whether you paraphrase the original source or quote it verbatim.

Citing Sources Orally

We have mentioned more than once in this chapter the importance of citing the sources of your supporting materials. Careful listeners are skeptical. They keep an ear out both for a speaker's information and for the sources of that information.

The bibliography in your speech outline should state the sources you used in constructing the speech (see Chapter 11). But listeners do not have access to your outline. You have to identify your sources orally, as you are speaking.

Unlike a written bibliography, oral source citations do not follow a standard format. What you include depends on your topic, your audience, the kind of supporting material you are using, and the claim you are making. The key is to tell your audience enough that they will know where you got your information and why they should accept it as qualified and credible. In most cases, you will need to identify some combination of the following:

- The book, magazine, newspaper, or web document you are citing
- The author or sponsoring organization of the document
- The author's qualifications with regard to the topic
- The date on which the document was published, posted, or updated

Here is an example of a speech citation that includes all the above:

> A CNN.com story of January 13, 2022, cites Doug Shapiro, executive director of the National Student Clearinghouse Research Center, on the 6.5 percent pandemic-related decline in college enrollment. It is, according to Shapiro, the largest two-year drop in the past half century and twice as steep as the previous largest drop.

Because this speaker was citing statistics, she needed to show that they were up-to-date and came from a credible source. In the following example, the speaker is using testimony, but notice how he also establishes the credibility of his source and the recency of his information:

> Human smuggling is big business, and the U.S. government has made little headway in stopping it. Just ask Scott Hatfield, chief of the Human Smuggling division at Immigration and Customs Enforcement, who was quoted last month in the *Houston Chronicle:* "Any time we shut down a smuggling organization, there's always somebody to take their place."

On the other hand, if you were quoting Abraham Lincoln's Gettysburg Address of November 19, 1863, about "government of the people, by the people, for the

checklist

Citing Sources Orally

YES	NO	
☐	☐	1. Do I identify all the print documents cited in my speech?
☐	☐	2. Do I identify all the web documents cited in my speech?
☐	☐	3. Do I identify the authors or sponsoring organizations of the documents I cite?
☐	☐	4. Do I establish the authors' credentials with regard to the topic?
☐	☐	5. Do I use documents from sponsoring organizations with established expertise and objectivity?
☐	☐	6. Do I include the dates on which the documents were published, posted, or updated?
☐	☐	7. Do I use a variety of methods in citing my sources?

FIGURE 8.2   Sample Oral Citations

Book

In her 2022 book, *South to America*, Princeton University professor Imani Perry argues that to understand the United States—its history, culture, politics, problems, and struggles—we need to start not with New England but with the American South.

Newspaper

A January 14, 2022, article in the *Washington Post* reveals just how big online sports betting has become. Thirty states currently allow online betting, with many more to follow. People in those states have already wagered almost $100 billion—a big number that will seem small in coming years.

Magazine

In this month's issue of *National Geographic,* science writer Tom Clynes explains how laser technology has revealed 60,000 previously unknown Mayan structures beneath the jungles of Guatemala. Over 1,200 years old, the structures include everything from small houses to grand palaces.

Academic journal

A recent study in the journal *Science Translational Medicine* by researchers at Stanford University shows that small vaccine injections might be an effective cancer therapy. These researchers were able to cure cancer in 97 percent of the mice they vaccinated.

Organization or institution

A February 2022 report from the U.S. Nuclear Regulatory Commission found that several nuclear power plants across the country are operating with counterfeit parts and equipment. According to the report, these parts and equipment pose a threat to "worker safety, facility performance, the public, and the environment."

Interview

In an interview I conducted for this speech, Professor Elinor Sanchez of the Political Science Department said that the impact of lobbyists has so corrupted the American political system that many people have lost their faith in government to serve the public good.

Television program

According to the February 9, 2022, episode of *PBS News Hour*, a group of Black scuba divers are combing the ocean floor to research some of the estimated 1,000 sunken ships from the international slave trade.

Website

A January 11, 2022, article on the World Economic Forum's website reports that last year, e-waste totaled 63 million tons. To put that in perspective, one year's worth of discarded cell phones, computers, and other gadgets weighed more than the Great Wall of China.

people," you would not need to explain Lincoln's qualifications (because he is so well known) or the date of his statement (because it does not affect the relevance of his words).

The same principles apply if you are citing online sources. It is not enough to say, "As I found on the web," or "As the Internet states." On the other hand, it is not necessary to recite the entire address of the web page. If you are citing a specific person, you should identify him or her and the name of the website on which you found the information—as in this example:

> In a January 17, 2022, story on NPR.org about the struggle for voting rights, former attorney for the U.S. Justice Department Laura Coates summarized the issue: "Our democracy is in peril every time we claw back the gains of the Voting Rights Act, because we dilute voting power, we dilute voting strength, we undermine the philosophy of one person, one vote."

If you are citing an organization, rather than an individual, you need to provide the name of the organization:

> The U.S. Department of Labor reports on its website that over 33 percent of people with disabilities are part of the labor force. That's the highest number ever recorded.

Finally, notice how skillfully the speakers quoted above blend their citations into their speeches. They do not always say "According to . . ." or "As stated by. . . ." Nor do they use words like "quote . . . unquote." Usually you can modify your tone of voice or use brief pauses to let your listeners know when you are making a direct quotation.

In Figure 8.2, you will find more examples of how you can cite different kinds of sources in your speeches. Keep in mind, however, that the examples are just that— examples. They are presented to give you a fuller sense of the various methods of oral citation. You can use *any* of the methods with any of the sources. As with other aspects of public speaking, citing sources orally in your speeches is not a matter of following a rigid formula, but of adapting general principles to specific circumstances.

Summary

Good speeches need strong supporting materials to bolster the speaker's point of view. The three basic types of supporting materials are examples, statistics, and testimony.

In the course of a speech you may use brief examples—specific instances referred to in passing—and sometimes you may want to give several brief examples in a row to create a stronger impression. Extended examples are longer and more detailed. Hypothetical examples describe imaginary situations and can be quite effective for relating ideas to the audience. All three kinds of examples help clarify ideas, reinforce ideas, or personalize ideas. To be most effective, they should be vivid and richly textured.

Statistics can be extremely helpful in conveying your message as long as you use them strategically and make them meaningful to your audience. Above all, you should understand your statistics and use them fairly. Make sure they are representative of what they claim to measure, that you use statistical measures correctly, and that you take statistics only from reliable sources.

Citing the testimony of experts is a good way to make your ideas more credible. You can also use peer testimony, from ordinary people who have firsthand experience on the topic. Regardless of the kind of testimony, you can either quote someone verbatim or paraphrase his or her words. Be sure to quote or paraphrase accurately and to use qualified, unbiased sources.

When citing sources in a speech, you need to let your audience know where you got your information and why they should accept it as qualified and credible. In most cases, this means identifying the document you are citing, its date of publication or posting, the author or sponsoring organization, and the author's credentials.

Key Terms

supporting materials (132)

example (134)

brief example (134)

extended example (134)

hypothetical example (135)

statistics (138)

mean (140)

median (140)

mode (140)

testimony (144)

expert testimony (145)

peer testimony (145)

direct quotation (145)

paraphrase (146)

quoting out of context (146)

Review Questions

After reading this chapter, you should be able to answer the following questions:

1. Why do you need supporting materials in your speeches?

2. What are the three kinds of examples discussed in this chapter? How might you use each kind to support your ideas?

3. What are four tips for using examples in your speeches?

4. Why is it so easy to lie with statistics? What three questions should you ask to judge the reliability of statistics?

5. What are five tips for using statistics in your speeches?

6. What is testimony? Explain the difference between expert testimony and peer testimony.

7. What are four tips for using testimony in your speeches?

8. What four pieces of information do you usually need to provide when making oral source citations in a speech?

Exercises for Critical Thinking

1. Each of the following statements violates at least one of the criteria for effective supporting materials discussed in this chapter. Identify the flaw (or flaws) in each statement.

   a. In the words of one expert, "the prevalence of online multi-tasking is reducing the ability of people to concentrate on a single task, no matter how important the task might be."

b. Figures compiled by the Bureau of Labor Statistics show that the median salary for petroleum engineers in the United States is $137,330. This shows that petroleum engineers average more than $137,000 a year in salary.

c. According to a poll conducted by AT&T, most people prefer AT&T's cellular service to that of T-Mobile or Verizon.

d. It's just not true that media violence has a strong influence on violent crimes. All my friends watch television, go to the movies, and play video games, and none of us has ever committed a violent crime.

e. As Ariana Grande stated in a recent interview, increasing offshore drilling for oil will harm the environment far more than it will help the economy.

f. According to the U.S. Census Bureau, California has the largest Native American population of any state in the Union—631,016. Oklahoma is second with 332,791 and Arizona is third with 319,512.

g. In a survey conducted last month among members of People for the Ethical Treatment of Animals, 99 percent of respondents opposed using animals for medical experiments. Clearly, then, the American people oppose such experiments.

2. Analyze "The Living-Wage Solution" in the appendix of sample speeches following Chapter 20. Identify the main points of the speech and the supporting materials used for each. Evaluate the speaker's use of supporting materials in light of the criteria discussed in this chapter.

End Notes

[1] Elliot Aronson, *The Social Animal,* 11th ed. (New York: Worth, 2011), pp. 92–93.

[2] This point was made by James A. Winans in his classic *Speech-Making* (New York: Appleton-Century-Crofts, 1922), p. 141.

[3] Mike Allen et al., "Testing the Persuasiveness of Evidence: Combining Narrative and Statistical Forms," *Communication Research Reports,* 17 (2000), pp. 331–336.

[4] Over the years there has been much debate about whether statistics or examples have more impact on listeners. For a review of perspectives on this subject, see Richard M. Perloff, *The Dynamics of Persuasion: Communication and Attitudes in the 21st Century,* 7th ed. (New York: Routledge, 2021), pp. 301–311.

[5] One implication of Bing Han and Edward L. Fink, "How Do Statistical and Narrative Evidence Affect Persuasion? The Role of Evidentiary Features," *Argumentation and Advocacy,* 48 (2012), pp. 39–58, is that multiple statistics tend to be more persuasive than single statistics.

[6] Tim Harford, *The Data Detective: Ten Easy Rules to Make Sense of Statistics* (New York: Riverhead Books, 2021), provides a fascinating look at the use and misuse of statistics. For a more technical approach, see Neil J. Salkind, *Statistics for People Who (Think They) Hate Statistics,* 7th ed. (Thousand Oaks, CA: Sage 2020).

[7] Bob Papper, "Research: TV Salaries Edge Up, Radio Salaries Dip," Radio Television Digital News Association (RTDNA). Web. May 18, 2021.

[8] On the importance of citing sources when presenting evidence, see Daniel J. O'Keefe, *Persuasion: Theory and Research,* 3rd ed. (Thousand Oaks, CA: Sage, 2016), pp. 216–220.

9

Organizing the Body of the Speech

Think about shopping in a store such as IKEA, Target, or Best Buy. Many of the items for sale are *organizers*—drawer organizers, desk organizers, closet organizers, kitchen organizers, bathroom organizers, office organizers, audio and video organizers. There is even a nationwide retail chain—The Container Store—devoted entirely to keeping things organized.

Why all this quest for organization? Obviously, when the objects you possess are well organized, they serve you better. Organization allows you to see what you have and to put your hands immediately on the garment, the tool, the piece of paper, the video you want without a frenzied search.

Much the same is true of your speeches. If they are well organized, they will serve you better. Organization allows you—and your listeners—to see what ideas you have and to put mental "hands" on the most important ones.

Organization Is Important

In a classic study, a college professor took a well-organized speech and scrambled it by randomly changing the order of its sentences. He then had a speaker deliver the original version to one group of listeners and the scrambled version to another group. After the speeches, he gave a test to see how well each group understood what they had heard. Not surprisingly, the group that heard the original, unscrambled speech scored much higher than the other group.[1]

A few years later, two professors repeated the same experiment at another school. But instead of testing how well the listeners comprehended each speech, they tested to see what effects the speeches had on the listeners' attitudes toward the

speakers. They found that people who heard the well-organized speech believed the speaker to be much more competent and trustworthy than did those who heard the scrambled speech.[2]

These are just two of many studies that show the importance of organization in effective speechmaking.[3] Listeners demand coherence. Unlike readers, they cannot flip back to a previous page if they have trouble grasping a speaker's ideas. In this respect a speech is much like a movie. Just as a director must be sure viewers can follow the plot of a film from beginning to end, so must a speaker be sure listeners can follow the progression of ideas in a speech from beginning to end. This requires that speeches be organized *strategically*. They should be put together in particular ways to achieve particular results with particular audiences.

strategic organization
Putting a speech together in a particular way to achieve a particular result with a particular audience.

Speech organization is important for other reasons as well. As we saw in Chapter 1, it is closely connected to critical thinking. When you work to organize your speeches, you gain practice in the general skill of establishing clear relationships among your ideas. This skill will serve you well throughout your college days and in almost any career you may choose. In addition, using a clear, specific method of speech organization can boost your confidence as a speaker and improve your ability to deliver a message fluently.

The first step in developing a strong sense of speech organization is to gain command of the three basic parts of a speech—introduction, body, and conclusion—and the strategic role of each. In this chapter we deal with the body of the speech. The next chapter will take up the introduction and the conclusion.

There are good reasons for talking first about the body of the speech. The body is the longest and most important part. Also, you will usually prepare the body first. It is easier to create an effective introduction after you know exactly what you will say in the body.

The process of organizing the body of a speech begins when you determine the main points.

Main Points

The main points are the central features of your speech. You should select them carefully, phrase them precisely, and arrange them strategically. Here are the main points of a student speech about the uses of hypnosis:

main points
The major points developed in the body of a speech.

Specific Purpose:	To inform my audience about some of the major uses of hypnosis.
Central Idea:	Three major uses of hypnosis today are to control pain in surgery, to help people stop smoking, and to help students improve their academic performance.
Main Points:	I. Hypnosis is used in surgery as an adjunct to chemical anesthesia.
	II. Hypnosis is used to help people stop smoking.
	III. Hypnosis is used to help students improve their academic performance.

These three main points form the skeleton of the body of the speech. If there are three major *uses* of hypnosis, then logically there can be three *main points* in the speech.

How do you choose your main points? Sometimes they will be evident from your specific purpose statement. Suppose your specific purpose is, "To inform my audience about the history, technology, and potential of quantum computers." Obviously, your speech will have three main points. The first will deal with the history of quantum computers, the second with the technology behind quantum computers, and the third with the uses of quantum computers. Written in outline form, they might be:

Specific Purpose: To inform my audience about the history, technology, and potential of quantum computers.

Central Idea: Once just a theory, quantum computers are developing quickly and have revolutionary potential.

Main Points:
    I. Quantum computers have long been in the imagination of scientists.
    II. Quantum computers are today a rapidly developing technology.
    III. Quantum computers have the potential to revolutionize the field of computing.

Even if your main points are not stated expressly in your specific purpose, they may be easy to project from it. Let's say your specific purpose is "To inform my audience of the basic steps in making stained-glass windows." You know each of your main points will correspond to a step in the window-making process. They might look like this in outline form:

Specific Purpose: To inform my audience of the basic steps in making stained-glass windows.

Central Idea: There are four steps in making stained-glass windows.

Main Points:
    I. The first step is designing the window.
    II. The second step is cutting the glass to fit the design.
    III. The third step is painting the glass.
    IV. The fourth step is assembling the window.

You will not always settle on your main points so easily. Often they will emerge as you research the speech and evaluate your findings. Suppose your specific purpose is "To persuade my audience that our city should not build a new convention center." You know that each main point in the speech will present a *reason* why a new convention center should not be built. But you aren't sure how many main points there will be or what they will be. As you research and study the topic, you decide there are two reasons to support your view. Each of these reasons will become a main point in your speech. Written in outline form, they might be:

Specific Purpose: To persuade my audience that our city should not build a new convention center.

| Central Idea: | Our city should not build a new convention center because it will cost too much and because online meeting technology makes it unnecessary. |

| Main Points: | I. Our city should not build a new convention center because it will cost too much. |
| | II. Our city should not build a new convention center because online meeting technology makes it unnecessary. |

NUMBER OF MAIN POINTS

You will not have time in your classroom speeches to develop more than four or five main points, and most speeches will contain only two or three. Regardless of how long a speech might run, if you have too many main points, the audience will have trouble sorting them out.

If, when you list your main points, you find that you have too many, you may be able to condense them into categories. Here is a set of main points for a speech about yoga:

| Specific Purpose: | To inform my audience about the practice of yoga. |

| Central Idea: | Yoga is an ancient practice that involves the whole body. |

Main Points:	I. Yoga breathing starts with deep inhalation.
	II. Yoga breathing requires slow exhalation.
	III. Yoga breathing includes prolonged pauses.
	IV. Yoga breathing provides many benefits.
	V. Yoga postures involve all parts of the body.
	VI. Yoga postures increase flexibility.
	VII. Yoga postures strengthen muscle tone.
	VIII. Yoga postures demand precise movements.

You have eight main points—which is too many. But if you look at the list, you see that the eight points fall into two broad categories: yoga breathing and yoga postures. You might, therefore, restate your main points this way:

I. One part of practicing yoga involves proper breathing.

II. Another part of yoga involves body postures.

STRATEGIC ORDER OF MAIN POINTS

Once you establish your main points, you need to decide the order in which you will present them. The most effective order depends on three things—your topic, your purpose, and your audience. Chapters 15 and 16 will cover special aspects of organizing informative speeches and persuasive speeches. Here we look briefly at the five basic patterns of organization used most often by public speakers.

Chronological Order

Speeches arranged chronologically follow a time pattern. They may narrate a series of events in the sequence in which they happened. For example:

| Specific Purpose: | To inform my audience about the rise of eSports. |

| Central Idea: | eSports has grown to become a worldwide billion-dollar industry. |

connect

View an excerpt from "Yoga: Uniting Mind, Body, and Spirit" in the online Media Library for this chapter (Video 9.1).

Clear organization is vital to effective public speaking. As in this address by NATO Secretary General Jens Stoltenberg, listeners must be able to follow the progression of ideas in a speech from beginning to end.

Kenzo Tribouillard/AFP/Getty Images

Main Points: I. eSports began in the 1980s as friendly competitions among friends.

II. eSports became a global phenomenon during the 1990s.

III. eSports flourished through official tournaments in the 2000s.

IV. eSports today draw more viewers than many traditional sports leagues.

Chronological order is also used in speeches explaining a process or demonstrating how to do something. For example:

Specific Purpose: To inform my audience of the steps in laser-assisted corrective eye surgery.

Central Idea: There are three main steps in laser-assisted corrective eye surgery.

Main Points: I. First, a thin layer is sliced off the surface of the eye to expose the cornea.

II. Second, an ultraviolet laser is used to reshape the cornea.

III. Third, the thin layer sliced off at the beginning of the surgery is reaffixed to the eye.

As this outline shows, chronological order is especially useful for informative speeches.

Spatial Order

Speeches arranged in spatial order follow a directional pattern. That is, the main points proceed from top to bottom, left to right, front to back, inside to outside, east to west, or some other route. For example:

Specific Purpose: To inform my audience about the structure of a hurricane.

Central Idea: A hurricane is made up of three parts going from inside to outside.

chronological order
A method of speech organization in which the main points follow a time pattern.

spatial order
A method of speech organization in which the main points follow a directional pattern.

Main Points:	I. At the center of a hurricane is the calm, cloud-free eye.
	II. Surrounding the eye is the eyewall, a dense ring of clouds that produces the most intense wind and rainfall.
	III. Rotating around the eyewall are large bands of clouds and precipitation called spiral rain bands.

connect

View an excerpt from "The Wrath of Hurricanes" in the online Media Library for this chapter (Video 9.2).

Or:

Specific Purpose:	To inform my audience about the three major regions in Italy.
Central Idea:	Northern, central, and southern Italy have their own identities and attractions.
Main Points:	I. Northern Italy is home to Venice and its world-famous canals.
	II. Central Italy is home to Rome and its historical treasures.
	III. Southern Italy is home to Sicily and its culinary traditions.

Spatial order, like chronological order, is used most often in informative speeches.

Causal Order

causal order

A method of speech organization in which the main points show a cause-effect relationship.

Speeches arranged in causal order organize main points so as to show a cause-effect relationship. When you put your speech in causal order, you have two main points—one dealing with the causes of an event, the other dealing with its effects. Depending on your topic, you can devote your first main point to the causes and the second to the effects, or you can deal first with the effects and then with the causes.

Suppose your specific purpose is "To persuade my audience that a growing shortage of nurses is a serious problem across the United States." Then you would begin with the causes of the shortage and work toward its effects:

Specific Purpose:	To persuade my audience that a growing shortage of nurses is a serious problem across the United States.
Central Idea:	The growing shortage of trained nurses is a problem for health care nationwide.
Main Points:	I. The United States faces a growing shortage of trained nurses in all parts of the country.
	II. If this shortage continues, it will strain the entire health care system.

When the effects you are discussing have already occurred, you may want to reverse the order and talk first about the effects and then about their causes—as in this speech about the Ancient Pueblo peoples that lived in what is now the southwestern United States:

Specific Purpose:	To inform my audience about possible causes for the collapse of the Ancient Pueblo civilization.
Central Idea:	The causes for the collapse of the Ancient Pueblo civilization have not yet been fully explained.
Main Points:	I. Ancient Pueblo civilization flourished for over a thousand years until 1200 A.D., when it mysteriously began to disintegrate.

The main points of a speech should be organized to communicate the speaker's message. Chronological order would work well for a speech on the history of the Chateau de Chenonceau.

Prosign/Shutterstock

II. Scholars have advanced three major explanations for the causes of this disintegration.

Because of its versatility, causal order can be used for both persuasive speeches and informative speeches.

Problem-Solution Order

Speeches arranged in problem-solution order are divided into two main parts. The first shows the existence and seriousness of a problem. The second presents a workable solution to the problem. For example:

Specific Purpose: To persuade my audience that action is needed to combat the abuses of puppy mills.

Central Idea: Puppy mills are a serious problem that can be solved by a combination of legislation and individual initiative.

Main Points: I. Puppy mills are a serious problem across the United States.

II. Solving the problem requires legislation and individual initiative.

Or:

Specific Purpose: To persuade my audience that the electoral college should be abolished.

Central Idea: Because the electoral college does not give equal weight to the vote of each citizen, it should be replaced with direct popular election of the president.

Main Points: I. The electoral college is a serious problem in the U.S. political system because it does not give equal weight to each citizen's vote in electing the president.

problem-solution order
A method of organizing persuasive speeches in which the first main point deals with the existence of a problem and the second main point presents a solution to the problem.

connect
View an excerpt from "The Horrors of Puppy Mills" in the online Media Library for this chapter (Video 9.3).

II. The problem can be solved by abolishing the electoral college and electing the president by popular vote.

As these examples indicate, problem-solution order is most appropriate for persuasive speeches.

Topical Order

Topical order results when you divide the speech topic into *subtopics,* each of which becomes a main point in the speech.

Let's say your topic is Josephine Baker, an African-American entertainer and social activist in the middle of the 20th century. You could organize your speech chronologically—by discussing Baker's exploits during each decade of her career. On the other hand, you could arrange the speech topically—by dividing Baker's accomplishments into categories. Then your central idea and main points might be:

Specific Purpose: To inform my audience about the achievements of Josephine Baker.

Central Idea: Josephine Baker was a multitalented figure in the fight for racial justice.

Main Points:
    I. As an entertainer, Baker captivated audiences in Europe and America.
    II. As a spy, Baker gathered information on Nazi activities in France during World War II.
    III. As a civil rights activist, Baker worked for racial equality on a variety of fronts.

Notice how the main points subdivide the speech topic logically and consistently. Each main point isolates one aspect of Baker's achievements. But suppose your main points look like this:

    I. As an entertainer, Baker captivated audiences in Europe and America.
    II. As a spy, Baker gathered information on Nazi activities in France during World War II.
    III. During the 1950s, Baker expanded her activities and the scope of her influence.

This would *not* be a good topical order because main point III is inconsistent with the rest of the main points. It deals with a *time period* in Baker's life, whereas main points I and II deal with fields of achievement.

The Josephine Baker example refers to an informative speech. But topical order also works for persuasive speeches. Usually the topical subdivisions are the *reasons* why a speaker believes in a certain point of view. Here, for example, are the main points for a speech on why the United States should continue its program of space exploration:

Specific Purpose: To persuade my audience that the United States should continue its program of space exploration.

Central Idea: The United States should continue its program of space exploration because it produces scientific knowledge, generates technological breakthroughs, and opens access to natural resources.

Main Points:

   I. The space program produces scientific knowledge about the nature of the solar system.

   II. The space program generates technological breakthroughs that benefit many aspects of human life.

   III. The space program opens access to natural resources that are in short supply on Earth.

Because it is applicable to almost any subject and to any kind of speech, topical order is used more often than any other method of speech organization.

TIPS FOR PREPARING MAIN POINTS

Keep Main Points Separate

Each main point in a speech should be clearly independent of the others. Compare these two sets of main points for a speech about the process of producing a Broadway play:

Ineffective	**More Effective**
I. The first step is choosing the play.	I. The first step is choosing the play.
II. The second step is selecting the cast.	II. The second step is selecting the cast.
III. The third step is conducting rehearsals and then performing the play.	III. The third step is conducting the rehearsals.
	IV. The fourth step is performing the play.

The problem with the left-hand list is that point III contains two main points. It should be divided, as shown in the right-hand list.

Try to Use the Same Pattern of Wording for Main Points

Consider the following main points for an informative speech about the benefits of karate:

Ineffective

I. Karate gives you better mental discipline.
II. You will become physically stronger through karate.
III. Taking karate lessons will teach you self-defense.

More Effective

I. Karate improves your mental discipline.
II. Karate increases your physical strength.
III. Karate teaches you self-defense.

The set of main points on the right follows a consistent pattern of wording throughout. Therefore, it is easier to understand and easier to remember than the set on the left.

You will find that it is not always possible to use this kind of parallel wording. Some speeches just don't lend themselves to such a tidy arrangement. But try to keep the wording parallel when you can; it's a good way to make your main points stand out from the details surrounding them.

Balance the Amount of Time Devoted to Main Points

Because your main points are so important, you want to be sure they all receive enough emphasis to be clear and convincing. This means allowing sufficient time to develop each main point. Suppose you discover that the proportion of time devoted to your main points is something like this:

I. 85 percent

II. 10 percent

III. 5 percent

A breakdown of this sort indicates one of two things. Either points II and III aren't really *main* points and you have only one main point, or points II and III haven't been given the attention they need. If the latter, you should revise the body of the speech to bring the main points into better balance.

This is not to say that all main points must receive exactly equal emphasis, but only that they should be roughly balanced. For example, either of the following would be fine:

I. 30 percent

II. 40 percent

III. 30 percent

I. 20 percent

II. 30 percent

III. 50 percent

The amount of time spent on each main point depends on the amount and complexity of supporting materials for each point.

Supporting Materials

By themselves, main points are only assertions. As we saw in Chapter 8, listeners need supporting materials to accept what a speaker says. The following outline demonstrates how supporting materials can be integrated into the body of a speech.

In Chapter 11, we'll look at requirements for a complete speech outline. For now, concentrate on how the supporting materials relate to the main points.

I. Hypnosis is used in surgery as an adjunct to chemical anesthesia.
   A. Hypnosis reduces both the physical and psychological aspects of pain.
      1. Hypnosis can double a person's pain threshold.
      2. It also reduces the fear that intensifies physical pain.
   B. Hypnosis is most useful in cases when the patient is known to have problems with general anesthesia.
      1. Quotation from Dr. Harold Wain of the Mayo Clinic.
      2. Story of Linda Kuay.
      3. Statistics from *Psychology Today*.

II. Hypnosis is used to help people stop smoking.
   A. Many therapists utilize hypnosis to help people break their addiction to cigarettes.
      1. The U.S. Department of Health and Human Services considers hypnosis a safe and effective means of stopping smoking.
      2. Success rates are as high as 70 percent.
         a. Story of Alex Hamilton.
         b. Quotation from New York psychiatrist Dr. Herbert Spiegel.
   B. Hypnosis does not work for all smokers.
      1. A person must want to stop smoking for hypnosis to work.
      2. A person must also be responsive to hypnotic suggestion.

III. Hypnosis is used to help students improve their academic performance.
   A. Hypnosis enables people to use their minds more effectively.
      1. The conscious mind utilizes about 10 percent of a person's mental ability.
      2. Hypnosis allows people to tap more of their mental power.
   B. Studies show that hypnosis can help people overcome many obstacles to academic success.
      1. It improves ability to concentrate.
      2. It increases reading speed.
      3. It reduces test anxiety.

supporting materials
The materials used to support a speaker's ideas. The three major kinds of supporting materials are examples, statistics, and testimony.

In Chapter 8, we discussed the major kinds of supporting materials and how to use them. Here, we need stress only the importance of *organizing* your supporting materials so they are directly relevant to the main points they are supposed to support. Misplaced supporting materials are confusing. Here's an example:

I. There are several reasons why people immigrate to the United States.
   A. Over the years, millions of people have immigrated to the United States.
   B. Many people immigrate in search of economic opportunity.
   C. Others immigrate to attain political freedom.
   D. Still others immigrate to escape religious persecution.

The main point deals with the reasons immigrants come to the United States, as do supporting points B, C, and D. Supporting point A ("Over the years, millions of people have immigrated to the United States") does not. It is out of place and should not be included with this main point.

If you find such a situation in your own speeches, try to reorganize your supporting points under appropriate main points, like this:

I. Over the years, millions of people have immigrated to the United States.
   A. Since the Civil War, 75 million people have immigrated to the United States.
   B. Today there are 45 million Americans who were born in other countries.

II. There are several reasons why people immigrate to the United States.
   A. Many people immigrate in search of economic opportunity.
   B. Others immigrate to attain political freedom.
   C. Still others immigrate to escape religious persecution.

Now you have two supporting points to back up your "millions of people" point and three supporting points to back up your "reasons" point.

Once you have organized your main points and supporting points, you must give attention to the third element in the body of a speech—connectives.

Connectives

Sierra Winston was speaking to her class about police-community relations. She had rehearsed the speech several times, had a well-defined central idea, three sharp main points, and strong evidence to support her position. But when Sierra delivered the

 **checklist**

Main Points

YES	NO	
☐	☐	1. Does the body of my speech contain two to five main points?
☐	☐	2. Are my main points organized according to one of the following methods of organization?
		Chronological order
		Spatial order
		Causal order
		Topical order
		Problem-solution order
☐	☐	3. Are my main points clearly separate from one another?
☐	☐	4. As much as possible, have I used the same pattern of wording for all my main points?
☐	☐	5. Have I roughly balanced the amount of time devoted to each main point?
☐	☐	6. Is each main point backed up with strong, credible supporting materials?
☐	☐	7. Do I use connectives to make sure my audience knows when I am moving from one main point to another?

speech, she said "All right" every time she moved from one thought to the next. After a while, her classmates started counting. By the end of the speech, most were too busy waiting for the next "All right" to pay attention to Sierra's message. Afterward, Sierra said, "I never even thought about saying 'All right.' I guess it just popped out when I didn't know what else to say."

We all have stock phrases that we use to fill the space between thoughts. In casual conversation they are seldom troublesome. But in speechmaking they distract listeners by calling attention to themselves.

What Sierra's speech lacked were strong *connectives*—words or phrases that join one thought to another and indicate the relationship between them. Without connectives, a speech is disjointed and uncoordinated—much as a person would be without ligaments and tendons to join the bones and hold the organs in place. Four types of speech connectives are transitions, internal previews, internal summaries, and signposts.

connective
A word or phrase that connects the ideas of a speech and indicates the relationships among them.

TRANSITIONS

Transitions are words or phrases that indicate when a speaker has just completed one thought and is moving on to another. Technically, transitions state both the idea the speaker is leaving and the idea she or he is coming up to. In the following examples, the transitional phrases are underlined:

transition
A word or phrase that indicates when a speaker has finished one thought and is moving on to another.

> Now that we have a clear understanding of the problem, let me share the solution with you.

> I have spoken so far of César Chávez the community organizer, but it was his work as a labor leader that truly etched his name into American history.

> Keeping these points in mind about sign language, let's return to the sentence I started with and see if we can learn the signs for "You are my friend."

Notice how these phrases remind the listener of the thought just completed, and reveal the thought about to be developed.

INTERNAL PREVIEWS

Internal previews let the audience know what the speaker will take up next, but they are more detailed than transitions. In effect, an internal preview works just like the preview statement in a speech introduction, except that it comes in the body of the speech—usually as the speaker is starting to discuss a main point. For example:

internal preview
A statement in the body of the speech that lets the audience know what the speaker is going to discuss next.

> In discussing how Asian Americans have been stereotyped in the mass media, we'll look first at the origins of the problem and second at its continuing impact today.

After hearing this, the audience knows exactly what to listen for as the speaker develops the "problem" main point.

Internal previews are often combined with transitions. For example:

> [*Transition*]: Now that we have seen how serious the problem of faulty credit reports is, let's look at some solutions. [*Internal Preview*]: I will focus

on three solutions—instituting tighter government regulation of credit bureaus, holding credit bureaus financially responsible for their errors, and giving individuals easier access to their credit reports.

You will seldom need an internal preview for each main point in your speech, but be sure to use one whenever you think it will help listeners keep track of your ideas.

INTERNAL SUMMARIES

internal summary
A statement in the body of the speech that summarizes the speaker's preceding point(s).

Internal summaries are the reverse of internal previews. Rather than letting listeners know what is coming up next, internal summaries remind listeners of what they have just heard. Such summaries are often used when a speaker finishes a complicated or particularly important main point or set of main points. For example:

> In short, palm reading is an ancient art. Developed in China more than 5,000 years ago, it was practiced in classical Greece and Rome, flourished during the Middle Ages, survived the Industrial Revolution, and remains popular today in many parts of the world.

Internal summaries are an excellent way to clarify and reinforce ideas. By combining them with transitions, you can also lead your audience smoothly into your next main point:

> [*Internal Summary*]: Let's pause for a moment to summarize what we have found so far. First, we have seen that keeping killer whales in captivity stunts their mental and physical development. Second, we have seen that keeping killer whales in captivity endangers other animals and human trainers. [*Transition*]: We are now in position to see what can be done to keep killer whales out of captivity.

SIGNPOSTS

signpost
A very brief statement that indicates where a speaker is in the speech or that focuses attention on key ideas.

Signposts are very brief statements that indicate exactly where you are in the speech. Frequently they are just numbers. Here is how one student used simple numerical signposts to help her audience keep track of the major causes for the continuing problem of famine in Africa:

> The first cause of this problem is inefficient agricultural production.
>
> The second cause is recurrent drought in the affected countries.
>
> The final cause is mismanagement of available food resources by local leaders.

Another way to accomplish the same thing is to introduce your main points with a question, as did one student in her speech on deteriorating public-school buildings in the United States. Her first main point showed that school buildings are crumbling in an alarming number of communities across the country. She introduced it this way:

> So how serious is the problem of decaying school buildings? Is it happening in just a few isolated districts, or is it widespread?

Experienced speakers include transitions and other connectives to help listeners keep track of their ideas. Here Alex Padilla speaks at a press conference on land and river conservation in California.

Carolyn Cole/Los Angeles Times/Getty Images

Her second main point dealt with ways to reinvest in public-school infrastructure. She introduced it by saying:

> So how can we solve this problem? Is there a way to save our schools while remaining financially responsible?

Questions are particularly effective as signposts because they invite subliminal answers that get the audience more involved with the speech.

Besides using signposts to indicate where you are in the speech, you can use them to focus attention on key ideas. You can do this with a simple phrase, as in the following example:

> The most important thing to remember about abstract art is that it is always based on forms in the natural world.

The underlined words alert the audience to the fact that an especially significant point is coming up. So do phrases such as these:

> Be sure to keep this in mind . . .
> This is crucial to understanding the rest of the speech . . .
> Above all, you need to know . . .

Depending on the needs of your speech, you may want to use two, three, or even all four kinds of connectives in combination. You needn't worry too much about what they are called—whether this one is a signpost and that a transition. The important thing is to be aware of their functions. Properly applied, connectives can make your speeches more unified and coherent.

Summary

Clear organization is vital to speechmaking. Listeners demand coherence. They get only one chance to grasp a speaker's ideas, and they have little patience for speakers who ramble aimlessly from one idea to another. A well-organized speech will enhance your credibility and make it easier for the audience to understand your message.

The process of planning the body of a speech begins when you determine the main points. You should choose them carefully, phrase them precisely, and organize them strategically. Because listeners cannot keep track of a multitude of main points, most speeches should contain no more than two to five. Each should focus on a single idea, should be worded clearly, and should receive enough emphasis to be clear and convincing.

You can organize main points in various ways, depending on your topic, purpose, and audience. Chronological order follows a time pattern, whereas spatial order follows a directional pattern. In causal order, main points are organized according to their cause-effect relationship. Topical order results when you divide your main topic into subtopics. Problem-solution order breaks the body of the speech into two main parts—the first showing a problem, the second giving a solution.

Supporting materials are the backup ideas for your main points. When organizing supporting materials, make sure they are directly relevant to the main points they are supposed to support.

Connectives help tie a speech together. They are words or phrases that join one thought to another and indicate the relationship between them. The four major types of speech connectives are transitions, internal previews, internal summaries, and signposts. Using them effectively will make your speeches more unified and coherent.

Key Terms

strategic organization (156)

main points (156)

chronological order (159)

spatial order (159)

causal order (160)

problem-solution order (161)

topical order (162)

supporting materials (165)

connective (167)

transition (167)

internal preview (167)

internal summary (168)

signpost (168)

Review Questions

After reading this chapter, you should be able to answer the following questions:

1. Why is it important that speeches be organized clearly and coherently?

2. How many main points will your speeches usually contain? Why is it important to limit the number of main points in your speeches?

3. What are the five basic patterns of organizing main points in a speech? Which are appropriate for informative speeches? Which is most appropriate for persuasive speeches? Which is used most often?

4. What are three tips for preparing your main points?

5. What is the most important thing to remember when organizing supporting materials in the body of your speech?

6. What are the four kinds of speech connectives? What role does each play in a speech?

Exercises for Critical Thinking

1. What organizational method (or methods) might you use to arrange main points for speeches with the following specific purpose statements?

   To inform my audience about the geographical regions of Argentina.

   To persuade my audience that the state legislature should enact tougher laws to curb the problem of predatory lending to college students.

   To inform my audience about the causes and effects of Lyme disease.

   To inform my audience about the major kinds of symbols used in Native American art.

2. Turn to the outline of main points and supporting materials for the speech about hypnosis on page 165. Create appropriate transitions, internal previews, internal summaries, and signposts for the speech.

3. Identify the organizational method used in each of the following sets of main points.

   I. Mardi Gras parades are lavish events that take place over the course of several weeks.
   II. Mardi Gras costumes include disguises, medallions, and the colors purple, green, and gold.
   III. Mardi Gras food features Cajun and Creole dishes common to southern Louisiana.

   I. In ancient Rome, the Colosseum hosted gladiatorial games and other kinds of popular entertainment.
   II. In the Middle Ages, the Colosseum was occupied by religious groups and used as a cemetery.
   III. In modern times, the Colosseum has been restored and turned into a tourist attraction.

   I. Human trafficking is a widespread national problem.
   II. The problem can be solved by a combination of national and international action.

End Notes

[1]Ernest C. Thompson, "An Experimental Investigation of the Relative Effectiveness of Organizational Structure in Oral Communication," *Southern Speech Journal,* 26 (1960), pp. 59–69.

[2]Harry Sharp Jr. and Thomas McClung, "Effects of Organization on the Speaker's Ethos," *Speech Monographs,* 33 (1966), pp. 182–183.

[3]See, for example, B. Scott Titsworth and Joseph P. Mazer, "Clarity in Teaching and Learning: Conundrums, Consequences, and Opportunities," in Deanna L. Fassett and John T. Warren (eds.), *Sage Handbook of Communication and Instruction* (Thousand Oaks, CA: Sage, 2010), pp. 241–261; Amber L. Finn and Paul Schrodt, "Students' Perceived Understanding Mediates the Effects of Teacher Clarity and Nonverbal Immediacy on Learner Environment," *Communication Education,* 61 (2012), pp. 111–130.

10 Beginning and Ending the Speech

The Introduction

The Conclusion

Amid silence, the famous line fades up on-screen—"A long time ago in a galaxy far, far away. . . ." Then the title *Star Wars* appears, accompanied by an orchestral blast from the musical score. As the title recedes, three paragraphs of backstory—known as the "opening crawl"—slide past viewers, and the music transforms into notes that sound like echoes of space.

Since the original *Star Wars* movie debuted in 1977, subsequent installments have had practically the same opener—same line of text, title effect, music, and three-paragraph crawl. Why? The opener indicates to audiences that they are about to watch a *Star Wars* movie. It captures their attention and orients them to the story about to unfold. Without it, the movie would seem incomplete, and viewers would not be "primed" for the experience.

Similarly, almost every *Star Wars* movie ends the same way. Fresh from a battle against forces of the dark side, the protagonists stand together and stare heroically into the distance. The music—a variation on the theme that played at the beginning—swells to a triumphant climax. Then the film quickly transitions to the name of the director and the credits roll. If there were no such conclusion, if the action suddenly stopped and the screen went blank, the audience would be left unsatisfied.

Just as movies like *Star Wars* need appropriate beginnings and endings, so do speeches. The beginning, or introduction, prepares listeners for what is to come. The conclusion ties up the speech and alerts listeners that the speech is going to end. Ideally, it is a satisfying conclusion.

In this chapter, we explore the roles played by an introduction and a conclusion in speechmaking. We also discuss techniques aimed at fulfilling those roles. If you apply these techniques imaginatively, you will take a big step toward elevating your speeches from the ordinary to the splendid.

The Introduction

First impressions are important. A poor beginning may so distract or alienate listeners that the speaker can never fully recover. Moreover, getting off on the right foot is vital to a speaker's self-confidence. What could be more encouraging than watching your listeners' faces begin to register interest, attention, and pleasure? A good introduction, you will find, is an excellent confidence booster.

In most speech situations, the introduction has four objectives:

- Get the attention and interest of your audience.
- Reveal the topic of your speech.
- Establish your credibility and goodwill.
- Preview the body of the speech.

We'll look at each of these objectives in turn.

GET ATTENTION AND INTEREST

"Unless a speaker can interest his audience at once, his effort will be a failure." So said the great lawyer Clarence Darrow. If your topic is not one of extraordinary interest, your listeners are likely to say to themselves, "So what? Who cares?" A speaker can quickly lose an audience if she or he doesn't use the introduction to get their attention and quicken their interest.

Getting the initial attention of your audience is usually easy—even before you utter a single word. After you are introduced and step to the lectern, your audience will normally give you their attention. If they don't, wait patiently. Look directly at the audience without saying a word. In a few moments all talking and physical commotion will stop. Your listeners will be attentive. You will be ready to start speaking.

Keeping the attention of your audience once you start talking is more difficult. Here are the methods used most often. Employed individually or in combination, they will help get the audience caught up in your speech.

Relate the Topic to the Audience

People pay attention to things that affect them directly. If you can relate the topic to your listeners, they are much more likely to be interested in it.

Suppose, for example, that one of your classmates begins his speech like this:

> Today I am going to talk about dreams, a subject that has always fascinated me. I will look first at why we dream and then at how psychologists interpret the meaning of dreams.

This is certainly a clear introduction, but it is not one to get you hooked on the speech. Now what if your classmate were to begin his speech this way—as one student actually did:

> You're being chased by an object of unspeakable horror, yet your legs can only move in slow motion. Each step takes unbearably long, and your frantic struggle to run faster is hopeless. Your pursuer gets closer, and your desperation turns to terror. You're completely helpless—eye to eye with death.

A good introduction will get your speech off to a strong start. To be most effective, it should gain attention, relate the topic to the audience, and be delivered with strong eye contact.

Derek White/Getty Images

Then you wake up, gasping for air, your heart pounding, your face clammy with sweat. It takes a few minutes for your heart and breathing to slow down. You reassure yourself that it was "just a dream." Soon you drift back to sleep.

Even when you use other interest-arousing lures, you should always relate your topic to the audience. At times this will test your ingenuity, but it is imperative for an effective introduction.

State the Importance of Your Topic

Presumably, you think your speech is important. Tell your audience why they should think so, too. Here is how António Guterres, Secretary General of the United Nations, used this method in a speech about climate change at the One Planet Summit:

> Climate change is moving much faster than we are. Atmospheric levels of carbon dioxide are higher than they have been for 800,000 years. . . . The past five years have been the hottest period on record. We are in a war for the very existence of life on our planet as we know it.

This technique is easy to use when discussing social and political issues, but it is appropriate for other topics as well. Here's how one student handled it in a speech about beach volleyball:

> Beach volleyball has grown from summer fun to an intensely competitive international sport, with 5 million participants in the United States alone. It's the fastest growing sport in NCAA history, with more than 75 sanctioned programs in its first decade. At the Summer Olympics, tickets to beach volleyball often sell out sooner than any other sport.

connect

View the beginning of "In Your Dreams" in the online Media Library for this chapter (Video 10.1).

Today, we'll look at the history of beach volleyball and some of the reasons for its spectacular growth.

Whenever you discuss a topic whose importance may not be clear to the audience, you should think about ways to demonstrate its significance in the introduction.

Startle the Audience

One surefire way to arouse interest quickly is to startle your listeners with an arresting or intriguing statement. Everyone in the audience paid close attention after this speaker's introduction:

> Take a moment and think of the three women closest to you. Who comes to mind? Your mother? Your sister? Your girlfriend? Your wife? Your best friend? Now guess which one will be sexually assaulted during her lifetime. It's not a pleasant thought, but according to the U.S. Department of Justice, one of every three American women will be sexually assaulted sometime during her life.

Notice the buildup to the speaker's arresting statement, "Now guess which one will be sexually assaulted during her lifetime." This statement startles the audience—especially the men—and drives home at a personal level the problem of sexual assault against women.

This technique is highly effective and easy to use. Just be sure the startling introduction relates directly to the subject of your speech. If you choose a strong opening simply for its shock value and then go on to talk about something else, your audience will be confused and possibly annoyed.

Arouse the Curiosity of the Audience

People are curious. One way to draw them into your speech is with a series of statements that progressively whet their curiosity about the subject of the speech. For example:

> This past month, more than 1 billion people around the world skipped lunch every day. They ate no food of any kind and drank no liquid of any kind from sunup to sunset. They did this every day during the month, and they do the same thing every year. I myself did it.
>
> Why? Last month was a time for tending to the mind, the body, and the spirit. Last month was the Muslim holy month of Ramadan.

By building suspense about her subject, the speaker pulls her audience into the speech. Notice how much less effective the introduction would have been if she had simply said, "Today I am going to talk about Ramadan."

Question the Audience

Asking a rhetorical question is another way to get your listeners thinking about your speech. Sometimes a single question will do:

> How would you respond if a loved one was the victim of terrorism?
>
> What would you think if you went to the doctor because you were ill and she told you to watch *It's Always Sunny in Philadelphia* as part of your treatment?

connect™
View the beginning of "Ramadan" in the online Media Library for this chapter (Video 10.2).

rhetorical question
A question that the audience answers mentally rather than aloud.

In other circumstances, you may want to pose a series of questions, each of which draws the audience deeper and deeper into the speech. Here is how one speaker used this method:

> Have you ever gone fishing and lost a lure? Do you think about what happens to the lure? Do you wonder what happens when large fishing boats lose their equipment? What do you think happens to the nets, buoys, hooks, and lines that they leave in the ocean every day?
>
> The problem of equipment abandoned at sea by commercial fishermen is wreaking havoc on our environment. A recent study in *Scientific Reports* found that this "ghost gear" is responsible for destroying habitats, spreading harmful microplastics, and aiding invasive animal species.

When using this technique, be sure to pause for just a moment after each question. This adds dramatic impact and gives the question time to sink in. The audience, of course, will answer mentally—not aloud.

Begin with a Quotation

Another way to arouse the interest of your audience is to start with an attention-getting quotation. You might choose your quotation from Shakespeare or Confucius, from the Bible or Talmud, from a poem, song, or film. Here is how one student used a humorous quotation to begin a speech about the need for political reform in the U.S. Congress:

> Mark Twain once said, "It could probably be shown by facts and figures that there is no distinctly American criminal class except Congress."

You need not use a famous quotation. The following made an effective introduction for a speech about birdwatching:

> "It is a moment I will never forget. I glimpsed a flash of color in the thicket, and then I saw it—a Bachman's Warbler, one of the rarest birds in all of America. I was so excited I could barely keep my binoculars from shaking."
>
> This statement was made by my father. He is just one of the millions of people who have discovered the joys of birdwatching.

Notice that both of the quotations used here as examples are relatively short. Opening your speech with a lengthy quotation is a sure way to set your audience yawning.

Tell a Story

We all enjoy stories, especially if they are provocative, dramatic, or suspenseful. When it comes to speech introductions, stories are sometimes about well-known events or public figures. But they can also be based on the speaker's personal experience. Here is how one pre-med student used such a story. She began by recounting the first time she observed doctors performing surgery in the operating room:

> There I stood, wearing a surgical mask, in the middle of a large, brightly lit room. In the center of the room were five figures huddled over a table. I found it difficult to see since everything was draped in blue sheets, yet I didn't dare take a step toward the table.

Then one of the figures called to me, "Angela, get over here and take a closer look." My knees buckled as I walked through the sterile environment. But eventually I was there, standing over an unconscious body in the operating room.

View the beginning of "Hoping to Heal" in the online Media Library for this chapter (Video 10.3).

The effectiveness of any story—especially a personal one—hinges on the speaker's delivery as well as the content. As you can see from the excerpt of this speech on Video 10.3, the speaker uses pauses, eye contact, and changes in her tone of voice to help draw her audience into the speech. See if you can do the same in your introduction.

Use Visual Aids

Visual aids are most often found in the body of a speech, but they can also be used in the introduction. They are most effective when they provide images that enhance the impact of the speaker's words.

Consider, for example, a speech on the subject of phony pharmaceuticals, drugs that look like legitimate prescription drugs but that have been illegally manufactured with counterfeit ingredients that can cause serious harm—perhaps even death—to a person who ingests them. Here is how one speaker opened her remarks on this topic:

Take a look at these two pills. Do you notice a difference between them? How about these two? Do you see a difference here? How about these?

✓ checklist

Speech Introduction

YES	NO	
☐	☐	1. Do I gain the attention and interest of my audience by using one or more of the methods discussed in this chapter?
☐	☐	2. Do I relate the speech topic to my audience?
☐	☐	3. Do I clearly reveal the topic of my speech?
☐	☐	4. Do I establish my credibility to speak on this topic?
☐	☐	5. If my topic is controversial, do I take steps to establish my goodwill toward the audience?
☐	☐	6. Do I define any key terms that will be necessary for the audience to understand the rest of my speech?
☐	☐	7. Do I provide a preview statement of the main points to be covered in the body of the speech?
☐	☐	8. Is the introduction limited to 10 to 20 percent of my entire speech?
☐	☐	9. Have I worked out the language of my introduction in detail?
☐	☐	10. Have I practiced the delivery of my introduction so I can present it fluently, confidently, and with strong eye contact?

As you work on your speeches, keep an eye out for quotations, stories, and other materials you can use to craft an introduction that will capture the attention of your listeners.

Cavan Images/Shutterstock

As she talked, the speaker showed photographs of three sets of pills. Each set looked identical. But in fact they were far from identical, as the speaker explained:

> To the naked eye, these pills are indistinguishable. But at a chemical level, they are very, very different. In each case, the pill on the left is real; it will help you get better. The pill on the right is counterfeit; it will not help you get better. In some cases, it may even kill you.

As you can see from Video 10.4, it was a creative—and compelling—way to start. The speaker used questions to arouse curiosity. She related to the audience by addressing them as "you." And she startled them by stating that a counterfeit pill could kill them. But it was her visual aids that pulled the whole introduction together and made it work.

If you are thinking about using visual aids in your introduction, keep in mind that they are effective only when they are chosen strategically, relate directly to the speech topic, and are in good taste. Using visual aids for their own sake or purely for shock value is always counterproductive. (See Chapter 14 for a full discussion of visual aids.)

The eight methods discussed in this section are those used most often by student speakers to gain attention and interest. Other methods include referring to the occasion, inviting audience participation, relating to a previous speaker, and using humor. For any given speech, try to use the method—or combination of methods—that is most suitable for the topic, the audience, and the occasion.

REVEAL THE TOPIC

In the process of gaining attention, be sure to state clearly the topic of your speech. If you do not, your listeners will be confused. And once they are confused, your chances of getting them absorbed in the speech are almost nil.

This is a basic point—so basic that it may hardly seem worth mentioning. Yet you would be surprised how many students need to be reminded of it. You may hear

connect

View the beginning of "Phony Pharmaceuticals" in the online Media Library for this chapter (Video 10.4).

speeches in your own class in which the topic is not clear by the end of the introduction. So you will know what to avoid, here is such an introduction, presented in a public speaking class:

> Imagine taking a leisurely boat ride along a peaceful waterway. The sun is high in the sky, reflecting brightly off the ripples around you. The banks are lush with mangrove and cypress trees. You see a stately pelican resting on a low-lying branch. You grab your camera, snap a shot, and check the result. The picture is perfect. But will it be perfect in the future?

What is the topic of this speech? Nature photography? No. Birding? No. Tourism in the tropics? No. The student was talking about efforts to restore the natural beauty of the Florida Everglades. But she did not make that clear to her audience. Suppose, instead, she had begun her speech differently:

> Alligators, panthers, otters, brown pelicans—these and other creatures have lost 50 percent of their habitat in south Florida over the past few decades. Now, however, there is a $10.5 billion program to preserve their home in the Florida Everglades. The largest restoration effort in the history of the world, it will rejuvenate one of America's most diverse ecosystems and protect it for future generations.

This opening would have provided a way to get the audience's attention, but it also would have related directly to the speech topic. If you beat around the bush in your introduction, you may lose your listeners. Even if they already know your topic, you should restate it clearly and concisely at some point in the introduction.

ESTABLISH CREDIBILITY AND GOODWILL

Besides getting attention and revealing the topic, there is a third objective you may need to accomplish in your introduction—establishing your credibility and goodwill.

credibility
The audience's perception of whether a speaker is qualified to speak on a given topic.

Credibility is mostly a matter of being qualified to speak on a given topic—and of being *perceived* as qualified by your listeners. Here is how one student established her credibility on the subject of meditation without sounding like a braggart:

> I've been practicing meditation for about four years, since my junior year of high school, and it has truly changed my life. I also did a great deal of research for this speech, and I hope to persuade each of you to begin daily meditation.
>
> It isn't a magic cure-all for every problem we face, but if your experience is like mine, you'll be pleasantly surprised by what it can do for you. Let's start by taking a closer look at the need to meditate.

connect
View this excerpt from the introduction of "Mindfulness Meditation" in the online Media Library for this chapter (Video 10.5).

Whether or not you have meditated yourself, you will probably be more interested in the speech when you realize that the speaker knows what she is talking about.

Your credibility need not be based on firsthand knowledge and experience. It can come from reading, from classes, from interviews, from friends—as in these cases:

> I have been interested in the myth of Atlantis for several years, and I have read a number of books and articles about it.

Telling a story is an excellent way to gain attention in a speech introduction. The story should be clearly relevant to the topic and should be delivered expressively and with strong eye contact.

FatCamera/Getty Images

> The information I'm going to share with you today comes mostly from my criminal justice class and an interview with Aisha Bigsby of the public defender's office.

Whatever the source of your expertise, be sure to let the audience know.

Establishing your *goodwill* is a slightly different challenge. It is often crucial outside the classroom, where speakers have well-established reputations and may be identified with causes that arouse hostility among listeners. In such a situation, the speaker must try to defuse that hostility right at the start of the speech.

Occasionally you may have to do the same thing in your classroom speeches. Suppose you advocate a potentially unpopular position. You will need to make a special effort to ensure that your classmates will consider your point of view. This is how one student tried to minimize her classmates' opposition in the introduction of a speech urging them to live without social media:

goodwill
The audience's perception of whether the speaker has the best interests of the audience in mind.

> I understand this sounds extreme. Who doesn't like to see photos of friends and videos of cute animals? Before I tried turning off my social-media accounts, I was really anxious about missing out on all the fun. But it ended up being one of the best decisions I've made. If you don't believe me, try it yourself—turn off social media for one month. I'm convinced you'll see a difference in your outlook on life.

The speaker was clear about her intentions and reasonable in her expectations. By the end of the introduction, the audience knew she had their best interests at heart.

PREVIEW THE BODY OF THE SPEECH

As we saw in Chapter 3, most people are poor listeners. Even good listeners need all the help they can get in sorting out a speaker's ideas. One way to help your listeners is to tell them in the introduction what they should listen for in the rest of the speech.

Here is an excellent example from a speech by Linda Thomas-Greenfield, U.S. Ambassador to the United Nations:

> Today, I'd like to talk about three aspects of the Middle East peace process: first, the United States' continued support for Israel; second, our desire to see both Israelis and Palestinians take steps toward a two-state solution; and third, our goal of delivering aid to the Palestinian people.

After this introduction, there was no doubt about Thomas-Greenfield's topic or the main points she would cover in her speech.

In some types of persuasive speeches, you may not want to reveal your central idea until later in the speech. But even in such a situation you must be sure your audience is not left guessing about the main points they should listen for as the speech unfolds. Nearly always, you should include a preview statement like the following:

> I've been fascinated by the Statue of Liberty since I was a kid, but I never knew how amazing it is until I researched it for this speech. This morning, I'd like to tell you about its symbolism, its history, and its architecture.

> I firmly believe in opening the doors of higher education to everyone. Today I hope to convince you that our state should make community college free for all residents. But before getting into the plan, let's look at the need to help more people attend college.

Preview statements such as these serve another purpose as well. Because they usually come at the very end of the introduction, they provide a smooth lead-in to the body of the speech. They signal that the body of the speech is about to begin.

There is one other aspect you may want to cover in previewing your speech. You can use your introduction to give specialized information—definitions or background—that your listeners will need if they are to understand the rest of the speech. Often you can do this very quickly, as in the following example:

> A triathlon is a race made up of three different events completed in succession. The events are usually swimming, biking, and running, though canoeing is sometimes substituted for one of these.

In other circumstances, you may have to explain an important term in more detail. Here is how one student handled the problem in a speech calling for the creation of a living-wage policy to replace the current minimum wage:

connect

View this excerpt from "The Living-Wage Solution" in the online Media Library for this chapter (Video 10.6).

> What is the living wage, you ask? Well, it's not the same as the minimum wage. The minimum wage is set by Congress and is the same in every part of the country. The living wage goes beyond the minimum wage.

> As the *Wall Street Journal* reports, the living wage is tied to the local cost of living and can vary from location to location. Its purpose is to help workers and their families meet a basic standard of living, even when that standard of living is higher than the minimum wage.

SAMPLE INTRODUCTION WITH COMMENTARY

So far we have seen many excerpts showing how to fulfill the various objectives of an introduction. Now here is a complete introduction from a student speech. The side comments indicate the principles used in developing the introduction.

Space Junk

COMMENTARY	SPEECH

The speaker begins by relating the topic to her audience. Then she arouses curiosity by referring to "something not so beautiful" that lurks just outside our atmosphere.

Tonight, after the sun goes down, I'd like you to step outside, lift your eyes to the heavens, and gaze at the night sky. If it's clear, you'll be able to see the moon, the stars, and distant planets. Yet right outside our atmosphere is something not so beautiful, something that *Scientific American* calls "a minefield in Earth orbit."

Now the speaker reveals her topic and defines what space junk is. The imagery of it as a floating landfill is very effective. Statistics from the European Space Agency quantify the amount of space junk.

Another name for this minefield is junk—space junk. Satellites that no longer work, pieces from spent rockets, debris from the collision of man-made objects—together they form a floating landfill that orbits the earth at speeds of over 18,000 miles per hour. The European Space Agency estimates that there are hundreds of thousands of pieces of space junk.

The speaker explains her interest in the topic and establishes her credibility.

I first learned about space junk last year in my physics class. Now, after doing research for this speech, I understand why there's an international effort to clean up the landfill whirling around our planet.

The introduction ends by previewing the main points to be discussed in the body.

Today we'll look first at the history of space junk, then at the way it's affecting space exploration, and finally at some proposals scientists have advanced to clean it up.

TIPS FOR THE INTRODUCTION

1. Keep the introduction relatively brief. Under normal circumstances it should not constitute more than 10 to 20 percent of your speech.

2. Be on the lookout for possible introductory materials as you do your research. File them with your notes so they will be handy when you are ready for them.

3. Be creative in devising your introduction. Experiment with two or three different openings and choose the one that seems most likely to get the audience interested in your speech.

4. Don't worry about the exact wording of your introduction until you have finished preparing the body of the speech. After you have determined your main points, it will be much easier to make final decisions about how to begin the speech.

5. Work out your introduction in detail. Some teachers recommend that you write it out word for word; others prefer that you outline it. Whichever method you use, practice the introduction over and over until you can deliver it smoothly from a minimum of notes and with strong eye contact.

6. When you present the speech, don't start talking too soon. Make sure the audience has quieted down and is focused on you before you begin. Establish eye contact, smile, and then launch into your opening words. Give yourself every chance to make sure your introduction has the desired impact.

connect
View the introduction of "Space Junk" in the online Media Library for this chapter (Video 10.7).

The Conclusion

"Great is the art of beginning," said Longfellow, "but greater the art is of ending." Longfellow was thinking of poetry, but his insight is equally applicable to public speaking. Many a speaker has marred an otherwise fine speech by a long-winded, silly, or antagonistic conclusion. Your closing remarks are your last chance to drive home your ideas. Moreover, your final impression will probably linger in your listeners' minds. Thus you need to craft your conclusion with as much care as your introduction.

No matter what kind of speech you are giving, the conclusion has two major functions:

- To let the audience know you are ending the speech.
- To reinforce the audience's understanding of, or commitment to, the central idea.

Let us look at each.

SIGNAL THE END OF THE SPEECH

It may seem obvious that you should let your audience know you are going to stop soon. However, you will almost certainly hear speeches in your class in which the speaker concludes so abruptly that you are taken by surprise. Too sudden an ending leaves the audience puzzled and unfulfilled.

How do you let an audience know your speech is ending? One way is through what you say. "In conclusion," "My purpose has been," "Let me end by saying"—these are all brief cues that you are getting ready to stop.

crescendo ending
A conclusion in which the speech builds to a zenith of power and intensity.

You can also let your audience know the end is in sight by your manner of delivery. The conclusion is the climax of a speech. A speaker who has carefully built to a peak of interest and involvement will not need to say anything like "in conclusion." By use of the voice—its tone, pacing, intonation, and rhythm—a speaker can build the momentum of a speech so there is no doubt when it is over.

One method of doing this has been likened to a musical crescendo. As in a symphony in which one instrument after another joins in until the entire orchestra is playing, the speech builds in force until it reaches a zenith of power and intensity.[1] (This does *not* mean simply getting louder and louder. It is a combination of many things, including vocal pitch, choice of words, dramatic content, gestures, pauses—and possibly loudness.)

A superb example of this method is the conclusion to Martin Luther King's "I've Been to the Mountaintop," the speech he delivered the night before he was assassinated in April 1968. Speaking to an audience of 2,000 people in Memphis, Tennessee, he ended his speech with a stirring declaration that the civil rights movement would succeed despite the many threats on his life. As the speech approached its climax, King stated that God had allowed him to climb the mountain and look over the Promised Land of equality and justice. Then, with soaring voice, he ended with the monumental words of the "Battle Hymn of the Republic": "Mine eyes have seen the glory of the coming of the Lord!" The audience erupted in thunderous applause.[2]

Another effective method might be compared to the dissolve ending of a concert song that evokes deep emotions: "The song seems to fade away while the light on the singer shrinks gradually to a smaller and smaller circle until it lights only the face, then the eyes. Finally, it is a pinpoint, and disappears with the last note of the song."[3]

The dissolve ending brings a speech to an emotional close by fading to a dramatic final statement. That's what one student did with great effect in a speech about visiting her grandparents' family farm as a young girl. During the body of her speech, the student spoke about the sights and sounds of the farm, the love and laughter she shared there as a child. Then, in conclusion, she evoked the images and sentiments of the farm one last time to create a moving dissolve ending:

dissolve ending
A conclusion that generates emotional appeal by fading step by step to a dramatic final statement.

> Now, as with so much of our childhood, the farm is no longer the same. Grandpa is gone. The barn has been rebuilt. The softball sits idly on the shelf. Grandma no longer cooks her huge family dinners. Going to the farm is different without these pleasures. But still the memories remain. I can still see the fields. I can still smell the hay. I can still hear the laughter. I can still feel the love.

Both the crescendo and dissolve endings must be worked out with great care. Practice until you get the words and the timing just right. The benefits will be well worth your time.

REINFORCE THE CENTRAL IDEA

The second major function of a conclusion is to reinforce the audience's understanding of, or commitment to, the central idea. There are many ways to do this. Here are the ones you are most likely to use.

Using public speaking in your CAREER

Your degree in civil engineering has served you well and you are now the chief city planner for a major metropolis. After studying the issue for more than a year, you and the planning commission have decided that the best way to relieve the city's growing traffic congestion is to build a new downtown freeway. Unfortunately, there is no way to build the freeway without knocking down a number of houses and businesses.

Not surprisingly, the neighborhood association that represents the area through which the new freeway will run has expressed a number of concerns about the proposal. Because of your excellent public speaking skills, you have been chosen to represent the city at a meeting of the neighborhood association. You know that if your speech is to be persuasive, you must use the introduction to establish your credibility and goodwill so your listeners will be willing to listen receptively to what you say in the body.

Write a draft of your introduction. Be sure to address all four functions of a speech introduction discussed in this chapter.

VGstockstudio/Shutterstock

The conclusion is your last chance to drive home your ideas. As you develop your conclusion, try to finish on a strong note that reinforces your main points and leaves a positive impression on listeners.
fizkes/Getty Images

Summarize Your Speech

Restating the main points is the easiest way to end a speech. One student used this technique effectively in his persuasive speech about the resurgence of tuberculosis as a worldwide killer:

> In conclusion, we have seen how tuberculosis has recently returned as a global health crisis. It is infecting and killing on an unprecedented scale. Especially in third-world countries, TB is decimating those who need the most help.
>
> But there is hope. The World Health Organization and privileged countries like the United States can expand their efforts to treat and prevent TB. We have the money and we have the know-how. Now we just need to come together and put an end to this epidemic.

connect

View the conclusion of "TB: An Ancient Plague Returns" in the online Media Library for this chapter (Video 10.8).

The value of a summary is that it explicitly restates the central idea and main points one last time. But as we shall see, there are more imaginative and compelling ways to end a speech. They can be used in combination with a summary or, at times, in place of it.

End with a Quotation

A quotation is one of the most common and effective devices to conclude a speech. Here is a fine example, from a speech on volunteering for Second Harvest Food Bank:

> None of us have the extra time that we'd like. But when you spend the precious little time that you have helping others, you'll know it was time well spent. In the words of the great poet Maya Angelou, "Try to be a rainbow in someone's cloud."

The closing quotation is particularly good because its hopeful tone is exactly suited to the speech. When you run across a *brief* quotation that so perfectly captures your central idea, keep it in mind as a possible conclusion.

Make a Dramatic Statement

Rather than using a quotation to give your conclusion force and vitality, you may want to devise your own dramatic statement. Some speeches have become famous because of their powerful closing lines. One is Patrick Henry's legendary "Liberty or Death" oration. It takes its name from the final sentences Henry uttered on March 23, 1775, as he exhorted his audience to resist British tyranny:

> Is life so dear, or peace so sweet, as to be purchased at the price of chains and slavery? Forbid it, Almighty God! I know not what course others may take; but as for me, give me liberty, or give me death!

Although your classroom speeches are not likely to become famous, you can still rivet your listeners—as Henry did—with a dramatic concluding statement. What follows is a particularly striking example, from a speech on suicide prevention. Throughout the speech, the student referred to a friend who had tried to commit suicide the previous year. Then, in the conclusion, she said:

> My friend is back in school, participating in activities she never did before—and enjoying it. I'm happy and proud to say that she's still fighting for her life and even happier that she failed to kill herself. Otherwise, I wouldn't be here today trying to help you. You see, I am my "friend," and I'm more than glad to say I've made it.

As you can imagine, the audience was stunned. The closing lines brought the speech to a dramatic conclusion. The speaker made it even more effective by pausing just a moment before the last words and by using her voice to give them just the right inflection.

✔ checklist

Speech Conclusion

YES	NO	
☐	☐	1. Do I signal that my speech is coming to an end?
☐	☐	2. Do I reinforce my central idea by:
		Summarizing the main points of my speech?
		Ending with a quotation?
		Making a dramatic statement?
		Referring to the introduction?
☐	☐	3. Is the conclusion limited to 5 to 10 percent of my entire speech?
☐	☐	4. Have I worked out the language of my conclusion in detail?
☐	☐	5. Have I practiced the delivery of my conclusion so I can present it fluently, confidently, and with strong eye contact?

Refer to the Introduction

An excellent way to give your speech psychological unity is to conclude by referring to ideas in the introduction. Here is how one student used the method in her speech about massive wildfires in the western United States:

connect

View the beginning and ending of "Raging Wildfires" in the online Media Library for this chapter (Video 10.9).

Introduction Toby Wait and his family saw the billowing smoke over the horizon, but it seemed far away from their home in Big Creek, California. That night, however, Toby woke up at 4 am to a pitch-black night vibrating with an intense orange. The wildfire was upon them. Toby, his family, and their three dogs hopped in their car and sped away, the hungry fire pursuing them down the mountain.

This was just one of countless scenes from the 2020 wildfire season in the western U.S. It was the biggest wildfire season on record, burning an estimated 10.3 million acres. At least 43 people died directly from the fires and the number of indirect deaths topped 3,000. These numbers are going to get worse before they get better.

In the body of her speech, the student looked in detail at the problem of wildfires and explained steps for reducing them. Then, in her closing words, she tied the whole speech together by returning to the story described in her introduction:

Conclusion Remember Toby Wait and his family from the introduction of my speech? They managed to escape the blaze with their lives, but their home and belongings went up in flames. So did the homes and belongings of over 10,000 other families that year.

We can't stop climate change in the short run. But we can reduce fire losses with better planning and regular management. It's up to us to create a future where devastating wildfires are the exception, not the norm.

Summarizing the speech, ending with a quotation, making a dramatic statement, referring to the introduction—all these techniques can be used separately. But you have probably noticed that speakers often combine two or more in their conclusions. Actually, all four techniques can be fused into one—for example, a dramatic quotation that summarizes the central idea while referring to the introduction.

One other concluding technique is making a direct appeal to your audience for action. This technique applies only to a particular type of persuasive speech, however, and will be discussed in Chapter 16. The four methods covered in this chapter are appropriate for all kinds of speeches and occasions.

SAMPLE CONCLUSION WITH COMMENTARY

How do you fit these methods together to make a conclusion? Here is an example, from the speech about space junk whose introduction we looked at earlier (page 183).

Space Junk

After signaling the end of her speech, the speaker gives an excellent summary of her main points. This is usually standard practice in an informative speech.

In conclusion, while humans have managed to boldly go where no one has gone before, we've left a lot of garbage behind. Space junk is growing every day, and it poses serious problems for the future of space exploration. Fortunately, scientists from NASA and the international community are exploring ingenious ways of taking out the trash.

By echoing her opening scenario, the speaker unifies the entire speech. The final sentence provides a dramatic ending.

So the next time you're outside at night, lift your gaze upward. You'll see the moon, the stars, and perhaps a couple planets. But now you'll know there's a lot more up there than meets the eye.

TIPS FOR THE CONCLUSION

1. As with the introduction, keep an eye out for possible concluding materials as you research and develop the speech.

2. Conclude with a bang, not a whimper. Be creative in devising a conclusion that hits the hearts and minds of your audience. Work on several possible endings, and select the one that seems likely to have the greatest impact.

3. Don't be long-winded. The conclusion will normally make up no more than 5 to 10 percent of your speech.

4. Don't leave anything in your conclusion to chance. Work it out in detail, and give yourself plenty of time to practice delivering it. Many students like to write out the conclusion word for word to guarantee it is just right. If you do this, make sure you can present it smoothly, confidently, and with feeling—without relying on your notes or sounding wooden. Make your last impression as forceful and as favorable as you can.

connect

View the conclusion of "Space Junk" in the online Media Library for this chapter (Video 10.10).

Summary

First impressions are important. So are final impressions. This is why speeches need strong introductions and conclusions.

In most speech situations you need to accomplish four objectives with your introduction—get the attention and interest of the audience, reveal the topic of your speech, establish your credibility and goodwill, and preview the body of the speech. Gaining attention and interest can be done in several ways. You can show the importance of your topic, especially as it relates to your audience. You can startle or question your audience or arouse their curiosity. You can begin with a quotation, a story, or visual aids.

Be sure to state the topic of your speech clearly in your introduction so the audience knows where the speech is going. Establishing credibility means that you tell the audience why you are qualified to speak on the topic at hand. Establishing goodwill may be necessary if your point of view is unpopular. Previewing the body of the speech helps the audience listen effectively and provides a smooth lead-in to the body of the speech.

The first objective of a speech conclusion is to let the audience know you are ending, which you can do by your words or by your manner of delivery. The second objective of a conclusion is to reinforce your central idea. You can accomplish this by summarizing the speech, ending with a quotation, making a dramatic statement, or referring to the introduction. Sometimes you may want to combine two or more of these techniques. Be creative in devising a vivid, forceful conclusion.

Key Terms

rhetorical question (176)

credibility (180)

goodwill (181)

preview statement (182)

crescendo ending (184)

dissolve ending (185)

Review Questions

After reading this chapter, you should be able to answer the following questions:

1. What are the four objectives of a speech introduction?
2. What are eight methods you can use in the introduction to get the attention and interest of your audience?
3. Why is it important to establish your credibility at the beginning of your speech?
4. What is a preview statement? Why should you nearly always include a preview statement in the introduction of your speech?
5. What are six tips for your introduction?
6. What are the major functions of a speech conclusion?
7. What are two ways you can signal the end of your speech?
8. What are four ways to reinforce the central idea when concluding your speech?
9. What are four tips for your conclusion?

Exercises for Critical Thinking

1. Here are six speech topics. Explain how you might relate each to your classmates in the introduction of a speech.

   roller coasters

   performance-enhancing drugs

   laughter

   high blood pressure

   Australia

   Social Security

2. Think of a speech topic (preferably one for your next speech in class). Create an introduction for a speech dealing with any aspect of the topic you wish. In your introduction, be sure to gain the attention of the audience, to reveal the topic and relate it to the audience, to establish your credibility, and to preview the body of the speech.

3. Using the same topic as in Exercise 2, create a speech conclusion. Be sure to let your audience know the speech is ending, to reinforce the central idea, and to make the conclusion vivid and memorable.

End Notes

[1]Dorothy Sarnoff, *Speech Can Change Your Life* (Garden City, NY: Doubleday, 1970), p. 189.

[2]Martin Luther King, "I've Been to the Mountaintop," in Stephen E. Lucas and Martin J. Medhurst (eds.), *Words of a Century: The Top 100 American Speeches, 1900-1999* (New York: Oxford University Press, 2009), p. 480.

[3]Sarnoff, *Speech Can Change Your Life,* p. 190.

11

Outlining the Speech

Think what might happen if you tried to build a house without a floor plan or an architect's blueprint. You install a cathedral ceiling so you can have big windows and a huge ceiling fan, but the roof is so high it blocks your bedroom window upstairs. You put in sliding doors to the yard, but they can't be opened because they're too close to the fireplace to slide back without hitting it. You think it's a wonderful idea to have almost no interior walls. But when the first snowfall comes, your (unsupported) roof collapses.

Plans and blueprints are essential to architecture. So, too, are outlines essential to effective speeches. An outline is like a blueprint for your speech. It allows you to see the full scope and content of your speech at a glance. By outlining, you can judge whether each part of the speech is fully developed, whether you have adequate supporting materials for your main points, and whether the main points are properly balanced. An outline helps you make sure that related items are together, that ideas flow from one to another, that the structure of your speech will "stand up"—and not collapse.

Probably you will use two kinds of outlines for your speeches—one very detailed, for the planning stage, and one very brief, for the delivery of the speech.

The Preparation Outline

The preparation outline is just what its name implies—an outline that helps you prepare the speech. Writing a preparation outline means putting your speech together—deciding what you will say in the introduction, how you will organize the main points and supporting materials in the body, and what you will say in the conclusion.

GUIDELINES FOR THE PREPARATION OUTLINE

Over the years, a relatively uniform system for preparation outlines has developed. It is explained in this section and is exemplified in the sample outline on pages 199–201. You should check with your teacher to see what format you are to follow.

State the Specific Purpose of Your Speech

The specific purpose statement should be a separate unit that comes before the outline itself. Including the specific purpose makes it easier to assess how well you have constructed the speech to accomplish your purpose.

Identify the Central Idea

Some instructors prefer that the central idea be given immediately after the purpose statement. Others prefer that it be given and identified in the text of the outline. Check to see which your instructor wants.

Label the Introduction, Body, and Conclusion

If you label the parts of your speech, you will be sure that you indeed *have* an introduction and conclusion and have accomplished the essential objectives of each. Usually the names of the speech parts are placed in the middle of the page or in the far left margin. They are technical labels only and are not included in the system of symbolization used to identify main points and supporting materials.

Use a Consistent Pattern of Symbolization and Indentation

In the most common system of outlining, main points are identified by Roman numerals and are indented equally so as to be aligned down the page. Subpoints (components of the main points) are identified by capital letters and are also indented equally so as to be aligned with each other.

Beyond this, there may be sub-subpoints and even sub-sub-subpoints. For example:

I. Main point
   A. Subpoint
   B. Subpoint
       1. Sub-subpoint
       2. Sub-subpoint
           a. Sub-sub-subpoint
           b. Sub-sub-subpoint

II. Main point
   A. Subpoint
       1. Sub-subpoint
       2. Sub-subpoint
   B. Subpoint
       1. Sub-subpoint
       2. Sub-subpoint

The clear *visual framework* of this outline immediately shows the relationships among the ideas of the speech. The most important ideas (main points) are

---

preparation outline
A detailed outline developed during the process of speech preparation that includes the title, specific purpose, central idea, introduction, main points, subpoints, connectives, conclusion, and bibliography of a speech.

As blueprints are essential to architecture, so outlines are essential to speechmaking. Developing an outline helps ensure that the structure of your speech is clear and coherent.

Tomazl/E+/Getty Images

farthest to the left. Less important ideas (subpoints, sub-subpoints, and so on) are progressively farther to the right. This pattern reveals the structure of your entire speech.

Once you have organized the body of your speech (see Chapter 9), you should have identified the main points. You need only flesh out your outline with subpoints and sub-subpoints, as necessary, to support the main points. But suppose, as sometimes happens, you find yourself with a list of statements and are not sure which are main points, which are subpoints, and so forth. Such a list might look like this:

There were 13 people at the Last Supper—Jesus and his 12 disciples.

Many superstitions revolve around numbers.

In the United States, 13 is often omitted in the floor numbering of hotels and skyscrapers.

The number 13 has meant bad luck as long as anyone can remember.

Which statement is the main point? The second statement ("Many superstitions revolve around numbers") is broader in scope than any of the other statements. This would be one of the main ideas of your speech. The fourth statement is the subpoint; it immediately supports the main point. The other two statements are sub-subpoints; they illustrate the subpoint. Rearranged properly, they look like this:

I. Many superstitions revolve around numbers.
    A. The number 13 has meant bad luck as long as anyone can remember.
        1. There were 13 people at the Last Supper—Jesus and his 12 disciples.
        2. In the United States, 13 is often omitted in the floor numbering of hotels and skyscrapers.

visual framework
The pattern of symbolization and indentation in a speech outline that shows the relationships among the speaker's ideas.

Above all, remember that all points at the same level should immediately support the point that is just above and one notch to the left in your outline. If this sounds confusing, think of it as a business organization chart:

I. President
  A. Vice president—Operations
    1. Manager—Domestic Operations
      a. Assistant manager—East
      b. Assistant manager—West
    2. Manager—International Operations
      a. Assistant manager—Europe
      b. Assistant manager—Asia
      c. Assistant manager—Americas
  B. Vice president—Administration
    1. Manager—Finance
    2. Manager—Personnel

As you can see, every person on this chart reports to the person who is above and one notch to the left—except, of course, the president, who is the "main point."

State Main Points and Subpoints in Full Sentences

Following are two sets of main points and subpoints for the same speech on the life of Martin Luther King.

Ineffective	**More Effective**
I. Montgomery	I. King began his civil rights career in the Montgomery bus boycott of 1955–1956.
II. 1960s	II. King's greatest triumphs came during the early 1960s.
A. Birmingham	A. In 1963, he campaigned against segregation in Birmingham, Alabama.
B. March	B. Later that year, he participated in the famous march on Washington, D.C.
1. 200,000	1. More than 200,000 people took part.
2. "Dream"	2. King gave his "I Have a Dream" speech.
C. Prize	C. In 1964, he received the Nobel Peace Prize.
III. Final years	III. King faced great turmoil during his final years.
A. Criticized	A. He was criticized by more militant Blacks for being nonviolent.
B. Vietnam	B. He protested against the war in Vietnam.
C. Assassination	C. He was assassinated in Memphis, Tennessee, on April 4, 1968.

The sample on the left might serve as a speaking outline, but it is virtually useless as a preparation outline. It gives only vague labels rather than distinct ideas. It does not indicate clearly the content of the main points and subpoints. Nor does it reveal whether the speaker has thought out his or her ideas. But there is no concern about any of these matters with the outline on the right.

In sum, a skimpy preparation outline is of little value. Stating your main points and subpoints in full sentences will ensure that you develop your ideas fully.

Label Transitions, Internal Summaries, and Internal Previews

One way to make sure you have strong transitions, internal summaries, and internal previews is to include them in the preparation outline. Usually they are not incorporated into the system of symbolization and indentation but are labeled separately and inserted in the outline where they will appear in the speech.

Attach a Bibliography

You should include with the outline a bibliography that shows all the books, magazines, newspapers, and Internet sources you consulted, as well as any interviews or field research you conducted.

bibliography
A list of all the sources used in preparing a speech.

The two major bibliographic formats are those developed by the Modern Language Association (MLA) and the American Psychological Association (APA). Both are widely used by communication scholars; ask your instructor which he or she prefers. No matter which format you adopt, make sure your statement of sources is clear, accurate, and consistent. For help, turn to page 128 in Chapter 7, where you will find sample citations for the kinds of sources used most frequently in classroom speeches.

Give Your Speech a Title, If One Is Desired

In the classroom you probably do not need a title for your speech unless your teacher requires one. In some other situations, however, a speech title is necessary—as when the speech is publicized in advance or is going to be published. Whatever the reason, if you do decide to use a title, it should (1) be brief, (2) attract the attention of your audience, and (3) encapsulate the main thrust of your speech.

A good title need not have what Madison Avenue would call "sex appeal"—lots of glitter and pizzazz. By the same token, there is certainly nothing wrong with a catchy title—as long as it is germane to the speech. Here are two groups of titles. Those on the left are straightforward and descriptive. Those on the right are figurative alternatives to the ones on the left.

Group I	**Group II**
Gambling Addiction	Against All Odds
The Rage to Diet	The Art of Wishful Shrinking
Living with Deafness	The Sounds of Silence
The United States Mint	The Buck Starts Here

Which group do you prefer? There are advantages and disadvantages to both. Those in the first group clearly reveal the topic, but they are not as provocative as those in the second group. Those in the second group are sure to arouse interest, but they do not give as clear an idea of what the speeches are about.

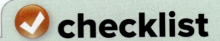

checklist

Preparation Outline

YES	NO	
☐	☐	1. Does my speech have a title, if one is required?
☐	☐	2. Do I state the specific purpose before the text of the outline itself?
☐	☐	3. Do I state the central idea before the text of the outline itself?
☐	☐	4. Are the introduction, body, and conclusion clearly labeled?
☐	☐	5. Are main points and subpoints written in full sentences?
☐	☐	6. Are transitions, internal summaries, and internal previews clearly labeled?
☐	☐	7. Does the outline follow a consistent pattern of symbolization and indentation?
☐	☐	8. Does the outline provide a clear visual framework that shows the relationships among the ideas of my speech?
☐	☐	9. Does the bibliography identify all the sources I consulted in preparing the outline?
☐	☐	10. Does the bibliography follow the format required by my instructor?

There is one other kind of title you should consider—the question. Phrasing your title as a question can be both descriptive and provocative. Using this method, we can construct a third set of titles combining the virtues of groups I and II:

Group III

Do You Really Think You Can Beat the Odds?

Diets: How Effective Are They?

Can You See What I'm Saying?

Where Is Making Money a Way of Life?

Sometimes you will choose a title for your speech very early. At other times you may not find one you like until the last minute. Either way, try to be resourceful about creating titles for your speeches. Experiment with several and choose the one that seems most appropriate.

SAMPLE PREPARATION OUTLINE WITH COMMENTARY

The following outline for a six-minute informative speech illustrates the principles just discussed. The commentary explains the procedures used in organizing the speech and writing the outline. (Check to see if your instructor wants you to include a title with your outline.)

Meadows of the Sea

Stating your specific purpose and central idea as separate units before the text of the outline makes it easier to judge how well you have constructed the outline to achieve your purpose and to communicate your central idea.

Labeling the introduction marks it as a distinct section that plays a special role in the speech.

The opening gets attention and, as it progresses, reveals the topic of the speech.

Here the speaker establishes her credibility and previews the main points of the body.

Including transitions ensures that the speaker has worked out how to connect one idea to the next.

Labeling the body marks it as a distinct section.

Main point I is phrased as a full sentence. The two subpoints of main point I are shown by the capital letters A and B and are also written in full sentences to ensure that the speaker has thought them out fully.

The progressive indentation shows visually the relationships among main points, subpoints, and sub-subpoints.

The transition shows how the speaker will get from main point I to main point II.

Specific Purpose: To inform my audience about the importance of seagrass to the environment.

Central Idea: Seagrass is a sprawling underwater organism that sustains marine life and can also help control climate change.

Introduction

I. It's one of the oldest living organisms on Earth, spanning some 116,000 square miles.
   A. What is it?
   B. None other than ordinary seagrass—the grass-looking plant that grows along seacoasts around the world.
II. From an ecological perspective, however, seagrass is anything but ordinary.
   A. Emmett Duffy of Smithsonian Marine Observatories compares seagrass to the famous Serengeti plain of Africa—except that seagrass exists totally underwater.
   B. Seagrass creates some of the most productive and vital ecosystems on the planet.
III. I learned about seagrass in my oceanography class, and I did additional research for this speech.
IV. Today I'd like to explain what seagrass is, its role in ocean life, and how it can combat climate change.

(*Transition:* Let's start by looking at what seagrass is.)

Body

I. Despite its name, seagrass is not technically a grass, but a unique underwater flowering plant.
   A. Unlike grass, it has roots, stems, and leaves, and it produces flowers and fruits.
   B. The National Oceanic and Atmospheric Administration explains that seagrass is the only flowering plant that can live completely submerged in marine environments.
      1. It has evolved to absorb oxygen and nutrients entirely from the water.
      2. It can pollinate and reproduce without ever touching the air.

(*Transition:* Now that you have a sense of what seagrass is, let's look at what it does.)

Like main point I, main point II is phrased as a full sentence.

II. Seagrass is vital to life in the oceans.
   A. First, seagrass provides a crucial food source.
      1. Some animals, like manatees and sea turtles, feed directly on seagrass.
      2. Other animals, including bottlenose dolphins, feed on the small organisms that live in seagrass.
   B. Second, seagrass provides a refuge for animals.
      1. Small fish, sea horses, clams, and others protect themselves by living in it.
      2. Some animals put their eggs and larvae in seagrass for protection from predators.
      3. Florida's Fish and Wildlife Conservation Commission calls seagrass an "essential nursery" for aquatic animals.

Points below the level of subpoint are indicated by Arabic numerals and lowercase letters.

The transition indicates that the speaker is moving to the next main point.

(*Transition:* But the importance of seagrass is not limited to life in the oceans.)

This main point, like the first two, is stated as a full sentence.

III. Properly cultivated, seagrass has the potential to combat climate change.
   A. As seagrass cycles nutrients and filters water, it also traps carbon dioxide in the seafloor.
      1. This is known as "carbon sequestration."
      2. The *Guardian* reports that seagrass can sequester carbon 35 times faster than rainforests.
      3. Seagrass accounts for 18 percent of the ocean's carbon sequestration, though it covers less than 1 percent of the ocean floor.
   B. This is why scientists are hard at work spreading seagrass to more parts of the ocean.
      1. One such scientist is Robert Orth of the Virginia Institute of Marine Science.
         a. As reported in *Smithsonian,* Orth and his team have been seeding areas where seagrass once dominated.
         b. Because of their efforts, we now have 13 square miles of new seagrass and carbon sequestration.
      2. The more seagrass scientists can plant, the better we can combat climate change.

Notice the pattern of subordination in this section. Subpoint B states that scientists are working on spreading seagrass. Sub-subpoint 1 notes that Robert Orth is a scientist leading this work. Because items a and b expand upon the point about Orth's work, they are subordinated to it.

Conclusion

I. In conclusion, the seas contain sprawling meadows of great importance.
   A. Seagrass is essential to life in the oceans.
   B. It can also help combat climate change.
II. So the next time you're at the beach enjoying the sun and the waves, think about those meadows of seagrass rolling beneath the surface.

Labeling the conclusion marks it as a distinct part of the speech.

Summarizing the main points is standard procedure in an informative speech.

The speaker's closing statement reinforces her central idea.

Bibliography

Courage, Katherine Harmon. "Prairies of the Sea." *Smithsonian,* Dec. 2020, www.smithsonianmag.com/science-nature/seagrass-ocean-secret-weapon. Accessed 14 Sept. 2022.

"Importance of Seagrass." Florida Fish and Wildlife Conservation Commission, myfwc.com/research/habitat/seagrasses/. Accessed 12 Sept. 2022.

Jiang, Zhijian, et al. "Home for Marine Species: Seagrass Leaves as Vital Spawning Grounds and Food Source." *Frontiers in Marine Science,* vol. 7, 2020, pp. 1–9.

McVeigh, Karen. "The Problem with Blue Carbon: Can Seagrass Be Replanted . . . by Hand?" *Guardian,* 5 Nov. 2021, www.theguardian.com/environment/ 2021/nov/05/. Accessed 14 Sept. 2022.

"Seagrass Are Flowering Plants That Grow Entirely Underwater." National Oceanic and Atmospheric Administration, floridakeys.noaa.gov/plants/seagrass.html. Accessed 12 Sept. 2022.

This is the final bibliography. It lists the sources actually used in writing the speech and is shorter than the preliminary bibliography compiled in the early stages of research. (See Chapter 7.)

This bibliography follows the Modern Language Association (MLA) format. Check with your instructor to see what format you should use for your bibliography.

Still have questions about outlining? If you log on to Connect, you will find additional resources to help you create effective preparation outlines. The Outline Tool will help you construct your own outlines from scratch following the guidelines in this chapter. There is also a program called EasyBib that can automatically format your speech bibliography in either APA or MLA format. Like many students before you, you can take advantage of these resources to improve your command of outlining principles and practices.

connect

The Outline Tool and EasyBib are available in Connect.

The Speaking Outline

"I was never so excited by public speaking before in my life," wrote one listener in 1820 after listening to Daniel Webster. "Three or four times I thought my temples would burst with the gush of blood. . . . I was beside myself, and am so still."[1]

Such reactions were not unusual among Webster's audiences. He thrilled two generations of Americans with his masterful orations. Incredible as it seems today, he did so while speaking for several hours at a time, often without using any notes! A reporter once asked how he managed this. "It is my memory," Webster said. "I can prepare a speech, revise and correct it in my memory, then deliver the corrected speech exactly as finished."[2]

Few people have Webster's remarkable powers of memory. Fortunately, it is no longer customary to speak from memory. Today most people speak extemporaneously—which means the speech is carefully prepared and practiced in advance, but much of the exact wording is selected while the speech is being delivered (see Chapter 13). Your speeches will probably be of this type. You should know, then, about the *speaking outline*—the most widely recommended form of notes for extemporaneous speeches.

The aim of a speaking outline is to help you remember what you want to say. In some ways, it is a condensed version of your preparation outline. It should contain

speaking outline
A brief outline used to jog a speaker's memory during the presentation of a speech.

key words or phrases to jog your memory, as well as essential statistics and quotations that you don't want to risk forgetting. But it should also include material *not* in your preparation outline—especially cues to direct and sharpen your delivery.

Most speakers develop their own variations on the speaking outline. As you acquire more experience, you, too, should feel free to experiment. But for now, your best bet is to follow the basic guidelines in this section and to use the sample speaking outline on pages 205–206 as your model. These guidelines are useful whether you're speaking to an in-person audience or an online audience.

GUIDELINES FOR THE SPEAKING OUTLINE

Follow the Visual Framework Used in the Preparation Outline

Your speaking outline should use the same visual framework—the same symbols and the same pattern of indentation—as your preparation outline. This will make it much easier to prepare the speaking outline. More important, it will allow you to see instantly where you are in the speech at any given moment while you are speaking. You will find this to be a great advantage. As you speak, you will look down at your outline periodically to make sure you are covering the right ideas in the right order.

Compare the following two versions of a partial speaking outline. They are from an informative speech about the history of the U.S. women's rights movement.

Ineffective	**More Effective**
I. 1840–1860	I. 1840–1860
A. World Anti-Slavery Convention	A. World Anti-Slavery Convention
B. Seneca Falls convention	B. Seneca Falls convention
1. Lucretia Mott	1. Lucretia Mott
2. Elizabeth Cady Stanton	2. Elizabeth Cady Stanton
3. Declaration of Sentiments	3. Declaration of Sentiments
II. 1900–1920	II. 1900–1920
A. National American Woman Suffrage Association	A. National American Woman Suffrage Association
1. Founding	1. Founding
2. Objectives	2. Objectives
B. Nineteenth Amendment	B. Nineteenth Amendment
1. Campaign	1. Campaign
2. Ratification	2. Ratification

The wording of both outlines is exactly the same. But the visual framework of the one on the right makes it easier to take in at a glance and reduces the odds of the speaker losing her or his place.

Make Sure the Outline Is Legible

Your speaking outline is all but worthless unless it is instantly readable at a distance. When you make your outline, use large lettering, leave extra space between lines, provide ample margins, and write or type on only one side of the paper.

Some speakers put their notes on index cards. Most find the 3 × 5 size too cramped and prefer the 4 × 6 or 5 × 8 size instead. Other people write their

Many experienced speakers are more comfortable with a brief set of notes, or no notes at all, which allows them to communicate directly with the audience.

Xuanyu Han/Getty Images

speaking outlines on regular paper. Either practice is fine, as long as your notes are immediately legible to you while you are speaking.

Keep the Outline as Brief as Possible

If your notes are too detailed, you will have difficulty maintaining eye contact with your audience. A detailed outline will tempt you to look at it far too often, as one student discovered:

> Khloe Nehls was speaking about America's opioid crisis. She had pre- pared the speech thoroughly and practiced it until it was nearly perfect. But when she delivered the speech in class, she referred constantly to her detailed notes. As a result, her delivery was choppy and strained. After the speech, Khloe's classmates remarked on how often she had looked at her notes, and she was amazed. "I didn't even know I was doing it," she said. "Most of the time I wasn't even paying attention to the outline. I knew the speech cold."

Many students have had the same experience. "As long as I have plenty of notes," they feel, "disaster will not strike." In fact, most beginning speakers use too many notes. Like Khloe, they don't need all of them to remember the speech, and they find that too many notes can actually interfere with good communication.

To guard against this, keep your speaking outline as brief as possible. It should contain key words or phrases to help you remember major points, subpoints, and connectives. If you are citing statistics, you will probably want to include them in your notes. Unless you are good at memorizing quotations, write them out fully as well. Finally, there may be two, three, or four key ideas whose wording is so important that you want to state them in simple complete sentences. The best rule is that your notes should be the *minimum* you need to jog your memory and keep you on track.

As the defense attorney in a car theft case, you need to prepare your closing argument to the jury before members begin their deliberations. After reviewing evidence from the trial, you decide to stress the following points to demonstrate the innocence of your client:

a. The stolen car was found abandoned three hours after the theft with the engine still warm; at the time the car was found, your client was at the airport to meet the flight of a friend who was flying into town.
b. Lab analysis of muddy shoe prints on the floor mat of the car indicates that the prints came from a size 13 shoe; your client wears a size 10.
c. Lab analysis shows the presence of cigarette smoke in the car, but your client does not smoke.
d. The only eyewitness to the crime, who was 50 feet from the car, said the thief "looked like" your client; yet the eyewitness admitted that at the time of the theft she was not wearing her glasses, which had been prescribed for improving distance vision.
e. The car was stolen at about 1 P.M.; your client testified that he was in a small town 250 miles away at 11 A.M.
f. In a statement to police, the eyewitness described the thief as blond; your client has red hair.

As you work on the outline of your speech, you see that these points can be organized into three main points, each with two supporting points. Compose an outline that organizes the points in this manner.

Stockbyte/Getty Images

Give Yourself Cues for Delivering the Speech

A good speaking outline reminds you not only of *what* you want to say but also of *how* you want to say it. As you practice the speech, you will decide that certain ideas and phrases need special emphasis—that they should be spoken more loudly, softly, slowly, or rapidly than other parts of the speech. You will also determine how you want to pace the speech—how you will control its timing, rhythm, and momentum. But no matter how you work these things out ahead of time, no matter how often you practice, it is easy to forget them once you get in front of an audience.

The solution is to include in your speaking outline delivery cues—directions for delivering the speech. One way to do this is by underlining or otherwise highlighting key ideas that you want to be sure to emphasize. Then, when you reach them in the outline, you will be reminded to stress them. Another way is to jot down on the outline explicit cues such as "pause," "repeat," "slow down," "louder," and so forth. Both techniques are good aids for beginning speakers, but they are also used by experienced speakers.

delivery cues
Directions in a speaking outline to help a speaker remember how she or he wants to deliver key parts of the speech.

SAMPLE SPEAKING OUTLINE WITH COMMENTARY

Following is a sample speaking outline for a six-minute informative talk about seagrass. By comparing it with the preparation outline for the same speech on pages 199–201, you can see how a detailed preparation outline is transformed into a concise speaking outline.

Eye Contact!!
Slow Down

Introduction

I. Oldest living organism—116,000 square miles.
   A. What is it?
   B. Ordinary seagrass.
II From ecological perspective—<u>not</u> ordinary.
   A. Emmett Duffy of Smithsonian Marine Observatories: seagrass vs Serengeti plain.
   B. Productive, vital ecosystems.
III. Learned in oceanography; did additional research.
IV. Today: what seagrass is, role in oceans, and combatting climate change

(Start with what seagrass is.)

—Pause—

Body

I. Not actually grass, but <u>flowering plant</u>.
   A. Roots, stems, leaves; produces flowers, fruits.
   B. Only flowering plant totally submerged.
      1. Absorbs oxygen, nutrients from water.
      2. Pollinates, reproduces w/o touching air.

(What it is—what it does.)

II. Vital to life in oceans.
   A. First: <u>food</u> source.
      1. Some animals feed directly on seagrass.
      2. Others on organisms in seagrass.
   B. Second: <u>refuge</u> for animals.
      1. Fish, sea horses, clams—live in it.
      2. Eggs, larvae—protection.
      3. Florida Fish and Wildlife Conservation Commission: "essential nursery."

(Importance not limited to life in oceans.)

III. Combats <u>climate change</u>.
   A. Traps carbon dioxide in seafloor.
      1. "Carbon sequestration."
      2. *Guardian*: seagrass sequesters <u>35 times faster</u>.
      3. <u>18 percent</u> total, <u>1 percent</u> of ocean floor.

COMMENTARY:

These comments remind the speaker to establish eye contact and not to race through the speech.

Including the main points of the introduction helps keep the speaker on track at the start of the speech.

It's usually a good idea to pause briefly before launching into the first main point. This is another way of signaling that you are moving from the introduction to the body.

Most speakers label the body in the speaking outline as well as in the preparation outline.

Notice how the body of the speech follows the same visual format as the preparation outline. This makes the outline easy to read at a glance.

Throughout the outline, key words are used to jog the speaker's memory. Because the final wording of an extemporaneous speech is chosen at the moment of delivery, it will not be exactly the same as that in the preparation outline.

Underlining reminds the speaker to stress key words.

Quotations are usually written out in the speaking outline.

Inserting transitions makes sure the speaker doesn't forget them.

B. Scientists working to spread seagrass.
   1. Robert Orth, Virginia Institute.
      a. *Smithsonian:* Orth seeding areas.
      b. 13 new square miles of seagrass.
   2. Increasing seagrass combats climate change.

—Pause—

Conclusion

I. In conclusion, meadows of seagrass in oceans.
   A. Essential to ocean life.
   B. Help combat climate change.
II. Next time at beach—remember seagrass beneath surface.

Summary

Outlines are essential to effective speeches. By outlining, you make sure that related ideas are together, that your thoughts flow from one to another, and that the structure of your speech is coherent. You will probably use two kinds of outlines for your speeches—a detailed preparation outline and a brief speaking outline.

In the preparation outline, you state your specific purpose and central idea; label the introduction, body, and conclusion; and designate transitions, internal summaries, and internal previews. You should identify main points, subpoints, and sub-subpoints by a consistent pattern of symbolization and indentation. Your instructor may require a bibliography with your preparation outline.

The speaking outline should contain key words or phrases to jog your memory, as well as essential statistics and quotations. Make sure your speaking outline is legible, follows the same visual framework as your preparation outline, and includes cues for delivering the speech.

Key Terms

preparation outline (194)
visual framework (195)
bibliography (197)

speaking outline (201)
delivery cues (204)

Review Questions

After reading this chapter, you should be able to answer the following questions:

1. Why is it important to outline your speeches?
2. What is a preparation outline? What are the eight guidelines discussed in this chapter for writing a preparation outline?
3. What is a speaking outline? What are four guidelines for your speaking outline?

Exercises for Critical Thinking

1. In the left-hand column below is a partially blank outline from a speech about chocolate. In the right-hand column, arranged in random order, are the subpoints to fill in the outline. Choose the appropriate subpoint for each blank in the outline.

Outline

I. Chocolate has a long and fascinating history.

   A.

      1.

      2.

   B.

      1.

      2.

   C.

II. There are four basic steps for turning cocoa beans into chocolate.

   A.

   B.

   C.

   D.

Subpoints

Fourth, this chocolate liquor product is used in making all genuine chocolate products.

The new heated and sweetened beverage soon became the rage of Europe.

In the 1500s, Spaniards introduced chocolate to Europe after returning from Central America.

Second, cocoa beans are then roasted, shelled, and cracked into small pieces called nibs.

The Maya used seeds of the cacao tree to brew a cold, bitter drink.

Chocolate was first used in Central America by the Maya and then by the Aztecs.

In the 1800s, chocolate became a popular candy as well as a beverage.

Third, nibs are ground to produce a rich brown liquid called chocolate liquor.

In Europe, Spaniards changed the beverage by heating it and adding sugar.

The Aztecs brewed a similar drink called "chocalatl."

First, cacao seeds are dried and fermented to become what are called cocoa beans.

2. From the preparation outline on chocolate you constructed in Exercise 1, create a speaking outline that you might use in delivering the speech. Follow the guidelines for a speaking outline discussed in this chapter.

End Notes

[1]Robert T. Oliver, *History of Public Speaking in America* (Boston, MA: Allyn and Bacon, 1965), p. 143.

[2]Oliver, *History of Public Speaking,* p. 145.

Using Language

Meanings of Words

Using Language Accurately

Using Language Clearly

Using Language Vividly

Using Language Appropriately

Contrary to popular belief, language does not mirror reality. It does not simply describe the world as it is. Instead, language helps create our sense of reality by giving meaning to events. The words we use to label an event determine to a great extent how we respond to it.

For example, if you see the current war on drugs as "socially beneficial," as "worth the cost," and as "fitting the crime," you will likely support it. However, if you see the current war on drugs as "socially harmful," as "a waste of money," and as "disproportionate to the crime," you will likely oppose it.

What separates these two viewpoints? Not the legality of street drugs; not the effects of drugs on individuals. Both are the same regardless of one's viewpoint. The difference is in the *meaning* given to them by the words that label them.[1]

Words are the tools of a speaker's craft. They have special uses, just like the tools of any other profession. Have you ever watched a carpenter at work? The job that would take you or me a couple of hours is done by the carpenter in 10 minutes—with the right tools. You can't drive a nail with a screwdriver or turn a screw with a hammer. It is the same with public speaking. You must choose the right words for the job you want to do.

Good speakers are aware of the meaning of words—both their obvious and their subtle meanings. They also know how to use language accurately, clearly, vividly, and appropriately. This chapter will explore each of these areas.

Meanings of Words

Words have two kinds of meanings—denotative and connotative. *Denotative* meaning is precise, literal, and objective. It describes the object, person, place, idea, or event to which the word refers. One way to think of a word's denotative meaning is as its dictionary definition. For example, denotatively, the noun "school" means "a place, institution, or building where instruction is given."

Connotative meaning is more variable, figurative, and subjective. The connotative meaning of a word is what the word suggests or implies. For instance, the connotative meaning of the word "school" includes all the feelings, associations, and emotions that the word touches off in different people. For some people, "school" might connote personal growth, childhood friends, and a special teacher. For others, it might connote frustration, discipline, and boring homework assignments.

Connotative meaning gives words their intensity and emotional power. It arouses in listeners feelings of anger, pity, love, fear, friendship, nostalgia, greed, guilt, and the like. Speakers, like poets, often use connotation to enrich their meaning. For example:

> Terrorists neither <u>listen to reason</u> nor engage in <u>reasoning</u> with others. Their aim is to generate <u>fear</u>—to <u>frighten</u> people into <u>submission</u>. They measure success by the magnitude of the <u>fear</u> they generate through <u>brutal, savage acts of violence</u>. <u>Terrorists</u> are prepared to <u>kill</u> to further whatever cause they claim to be pursuing. And the <u>heinousness</u> of these <u>murders</u> is accentuated by the fact that <u>terrorists murder without passion</u>. They <u>murder with cool deliberation and deliberate planning</u>. They are <u>utterly amoral</u>.

The underlined words in this passage have powerful connotations that are almost certain to produce a strong emotional revulsion to terrorism.

Here, in contrast, is another version of the same statement—this time using words with a different set of connotations:

> Terrorists do not seek to negotiate with their opponents. They seek victory by using political and psychological pressure, including acts of violence that may endanger the lives of some people. To the terrorist, ultimate objectives are more important than the means used to achieve them.

With the exception of "terrorist," the words in this statement are less likely to evoke an intensely negative response than those in the first statement.

Which statement is preferable? That depends on the audience, the occasion, and the speaker's purpose. Do you want to stir up your listeners' emotions, rally them to some cause? Then select words with more intense connotative meanings. Or are you addressing a controversial issue and trying to seem completely impartial? Then stick with words that touch off less intense reactions. Choosing words skillfully for their denotative and connotative meanings is a crucial part of the speaker's craft.

denotative meaning
The literal or dictionary meaning of a word or phrase.

connotative meaning
The meaning suggested by the associations or emotions triggered by a word or phrase.

Words are the tools of the speaker's craft. Good speakers use them accurately and correctly. They also use language that will be clear, vivid, and appropriate for their listeners.

Mark Mitchell/Getty Images

Using Language Accurately

Using language accurately is as vital to a speaker as using numbers accurately is to an accountant. One student learned about this the hard way. In a speech about the U.S. legal system, he referred several times to evidence that would "collaborate" the guilt or innocence of a defendant. What he meant, of course, was "corroborate." When this was pointed out to him afterward, he was noticeably embarrassed; worse, the error diminished his credibility and reduced the effectiveness of his speech.

Fortunately, such outright blunders are relatively rare among college students. However, we all commit more subtle errors—especially using one word when another will capture our ideas more precisely. Every word has shades of meaning that distinguish it from every other word. As Mark Twain said, "The difference between the right word and the almost right word is the difference between lightning and the lightning bug."

If you look in a thesaurus, you'll find the following words given as synonyms:

thesaurus
A book of synonyms.

    knowledge   expertise   education

All mean roughly the same thing—special grasp of a subject matter or skill. But all these words have different shades of meaning. See if you can fill in the best word to complete each of the following sentences:

1. Because he won a scholarship to a top university, Enrique received an excellent _____ .

2. Sophie acquired her _____ of Chinese history by reading a number of books on the subject.

3. Nina's _____ as a business consultant comes from having worked with many clients over the years.

The best answers for the three statements are:

1. education   2. knowledge   3. expertise

Each of the words means something a little different from the others, and each says something special to listeners.

As you prepare your speeches, ask yourself constantly, "What do I *really* want to say? What do I *really* mean?" When in doubt, consult a dictionary or thesaurus to make sure you have the best words to express your ideas.

Using Language Clearly

People are different. What makes perfect sense to some may be gobbledygook to others. You cannot assume that what is clear to you is clear to your audience. Listeners, unlike readers, cannot turn to a dictionary or reread an author's words to discover their meaning. A speaker's meaning must be *immediately* comprehensible; it must be so clear that there is no chance of misunderstanding. You can ensure this by using familiar words, by choosing concrete words over abstract words, and by eliminating verbal clutter.

USE FAMILIAR WORDS

One of the biggest barriers to clear speech is using big, bloated words where short, sharp ones will do the job better.[2] This is especially true when it comes to technical language that may be familiar to the speaker but not to the audience. Yet, if you work at it, you will almost always be able to translate even the most specialized topic into clear, familiar language.

Here, for instance, are two passages explaining the devastating effects of a pregnant woman's drinking on her unborn child. The first passage is technically accurate, but it contains too many obscure words.

> The deleterious effects of alcohol on the unborn child are very serious. When a pregnant mother consumes alcohol, the ethanol in the bloodstream easily crosses the placenta from mother to child and invades the amniotic fluid. This can produce a number of abnormal birth syndromes, including central-nervous-system dysfunctions, growth deficiencies, a cluster of facial aberrations, and variable major and minor malformations.

Well-informed listeners can probably figure out "deleterious effects," "central-nervous-system dysfunctions," and "facial aberrations." But these terms don't create sharp mental images of what the speaker is trying to say.

Here, in contrast, is the second passage. It is utterly clear and shows what can be done with work, imagination, and a healthy respect for everyday words:

> When the expectant mother drinks, alcohol is absorbed into her bloodstream and distributed throughout her entire body. After a few beers or a couple of martinis, she begins to feel tipsy and decides to sober up. She grabs a cup of coffee, two aspirin, and takes a little nap. After a while she'll be fine.

But while she sleeps, the fetus is surrounded by the same alcoholic content as its mother had. After being drowned in alcohol, the fetus begins to feel the effect. But it can't sober up. It can't grab a cup of coffee. It can't grab a couple of aspirin. For the fetus's liver, the key organ in removing alcohol from the blood, is just not developed. The fetus is literally pickled in alcohol.[3]

This kind of plain talk is what listeners want. You cannot go wrong by following the advice of Winston Churchill to speak in "short, homely words of common usage." If you think big words (or a lot of words) are needed to impress listeners, bear in mind that the Gettysburg Address—considered the finest speech in the English language—contains 271 words, of which 251 have only one or two syllables.

CHOOSE CONCRETE WORDS

Concrete words refer to tangible objects—people, places, and things. They differ from abstract words, which refer to general concepts, qualities, or attributes. "Carrot," "pencil," "nose," and "door" are concrete words. "Humility," "science," "progress," and "philosophy" are abstract words.

Of course, few words are completely abstract or concrete. "Apple pie" is concrete, but in the United States, the phrase also has abstract values of patriotism and conventional morals. Usually, the more specific a word, the more concrete it is. Let us say you are talking about basketball. Here are several words and phrases you might use:

physical activity	abstract/general
sports	
basketball	
professional basketball	
Stephen Curry	concrete/specific

As you move down the list, the words become less abstract and more concrete. You begin with a general concept (physical activity), descend to one type of activity (sports), to a particular sport (basketball), to a division of that sport (professional basketball), to one specific professional basketball player (Stephen Curry).

Although abstract words are necessary to express certain kinds of ideas, they are much easier to misinterpret than are concrete words. Also, concrete words are much more likely to claim your listeners' attention. Suppose you make a speech about Asian carp, which are plaguing waterways in the United States from coast to coast. Here are two ways you could approach the subject—one featuring abstract words, the other concrete words:

Abstract Words

Asian carp have become a big problem. They can grow to an enormous size and eat a lot of food in the process. When that happens, other fish don't have much to eat. Asian carp can now be found in rivers, lakes, and streams in a number of different states, some down South and others up North.

concrete words
Words that refer to tangible objects.

abstract words
Words that refer to ideas or concepts.

Concrete Words

Asian carp are one of the most destructive invasive species in the United States. These insatiable eaters can devour 20 percent of their body weight in plankton every day. Because they grow up to 100 pounds, their endless appetites are starving native fish of the food they need to survive.

Large and aggressive, Asian carp have taken over rivers, lakes, and streams from the Gulf Coast to the Canadian border. They now look poised to attack the Great Lakes, where they could decimate the existing ecosystem and destroy the fishing industry.

Federal and state governments have spent millions of dollars trying to contain Asian carp, but so far the invaders continue their relentless advance.

Notice how much more persuasive the second version is. A speech dominated by concrete words will almost always be clearer, more interesting, and easier to recall than one dominated by abstract words.

ELIMINATE CLUTTER

Cluttered speech has become a national epidemic. Whatever happened to such simple words as "before," "if," and "now"? When last seen they were being routed by their cluttered counterparts: "prior to," "in the eventuality of," and "at this point in time." By the same token, why can't politicians say "We have a crisis," instead of saying "We are facing a difficult crisis situation that will be troublesome to successfully resolve"?

This type of clutter forces listeners to hack through a tangle of words to discover the meaning. When you make a speech, keep your language lean and lively. Beware of using several words where one or two will do. Avoid flabby phrases. Let your ideas emerge sharply and firmly. Above all, watch out for redundant adjectives and adverbs. Inexperienced speakers (and writers) tend to string together two or three synonymous adjectives, such as "a learned and educated person" or "a hot, steamy, torrid day."

Here is part of a student speech that has been revised to eliminate clutter:

Sitting Bull was one of the most important ~~and significant of all~~ Native American leaders. He was born in ~~the year of~~ 1831 near Grand River, in ~~an area that is now part of the state of~~ *present-day* South Dakota. A fearless ~~and courageous~~ warrior, he ~~ended up being~~ *was* elected chief of the Hunkpapa Sioux in 1867. In the following years, he also attracted a large ~~and numerous~~ following among the ~~tribes of the~~ Cheyenne and Arapaho. He is best known ~~to people in this day and age~~ *today* for his instrumental role in ~~helping to lead the defeat of~~ *defeating* General Custer at the Battle of Little Big Horn in 1876. Although eventually ~~required against his will~~ *forced* to live ~~his life~~ on the Standing Rock Reservation in South Dakota, he never surrendered ~~to anyone~~ his dignity or his ~~personal~~ devotion to the Sioux way of life.

connect

View this excerpt from "The Plague of Asian Carp" in the online Media Library for this chapter (Video 12.1).

clutter

Discourse that takes many more words than are necessary to express an idea.

Even when discussing technical subjects, effective speakers such as renowned scholar Henry Louis Gates look for ways to communicate their ideas in clear, familiar language.

Amy Sussman/Getty Images

Notice how much cleaner and easier to follow the revised version is. No longer are the speaker's ideas hidden in a thicket of wasted words.

This kind of pruning is easy once you get the knack of it. The hardest part—and it is often very hard—is recognizing clutter and forcing yourself to throw away the unnecessary words. Watch for clutter when you write your speech outlines. Be prepared to revise the outline until your ideas emerge clearly and crisply.

You can also help eliminate clutter by practicing your speeches with a digital recorder. As you play back the speech, keep an ear out not just for flabby phrases but for verbal fillers such as "you know," "like," and "really." Practice delivering the speech again, this time making a special effort to trim it of wasted or distracting words. This will not only make you a better public speaker, it will also help you present ideas more effectively in meetings, conversations, and group discussions.[4]

Using Language Vividly

Just as you can be accurate without being clear, so you can be both accurate and clear without being interesting. Here, for example, is how Barack Obama *might* have phrased part of his acclaimed presidential speech commemorating the 1965 civil rights march across Edmund Pettus Bridge in Selma, Alabama:

> We are very proud of the people who acted in support of civil rights. They were brave, patriotic, and religious. They suffered greatly, but they remained committed to their principles.

Here is what Obama *actually* said:

> We gather here to honor the courage of ordinary Americans willing to endure billy clubs and the chastening rod; tear gas and the trampling

hoof; men and women who despite the gush of blood and splintered bone would stay true to their North Star and keep marching toward justice.

They did as Scripture instructed: "Rejoice in hope, be patient in tribulation, be constant in prayer." And in the days to come, they went back again and again. When the trumpet call sounded for more to join, the people came—Black and white, young and old, Christian and Jew, waving the American flag and singing the same anthems full of faith and hope.

Much more stirring, isn't it? If you want to move people with your speeches, use vivid, animated language. Although there are several ways to do this, two of the most important are imagery and rhythm.

IMAGERY

One sign of a good novelist is the ability to create word pictures that let you "see" the haunted house, or "hear" the birds chirping on a warm spring morning, or "taste" the hot enchiladas at a Mexican restaurant.

Speakers can use imagery in much the same way to make their ideas come alive. Three ways to generate imagery are by using concrete words, simile, and metaphor.

imagery
The use of vivid language to create mental images of objects, actions, or ideas.

Concrete Words

As we saw earlier in this chapter, choosing concrete words over abstract words is one way to enhance the clarity of your speeches. Concrete words are also the key to effective imagery. Consider the following excerpt from Ronald Reagan's famous address commemorating the 40th anniversary of D-Day. Speaking at the scene of the battle, Reagan dramatically recounted the heroism of the U.S. Rangers who scaled the cliffs at Pointe du Hoc to help free Europe from Hitler's stranglehold:

> We stand on a lonely, windswept point on the northern shore of France. The air is soft, but 40 years ago at this moment, the air was dense with smoke and the cries of men, and the air was filled with the crack of rifle fire and the roar of cannon.
>
> At dawn, on the morning of the 6th of June, 1944, 225 Rangers jumped off the British landing craft and ran to the bottom of these cliffs. . . . The Rangers looked up and saw the enemy soldiers—at the edge of the cliffs shooting down at them with machine guns and throwing grenades. And the American Rangers began to climb. They shot rope ladders over the face of these cliffs and began to pull themselves up.
>
> When one Ranger fell, another would take his place. When one rope was cut, a Ranger would grab another and begin his climb again. They climbed, shot back, and held their footing. Soon, one by one, the Rangers pulled themselves over the top, and in seizing the firm land at the top of these cliffs, they began to seize back the continent of Europe.[5]

Concrete words call up mental impressions of sights, sounds, touch, smell, and taste. In Reagan's speech, we do not merely learn that the U.S. Rangers helped win the battle of D-Day. We visualize the Rangers landing at the foot of the cliffs. We see them fighting their way up the cliffs in the face of enemy grenades and machine guns. We hear the crack of rifle fire and the cries of the soldiers. The concrete words create images that pull us irresistibly into the speech.

Simile

Another way to create imagery is through the use of simile. Simile is an explicit comparison between things that are essentially different yet have something in common. It always contains the word "like" or "as." Here are some examples from student speeches:

> Walking into my grandparents' home when I was a child was like being wrapped in a giant security blanket.

> With eyes glued on their phones, pedestrians walk the streets like zombies after the apocalypse.

These are bright, fresh similes that clarify and vitalize ideas. Some similes, however, have become stale through overuse. Here are a few:

fresh as a daisy	hungry as a bear
fit as a fiddle	busy as a bee
strong as an ox	happy as a lark

Such clichés are fine in everyday conversation, but you should avoid them in speechmaking. Otherwise, you are likely to be "dull as dishwater" and to find your audience "sleeping like a log"!

Metaphor

You can also use metaphor to create imagery in your speeches. Metaphor is an implicit comparison between things that are essentially different yet have something in common. Unlike simile, metaphor does not contain the word "like" or "as." For example:

> Being a fish out of water is tough, but that's how you evolve. (Kumail Nanjiani)

> A pandemic is a marathon, not a sprint. (Ursula von der Leyen)

simile
An explicit comparison, introduced with the word "like" or "as," between things that are essentially different yet have something in common.

cliché
A trite or overused expression.

metaphor
An implicit comparison, not introduced with the word "like" or "as," between two things that are essentially different yet have something in common.

Audience-oriented speakers put a premium on clear, vivid, uncluttered language. They give a great deal of thought to finding just the right words to express their ideas.

Jörg Carstensen/picture alliance/ Getty Images

These are both brief metaphors. Sometimes, however, a speaker will develop a longer metaphor. Here is an excellent example, from Al Gore's speech accepting the Nobel Peace Prize for his efforts to help the world deal with climate change:

> The earth has a fever. And the fever is rising. The experts have told us it is not a passing affliction that will heal by itself. We asked for a second opinion. And a third. And a fourth. And the consistent conclusion, restated with increasing alarm, is that something basic is wrong.

When used effectively, metaphor—like simile—is an excellent way to bring color to a speech, to make abstract ideas concrete, to clarify the unknown, and to express feelings and emotions.

RHYTHM

rhythm

The pattern of sound in a speech created by the choice and arrangement of words.

Language has a rhythm created by the choice and arrangement of words. Speakers, like poets, sometimes seek to exploit the rhythm of language to enhance the impact of their words. Winston Churchill was a master at this. Here is a passage from one of his famous speeches during World War II. To emphasize its cadence, the passage has been printed as if it were poetry rather than prose:

> We cannot tell what the course
>   of this fell war will be. . . .
> We cannot yet see
>   how deliverance will come,
> or when it will come.
>   But nothing is more certain
> than that every trace of Hitler's footsteps,
>   every stain of his infected and corroding fingers,
> will be sponged and purged
>   and, if need be,
> blasted from the surface of the earth.

The impact of the passage was heightened by Churchill's superb delivery; but even by themselves the words take on an emphatic rhythm that reinforces the message. You can see why one observer said that Churchill "mobilized the English language and sent it into battle."[6]

A speech, however, is not a poem. You should never emphasize sound and rhythm at the expense of meaning. The aim is to think about ways you can use the rhythm and flow of language to enhance your meaning. Although you may never have paid much conscious attention to this subject, you can develop an ear for vocal rhythms by study and practice. What's more, you can easily begin now to use four basic stylistic devices employed by Churchill and other fine speakers to improve the rhythm of their prose.

Parallelism

The first device is parallelism—the similar arrangement of a pair or series of related words, phrases, or sentences. For example:

> *Rich and poor, intelligent and ignorant, wise and foolish, virtuous and vicious, man and woman*—it is ever the same, each soul must depend wholly on itself. (Elizabeth Cady Stanton)

Since graduating from college, you have developed a successful business that is located near the campus. As part of its plan to involve more alumni and community members in college affairs, the school has asked you to speak with new students during registration week for the fall term. In the opening section of your speech, you want the audience to feel what you felt the first few days you were on campus as a new student. The best strategy, you decide, is to present two or three similes that complete the sentence "Beginning college is like. . . ." Write your similes.

Tom Grill/JGI/Blend Images/Getty Images

The effects of parallelism are perhaps best illustrated by seeing what happens when it is absent. For instance, compare this statement:

> I speak as a Republican. I speak as a woman. I speak as a United States Senator. I speak as an American. (Margaret Chase Smith)

with this one:

> I speak as a Republican. I speak as a woman. I speak as a United States Senator. And I am also addressing you as an American.

The first statement is clear, consistent, and compelling. The second is not. By violating the principle of parallel structure, its final sentence ("And I am also addressing you as an American") destroys the progression begun by the preceding three sentences. It turns a strong, lucid, harmonious statement into one that is fuzzy and jarring.

parallelism
The similar arrangement of a pair or series of related words, phrases, or sentences.

Repetition

Repetition means reiterating the same word or set of words at the beginning or end of successive clauses or sentences. For example:

> *Without* facts, *you can't have* truth. *Without* truth, *you can't have* trust. *Without* trust, we have no shared reality. (Maria Ressa)

> *Here is the price of* freedom, *here is the price of* independence. (Volodymyr Zelensky)

As you can see, repetition usually results in parallelism. In addition to building a strong cadence, it unifies a sequence of ideas, emphasizes an idea by stating it more than once, and helps create a strong emotional effect.

repetition
Reiteration of the same word or set of words at the beginning or end of successive clauses or sentences.

Alliteration

The third device you can use to enhance the rhythm of your speeches is alliteration. The most common method of alliteration is repeating the initial consonant sound of close or adjoining words. For example:

> Our alliances are an *un*matched and *un*rivaled source of strength and security. (Lloyd Austin)

alliteration
Repetition of the initial consonant sound of close or adjoining words.

Nothing great is accomplished without cooperation, compromise, and common cause. (Ban Ki-moon)

By highlighting the sounds of words, alliteration catches the attention of listeners and can make ideas easier to remember. Used sparingly, it is a marvelous way to spruce up your speeches. Used to excess, however, it can draw attention to itself, so that listeners get more involved in listening for the next alliteration than in absorbing the content of the speech.

Antithesis

antithesis
The juxtaposition of contrasting ideas, usually in parallel structure.

Finally, you might try using antithesis—the juxtaposition of contrasting ideas, usually in parallel structure. For example:

Ask not what your country can do for you; ask what you can do for your country. (John F. Kennedy)

Let us never negotiate out of fear. But let us never fear to negotiate. (John F. Kennedy)

It is no accident that both of these examples are from speeches by President Kennedy. Antithesis was one of his favorite language devices, and the one he used in his most memorable phrases. Because it nearly always produces a neatly turned phrase, it is a fine way to give your speeches a special touch of class.

You may be thinking that imagery and rhythm are too fancy for ordinary speeches like yours. This is not true. Take a look at the following excerpt from one student's speech about Ida B. Wells, a pioneering civil rights activist who fought against the injustices of her time:

connect

View this excerpt from "Ida B. Wells" in the online Media Library for this chapter (Video 12.2).

Ida B. Wells had the courage to stand up—to stand up for herself and for equality under the law. Born in muggy Mississippi in the dark days of the Civil War, Wells faced segregation every day, but she refused to accept it.

In 1883 she bought a first-class ticket for a train ride from Memphis to Nashville. Even though she paid just as much as the white, first-class passengers, and had already taken her seat, crew members told her to move to the crowded, run-down smoking car reserved for Blacks. When she refused and stayed in her seat, she was dragged away and forcibly removed from the train.

Seventy years before Rosa Parks ignited the civil rights movement by refusing to give up her bus seat, Wells stood up for equality—also by staying seated.

This is vivid, moving language. The imagery is sharp and poignant, the rhythm strong and insistent. Think of how you can do similar things in your own speeches.

Using Language Appropriately

Here is part of a famous oration given by John Hancock in 1774, during the American Revolution. Speaking of the British soldiers who killed five Americans in the Boston Massacre, Hancock exclaimed:

Language needs to be appropriate to a speaker's topic, as well as to the audience. A speech on thoroughbred horse racing would use more action-oriented words than would a speech about theories of psychology.

Vince Caligiuri/Getty Images

> Ye dark designing knaves, ye murderers, parricides! How dare you tread upon the earth, which has drank in the blood of slaughtered innocents shed by your wicked hands? . . . Tell me, ye bloody butchers, ye villains high and low, ye wretches, do you not feel the goads and stings of conscious guilt pierce through your savage bosoms?

This is certainly vivid language—and Hancock's audience loved it. But can you imagine speaking the same way today? Norms about language are constantly changing as society itself changes. In addition to being accurate, clear, and vivid, language should be appropriate—to the occasion, to the audience, to the topic, and to the speaker.

APPROPRIATENESS TO THE OCCASION

Language that is appropriate for some occasions may not be appropriate for others. As a simple example, a coach might address the football team as "you guys" (or worse!), whereas the speaker in a more formal situation would begin with "distinguished guests." Try reversing these two situations, and see how ridiculous it becomes. It's only common sense to adjust your language to different occasions.

APPROPRIATENESS TO THE AUDIENCE

Appropriateness also depends on the audience. If you keep this in mind, it will help you greatly when dealing with technical topics. When addressing an audience of physicians, you might say "parotitis" to refer to a viral disease marked by the swelling of the parotid glands. Your audience would know just what you meant. But when talking to a nonmedical audience, such as your classmates, you would appropriately say "mumps."

You should be especially careful to avoid language that might offend your audience. Off-color humor or profanity might be appropriate in a comedy routine, but most listeners would find it offensive in a formal public speech. Remember, speakers are expected to elevate and polish their language when addressing an audience.

Speakers are also expected to use inclusive language that is respectful of the different groups that make up American society. As the United States has become more diverse, our language has evolved to reflect that diversity. Public speakers should strive to use language that avoids stereotypes based on age, race, religion, ethnicity, gender, and other factors. Just as in conversation you would be sensitive to a person with a different background, condition, or identity than yours, so you should accord the same respect when giving a speech. Using inclusive language is not a matter of political correctness, but it is a matter of P.C.—personal courtesy.[7]

APPROPRIATENESS TO THE TOPIC

Language should also be appropriate to the topic. You would not use metaphor, antithesis, and alliteration when explaining how to change a bicycle tire. But you might use all three in a speech honoring U.S. soldiers who have died in defense of their country. The first topic calls for straightforward description and explanation. The second calls for special language skills to evoke emotion, admiration, and appreciation.

APPROPRIATENESS TO THE SPEAKER

No matter what the occasion, audience, or topic, language should also be appropriate to the speaker. Every public speaker develops his or her own language style.

"Terrific," you may be thinking. "I have my own style, too. I feel more comfortable using abstract words, slang, and technical jargon. That's *my* way of speaking." But to say that language should be appropriate to the speaker does not justify ignoring the other needs for appropriateness. There is a difference between one's everyday style and one's *developed* style as a public speaker. Accomplished speakers have developed their speaking styles over many years of trial, error, and practice. They have *worked* at using language effectively.

You can do the same if you become language-conscious. One way to develop this consciousness is to read and listen to effective speakers. Study their techniques for achieving accuracy, clarity, and vividness, and try to adapt those techniques to your own speeches. But do not try to "become" someone else when you speak. Learn from other speakers, blend what you learn into your own language style, and seek to become the best possible you.

Summary

Good speakers have respect for language and how it works. As a speaker, you should be aware of the meanings of words and know how to use language accurately, clearly, vividly, and appropriately.

Words have two kinds of meanings—denotative and connotative. Denotative meaning is precise, literal, and objective. Connotative meaning is more variable, figurative, and subjective. It includes all the feelings, associations, and emotions that a word touches off in different people.

Using language accurately is vital to a speaker. Never use a word unless you are sure of its meaning. If you are not sure, look up the word in a dictionary. As you prepare your speeches, ask yourself constantly, "What do I *really* want to say? What do I *really* mean?" Choose words that are precise and accurate.

Using language clearly allows listeners to grasp your meaning immediately. You can ensure this by using words that are known to the average person and require no specialized background, by choosing concrete words in preference to more abstract ones, and by eliminating verbal clutter.

Using language vividly helps bring your speech to life. One way to make your language more vivid is through imagery, which you can develop by using concrete language, simile, and metaphor. Another way to make your speeches vivid is by exploiting the rhythm of language with parallelism, repetition, alliteration, and antithesis.

Using language appropriately means adapting to the particular occasion, audience, and topic at hand. It also means developing your own language style instead of trying to copy someone else's.

Key Terms

denotative meaning (210)

connotative meaning (210)

thesaurus (211)

concrete words (213)

abstract words (213)

clutter (214)

imagery (216)

simile (217)

cliché (217)

metaphor (217)

rhythm (218)

parallelism (218)

repetition (219)

alliteration (219)

antithesis (220)

Review Questions

After reading this chapter, you should be able to answer the following questions:

1. How does language help create our sense of reality?

2. What is the difference between denotative and connotative meaning? How might you use each to convey your message most effectively?

3. What are four criteria for using language effectively in your speeches?

4. What are three things you should do to use language clearly in your speeches?

5. What are two ways to bring your speeches to life with vivid, animated language?

6. What does it mean to say you should use language appropriately in your speeches?

Exercises for Critical Thinking

1. Arrange each of the following sequences in order, from the most abstract word to the most concrete word.

   a. housing complex, building, dining room, structure, apartment

   b. *Mona Lisa,* art, painting, creative activity, portrait

   c. automobile, vehicle, Ferrari, transportation, sports car

2. Rewrite each of the following sentences using clear, familiar words.

   a. My employment objective is to attain a position of maximum financial reward.

   b. All professors at this school are expected to achieve high standards of excellence in their instructional duties.

   c. In the eventuality of a fire, it is imperative that all persons evacuate the building without undue delay.

3. Each of the following statements uses one or more of these stylistic devices: metaphor, simile, parallelism, repetition, alliteration, antithesis. Identify the device(s) used in each statement.

   a. "We are a people in a quandary about the present. We are a people in search of our future. We are a people in search of a national community." (Barbara Jordan)

   b. "The vice presidency is the sand trap of American politics. It's near the prize, and designed to be limiting." (Howard Fineman)

   c. "I want you to make history, not be history. I want your work to be remembered, not be forgotten. I want you to power and steer the academic current, not be engulfed by it." (Ibram X. Kendi)

   d. "I speak so those without a voice can be heard. Those who have fought for their rights: Their right to live in peace. Their right to be treated with dignity. Their right to equality of opportunity." (Malala Yousafzai)

End Notes

[1] For a valuable collection of essays on language, meaning, and culture, see Susan D. Blum (ed.), *Making Sense of Language,* 3rd ed. (New York: Oxford University Press, 2017).

[2] Dorothy Sarnoff, *Speech Can Change Your Life* (New York: Doubleday, 1970), p. 71.

[3] Annmarie Mungo, "A Child Is Born," *Winning Orations, 1980* (Mankato, MN: Interstate Oratorical Association, 1980), pp. 49–50.

[4] See Joseph M. Williams and Joseph Bizup, *Style: Lessons in Clarity and Grace,* 12th ed. (New York: Longman, 2016), for more on the principles of verbal clarity.

[5] Ronald Reagan, "Address on the Fortieth Anniversary of D-Day," in Stephen E. Lucas and Martin J. Medhurst (eds.), *Words of a Century: The Top 100 American Speeches, 1900–1999* (New York: Oxford University Press, 2009), pp. 552–555.

[6] Edward Bliss Jr. (ed.), *In Search of Light: The Broadcasts of Edward R. Murrow, 1938–1961* (New York: Knopf, 1967), p. 276.

[7] Rosalie Maggio, *Talking About People: A Guide to Fair and Accurate Language* (Phoenix, AZ: Oryx Press, 1997), p. 26.

Delivery

> What Is Good Delivery?
>
> Methods of Delivery
>
> The Speaker's Voice
>
> The Speaker's Body
>
> Practicing Delivery
>
> Answering Audience Questions

f you were to record one of Stephen Colbert's monologues, memorize it word for word, and stand up before your friends to recite it, would you get the same response Colbert does? Not very likely. And why not? Because you would not *deliver* the jokes as Colbert does. Of course, the jokes are basically funny. But Stephen Colbert brings something extra to the jokes—his manner of presentation, his vocal inflections, his perfectly timed pauses, his facial expressions, his gestures. All these are part of an expert delivery. It would take you years of practice—as it took Colbert—to duplicate his results.

No one expects your speech class to transform you into a multimillion-dollar talk show host. Still, this example demonstrates how important delivery can be to any public speaking situation. Even a mediocre speech will be more effective if it is presented well, whereas a wonderfully written speech can be ruined by poor delivery.

This does not mean dazzling delivery will turn a mindless string of nonsense into a triumphant oration. You cannot make a good speech without having something to say. But having something to say is not enough. You must also know *how* to say it.

nonverbal communication
Communication based on a person's use of voice and body, rather than on the use of words.

Speech delivery is a matter of nonverbal communication. It is based on how you use your voice and body to convey the message expressed by your words. There is a great deal of research showing that the impact of a speaker's words is powerfully influenced by his or her nonverbal communication. In this chapter, we will explain how you can use nonverbal communication to deliver your speeches effectively and to increase the impact of your verbal message.

Randy Shropshire/Getty Images

What Is Good Delivery?

Wendell Phillips was a leader in the movement to abolish slavery in the United States during the 1800s. Some people considered him the greatest speaker of his time. The following story suggests one reason why:

> Shortly before the Civil War an Andover student, learning that Phillips was to lecture in Boston, made a 22-mile pilgrimage on foot to hear him. At first the trip seemed hardly worthwhile, for the student discovered that Phillips was not an orator in the grand manner, but spoke in an almost conversational style. He stood on the platform, one hand lightly resting on a table, talked for what seemed to be about 20 minutes, concluded, and sat down. When the student looked at his watch, he found to his astonishment that he had been listening for an hour and a half![1]

Good delivery does not call attention to itself. It conveys the speaker's ideas clearly, interestingly, and without distracting the audience. Most audiences prefer delivery that combines a certain degree of formality with the best attributes of good conversation—directness, spontaneity, animation, vocal and facial expressiveness, and a lively sense of communication.

Speech delivery is an art, not a science. What works for one speaker may fail for another. And what succeeds with today's audience may not with tomorrow's. You cannot become a skilled speaker just by following a set of rules in a textbook. In the long run, there is no substitute for experience. But take heart! A textbook *can* give you basic pointers to get you started in the right direction.

When you plan your first speech (or your second or third), you should concentrate on such basics as speaking intelligibly, avoiding distracting mannerisms, and establishing eye contact with your listeners. Once you get these elements under control and begin to feel fairly comfortable in front of an audience, you can work on polishing your delivery to enhance the impact of your ideas. Eventually, you may find yourself able to control the timing, rhythm, and momentum of a speech as skillfully as a conductor controls an orchestra.

Methods of Delivery

There are four basic methods of delivering a speech: (1) reading verbatim from a manuscript, (2) reciting a memorized text, (3) speaking impromptu, and (4) speaking extemporaneously. Let us look at each.

READING FROM A MANUSCRIPT

manuscript speech
A speech that is written out word for word and read to the audience.

Certain speeches *must* be delivered word for word, according to a meticulously prepared manuscript. Examples include a Pope's religious proclamation, an engineer's report to a professional meeting, or a president's message to Congress. In such situations, absolute accuracy is essential. Every word of the speech will be analyzed by the press, by colleagues, perhaps by enemies. In the case of the president, a misstated phrase could cause an international incident.

Although it looks easy, delivering a speech from manuscript requires great skill. Some people do it well. Their words "come alive as if coined on the spot."[2] Others ruin it every time. Instead of sounding vibrant and conversational, they come across as wooden and artificial. They falter over words, pause in the wrong places, read too quickly or too slowly, speak in a monotone, and march through the speech without even glancing at their audience. In short, they come across as *reading to* their listeners, rather than *talking with* them.

If you are in a situation where you must speak from a manuscript, practice aloud to make sure the speech sounds natural. Work on establishing eye contact with your listeners. Be certain the final manuscript is legible at a glance. Above all, reach out to your audience with the same directness and sincerity that you would if you were speaking extemporaneously.

RECITING FROM MEMORY

Among the feats of the legendary orators, none leaves us more in awe than their practice of presenting even the longest and most complex speeches entirely from memory. Nowadays it is no longer customary to memorize any but the shortest of speeches—toasts, congratulatory remarks, acceptance speeches, introductions, and the like.

If you are giving a speech of this kind and want to memorize it, by all means do so. However, be sure to memorize it so thoroughly that you will be able to concentrate on communicating with the audience, not on trying to remember the words. Speakers who gaze at the ceiling or stare out the window trying to recall what they have memorized are no better off than those who read dully from a manuscript.

SPEAKING IMPROMPTU

An impromptu speech is delivered with little or no immediate preparation. Few people choose to speak impromptu, but sometimes it cannot be avoided. In fact, many of the speeches you give in life will be impromptu. You might be called on suddenly to "say a few words" or, in the course of a class discussion, business meeting, or committee report, want to respond to a previous speaker.

When such situations arise, don't panic. No one expects you to deliver a perfect speech on the spur of the moment. If you are in a meeting or discussion, pay close attention to what the other speakers say. Take notes of major points with which you agree or disagree. In the process, you will automatically begin to formulate what you will say when it is your turn to speak.

Whenever you are responding to a previous speaker, try to present your speech in four simple steps: First, state the point you are answering. Second, state the point you wish to make. Third, support your point with appropriate statistics, examples, or testimony. Fourth, summarize your point. This four-step method will help you organize your thoughts quickly and clearly.

If time allows, sketch a quick outline of your remarks on a piece of paper before you start to speak. This will help you remember what you want to say and will keep you from rambling.

If the situation calls for you to speak from a lectern, walk to it calmly, take a deep breath or two (not a visible gasp), establish eye contact with your audience, and begin speaking. If you're speaking online, establish an upright posture and check your framing in the webcam to make sure you are properly centered with appropriate headroom. No matter how nervous you are inside, do your best to look calm and assured on the outside.

impromptu speech
A speech delivered with little or no immediate preparation.

Once you begin speaking, maintain eye contact with the audience. Help the audience keep track of your ideas with signposts such as "My first point is . . . ; second, we can see that . . . ; in conclusion, I would like to say. . . ." By stating your points clearly and concisely, you will come across as organized and confident.

As with other kinds of public speaking, the best way to become a better impromptu speaker is to practice. You can do this on your own. Simply choose a topic on which you are already well informed, and give a one- or two-minute impromptu talk on some aspect of that topic. Any topic will do, no matter how serious or frivolous it may be. You don't even need an audience—you can speak to an empty room. Better yet, record the speech and play it back to hear how you sound. The purpose is to gain experience in pulling your ideas together quickly and stating them succinctly.

SPEAKING EXTEMPORANEOUSLY

In popular usage, extemporaneous means the same as impromptu. But technically the two are different. Unlike an impromptu speech, which is delivered off-the-cuff, an extemporaneous speech is carefully prepared and practiced in advance. In presenting the speech, the extemporaneous speaker uses only a brief set of notes or a speaking outline to jog the memory (see Chapter 11). The exact wording is chosen at the moment of delivery.

This is not as hard as it sounds. Once you have your outline (or notes) and know what topics you are going to cover and in what order, you can begin to practice the speech. Every time you run through it, the wording will be slightly different. As you practice the speech over and over, the best way to present each part will emerge and stick in your mind.

The extemporaneous method has several advantages. It gives more precise control over thought and language than does impromptu speaking; it offers greater spontaneity and directness than does speaking from memory or from a full manuscript; and it is adaptable to a wide range of situations. It also encourages the conversational quality audiences look for in speech delivery.

Conversational quality means that no matter how many times a speech has been rehearsed, it still *sounds* spontaneous. When you speak extemporaneously—and have prepared properly—you have full control over your ideas, yet you are not tied to a manuscript. You are free to establish strong eye contact, to gesture naturally, and to concentrate on talking *with* the audience rather than declaiming *to* them.

For an example of extemporaneous delivery, watch Video 13.1. The student is presenting her speech on supervolcanoes. She clearly has rehearsed a great deal, and she knows what she wants to say, but she has not memorized the speech. She has a brief set of speaking notes but is not tied to them. Rather, she selects her words as she goes along, maintains eye contact with the audience, and has excellent conversational quality.

Like thousands of previous students, you can become adept at speaking extemporaneously by the end of the term. As one student commented in looking back at his class: "At the start, I never thought I'd be able to give my speeches without a ton of notes, but I'm amazed at how much progress I've made. It's one of the most valuable things I learned in the entire class."

Most experienced speakers prefer the extemporaneous method, and most teachers emphasize it. Later in this chapter (pages 238–239), we'll look at a step-by-step program for practicing your extemporaneous delivery.

extemporaneous speech
A carefully prepared and rehearsed speech that is presented from a brief set of notes.

conversational quality
Presenting a speech so it sounds spontaneous no matter how many times it has been rehearsed.

connect
View an excerpt from "Supervolcanoes: The Sleeping Giants" in the online Media Library for this chapter (Video 13.1).

Extemporaneous speeches are prepared ahead of time, but the exact words are chosen at the moment of presentation. This allows for more direct delivery than reading from a manuscript.

Stefan Puchner/picture alliance/ Getty Images

The Speaker's Voice

What kind of voice do you have? Is it rich and resonant? Soft and alluring? Loud and irritating? Whatever the characteristics of your voice, you can be sure it is unique. Because no two people are exactly the same physically, no two people have identical voices.

A golden voice is certainly an asset for a public speaker, but some of the most famous speakers in history have had undistinguished voices. Abraham Lincoln had a harsh and penetrating voice; Winston Churchill suffered from a slight lisp and an awkward stammer. Like them, you can overcome natural disadvantages and use your voice to the best effect. Lincoln and Churchill learned to *control* their voices. You can do the same thing.

The aspects of voice you should work to control are volume, pitch, rate, pauses, vocal variety, pronunciation, articulation, and dialect.

VOLUME

At one time, a powerful voice was essential for an orator. Today, electronic amplification allows even a soft-spoken person to be heard in any setting. In the classroom, volume is essential, because you will speak without a microphone. When you do, be sure to adjust your voice to the acoustics of the room, the size of the audience, and the level of background noise. If you speak too loudly, your listeners will think you boorish. If you speak too softly, they will not understand you.

Remember that your own voice always sounds louder to you than to a listener. Soon after beginning your speech, glance at the people farthest away from you. If they look puzzled, are leaning forward in their seats, or are otherwise straining to hear, you need to talk louder.

Unlike in-person speeches, online speeches require a microphone to carry your voice across the Internet. Presentation software like Zoom allows you to set your audio level so your voice is transmitted at just the right volume. This is usually done in the software's preferences pane. Before your speech, check the volume and adjust as needed.

volume
The loudness or softness of the speaker's voice.

PITCH

pitch
The highness or lowness of the speaker's voice.

Pitch is the highness or lowness of a speaker's voice. The faster sound waves vibrate, the higher their pitch; the slower they vibrate, the lower their pitch.

Changes in pitch are known as inflections. Inflection is what makes the difference between the "Aha!" triumphantly exclaimed by Sherlock Holmes upon discovering a seemingly decisive clue and the "Aha" he mutters when he learns the clue is not decisive after all. If you were to read the preceding sentence aloud, your voice would probably go up in pitch on the first "Aha" and down on the second.

inflections
Changes in the pitch or tone of a speaker's voice.

In ordinary conversation, we instinctively use inflections to convey meaning and emotion. People who use no variation in pitch are said to speak in a monotone, a trait whose only known benefit is to cure insomnia in one's listeners.

monotone
A constant pitch or tone of voice.

Although few people speak in an absolute monotone, many fall into repetitious pitch patterns that are just as hypnotic. You can guard against this by recording your speeches as you practice them. If all your sentences end on the same inflection—either upward or downward—work on varying your pitch patterns to fit the meaning of your words.

RATE

rate
The speed at which a person speaks.

Rate refers to the speed at which a person talks. People in the United States usually speak at a rate between 120 and 150 words per minute, but there is no uniform rate for effective speechmaking. Franklin Roosevelt spoke at 110 words per minute, John Kennedy at 180. Martin Luther King opened his "I Have a Dream" speech at 92 words per minute and finished it at 145. The best rate of speech depends on several things—the vocal attributes of the speaker, the mood she or he is trying to create, the composition of the audience, and the nature of the occasion.

Two obvious faults to avoid are speaking so slowly that your listeners become bored or so quickly that they lose track of your ideas. Novice speakers are particularly prone to racing through their speeches at a frantic rate. Fortunately, this is usually an easy habit to break, as is the less common one of crawling through one's speech at a snail's pace.

The key in both cases is becoming aware of the problem and concentrating on solving it. Use a recording device to check how fast you speak. Pay special attention to rate when practicing your speech. Finally, be sure to include reminders about delivery on your speaking outline so you won't forget to make the adjustments when you give your speech in class.[3]

PAUSES

pause
A momentary break in the vocal delivery of a speech.

Learning how and when to pause is a major challenge for most beginning speakers. Even a moment of silence can seem like an eternity. As you gain more poise and confidence, however, you will discover how useful the pause can be. It can signal the end of a thought unit, give an idea time to sink in, and lend dramatic impact to a statement. "The right word may be effective," said Mark Twain, "but no word was ever as effective as a rightly timed pause."

Developing a keen sense of timing is partly a matter of common sense, partly a matter of experience. You will not always get your pauses just right at first, but keep trying. Listen to accomplished speakers to see how they use pauses to modulate the rate and rhythm of their messages. Work on pauses when you practice your speeches.

Make sure you pause at the end of thought units and not in the middle. Otherwise, you may distract listeners from your ideas. Most important, do not fill the silence

The best rate of speech depends partly on the mood a speaker wants to create. To communicate the beauty of Switzerland's Lake Geneva, you would probably speak at a slower-than-normal rate.

Christian D/Getty Images

with "uh," "er," or "um." These vocalized pauses can create negative perceptions about a speaker's intelligence and often make a speaker appear deceptive.[4]

VOCAL VARIETY

Just as variety is the spice of life, so is it the spice of public speaking. A flat, listless, unchanging voice is as deadly to speechmaking as a flat, listless, unchanging routine is to daily life. When giving a speech, you should strive for vocal variety—changes in rate, pitch, and volume that will give your voice interest and expressiveness.

For an excellent example of vocal variety, watch Video 13.2. The speaker, Sajjid Zahir Chinoy, was born and raised in Bombay, India, before coming to the United States to attend college at the University of Richmond. At the end of his senior year, Chinoy was selected as the student commencement speaker in a campus-wide competition. He spoke of the warm reception he received at Richmond and of how cultural differences can be overcome by attempting to understand other people.

At the end of his speech, Chinoy received thunderous applause—partly because of what he said, but also because of how he said it. Addressing the audience of 3,000 people without notes, he spoke extemporaneously with strong eye contact and excellent vocal variety. The speech was so inspiring that the main speaker, Harvard psychiatrist Robert Coles, began his presentation by paying tribute to Chinoy. "I've been to a number of commencements," said Coles, "but I've never heard a speech quite like that!"

How can you develop a lively, expressive voice? Above all, by approaching every speech as Chinoy approached his—as an opportunity to share with your listeners ideas that are important to you. Your sense of conviction and your desire to communicate will give your voice the same spark it has in spontaneous conversation.

PRONUNCIATION

We all mispronounce words now and again. Here, for example, are four words with which you are probably familiar. Say each one aloud.

vocalized pause
A pause that occurs when a speaker fills the silence between words with vocalizations such as "uh," "er," and "um."

vocal variety
Changes in a speaker's rate, pitch, and volume that give the voice variety and expressiveness.

connect

View an excerpt from "Questions of Culture" in the online Media Library for this chapter (Video 13.2).

The Speaker's Voice   **233**

genuine	arctic
err	nuclear

Very likely you made a mistake on at least one, for they are among the most frequently mispronounced words in the English language. Let's see:

Word	Common Error	Correct Pronunciation
genuine	gen-u-wine	gen-u-win
arctic	ar-tic	arc-tic
nuclear	nu-cu-lar	nu-cle-ar
err	air	ur

Every word leads a triple life: It is read, written, and spoken. Most people recognize and understand many more words in reading than they use in ordinary writing, and about three times as many as occur in spontaneous speech.[5] This is why we occasionally stumble when speaking words that are part of our reading or writing vocabularies. In other cases, we may mispronounce the most commonplace words out of habit.

The problem is that we usually don't *know* when we are mispronouncing a word. If we are lucky, we learn the right pronunciation by hearing someone else say the word properly or by having someone gently correct us in private. If we are unlucky, we mispronounce the word in front of a roomful of people, who may raise their eyebrows, groan, or laugh.

All of this argues for practicing your speech in front of as many trusted friends and relatives as you can corner. If you have any doubts about the proper pronunciation of certain words, be sure to check a dictionary.

ARTICULATION

articulation
The physical production of particular speech sounds.

Articulation and pronunciation are not identical. Sloppy articulation is the failure to form particular speech sounds crisply and distinctly. It is one of several causes of mispronunciation, but you can articulate a word sharply and still mispronounce it. For example, if you say the "s" in "Illinois" or the "p" in "pneumonia," you are making a mistake in pronunciation, regardless of how precisely you articulate the sounds.

Among U.S. college students, poor articulation is more common than ignorance of correct pronunciation. We know that "let me" is not "lemme," that "going to" is not "gonna," that "did you" is not "didja," yet we persist in articulating these words improperly. Here are some other common errors in articulation you should work to avoid:

Word	Misarticulation
ought to	otta
didn't	dint
don't know	dunno
have to	hafta
want to	wanna
will you	wilya

pronunciation
The accepted standard of sound and rhythm for words in a given language.

If you have sloppy articulation, work on identifying and eliminating your most common errors. Like other bad habits, careless articulation can be broken only by persistent effort—but the results are well worth it. As Shakespeare advised, "Mend your speech a little, lest you may mar your fortunes."

DIALECT

Most languages have dialects, each with a distinctive accent, grammar, and vocabulary. Dialects are usually based on regional or ethnic speech patterns. The United States has four major regional dialects—Eastern, New England, Southern, and General American. We also have multiple ethnic dialects. As the nation has become more diverse culturally, it has also become more diverse linguistically.

Linguists have concluded that no dialect is inherently better or worse than another. Dialects are not linguistic badges of superiority or inferiority. They are usually shaped by our regional or ethnic background, and every dialect is "right" for the community of people who use it.

When is a given dialect appropriate in public speaking? The answer depends above all on the composition of your audience. Heavy use of any dialect—regional or ethnic—can be troublesome when the audience does not share that dialect. In such a situation, the dialect may cause listeners to make negative judgments about the speaker's personality, intelligence, and competence. This is why professional speakers have been known to invest large amounts of time (and money) to master the General American dialect used by most television news broadcasters.

Does this mean you must talk like a television news broadcaster if you want to be successful in your speeches? Not at all. Regional or ethnic dialects do not pose a problem as long as the audience is familiar with them and finds them appropriate. When speaking in the North, for example, a southern politician may avoid regional dialect. But when addressing audiences in the South, the same politician may intentionally include regional dialect as a way of creating common ground with listeners.

Although not strictly speaking a matter of dialect, the proficiency of non-native speakers of English often arises in the speech classroom. Fortunately, teachers and students alike usually go out of their way to be helpful and encouraging to international students and others for whom English is not the primary language. Over the years, many non-native speakers of English have found speech class a supportive environment in which to improve their proficiency in spoken English.[6]

dialect
A variety of a language distinguished by variations of accent, grammar, or vocabulary.

The Speaker's Body

Imagine yourself at a party. During the evening you form impressions about the people around you. Jonte seems relaxed and even-tempered, Nicole tense and irritable. Kyndra seems open and straightforward, Sun Hi hostile and evasive. Amin seems happy to see you; Seth definitely is not.

How do you reach these conclusions? To a surprising extent, you reach them not on the basis of what people say with words, but because of what they say with their posture, gestures, eyes, and facial expressions. Suppose you are sitting next to Amin, and he says, "This is a great party. I'm really glad to be here with you." However, his body is turned slightly away from you, and he keeps looking at someone across the room. Despite what he says, you know he is *not* glad to be there with you.

Much the same thing happens in speechmaking. Posture, facial expression, gestures, eye contact—all affect the way listeners respond to a speaker. How we use these and other body motions to communicate is the subject of a fascinating area of study called kinesics. One of its founders, Ray Birdwhistell, estimated that more than 700,000 physical signals can be sent through bodily movement. Studies have shown that these signals have a significant impact on the meaning communicated by speakers.

kinesics
The study of body motions as a systematic mode of communication.

Research has also lent support to what the Greek historian Herodotus observed more than 2,400 years ago: "People trust their ears less than their eyes." When a speaker's body language is inconsistent with his or her words, listeners may well believe the body language rather than the words. Here are the major aspects of physical action that will affect the outcome of your speeches.

PERSONAL APPEARANCE

Many studies have confirmed that personal appearance plays an important role in speechmaking.[7] As with many aspects of public speaking, how you dress will depend a lot on the audience and the occasion. If you're addressing a group of Wall Street executives, you'll likely wear a business suit. If you're addressing Silicon Valley coders, you'll doubtless wear something more casual. You'll make still different choices if you're speaking at a sales event or a retirement celebration.

A good rule of thumb is to dress a half-step up from your audience. If your audience will be in casual clothing, you should opt for "smart casual" or "business casual." If they will be in business clothing, you should appear slightly more formal. Keep in mind that listeners always see you before they hear you, so try to evoke a favorable first impression.

Personal appearance is as important for online speeches as it is for in-person speeches. Some people think that because much of their online communication is informal, their online speeches can be, too. But that's not the case. Even if you're speaking from your dorm or apartment, you can't wear what you would normally wear around the house. Instead, follow this simple rule: Your personal appearance in an online speech should be the same as it would be if you were giving the speech to an in-person audience.

MOVEMENT

Novice speakers are often unsure about what to do with their body while giving a speech. Some shift their weight uneasily, fidget with their notes, or jingle coins in their pockets. Still others turn into statues, standing rigid and expressionless from beginning to end.

Such quirks usually stem from nervousness. If you are prone to distracting mannerisms, your teacher will identify them so you can work on controlling them. With a little concentration, these mannerisms should disappear as you become more comfortable speaking in front of an audience.

As important as how you act during the speech is what you do just *before* you begin and *after* you finish. As you get ready to speak, try to appear calm, poised, and confident, despite the butterflies in your stomach. Don't rush to get the speech started. Give yourself time to get set. Arrange your notes just the way you want them. Establish eye contact with your listeners. Then—and only then—should you start to talk.

Good speakers use a lively voice to bring their ideas to life. They also use eye contact and facial expressions to create a bond with their audience.
SDI Productions/Getty Images

When you reach the end of your speech, maintain eye contact for a few moments after you stop talking. This will give your closing line time to sink in. As it does, maintain your cool, collected demeanor. Whatever you do, don't start to gather your notes before you have finished talking, and don't cap off your speech with a huge sigh of relief or some remark like, "Whew! Am I glad that's over!"

When practicing your speeches, spend a little time rehearsing how you will behave at the beginning and at the end. It is one of the easiest—and one of the most effective—things you can do to improve your image with an audience.

GESTURES

Few aspects of delivery cause students more anguish than deciding what to do with their hands. "Should I clasp them behind my back? Let them hang at my sides? Rest them on the lectern? And what about gesturing? When should I do that—and how?" Even people who use their hands expressively in everyday conversation seem to regard them as awkward appendages when speaking before an audience.

Over the years, more nonsense has been written about gesturing than any other aspect of speech delivery. Adroit gestures *can* add to the impact of a speech; but effective speakers do not need a vast repertoire of gestures. Some accomplished speakers gesture frequently, others hardly at all. The primary rule is this: Whatever gestures you make should not distract from your message. They should *appear* natural and spontaneous, help clarify or reinforce your ideas, and be suited to the audience and occasion. For a good example, watch Video 13.3.

Gesturing tends to work itself out as you acquire experience and confidence. For now, make sure your hands do not upstage your ideas. Avoid flailing them about, wringing them together, or toying with your rings. Once you have eliminated these distractions, forget about your hands. Think about communicating with your listeners, and your gestures will take care of themselves—just as they do in conversation.

gestures
Motions of a speaker's hands or arms during a speech.

connect

View an excerpt from "Third-Culture Kid" in the online Media Library for this chapter (Video 13.3).

EYE CONTACT

The eyes have been called "the windows of the soul." We look to them to help gauge a speaker's truthfulness, intelligence, attitudes, and feelings.

eye contact

Direct visual contact with the eyes of another person.

Although patterns of eye contact in everyday conversation vary from culture to culture, there is wide agreement across cultures on the importance of eye contact in public speaking. In most circumstances, one of the quickest ways to establish a communicative bond with your listeners is to look at them personally and pleasantly. Avoiding their gaze is one of the surest ways to lose them.

Speakers in the United States who fail to establish eye contact are perceived as tentative or ill at ease and may be seen as insincere or dishonest. It is no wonder, then, that teachers urge students to look at the audience 80 to 90 percent of the time they are talking. You may find this disconcerting at first. But after one or two speeches, you should be able to meet the gaze of your audience fairly comfortably.

It isn't enough just to look at your listeners; *how* you look at them also counts. Beware of the tendency to gaze intently at one part of the audience while ignoring the rest. In speech class, some students look only at the section of the room where the teacher is sitting. Others avoid looking anywhere near the teacher and focus on one or two sympathetic friends. You should try to establish eye contact with your whole audience.

When addressing a small audience such as your class, you can usually look briefly from one person to another. For a larger group, you can scan the audience rather than trying to engage the eyes of each person individually. No matter the size of your audience, you want your eyes to convey confidence, sincerity, and conviction.

connect

View an excerpt from "Making a Difference Through the Special Olympics" in the online Media Library for this chapter (Video 13.4).

Watch Video 13.4 to see a fine example of eye contact. The speaker is telling her classmates how they can become volunteers for the Special Olympics. Notice how she uses her eyes to connect with her listeners at a personal level. This is the kind of strong communication you should strive for in your speeches. (For special aspects of eye contact in online speaking, check Chapter 19, pages 356–358.)

Practicing Delivery

Popular wisdom promises that practice makes perfect. This is true, but only if we practice properly. You will do little to improve your speech delivery unless you practice the right things in the right ways. Here is a five-step method that has worked well for many students:

1. Go through your preparation outline *aloud* to check how what you have written translates into spoken discourse. Is it too long? Too short? Are the main points clear when you speak them? Are the supporting materials distinct, convincing, interesting? Do the introduction and conclusion come across well? As you answer these questions, revise the speech as needed.

2. Prepare your speaking outline. In doing so, be sure to follow the guidelines in Chapter 11. Use the same visual framework as in the preparation outline. Make sure the speaking outline is easy to read at a glance. Give yourself cues on the outline for delivering the speech.

Regardless of the audience and situation, you should use your delivery to establish a strong bond with your listeners. Their responses will help you judge how you are coming across.

Jeffbergen/Getty Images

3. Practice the speech aloud several times using only the speaking outline. Be sure to "talk through" all examples and to recite in full all quotations and statistics. If your speech includes visual aids, use them as you practice. The first couple of times, you will probably forget something or make a mistake, but don't worry. Keep going and complete the speech as well as you can. Concentrate on gaining control of the *ideas;* don't try to learn the speech word for word. After a few tries you should be able to get through the speech extemporaneously with surprising ease.

4. Now begin to polish and refine your delivery. Practice the speech in front of a mirror to check for eye contact and distracting mannerisms. Record the speech to gauge volume, pitch, rate, pauses, and vocal variety. Most important, try it out on friends, roommates, family members—anyone who will listen and give you an honest appraisal. Because your speech is designed for people rather than for mirrors or recorders, you need to find out ahead of time how it goes over with people.

5. Finally, give your speech a dress rehearsal under conditions as close as possible to those you will encounter on speech day. Some students like to try the speech a couple times in an empty classroom the day before the speech is due. If you're speaking online, practice delivering your speech to a remote audience of family and friends—as though they are your classmates on the other side of the webcam. No matter where you hold your last practice session, you should leave it feeling confident and looking forward to delivering the final version of your speech.

If this or any practice method is to work, you must start early. Don't wait until the night before your speech to begin working on delivery. A single practice session—no matter how long—is rarely enough. Allow yourself *at least* a couple days, preferably more, to gain command of the speech and its presentation.

Answering Audience Questions

If you have ever watched a press conference or heard a speaker answer questions after a talk, you know the question-and-answer session can make or break a presentation. A speaker who handles questions well can strengthen the impact of his or her speech. On the other hand, a speaker who evades questions or shows annoyance will almost certainly create the opposite effect.

The question-and-answer session is a common part of public speaking, whether the occasion is a press conference, an online business presentation, a public hearing, or a classroom assignment. An answer to a question is often the final word an audience hears and is likely to leave a lasting impression.

PREPARING FOR THE QUESTION-AND-ANSWER SESSION

The first step to doing well in a Q&A session is to take it as seriously as the speech itself. The two major steps in preparing are working out answers to possible questions and practicing the delivery of those answers.

Formulate Answers to Possible Questions

Once you know that your presentation will include questions from the audience, you should be thinking about possible questions even as you are writing your speech. If you practice your speech in front of friends, family, or coworkers, ask them to jot down questions. Keep track of all the questions and formulate answers. Write your answers in full to make sure you have thought them through completely.

If you are giving a persuasive speech, be sure to work out answers to objections the audience may have to your proposal. No matter how careful you are to deal with those objections in your speech, you can be sure they will come up in the Q&A session.

If you are speaking on a topic with technical aspects, be ready to answer specialized inquiries about them, as well as questions that seek clarification, in nontechnical terms. You might even prepare a handout that you can distribute afterward for people who want more information.

Practice the Delivery of Your Answers

You would not present a speech to a room full of people without rehearsing. Neither should you go into a Q&A session without practicing the delivery of your answers.

One possibility is to have a friend or colleague listen to your presentation, ask questions, and critique your answers. This method is used by political candidates and business leaders before debates or press conferences. Another possibility is to record your answers to anticipated questions, play them back, and revise them until they are just right.

As you rehearse, work on making your answers brief and to the point. Many simple questions can be answered in 30 seconds, and even complex ones should usually be answered in a minute or two. If you practice answering questions beforehand, you will find it much easier to keep to these time limits.

Of course, there is no way to predict every question you will receive. But if you go into the Q&A period fully prepared, you will be able to adapt to whatever occurs.

Question-and-answer sessions are an important part of public speaking in many situations, including business meetings, education conventions, and international conferences.

PeopleImages/Digital Vision/Getty Images

MANAGING THE QUESTION-AND-ANSWER SESSION

If you have ever watched a skillful speaker field inquiries from the audience, you know there is an art to managing a Q&A session. Entire books have been written on this subject, but the following suggestions will get you started on the right foot.

Approach Questions with a Positive Attitude

A positive attitude will help you answer questions graciously and respectfully. Try to view questions from the audience as signs of genuine interest and a desire to learn more about your subject. If someone asks about a point that seems clear to you, don't respond by saying "I discussed that at the beginning of my talk," or "The answer seems obvious." Instead, use moments like these to reiterate or expand upon your ideas.

A speaker who adopts a sharp or defensive tone while answering questions will alienate many people in the audience. Even if you are asked a hostile question, keep your cool. Avoid the temptation to answer defensively, sarcastically, or argumentatively. Most people in the audience will respect you for trying to avoid a quarrel.

Listen Carefully

It's hard to answer a question well if you don't listen carefully to it. Give the questioner your full attention. When faced with an unclear or unwieldy question, try to rephrase it by saying something like, "If I understand your question, it seems to me that you are asking. . . ." Another option is simply to ask the audience member to repeat the question. Most people will restate it more succinctly and clearly.

Direct Answers to the Entire Audience

When you are being asked a question, look at the questioner. Direct your answer, however, to the entire audience. Make occasional eye contact with the questioner as

Utilizing your business degree and computer savvy, you have made a success of the online marketing company you started after graduating from college. Now in its third year, the company has prepared a proposal to design the e-commerce site for a major sporting goods retailer. In your 30-minute presentation to the retailer's management team, you will review the homepage designs, site maps, and security protocols.

You notice on the agenda that another 30 minutes has been allotted after your presentation for questions and answers. Knowing from your previous experience with clients how important the Q&A session can be, you want to be sure you are ready for it. What steps will you take to prepare?

Nick David/Getty Images

you answer, but speak primarily to the audience as a whole. If you speak just to the questioner, the rest of your audience may drift off.

When speaking to a large audience, repeat or paraphrase each question after it is asked. This involves the entire audience and ensures that they know the question. In addition, repeating or paraphrasing the question gives you a moment to frame an answer before you respond.

In an online speech, you may be answering questions posed in the chat area of the presentation software. If so, be sure to restate the question for those who are not monitoring the chat. You can say something like, "Here's a question I just received in the chat. . . ." Then answer it for the whole audience.

Be Honest and Straightforward

If you don't know the answer to a question, say so. Don't apologize, don't evade, and most important, don't try to bluff. Do, however, let the questioner know that you take the question seriously. Offer to check into the answer as soon as possible after the speech. If a more knowledgeable person is at hand, ask if she or he knows the answer.

Stay on Track

It's easy to get diverted or lose control of time in a lively Q&A session. Unless there is a moderator, the speaker is responsible for keeping things on track. Allow one follow-up question from each person, and don't let yourself be dragged into a personal debate with any questioner. If someone attempts to ask more than two questions, respond graciously yet firmly by saying, "This is an interesting line of questioning, but we need to give other people a chance to ask questions."

Sometimes, a listener will launch into an extended monologue instead of posing a question. When this happens, you can retain control of the situation by saying something like, "Those are very interesting ideas, but do you have a specific question I can answer?" If the person persists, offer to talk individually with him or her after the session.

On some occasions, the length of the question-and-answer session is predetermined. On other occasions, it's up to the speaker. Make sure you allow enough time to get through issues of major importance, but don't let things drag on after the momentum of the session has started winding down. As the end approaches, offer to respond to another question or two. Then wrap things up by thanking the audience for its time and attention.[8]

Summary

Speech delivery is a matter of nonverbal communication. It is based on how you use your voice and body to convey the message expressed by your words. Rather than calling attention to itself, effective delivery conveys the speaker's ideas clearly, engagingly, and without distracting the audience.

There are four basic methods of delivering a speech: reading verbatim from a manuscript, reciting a memorized text, speaking impromptu, and speaking extemporaneously. When speaking extemporaneously, you will have a brief set of notes or a speaking outline and will choose the exact wording of your speech at the moment of delivery.

To use your voice effectively you should work on controlling your volume, pitch, rate, pauses, vocal variety, pronunciation, articulation, and dialect. Volume is the relative loudness of your voice, and pitch is the relative highness or lowness. Rate refers to the speed at which you talk. Pauses, when carefully timed, can add punch to your speech, but you should avoid vocalized pauses ("er," "um," and the like).

Vocal variety refers to changes in volume, pitch, rate, and pauses, and is crucial to making your voice lively and animated. You also need correct pronunciation and distinct articulation. Avoid heavy use of dialect in situations where the audience does not share the dialect or will find it inappropriate.

Posture, personal appearance, facial expression, gestures, and eye contact also affect the way listeners respond to speakers. Dress and groom appropriately, use gestures and bodily movement to enhance your message, and make eye contact with your listeners.

You should practice all these aspects of delivery along with the words of your speech. Start your practice sessions early so you will have plenty of time to gain command of the speech and its presentation.

If your speech includes a question-and-answer session, anticipate the most likely questions, prepare answers to them, and practice delivering those answers. During the Q&A period, listen carefully to the questions, approach them positively, and respond to them briefly, graciously, and straightforwardly. Direct your answers to the full audience, rather than to the questioner alone, and make sure to end the session in a timely fashion.

Key Terms

nonverbal communication (226)
manuscript speech (228)
impromptu speech (229)
extemporaneous speech (230)
conversational quality (230)

volume (231)
pitch (232)
inflections (232)
monotone (232)
rate (232)

pause (232)   dialect (235)

vocalized pause (233)   kinesics (236)

vocal variety (233)   gestures (237)

pronunciation (234)   eye contact (238)

articulation (234)

Review Questions

After reading this chapter, you should be able to answer the following questions:

1. What is nonverbal communication? Why is it important to effective public speaking?

2. What are the elements of good speech delivery?

3. What are the four methods of speech delivery?

4. What are the eight aspects of voice usage you should concentrate on in your speeches?

5. What are four aspects of bodily action you should concentrate on in your speeches?

6. What are the five steps you should follow when practicing your speech delivery?

7. What steps should you take when preparing for a question-and-answer session? What should you concentrate on when responding to questions during the session?

Exercises for Critical Thinking

1. An excellent way to improve your vocal variety is to read aloud selections from poetry that require emphasis and feeling. Choose one of your favorite poems that falls into this category, or find one by leafing through a poetry anthology.

   Practice reading the selection aloud. As you read, use your voice to make the poem come alive. Vary your volume, rate, and pitch. Find the appropriate places for pauses. Underline the key words or phrases you think should be stressed. Modulate your tone of voice; use inflections for emphasis and meaning.

   For this to work, you must overcome your fear of sounding affected or "dramatic." Most beginning speakers do better if they exaggerate changes in volume, rate, pitch, and expression. This will make you more aware of the ways you can use your voice to express a wide range of moods and meanings. Besides, what sounds overly "dramatic" to you usually does not sound that way to an audience. By adding luster, warmth, and enthusiasm to your voice, you will go a long way toward capturing and keeping the interest of your listeners.

   If possible, practice reading the selection into a digital recorder. Listen to the playback. If you are not satisfied with what you hear, practice the selection some more and record it again.

2. Watch a 10-minute segment of a televised or streaming drama with the sound turned off. What do the characters say with their dress, gestures, facial expressions, and the like? Do the same with a comedy. How do the nonverbal messages in the two shows differ? Be prepared to report your observations in class.

3. Attend a speech sponsored by a campus organization. You may choose either a presentation by a guest speaker from outside your school or by someone at your school who has a reputation as a good lecturer. Prepare a brief report on the speaker's delivery.

In your report, first analyze the speaker's volume, pitch, rate, pauses, vocal variety, pronunciation, and articulation. Then evaluate the speaker's personal appearance, bodily action, gestures, and eye contact. Explain how the speaker's delivery added to or detracted from what the speaker said. Finally, note at least two techniques of delivery used by the speaker that you might want to try in your next speech.

End Notes

[1]Irving Bartlett, *Wendell Phillips: Boston Brahmin* (Boston, MA: Beacon Press, 1961), p. 192.

[2]A. Craig Baird, *Rhetoric: A Philosophical Inquiry* (New York: Ronald Press, 1965), p. 207.

[3]For more on how speech rate affects audience perception, see Richard M. Perloff, *The Dynamics of Persuasion: Communication and Attitudes in the 21st Century,* 7th ed. (New York: Routledge, 2021), pp. 315–317.

[4]Daniel J. O'Keefe, *Persuasion: Theory and Research,* 3rd ed. (Thousand Oaks, CA: Sage, 2016), p. 191.

[5]Dorothy Sarnoff, *Speech Can Change Your Life* (Garden City, NY: Doubleday, 1970), p. 73.

[6]For more detail on various aspects of dialect, see Walt Wolfram and Natalie Schilling, *American English: Dialects and Variation,* 3rd ed. (West Sussex, UK: Wiley Blackwell, 2016).

[7]See, for example, Perloff, *Dynamics of Persuasion,* pp. 282–292; O'Keefe, *Persuasion: Theory and Research,* pp. 204–206.

[8]Thomas F. Calcagni, *Tough Questions—Good Answers: Taking Control of Any Interview* (Sterling, VA: Capital Books, 2008), provides many practical tips on managing question-and-answer sessions.

Using Visual Aids

Every year, usually in September, Apple unveils a new iPhone. If you watch the unveiling, you'll see the phone's captivating features. You'll also witness a masterclass in the use of visual aids.

Every time a new phone arrives, Apple executives create a dazzling story about it. You'll see video clips of users handling the phone with smiles on their faces. You'll see the presenters reinforce their pitch with dramatic images and succinct text. You'll see complex information conveyed in spectacular, easy-to-understand charts and graphs showing the phone's speed, battery life, options, and camera system.

What you won't see are the months of planning and practice that went into the event. Apple executives rehearse their speeches countless times before the day the new phone is revealed. They go through their speeches time and again to make sure what they say is perfectly coordinated with what the audience will see, creating a presentation with optimal impact.

By the day of the unveiling, they have crafted a visually rich story expertly designed to do one thing—sell the new iPhone. And they will sell plenty.

When Apple debuts a new iPhone, they spend months and millions of dollars getting their message and visual aids just right. You won't have that luxury in your speech class. But you can take several cues from the introduction of a new iPhone to create visual aids that will help make your speeches engaging and perhaps even dazzling.

People find a speaker's message more interesting, grasp it more easily, and retain it longer when it is presented visually as well as verbally. In fact, when used properly, visual aids can enhance almost *every* aspect of a speech. An average speaker who

uses visual aids will come across as better prepared, more credible, and more professional than a dynamic speaker who does not use visual aids. Visual aids can even help you combat stage fright. They heighten audience interest, shift attention away from the speaker, and give the speaker greater confidence in the presentation as a whole.[1]

For all these reasons, you will find visual aids of great value in your speeches, whether you're addressing an in-person audience or an online audience. In this chapter, we will concentrate on general principles for visual aids. In Chapter 19, we'll attend to special aspects of using visual aids in online speeches.

Let us look first at the kinds of visual aids you are most likely to use, then at guidelines for preparing visual aids, and finally at guidelines for using visual aids.

Kinds of Visual Aids

OBJECTS AND MODELS

Bringing the object of your speech to class can be an excellent way to clarify your ideas and give them dramatic impact. If your specific purpose is "To inform my audience how to choose the right ski equipment," why not bring the equipment to class to show your listeners? Or suppose you want to inform your classmates about the Peruvian art of doll making. You could bring several dolls to class and explain how they were made.

Some objects, however, cannot be used effectively in classroom speeches. Some are too big. Others are too small to be seen clearly. Still others may not be available to you. If you were speaking about a rare suit of armor in a local museum, you could, theoretically, transport it to class, but it is most unlikely that the museum would let you borrow it.

If the object you want to discuss is too large, too small, or unavailable, you may be able to work with a model. For an example, check Video 14.1. The speaker is talking about CPR, which he demonstrates on a training dummy he borrowed from the local Red Cross.

connect

View an excerpt from "CPR" in the online Media Library for this chapter (Video 14.1).

PHOTOGRAPHS AND DRAWINGS

In the absence of an object or a model, you may be able to use photographs or drawings. Neither, however, will work effectively unless they are large enough for the audience to see without straining. Normal-size photos are too small to be seen clearly without being passed around—which only diverts the audience from what you are saying. The same is true of photographs and drawings in books.

The most effective way to show drawings and photographs is with a presentation program such as PowerPoint or Google Slides. Notice, for example, how the speaker in Video 14.2 uses PowerPoint to present a photograph of the famous ruins at Angkor Wat in Cambodia. No other method of showing the photograph would work as well.

For another example, take a look at Figure 14.1 (page 249), which shows a drawing used in a speech about the kinds of problems faced by people who have dyslexia. It allowed the speaker to translate complex ideas into visual terms the audience could grasp immediately.

connect

View an excerpt from "The Splendor of Angkor Wat" in the online Media Library for this chapter (Video 14.2).

Photographs make excellent visual aids if they are large enough to be seen easily. Check Video 14.2 in the online Media Library for this chapter to see how one speaker used this photograph of the famous ruins at Angkor Wat.

Andrew Gunners/Getty Images

GRAPHS

Audiences often have trouble grasping a complex series of numbers. You can ease their difficulty by using graphs to show statistical trends and patterns.

The most common type is the *line graph*. Figure 14.2 (page 250) shows such a graph, used in a speech about food spending in the United States. If you watch Video 14.3, you can see how the speaker explained the graph. She said:

> According to figures from the U.S. Census Bureau, Americans now spend more money on restaurant food than on food in grocery stores. The blue line on this graph represents money spent in grocery stores. Historically it has always been higher than money spent in restaurants. But that changed in 2015.
>
> As the red line shows, that's when, for the first time in our nation's history, we spent more at restaurants than at grocery stores. If projections are accurate, the gap between restaurant and grocery spending will continue to grow in coming years.

graph
A visual aid used to show statistical trends and patterns.

connect
View an excerpt from "How We Eat" in the online Media Library for this chapter (Video 14.3).

FIGURE 14.1

This si wнat a qerson with dyslexia mihgt ƨe wнem reding this ƨentnce.

FIGURE 14.2

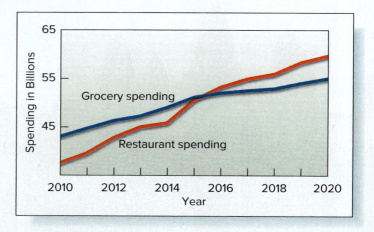

line graph
A graph that uses one or more lines to show changes in statistics over time or space.

The *pie graph* is best suited for illustrating simple distribution patterns. Figure 14.3 shows how one speaker used a pie graph to help listeners visualize changes in marital status among working women in the past century. The graph on the left shows the percentages of working women who were single, married, and widowed or divorced in 1920. The graph on the right shows percentages for the same groups in 2020.

Because a pie graph is used to dramatize relationships among the parts of a whole, you should keep the number of different segments in the graph as small as possible. A pie graph should ideally have from two to five segments; under no circumstances should it have more than eight.

The *bar graph* is a particularly good way to show comparisons among two or more items. It also has the advantage of being easy to understand, even by people who have no background in reading graphs.

FIGURE 14.3

Women in the Workforce

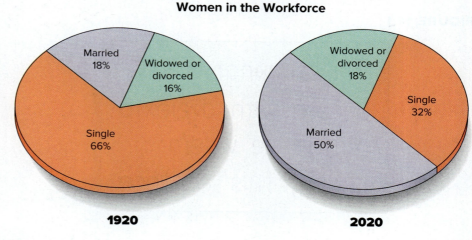

pie graph
A graph that highlights segments of a circle to show simple distribution patterns.

FIGURE 14.4

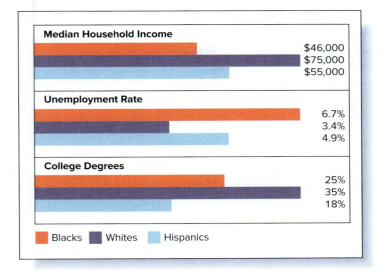

bar graph

A graph that uses vertical or horizontal bars to show comparisons among two or more items.

Figure 14.4 is an example of a bar graph from a speech titled "The Politics of Race in America." It shows visually the relative standing of Blacks, Whites, and Hispanics with respect to median household income, unemployment, and college education. By using a bar graph, the speaker made her points more vividly than if she had just cited the numbers orally.

CHARTS

Charts are particularly useful for summarizing large blocks of information. One student, in a speech titled "Risks and Rewards of Work," used a chart to show the most dangerous jobs in the United States (Figure 14.5, page 252). These are too many categories to be conveyed in a pie graph. By listing them on a chart, the speaker made it easier for listeners to keep the information straight. Look at Video 14.4 to see how the student presented the chart during his speech.

The biggest mistake made by beginning speakers when using a chart is to include too much information. As we will discuss later, visual aids should be clear, simple, and uncluttered. Lists on a chart should rarely exceed seven or eight items, with generous spacing between items. If you cannot fit everything on a single chart, make a second one.

connect

View an excerpt from "Risks and Rewards of Work" in the online Media Library for this chapter (Video 14.4).

VIDEO

If you are talking about the impact caused by a low-speed automobile accident, what could be more effective than showing slow-motion video of crash tests? Or suppose you are explaining the different kinds of roller coasters found in amusement parks. Your best visual aid would be a video showing those coasters in action.

Despite its advantages, however, adding video to a speech can cause more harm than good if it is not done carefully and expertly. First, make sure the clip is not too long. While a 30-second video can illustrate your ideas in a memorable way, anything much longer will distract attention from the speech itself. Second, make sure the video is cued to start exactly where you want it. Third, if necessary, edit the video to

FIGURE 14.5

Most Dangerous Jobs in the U.S.

Occupation	Fatal Work Injuries*
Loggers	133
Fishing workers	55
Aircraft pilots & engineers	40
Roofers	40
Refuse collectors	39
Structural iron & steel workers	30
Professional drivers & truck drivers	24

*per 100,000 workers

Source: U.S. Department of Labor Statistics, USDL-17-1667

chart
A visual aid that summarizes a large block of information, usually in list form.

the precise length you need so it will blend smoothly into your speech. Fourth, beware of low-resolution video that may look fine on a computer but is blurry and distorted when projected on a screen or monitor.

THE SPEAKER

Sometimes you can use your own body as a visual aid—by illustrating how a conductor directs an orchestra, by revealing the secrets behind magic tricks, by showing how to perform sign language, and so forth. In addition to clarifying a speaker's ideas, doing some kind of demonstration helps keep the audience involved. It also can reduce a speaker's nervousness by providing an outlet for extra adrenaline.

connect

View an excerpt from "Using a Tourniquet to Save a Life" in the online Media Library for this chapter (Video 14.5).

Doing a demonstration well requires special practice to coordinate your actions with your words and to control the timing of your speech. You can see an excellent example on Video 14.5. After talking about when a tourniquet is useful in emergency situations, the speaker demonstrates how to apply a tourniquet. Notice how clearly he explains the five steps of application, communicates directly with the audience, and maintains eye contact throughout his demonstration.

Special care is required if you are demonstrating a process that takes longer to complete than the time allotted for your speech. If you plan to show a long process, you might borrow the techniques of television chefs. They work through most of the steps in making a perfect marinated chicken, but they have a second, finished chicken ready to show you at the last minute.

Presentation Technology

Presentation technology allows you to integrate a variety of visual aids—including charts, graphs, photographs, and video—in the same talk. The most widely used presentation program is PowerPoint, but in recent years it has been joined by a host of competitors, including Google Slides, Keynote, Prezi, and Haiku Deck. Depending on the resources at your school, you may be able to use one of these

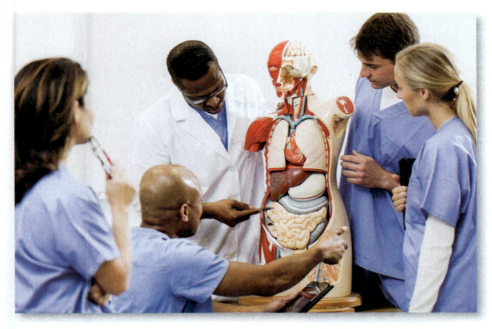

Visual aids make a speaker's message clearer, more interesting, and easier to retain. In this case, a doctor uses a model to help medical students see the location of internal organs in the human body.
Kali9/Getty Images

programs in your speech class. If so, it will provide training for speeches outside the classroom—especially in business settings, where presentation technology is used every day.

Later in this chapter, we will look at guidelines for preparing and presenting visual aids effectively. In the process, we'll pay special attention to what you can do to create and deliver high-quality slides. For now, consider the following factors when thinking about employing presentation technology in your speeches.

PLUSES AND MINUSES OF PRESENTATION TECHNOLOGY

When used well, presentation technology is a great boon to communication. Unfortunately, it is not always used well. Too often speakers allow it to dominate their talks, wowing the audience with their technical proficiency while losing the message in a flurry of sounds and images.

This can be especially true with some of the new presentation programs. Prezi, for example, promises that you can "captivate your audience by zooming through your story." The danger is that Prezi's zooming, panning, and transition effects can become a barrier to communication, especially in a brief classroom speech. As one leading expert on presentation technology warns, Prezi too often turns speeches into "heavily decorated and animated affairs with excessive motion that distracts from even well-researched content."[2]

At the other extreme are mind-numbing presentations that gave rise to the phrase "Death by PowerPoint." In such cases, the speaker plods through one poorly designed slide after another, virtually reading the speech to the audience as the words appear on-screen. This is no more effective than reading dully from a manuscript.

PLANNING TO USE PRESENTATION TECHNOLOGY

If you are going to employ presentation technology effectively, you need a clear idea of exactly why, how, and when to use it. Rather than putting everything you say

As a veterinarian and owner of a small-animal practice, you work closely with your local humane society to help control a growing population of unwanted dogs and cats. You and your staff devote many hours annually in free and reduced-cost medical services to animals adopted from the society. Now you have been asked to speak to the city council in support of legislation proposed by the society for stronger enforcement of animal licensing and leash laws.

In your speech, you plan to include statistics that (1) compare estimates of the city's dog population with the number of licenses issued during the past five years and (2) show the small number of citations given by local law enforcement for unleashed pets during the same period of time. Knowing from your college public speaking class how valuable visual aids can be in presenting statistics, you decide to illustrate one set of statistics with a chart and the other with a graph.

For which set of statistics will a chart be more appropriate? For which set will a graph be more appropriate? Of the three kinds of graphs discussed in this chapter—bar, line, pie—which will work best for your statistics, and why?

G-stockstudio/Getty Images

on-screen for the audience to read, you need to choose which aspects of your speech to illustrate. This requires careful planning.

The first step is deciding where you can use PowerPoint, Keynote, or some other program to greatest advantage. After you have finished developing the speech, think about where well-chosen slides will clarify or strengthen your ideas. Rather than using slides to illustrate every thought, look for spots where they will genuinely enhance your message.

connect
View this excerpt from "Medical Robots: From Science Fiction to Science Fact" in the online Media Library for this chapter (Video 14.6).

One student, for example, used PowerPoint splendidly in a speech on medical robots. Part of the speech dealt with orderly robots, which transport medicine, food, and lab supplies around the hospital without a human by their side. The robots navigate by using "light whiskers"—invisible beams of sonar, infrared, and laser that constantly scan the environment to avoid collisions. Because the light whiskers are invisible, the speaker needed to find a way to make them visible for his audience. He did so by creating a PowerPoint slide in which colored lines representing the light whiskers popped on-screen in perfect coordination with the speaker's words. As you can see from Video 14.6, it was an ingenious solution.

As you plan your speeches, think about how you can use presentation technology to enhance your ideas. At the same time, remember that too many visuals—or poor visuals—can do more harm than good. Be creative and resourceful without allowing technology to overpower your entire speech.

Guidelines for Preparing Visual Aids

Whether you are creating visual aids by hand or with presentation technology, the following guidelines will help you design aids that are clear and visually appealing.

PREPARE VISUAL AIDS WELL IN ADVANCE

Preparing visual aids well in advance has two advantages. First, it means you will have the time and resources to devise creative, attractive aids. Second, it means you can use them while practicing your speech. Visual aids are effective only when they are integrated smoothly with the rest of the speech. If you lose your place, drop your aids, or otherwise stumble around when presenting them, you will distract your audience and shatter your concentration.

KEEP VISUAL AIDS SIMPLE

Visual aids should be simple, clear, and to the point. If you look back at the aids presented earlier in this chapter, you will see that all of them are clear and uncluttered. They contain enough information to communicate the speaker's point, but not so much as to confuse or distract the audience.

Limit your slides to a manageable amount of information, and beware of the tendency to go overboard. It is possible to create a graphic that displays two charts, a photograph, and 10 lines of text in five different typefaces with 250 colors. But who would be able to read it?

MAKE SURE VISUAL AIDS ARE LARGE ENOUGH

A visual aid is useless if no one can see it. Keep in mind the size of the room in which you will be speaking and make sure your aid is big enough to be seen easily by everyone. As you prepare the aid, check its visibility by moving to a point as far away from it as your most distant listener will be sitting.

If you are using a presentation program such as PowerPoint or Google Slides, make sure your text and images are easy for everyone in your audience to see. By making sure your visual aid is large enough, you will avoid having to introduce it with the comment, "I know some of you can't see this, but. . . ."

What about using all capital letters? That might seem a great way to ensure that your print is large enough to be read easily. But research has shown that a long string of words in ALL CAPS is actually harder to read than normal text. Reserve ALL CAPS for titles or for individual words that require special emphasis.

USE A LIMITED AMOUNT OF TEXT

When displaying text on visual aids, follow this general rule: Briefer is better. Succinct phrases containing only essential key words will help listeners grasp your basic point and process the information as you're speaking.

One of the biggest mistakes people make with presentation technology is putting too much text on a single slide. A general rule for slides that contain only text is to include no more than a half-dozen lines of type. If you are combining text with images, you may need to limit yourself to fewer lines to keep the text from getting too small. If you have a number of important points to cover, spread them out over multiple slides.

Figure 14.6 (page 256) shows a slide from a speech about the Iditarod Sled Dog Race, held each year in Alaska. Notice that the slide is not bogged down with information. It presents only an image of sled dogs, plus a title and text noting the number of dogs per team, the length of the race, and the start and ends points in Alaska. Because the slide is simple and clear, the speaker was able to present it succinctly and move on to her next point.

FIGURE 14.6

Alaska Photography/Moment/Getty Images

USE FONTS EFFECTIVELY

font
A complete set of type of the same design.

Not all fonts are suitable for visual aids. For the most part, you should avoid decorative fonts such as those on the left in Figure 14.7. Those on the right of the figure, however, will help make your aids audience-friendly.

Using fonts effectively can make a huge difference in your slides. In general, keep the following guidelines in mind when selecting fonts:

- Choose fonts that are clear and easy to read.
- Make sure lettering is large enough to be read easily by the entire audience.
- Avoid using ALL CAPS because they are difficult to read.
- Don't use more than two fonts on a single slide—one for the title or major heading and another for subtitles or other text.
- Use the same fonts on all your slides.

If you use one of the built-in themes in Keynote or PowerPoint, you can be confident that the fonts, which have been preselected according to the design of the theme, are clear, legible, and consistent.

USE COLOR EFFECTIVELY

When used effectively, color can dramatically increase the impact of a visual aid. The key words, of course, are "when used effectively." Some colors do not work well together. Red and green are a tough combination for anyone to read, and they look the same to people who are color-blind. Many shades of blue and green are too close to each other to be easily differentiated—as are orange and red, blue and purple.

You can use either dark print on a light background or light print on a dark background, but in either case make sure there is enough contrast between the background and the text so listeners can see everything clearly. Avoid such colors as yellow on a white background or purple on a red background.

Also, stick to a limited number of colors and use them consistently. Use one color for background, one color for titles, and one color for other text throughout all your slides. This consistency will unify the slides and give your speech a professional appearance.

FIGURE 14.7

USE IMAGES STRATEGICALLY

One of the benefits of presentation technology is the ease with which it allows you to include photographs, charts, graphs, and other images, including video. Unfortunately, some speakers are prone to adding images simply because it is easy, rather than because it is essential for communicating their message. You should *never* add images of any sort to a slide unless they are truly needed. There is a great deal of research showing that extraneous images distract listeners and reduce comprehension of the speaker's point.[3]

In addition to keeping your slides free of extraneous images, keep these guidelines in mind:

- Make sure images are large enough to be seen clearly.
- Choose high-resolution images that will project without blurring.
- Keep graphs and charts clear and simple.
- In most cases, include a title above charts and graphs so the audience knows what they are viewing.
- Edit video so it is integrated seamlessly into your slides.

Guidelines for Presenting Visual Aids

No matter how well designed your visual aids may be, they will be of little value unless you display them properly, discuss them clearly, and integrate them effectively with the rest of your presentation. Here are seven guidelines that will help you get the maximum impact out of your visual aids.

DISPLAY VISUAL AIDS WHERE LISTENERS CAN SEE THEM

Check the speech room ahead of time to decide exactly where you will display your visual aids. If you are displaying an object or a model, be sure to place it where it can be seen easily by everyone in the room. If necessary, hold up the object or model while you are discussing it.

Once you have set the aid in the best location, don't undo all your preparation by standing where you block the audience's view of the aid. Stand to one side of the aid, and point with the arm nearest it. Using a pen, a ruler, or some other pointer will allow you to stand farther away from the visual aid, thereby reducing the likelihood that you will obstruct the view.

If you are using a projection screen, check ahead of time to make sure it is not located where you will cast a shadow on it while you are speaking. If necessary, move the lectern to the side of the screen.

AVOID PASSING VISUAL AIDS AMONG THE AUDIENCE

Once visual aids get into the hands of your listeners, you are in trouble. At least three people will be paying more attention to the aid than to you—the person who has just had it, the person who has it now, and the person waiting to get it next. By the time the visual aid moves on, all three may have lost track of what you are saying.[4]

Nor do you solve this problem by preparing a handout for every member of the audience. They are likely to spend a good part of the speech looking over the handout at their own pace, rather than listening to you. Although handouts can be valuable, they usually just create competition for beginning speakers.

Every once in a while, of course, you will want listeners to have copies of some material to take home. When such a situation arises, keep the copies until after you've finished talking and distribute them at the end. Keeping control of your visual aids is essential to keeping control of your speech.

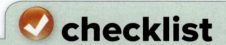 **checklist**

Preparing Visual Aids

YES	NO	
☐	☐	1. Have I prepared my visual aids well in advance?
☐	☐	2. Are my visual aids clear and easy to comprehend?
☐	☐	3. Does each visual aid contain only the information needed to make my point?
☐	☐	4. Are my visual aids large enough to be seen clearly by the entire audience?
☐	☐	5. Do the colors on my visual aids work well together?
☐	☐	6. Is there a clear contrast between the lettering and background on my charts, graphs, and drawings?
☐	☐	7. Do I use line graphs, pie graphs, and bar graphs correctly to show statistical trends and patterns?
☐	☐	8. Do I limit charts to no more than eight items?
☐	☐	9. Do I use fonts that are easy to read?
☐	☐	10. Do I use a limited number of fonts?

Speakers should display visual aids where they can be seen clearly by all members of the audience. They should also remember to maintain eye contact with the audience while discussing their aids.

Hero Images/Getty Images

DISPLAY VISUAL AIDS ONLY WHILE DISCUSSING THEM

Just as circulating visual aids distracts attention, so does displaying them throughout a speech. If you are using an object or a model, keep it out of sight until you are ready to discuss it. When you finish your discussion, place the object or model back out of sight.

The same principle applies to presentation slides. They should be visible only while you are discussing them. You can accomplish this by adding blank slides as needed, so the audience's attention will not be diverted by the previous slide. It is also a good idea to add a blank slide at the end of your presentation, so your last content slide will not continue to be exposed after you have finished discussing it.

EXPLAIN VISUAL AIDS CLEARLY AND CONCISELY

Visual aids don't explain themselves. Like statistics, they need to be translated and related to the audience. For example, Figure 14.8 (page 260) is an excellent visual aid, but do you know what it represents? Probably not, unless you've researched the supervolcano beneath Yellowstone National Park. But even then, the full meaning of the map may not be clear until it is explained to you.

A visual aid can be of enormous benefit—but only if the viewer knows what to look for and why. Unfortunately, speakers often rush over their visual aids without explaining them clearly and concisely. Don't just say, "As you can see . . ." and then pass quickly over the aid. Tell listeners what the aid means. Describe its major features. Spell out the meaning of charts and graphs. Interpret statistics and percentages. Remember, a visual aid is only as useful as the explanation that goes with it.

As you can see from Video 14.7, the speaker who used the map about past eruptions of the Yellowstone supervolcano did an excellent job explaining that each colored area corresponds to a different eruption. Having used the map during her practice sessions, she was able to work it into the speech smoothly and skillfully—and to maintain eye contact with the audience throughout her discussion of it. You should strive to do the same when you present visual aids in your speeches.

FIGURE 14.8

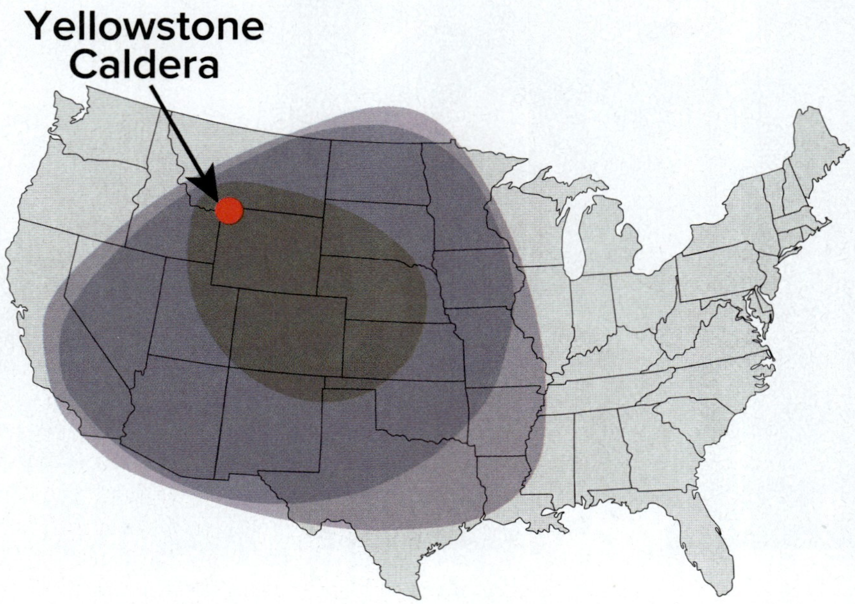
Yellowstone
Caldera

connect

View an excerpt from "Supervolcanoes: The Sleeping Giants" in the online Media Library for this chapter (Video 14.7).

TALK TO YOUR AUDIENCE, NOT TO YOUR VISUAL AID

When explaining a visual aid, it is easy to break eye contact with your audience and speak to the aid. Of course, your listeners are looking primarily at the aid, and you may need to glance at it periodically as you talk. But if you keep your eyes fixed on the visual aid, you will lose your audience. By keeping eye contact with your listeners, you can also pick up feedback about how the visual aid and your explanation of it are coming across.

PRACTICE WITH YOUR VISUAL AIDS

This chapter has mentioned several times the need to practice with visual aids, but the point bears repeating. No matter what kind of visual aid you choose, be sure to employ it when you practice. Go through the speech multiple times, rehearsing how you will show your aids, the gestures you will make, and the timing of each move. In using visual aids, as in other aspects of speechmaking, there is no substitute for preparation.

connect

View an excerpt from "Eyewitness Misidentification" in the online Media Library for this chapter (Video 14.8).

If you are using presentation technology, don't just click the mouse casually or rush quickly over your words when you practice. Make sure you know exactly when you want each slide to appear and disappear, and what you will say while each is on-screen. Mark your speaking notes with cues that will remind you when to display each slide and when to remove it.

Rehearse with the mouse, keyboard, or iPad until you can use them without looking down for more than an instant when advancing your slides. Also concentrate on presenting the speech without looking back at the screen to see what is being projected. For a good example, check Video 14.8. Notice how the speaker's visual aids are perfectly coordinated with her words and how she keeps eye contact with her audience while she is presenting the aids.

Given all the things you have to work on when practicing a speech with any kind of presentation technology, you need to allow extra time for rehearsal. So get an early start and give yourself plenty of time to ensure that your delivery is as impressive as your slides.[5]

CHECK THE ROOM AND EQUIPMENT

For classroom speeches, you will already be familiar with the room and equipment. If any of the technology fails, a technician can make the necessary adjustments. For speeches outside the classroom, however, the situation is very different. There is wide variation among computers and projectors, as well as among rooms equipped with multimedia connections. Even if you have used PowerPoint or Google Slides on previous occasions, you need to check the setup in the room where you will be speaking.

If possible, look at the room and equipment before the day of your speech. Hook up your computer to make sure everything works properly. If you are using a computer that is installed in the room, bring your slides on a flash drive so you can see how they work with that computer. If your presentation includes audio or video, double-check them using the room's audiovisual system. Arrange ahead of time to have a technician present so he or she can take care of any problems.

Sometimes, of course, it is not possible to visit the room before the day of your speech. In that case, plan to arrive an hour early to familiarize yourself with the equipment and to make sure it's working properly. Never assume that everything will

 **checklist**

Presenting Visual Aids

YES	NO	
☐	☐	1. Have I checked the speech room to decide where I can display my visual aids most effectively?
☐	☐	2. Have I practiced presenting my visual aids so they will be clearly visible to everyone in the audience?
☐	☐	3. Have I practiced presenting my visual aids so they are perfectly timed with my words and actions?
☐	☐	4. Have I practiced keeping eye contact with my audience while presenting my visual aids?
☐	☐	5. Have I practiced explaining my visual aids clearly and concisely in terms my audience will understand?
☐	☐	6. If I am using handouts, have I planned to distribute them after the speech rather than during it?
☐	☐	7. Have I double-checked all equipment to make sure it works properly?
☐	☐	8. If I am using presentation technology, do I have a backup of my slides that I can take to the speech with me?

be "just fine." Instead, assume that things will not be fine and that they need to be checked ahead of time.

Finally, *always* bring a backup of your slides on a flash drive or in a cloud storage folder even if you plan on using your own computer during the speech. This may seem like a lot of fuss and bother, but anyone who has given speeches using any kind of presentation technology will tell you that it is absolutely essential.

Summary

There are many kinds of visual aids. Most obvious is the object about which you are speaking, or a model of it. Diagrams, sketches, and other kinds of drawings are valuable because you can design them to illustrate your points exactly. Photographs should be large enough to be seen clearly by all your listeners. Graphs are an excellent way to illustrate any subject dealing with numbers, while charts are used to summarize large blocks of information. Video can be useful as a visual aid, but it needs to be carefully edited and integrated into the speech. You can act as your own visual aid by performing actions that demonstrate processes or ideas.

If you use presentation technology such as PowerPoint, Keynote, or Google Slides, plan carefully why, how, and when you will utilize it. Rather than putting everything you say on-screen for your audience to read, use the technology only when it will genuinely enhance your message.

No matter what kind of visual aid you use, you need to prepare it carefully. You will be most successful if you prepare your aids well in advance, keep them simple, make sure they are large enough to be seen clearly, and use a limited amount of text. If you are creating visual aids on a computer, use fonts, color, and images strategically and effectively.

In addition to being designed with care, visual aids need to be presented skillfully. Avoid passing visual aids among the audience. Display each aid only while you are talking about it, and be sure to place it where everyone can see it without straining. When presenting a visual aid, maintain eye contact with your listeners and explain the aid clearly and concisely. If you are using presentation technology, make sure you check the room and equipment prior to the time of delivery. Above all, practice with your visual aids so they fit into your speech smoothly and expertly.

Key Terms

graph (249)   bar graph (251)
line graph (250)   chart (252)
pie graph (250)   font (256)

Review Questions

After reading this chapter, you should be able to answer the following questions:

1. What are the major advantages of using visual aids in your speeches?
2. What kinds of visual aids might you use in a speech?

3. What factors should you consider when planning to use presentation technology in a speech?

4. What guidelines are given in the chapter for preparing visual aids?

5. What guidelines are given in the chapter for presenting visual aids?

Exercises for Critical Thinking

1. Watch a how-to video (a cooking show, for example) or the weather portion of a local newscast. Notice how the speaker uses visual aids to help communicate the message. What kinds of visual aids are used? How do they enhance the clarity, interest, and retainability of the speaker's message? What would the speaker have to do to communicate the message effectively without visual aids?

2. Consider how you might use visual aids to explain each of the following:

   a. How to stretch before and after exercise.

   b. The proportion of the electorate that votes in major national elections in the United States, France, Germany, England, and Japan, respectively.

   c. Where to obtain information about student loans.

   d. The wing patterns of various species of butterflies.

   e. The decrease in the amount of money spent by public schools on arts education since 2005.

   f. How to play the ukulele.

   g. The basic equipment and techniques of rock climbing.

3. Plan to use visual aids in at least one of your classroom speeches. Be creative in devising your aids, and be sure to follow the guidelines discussed in the chapter for using them. After the speech, analyze how effectively you employed your visual aids, what you learned about the use of visual aids from your experience, and what changes you would make in using visual aids if you were to deliver the speech again.

End Notes

[1] For a review of research on these subjects, see Richard E. Mayer, "Instruction Based on Visualizations," in Richard E. Mayer and Patricia A. Alexander (eds.), *Handbook of Research on Learning and Instruction,* 2nd ed. (New York: Routledge, 2017), pp. 483–501.

[2] Garr Reynolds, *Presentation Zen: Simple Ideas on Presentation and Delivery,* 2nd ed. (Berkeley, CA: New Riders Press, 2012), p. 11.

[3] See Mayer, "Instruction Based on Visualization," pp. 491–492.

[4] Bert E. Bradley, *Fundamentals of Speech Communication: The Credibility of Ideas,* 6th ed. (Dubuque, IA: William C. Brown, 1991), p. 280.

[5] For a fascinating look at the principles of information graphics in general, see Alberto Cairo, *How Charts Lie: Getting Smarter about Visual Information* (New York: W. W. Norton and Company, 2019).

Speaking to Inform

Types of Informative Speeches: Analysis and Organization

Guidelines for Informative Speaking

Sample Speech with Commentary

Courtney Roddick is the chief marketer at a fast-growing company that sells eco-friendly camping equipment. On a bright Thursday morning in March, Courtney begins her workday by talking to a colleague from tech support about problems on her mobile device and what goes wrong when she tries to view files on the company's internal messaging system.

Later that morning, Courtney has a long Zoom meeting with members of her marketing team, who operate in different regions of North America. They discuss the company's new line of camping chairs, going over everything from the recycled fabric materials to potential advertising ideas. As the other team members talk, Courtney takes careful notes and asks questions to make sure she doesn't miss anything.

In the afternoon, Courtney rushes to a meeting with the company president, so she can report on what the marketing team discussed earlier in the day. She reviews the low environmental impact of the new camping chairs, discusses the distribution chain, and explains different advertising ideas. Afterward, the president compliments Courtney for giving such a clear presentation. "Anyone who can communicate that well," the president says, "is going to go a long way in this company."

Courtney doesn't consider herself a "public speaker," but much of her job involves absorbing and communicating information clearly and effectively. Although Courtney is only one person, her experience is not unusual. In one survey, graduates from five U.S. colleges were asked to rank the speech skills most important to their jobs. They rated informative speaking number one. In another survey, 62 percent of the respondents said they used informative speaking "almost constantly."[1]

Public speaking to inform occurs in a wide range of everyday situations. The business manager explains next year's budget. The architect reviews plans for a new building. The union leader informs members about a new contract. The church worker outlines plans for a fund drive. There are endless situations in which people need to inform others. Competence in this form of communication will prove valuable to you throughout your life.

One of your first classroom assignments probably will be to deliver an informative speech in which you will act as a lecturer or teacher. You may describe an object, show how something works, report on an event, explain a concept. Your aim will be to convey knowledge and understanding—not to advocate a cause. Your speech will be judged in light of three general criteria:

Is the information communicated accurately?

Is the information communicated clearly?

Is the information made meaningful and interesting to the audience?

In this chapter, we will look at four types of informative speeches and the basic principles of informative speaking. Along the way, we will apply various general principles discussed in previous chapters.

informative speech
A speech designed to convey knowledge and understanding.

Types of Informative Speeches: Analysis and Organization

There are many ways to classify informative speeches. Here we focus on the kinds you are most likely to give in your speech class: (1) speeches about objects, (2) speeches about processes, (3) speeches about events, and (4) speeches about concepts.

SPEECHES ABOUT OBJECTS

As the word is used here, "objects" include anything that is visible, tangible, and stable in form. Objects may have moving parts or be alive; they may include places, structures, animals, even people. Here are examples of subjects for speeches about objects:

object
Anything that is visible, tangible, and stable in form.

Galapagos Islands	stock market
Joan of Arc	Webb Space Telescope
musical instruments	dreamcatchers

You will not have time to tell your classmates everything about any of these subjects. Instead, you will choose a specific purpose that focuses on one aspect of your subject. Working from the topics listed above, the following are examples of good specific purpose statements for informative speeches about objects:

To inform my audience about the scientific uses of the Webb Space Telescope.

To inform my audience about the role of dreamcatchers in Native American cultures.

To inform my audience about the major ecological features of the Galapagos Islands.

Notice how precise these statements are. As we saw in Chapter 5, you should select a specific purpose that is not too broad to achieve in the allotted time. "To inform my audience about Pablo Picasso" is far too general for a classroom speech.

"To inform my audience about the major contributions of Pablo Picasso to modern art" is more precise and is a purpose you could reasonably hope to achieve in a brief talk.

If your specific purpose is to explain the history or evolution of your subject, you will put your speech in *chronological* order. For example:

Specific Purpose: To inform my audience about the major achievements of Frederick Douglass.

Central Idea: Although born in slavery, Frederick Douglass became one of the greatest figures in American history.

Main Points:

    I. Douglass spent the first 20 years of his life as a slave in Maryland.

    II. After escaping to the North, Douglass became a leader in the abolitionist movement to end slavery.

    III. During the Civil War, Douglass helped establish Black regiments in the Union Army.

    IV. After the war, Douglass was a tireless champion of equal rights for his race.

If your specific purpose is to describe the main features of your subject, you may organize your speech in *spatial* order:

Specific Purpose: To inform my audience about the geographical regions of the Mississippi River.

Central Idea: The Mississippi River is divided into three sections, each with its own unique features.

Main Points:

    I. The upper Mississippi is known for its scenic parks and system of dams and locks.

    II. The middle Mississippi is known for its wildlife refuges and fishing opportunities.

    III. The lower Mississippi is known for its heavy river traffic and connection to the Gulf of Mexico.

As often as not, you will find that speeches about objects fall into *topical* order. For example:

Specific Purpose: To inform my audience about the three major features of the Taj Mahal.

Central Idea: The three major features of the Taj Mahal are the mausoleum, the garden, and the reflecting pool.

Main Points:

    I. The Taj Mahal's mausoleum is famous for its brilliant white marble and massive dome.

    II. The Taj Mahal's garden is famous for its symmetry and carefully sculpted greenery.

    III. The Taj Mahal's reflecting pool is famous for its mirrorlike surface and expansive layout.

No matter which of these organizational methods you use—chronological, spatial, or topical—be sure to follow the guidelines discussed in Chapter 9: (1) Limit your speech to between two and five main points; (2) keep main points separate; (3) try to use the same pattern of wording for all main points; (4) balance the amount of time devoted to each main point.

SPEECHES ABOUT PROCESSES

process
A systematic series of actions that leads to a specific result or product.

A process is a systematic series of actions that leads to a specific result or product. Speeches about processes explain how something is made, how something is done, or how something works. Here are examples of good specific purpose statements for speeches about processes:

> To inform my audience how to write an effective job resumé.
>
> To inform my audience how tsunamis develop.
>
> To inform my audience how to read Braille.

As these examples suggest, there are two kinds of informative speeches about processes. One kind explains a process so listeners will *understand* it better. Your goal is to have your audience know the steps of the process and how they relate to one another. If your specific purpose is "To inform my audience how a nuclear power plant works," you will explain the basic procedures of a nuclear power plant. You will not instruct your listeners on how they can *operate* a nuclear power plant.

A second kind of speech explains a process so listeners will be better able to *perform* the process themselves. Your goal in this kind of speech is to have the audience learn a skill. Suppose your specific purpose is "To inform my audience how to take pictures like a professional photographer." You will present photographic techniques and show your listeners how they can utilize them. You want the audience to be able to *use* the techniques as a result of your speech.

Both kinds of speeches about processes may require visual aids. At the very least, you should prepare a chart outlining the steps or techniques of your process. In some cases you will need to demonstrate the steps or techniques by performing them in front of your audience. One student did sleight-of-hand magic tricks to show the techniques behind them. Another student executed elementary tai chi maneuvers. In each case, the demonstration not only clarified the speaker's process but captivated the audience as well. (If you are using visual aids of any kind, be sure to review Chapter 14.)

When informing about a process, you will usually arrange your speech in *chronological* order, explaining the process step by step from beginning to end. For example:

Specific Purpose: To inform my audience about the three major stages in the development of type 2 diabetes.

Central Idea: Type 2 diabetes is a life-threatening disease that develops through early, middle, and late stages.

Main Points: I. The early stage of type 2 diabetes includes blurred vision, numbness, and weight loss.

    II. The middle stage of type 2 diabetes includes poor circulation, nerve damage, and kidney failure.

    III. The late stage of type 2 diabetes includes blindness, increased risk of stroke, and loss of limbs.

Informative speeches can be organized in many ways. A speech on the history of Istanbul's famous Hagia Sophia would likely be in chronological order, while a speech on its major features would fall into topical order.

Emad Aljumah/Getty Images

Sometimes, rather than moving through a process step by step, you will focus on the major principles or techniques involved in performing the process. Then you will organize your speech in *topical* order. Each main point will deal with a separate principle or technique. For example:

Specific Purpose:	To inform my audience of the common methods used by stage magicians to perform their tricks.
Central Idea:	Stage magicians use two common methods to perform their tricks—mechanical devices and sleight of hand.
Main Points:	I. Many magic tricks rely on mechanical devices that may require little skill by the magician.
	II. Other magic tricks depend on the magician's skill in fooling people by sleight-of-hand manipulation.

Concise organization is especially important in speeches about processes. You must make sure each step is clear and easy to follow. If your process has more than four or five steps, group the steps into units to limit the number of main points. For example, in a speech explaining how to set up a home aquarium, a student presented the following main points:

I. First you must choose the size of your tank.
II. Then you must determine the shape of your tank.
III. You must also decide how much you can afford to pay for a tank.
IV. Once you have the tank, you need a filter system.
V. A heater is also absolutely necessary.
VI. You must also get an air pump.
VII. Once this is done, you need to choose gravel for the tank.
VIII. You will also need plants.

IX. Other decorations will round out the effects of your aquarium.

X. Now you are ready to add the fish.

XI. Freshwater fish are the most common.

XII. Saltwater fish are more expensive and require special care.

Not surprisingly, this was too much for the audience to follow. The speaker should have organized the points something like this:

I. The first step in establishing a home aquarium is choosing a tank.

A. The size of the tank is important.

B. The shape of the tank is important.

C. The cost of the tank is important.

II. The second step in establishing a home aquarium is equipping the tank.

A. You will need a filter system.

B. You will need a heater.

C. You will need an air pump.

D. You will need gravel.

E. You will need plants.

F. You may also want other decorations.

III. The third step in establishing a home aquarium is adding the fish.

A. Freshwater fish are the most common for home aquariums.

B. Saltwater fish are more expensive and require special care.

The subpoints cover the same territory as the original twelve points, but three main points are much easier to understand and remember.

SPEECHES ABOUT EVENTS

The *Random House Dictionary* defines an event as "anything that happens or is regarded as happening." By this definition, the following are examples of suitable topics for informative speeches about events:

Carnival	music festivals
flash floods	seasonal affective disorder
cheerleading	civil rights movement

As usual, you will need to narrow your focus and pick a specific purpose you can accomplish in a short speech. Here are examples of good specific purpose statements for informative speeches about events:

event

Anything that happens or is regarded as happening.

To inform my audience about the major events at Carnival in Rio de Janeiro.

To inform my audience about the causes, symptoms, and treatment of seasonal affective disorder.

To inform my audience about the experience of being a university cheerleader.

There are many ways to discuss events. If your specific purpose is to recount the history of an event, you will organize your speech in *chronological* order, relating the incidents one after another in the order they occurred. For example:

Specific Purpose:	To inform my audience about the history of the Paralympics.
Central Idea:	Olympic-style games for athletes with physical disabilities have made great strides since the first competition more than 60 years ago.
Main Points:	I. What would eventually become the Paralympics began in 1948 with a sports competition in Great Britain involving World War II veterans with spinal cord injuries.
	II. In 1952, the event expanded when athletes from the Netherlands took part.
	III. In 1960, the first Paralympic Games for international athletes took place in Rome.
	IV. In 2001, an agreement was signed officially holding the Paralympic Games alongside the summer and winter Olympic Games.

You can approach an event from almost any angle or combination of angles—features, origins, implications, benefits, future developments, and so forth. In such cases, you will put your speech together in *topical* order. And you should make sure your main points subdivide the subject logically and consistently. For instance:

Specific Purpose:	To inform my audience about three aspects of Japan's Obon festival.
Central Idea:	Japan's Obon festival is famous for its lanterns, historic dances, and graveside gatherings.
Main Points:	I. Paper lanterns are hung outside homes to guide the spirits of departed family members.
	II. Historic dances are performed in public areas with special music and choreography.
	III. Graveside gatherings are held by families to maintain the burial sites of their ancestors.

SPEECHES ABOUT CONCEPTS

Concepts include beliefs, theories, ideas, principles, and the like. They are more abstract than objects, processes, or events. The following are examples of subjects for speeches about concepts:

concept
A belief, theory, idea, notion, principle, or the like.

astrology	human rights
freeganism	original-intent doctrine
military theory	Confucianism

Taking a few of these general subjects, here are some specific purpose statements for speeches about concepts:

To inform my audience about the philosophy of freeganism.

To inform my audience about the basic principles of Confucianism.

To inform my audience about the original-intent doctrine in constitutional interpretation.

Speeches about concepts are usually organized in *topical* order and focus on the main features or aspects of your concept. For example:

Specific Purpose: To inform my audience about the basic principles of nonviolent resistance.

Central Idea: The basic principles of nonviolent resistance stress using moral means to achieve social change, refusing to inflict violence on one's enemies, and using suffering as a social force.

Main Points:
I. The first major principle of nonviolent resistance is that social change must be achieved by moral means.
II. The second major principle of nonviolent resistance is that one should not inflict violence on one's enemies.
III. The third major principle of nonviolent resistance is that suffering can be a powerful social force.

Another approach is to define the concept you are dealing with, identify its major elements, and illustrate it with specific examples. An excellent instance of this came in a student speech about homeschooling:

Specific Purpose: To inform my audience about different philosophies of homeschooling.

Central Idea: Approaches to homeschooling include the classical model, the Montessori model, and the unschooling model.

Main Points:
I. The classical model focuses on language, critical thinking, and communication skills.
II. The Montessori model focuses on an interactive environment that children navigate on their own.
III. The unschooling model focuses on escaping formal instruction and letting children learn through experience.

Speeches about concepts are often more complex than other kinds of informative speeches. When dealing with concepts, pay special attention to avoiding technical language, to defining terms clearly, and to using examples and comparisons to illustrate the concepts.

Look, for example, at Video 15.1 in the online Media Library for this chapter, which presents an excerpt from a student speech about the Chinese philosophy of Confucianism. Notice how the student defines Confucianism and then explains its unifying principle of *jen.* If you give an informative speech about a concept, give special thought to how you can make that concept clear and comprehensible to your listeners.

The lines dividing speeches about objects, processes, events, and concepts are not absolute. Some subjects could fit into more than one category, depending on how you develop the speech. For example, a speech about the Great Pyramid of Giza would probably deal with its subject as an object, but a speech on how pyramids were built would most likely treat its subject as a process. The important step is to decide whether you will handle your subject as an object, a process, an event, or a concept. Once you do that, you can develop the speech accordingly.

Regardless of how you approach your topic, be sure to give listeners plenty of help in sorting out facts and ideas. One way is by using enough transitions, internal

connect
View an excerpt from "Confucianism" in the online Media Library for this chapter (Video 15.1).

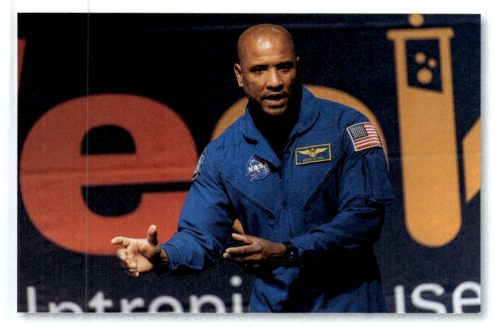

Speaking to inform plays a role in many occupations. Here U.S. astronaut Victor J. Glover Jr. talks at the Intrepid Sea, Air, and Space Museum about the importance of STEM education.

Lev Radin/Pacific Press/LightRocket/ Getty Images

previews, internal summaries, and signposts (see Chapter 9). Another way is to follow the old maxim, "Tell 'em what you're going to say; say it; then tell 'em what you've said." In other words, preview the main points of your speech in the introduction and summarize them in the conclusion. This will make your speech easier to understand and easier to remember.

Guidelines for Informative Speaking

All the previous chapters of this book relate to the principles of informative speaking. Selecting a topic and specific purpose, analyzing the audience, gathering materials, choosing supporting details, organizing the speech, using words to communicate meaning, delivering the speech—all must be done effectively if an informative speech is to be a success. Here we emphasize six additional points that will help make yours a success.

DON'T OVERESTIMATE WHAT THE AUDIENCE KNOWS

In a speech about meteorology, a student said, "If modern methods of weather forecasting had existed in 1900, the Galveston hurricane disaster would never have taken place." Then he was off to other matters, leaving his listeners to puzzle over what the Galveston hurricane was, when it happened, and what kind of destruction it wreaked.

The speaker assumed his audience already knew these things. But they were not experts on meteorology or on American history. Even those who had heard of the hurricane had only a fuzzy notion of it. Only the speaker knew that the hurricane, which killed more than 6,000 people when it unexpectedly struck on September 8, 1900, is still the deadliest natural disaster in American history.

As many speakers have discovered, it is easy to overestimate the audience's stock of information. In most informative speeches, your listeners will be only vaguely knowledgeable (at best) about the details of your topic. You cannot *assume* they will know what you mean. Rather, you must be *sure* to explain everything so thoroughly that they cannot help but understand. As you work on your speech, always consider whether it will be clear to someone who is hearing about the topic for the first time.

Suppose you are talking about night-vision goggles—the kind you might see in a spy movie. Surely all of your classmates have heard of night-vision goggles, but most probably don't know how the goggles work. How will you tell them? Here's one way:

> Night-vision goggles rely on an image-intensifying tube that moves infrared and visible light through a photocathode and a microchannel plate, where photons are converted to electrons and multiplied. Those electrons then hit a screen coated with phosphors that keep the electrons in the proper position—only with many more of them serving as light points.

To someone who knows a lot about physics and imaging, this may be perfectly clear. But someone who does not will almost surely get lost along the way. The tone of the statement is that of a speaker reviewing information already familiar to the audience—not of a speaker introducing new information.

Here, in contrast, is another explanation of night-vision goggles:

> So how do night-vision goggles allow you to see in the dark? Imagine a secret agent on a nighttime mission. She quietly approaches the building she must infiltrate, but it's shrouded in darkness. Fortunately, she brought along her trusty night-vision goggles.
>
> Once they're powered on, the goggles capture whatever light is in the immediate environment. But instead of stopping there, as human eyes do, the goggles send the light to a special tube that converts the light into electrons and multiplies the electrons thousands of times over. The electrons are then displayed on a small screen inside the goggles, thereby allowing the wearer to see shapes in the darkness.
>
> With the aid of her night-vision goggles, our secret agent can now complete her mission.

This explanation is clear and simple. Its tone is that of a teacher unraveling a new subject.

Is it too simple? Not at all. The test of a good speaker is to communicate even the most complex ideas clearly and simply. Anyone can go to a book and find a learned-sounding definition of night-vision goggles. But to say in plain English how night-vision goggles work—that takes effort and creative thinking.

Also, remember that readers can study a printed passage again and again until they extract its meaning, but listeners don't have that luxury. They must understand what you say in the time it takes you to say it. The more you assume they know about the topic, the greater your chances of being misunderstood.

RELATE THE SUBJECT DIRECTLY TO THE AUDIENCE

> The British dramatist Oscar Wilde arrived at his club after the disastrous opening-night performance of his new play.
>
> "Oscar, how did your play go?" asked a friend.
>
> "Oh," Wilde quipped, "the play was a great success, but the audience was a failure."

Informative speaking takes place in a wide range of situations. Here structural engineers discuss details of an ongoing building project.

Gorodenkoff/Shutterstock

Speakers have been known to give much the same answer in saving face after a dismal informative speech. "Oh," they say, "the speech was fine, but the audience just wasn't interested." And they are at least partly right—the audience *wasn't* interested. But there is no such thing as a fine speech that puts people to sleep. It is the speaker's job to get listeners interested—and to keep them interested.

Informative speakers have one big hurdle to overcome. They must recognize that what is fascinating to them may not be fascinating to everybody. Once you have chosen a topic that could possibly be interesting to your listeners, you should take special steps to relate it to them. You should tie it in with their interests and concerns.

Start in the introduction. Instead of saying,

> I want to talk with you about the Ironman competition.

you could say:

> Your body can't go any further. Your toenails fell off long ago. Your lungs are on fire. Your heart is one beat away from exploding. Are you dying? Are you dreaming? Neither. You're about to cross the finish line of your first Ironman competition—and nothing could feel better.

But don't stop with the introduction. Whenever you can, put your listeners into the body of the speech. After all, nothing interests people more than themselves. Find ways to talk about your topic in terms of your listeners. Bring your material home to them. Get it as close to them as possible.

Here's an example. Let's say you are discussing the artistic technique known as encaustics, which involves painting with hot wax. You have plenty of facts and could recite them like this:

> Dating back to the ancient Greeks, encaustic painting is a mixed-media method that combines melted wax, resin, and colored pigments. In encaustic painting, the artist first melts beeswax, then adds resin on a solid flat surface. After that, the artist adds pigment, which is fused to the wax and resin with a heat gun. After layer upon layer, the result is a rich, textured artwork.

connect

View this excerpt from "Not Your Everyday Competition" in the online Media Library for this chapter (Video 15.2).

This is valuable information, but it is not related to the audience. Let's try again:

> Picture yourself as an artist, ready to create an encaustic painting like people have done for thousands of years. You start by melting beeswax and adding resin, then you apply it in layers to your wood panel or similar surface. As you apply layers of wax and resin, you fuse them together with a heat gun or torch. That makes the layers workable.
>
> Then it's time to add color. You might use oil paint or blocks of pigment. You melt the pigment down and layer it on top of the wax. With a little more heat from your handy heat gun, the colors combine with the wax for a vibrant, textured, layered masterpiece. Now you're part of the long history of encaustic painting.

connect

View this excerpt from "The Genius of Encaustics" in the online Media Library for this chapter (Video 15.3).

Look at the frequent use of "you" and "your." The facts are the same, but now they are pointed directly at the audience. Research shows that using personal terms such as "you" and "your" in an informative speech significantly increases audience understanding of the speaker's ideas.[2]

DON'T BE TOO TECHNICAL

What does it mean to say that an informative speech is too technical? It may mean the subject matter is too specialized for the audience. Any subject can be popularized—but only up to a point. The important thing for a speaker to know is what can be explained to an ordinary audience and what cannot.

Say your subject is power amplifiers. It's no trick to demonstrate how to operate an amplifier (how to turn it on and off, adjust the volume, set the tone and balance controls). It's also relatively easy to explain what an amplifier does (it boosts the sound received from a digital file, mobile device, or live performance). But to give a full scientific account of how an amplifier works cannot be done in any reasonable time unless the audience knows the principles of audio technology. The material is just too technical for a general audience.

Even when the subject matter is not technical, the language used to explain it may be. Every activity has its jargon, whether it be golf (bogey, wedge, match play); chemistry (colloid, glycogen, heavy water); or financial analysis (covered call, reverse bid, toehold acquisition). If you are talking to a group of specialists, you can use technical words and be understood. But you must do all you can to avoid technical words when informing a general audience such as your speech class.

Here, for instance, are two statements explaining aquamation, an eco-friendly alternative to cremation and traditional burial. The first is heavily laden with specialized language that would have little impact on ordinary listeners:

> Aquamation, also known as alkaline hydrolysis, is a water-based process that promotes natural decomposition of a body. More eco-friendly than cremation and burial, aquamation begins by placing a body in a pressurized metal container, then heating a solution of water and alkali, often potassium hydroxide, inside the container. The process dissolves tissue and, like cremation, reduces bones to dusty ashes.

The second statement is perfectly understandable and shows how technical information can be made clear to the average person:

As a financial planner at a local investment firm, you have been asked to speak to a group of recent college graduates about long-term financial planning. After considering what recent college graduates need to know about saving for their future, you decide to organize your presentation around four general stages of investing:

1. The early years of investing, which include putting aside small amounts of money that will grow over time.
2. The years of acquisition, which include balancing investments with large expenses such as raising children and paying a mortgage.
3. The years of accumulation, which include putting away as much money as possible in anticipation of retirement.
4. The retirement years, which include living off of savings and adjusting investments as needed.

As you look over these stages of investing, you think back to the public speaking course you took in college. You remember that informative speakers should relate their speech directly to the audience, should not be too technical, should not overestimate what the audience knows about the subject, and should be creative. How might each of these guidelines influence your presentation to recent college graduates? Be specific.

Jim Craigmyle/Getty Images

It's an environmentally friendly way to handle a body after a loved one has passed away. The *Washington Post* calls it central to the growing "green burial" movement. Although the name might sound strange, you'll be hearing a lot more about it in the coming years—aquamation.

Writing in *Science, Technology, & Human Values*, Philip Olson of Virginia Tech University explains how aquamation works. While cremation burns a body at extremely high temperatures and releases toxins into the air, aquamation uses a mixture of water and acid to speed up natural decomposition.

The body is liquefied under pressure, and the bones are turned to dust that can be put in an urn and given to the family to remember their loved one. Some advocates say it uses up to 90 percent less energy than traditional cremation.

Much clearer, isn't it? The only specialized word in the whole passage is "aquamation." The rest of the language is straightforward, the ideas easy to grasp. This is what you should strive for in your informative speeches.

AVOID ABSTRACTIONS

"My task," said novelist Joseph Conrad, "is, before all, to make you see." And make the reader see is just what Conrad did. Witness this passage, in which Conrad describes the aftermath of an explosion aboard a ship:

The first person I saw was Mahon, with eyes like saucers, his mouth open, and the long white hair standing straight on end round his head like a silver halo. . . . I stared at him in unbelief, and he stared at me with a queer kind of shocked curiosity. I did not know that I had no hair, no eyebrows, no eyelashes, that my young mustache was burnt off, that my face was black, one cheek laid open, my nose cut, and my chin bleeding.[3]

A speech is not a novel. Still, many informative speeches would be vastly improved by the novelist's bent for color, specificity, and detail.

One way to avoid abstractions is through *description*. When we think of description, we usually think of external events such as the explosion described by Conrad. But description is also used to communicate internal feelings. Here is how one student tried to convey to his audience the sensations he experienced when he first began sky diving:

> As we wait for the plane to climb to the jump altitude of 12,000 feet, my mind races with a frenzied jumble of thoughts: "OK, this is the moment you've been waiting for. It's going to be great. Am I really going to jump out of an airplane from 12,000 feet? What if something goes wrong? Can I still back out? Come on now, don't worry. It'll be fine."

Even if we have not been sky diving, we have all had the same kinds of emotions on similar occasions. So what happened next?

> Now it is time to jump. My palms are sweating and my heart is pounding so hard I think it may burst. "Get ready," yells the instructor. As I jump into the blue, I wonder, "What am I doing here?"

Yes—and then what?

> The blast of air resistance blows me backward like a leaf at the mercy of an autumn wind. In about 10 seconds my body levels out and accelerates to a speed of 120 miles an hour. The air supports my body like an invisible flying carpet. There is no sound except for the wind rushing around my face. Any fears or doubts I had are gone in the exhilaration of free flight. Every nerve in my body is alive with sensation; yet I am overcome by a peaceful feeling and the sense that I am at one with the sky.

As we listen to the speaker we share his thoughts, feel his heart pound, and join his exhilaration as he floats effortlessly through the sky. The vivid description lends reality to the speech and draws us further in.

Another way to escape abstractions is with *comparisons* that put your subject in concrete, familiar terms. Do you want to convey the fact that sharks very seldom attack people? You could say this:

> Despite all the negative publicity, sharks pose little danger to human beings.

True, but the statement is vague and abstract. It does not communicate your meaning clearly and concretely. Now suppose you add this:

> According to *National Geographic,* the United States averages less than one fatal shark attack every two years. In comparison, more than 41 people die every year from lightning strikes in the coastal states alone.

Now you have made the abstract specific and given us a sharp, new slant on things.

description

A statement that depicts a person, event, idea, or the like with clarity and vividness.

comparison

A statement of the similarities among two or more people, events, ideas, etc.

Whatever the subject of your informative speech, you will need strong supporting materials and clear organization. The more carefully you prepare your speech, the more likely you are to be successful.

Steve Debenport/E+/Getty Images

Like comparison, *contrast* can put an idea into concrete terms. Suppose you want to illustrate the popularity of World Cup soccer. You could say, "The championship game of the most recent World Cup was seen by a staggering 1 billion people." The word "staggering" suggests that you consider 1 billion a significant number, but significant in comparison to what? One speaker offered this contrast:

> The championship match of the most recent World Cup was seen by 1 billion people. In contrast, the most recent Super Bowl was seen by 112 million people. Think about it—almost ten times more people watched the final game of the World Cup than watched the Super Bowl.

contrast
A statement of the differences among two or more people, events, ideas, etc.

This puts an abstract fact into meaningful perspective.

PERSONALIZE YOUR IDEAS

Listeners want to be entertained as they are being enlightened.[4] Nothing takes the edge off an informative speech more than an unbroken string of facts and figures. And nothing enlivens a speech more than personal illustrations. When possible, you should try to *personalize* your ideas and dramatize them in human terms.

Let's say you are talking about family homelessness, which most often involves mothers and their children living on the streets, in cars, or in shelters. You would surely note that 34 percent of the homeless population consists of families, leaving 1.6 million children without a home. You would also note that these children are much more likely than their peers to experience violence, physical and mental health problems, and developmental difficulties.

But these are dry facts and figures. If you really want to get your audience involved, you will weave in some examples of families who have experienced homelessness. One speaker began by telling this story:

personalize
To present one's ideas in human terms that relate in some fashion to the experience of the audience.

> Lydia. She was the new girl in school. We were in a couple of the same classes, sometimes we sat together at lunch, and we would see each

other during recess. Lydia was kind, funny, and supportive. But for six months, I didn't know the secret she was hiding.

Lydia didn't like to talk about her family. She never wanted me to meet her mom, and she never invited me over to her house. She always insisted that we meet somewhere like the mall. But then one day I found out why: Lydia never invited me to her house because she did not have a house. For more than a year she, her mother, and her little brother had been homeless. They had been living in shelters, staying with relatives, and resting their heads wherever they could.

During the body of the speech, the speaker mentioned Lydia twice more to illustrate different aspects of family homelessness. Then, at the end of the speech, she brought Lydia's story to a hopeful conclusion:

connect
View this excerpt from "Family Homelessness" in the online Media Library for this chapter (Video 15.4).

We have seen how family homelessness affects millions of Americans and can lead to poor physical and mental health, episodes of violence, and a range of developmental difficulties. Homelessness is not just the disheveled man sitting by himself on the street—the image we've seen countless times in the media. Homelessness affects families; it affects people like Lydia.

Or, I should say, it *used* to affect Lydia. After two difficult years, her mother found a job that paid her enough to rent an apartment. Lydia herself now works part time and takes classes at a community college. She made it through the stressful time that affects far too many families. And she remains my friend.

It was a powerful ending. By putting a human face on the topic, the speaker took family homelessness out of the realm of statistics and social services and communicated it in personal terms.

BE CREATIVE

Whether you are seeking alternatives to technical language, avoiding abstractions, personalizing ideas, or adapting to the audience's knowledge about the topic, you need to be creative in thinking about ways to achieve your objectives. A good informative speech is not an oral encyclopedia article. Like any other kind of speech, it requires a healthy dose of creativity.

connect
View an excerpt from "Lady Liberty" in the online Media Library for this chapter (Video 15.5).

If you look back at the examples on the previous few pages, you will see that all of them involve creative thinking by the speaker. As in these examples, creativity is often a matter of using language imaginatively and resourcefully. But creativity can involve *any* aspect of an informative speech, including visual aids—as can be seen in the speech on the Statue of Liberty that is reprinted in the appendix following Chapter 20.

Part of the speech deals with the architecture of the statue. The exterior of the Statue of Liberty is made of thin copper, which is supported by a massive iron skeleton. Because the skeleton can't be seen in photographs, the speaker needed to find a way to make it visible for his audience. He did so by using a PowerPoint slide in which a photograph of the statue faded away and black lines representing the iron skeleton appeared in coordination with the speaker's words. The black lines seemed to "build" the skeleton right before the audience's eyes. As you can see from Video 15.5, it was an effective—and creative—solution.

If, like this speaker, you think creatively when constructing your informative speech, you are much more likely to be successful.

Sample Speech with Commentary

The following speech provides an excellent example of how to apply the principles of informative speaking discussed in this chapter. Notice how clearly the speech is organized, how the speaker discusses it in everyday, nontechnical language, and how he personalizes it by relating the subject to his classmates. He also uses a wide range of visual aids—drawings, maps, and photographs—to help the audience grasp his ideas.

As you can see by watching Video 15.6, the speech also exemplifies the methods of an effective online presentation. It was recorded by the speaker and then uploaded for viewing by his classmates and instructor. The content is identical to what would have been presented in class, but the visual aids are presented with the GoReact Video Capture software that is available on the Connect platform with *The Art of Public Speaking.*

If you are presenting an online informative speech for your class, be sure to read Chapter 19, Presenting Your Speech Online, as part of your preparation.

View "The Great Mesoamerican Ballgame" in the online Media Library for this chapter (Video 15.6).

The Great Mesoamerican Ballgame

COMMENTARY	SPEECH

The roar of the fans. The smell of the field. The competitors clashing before your eyes. I love watching sports in person, and I'm sure many of you do, too. It's something we share with people across the world going back thousands of years. Around 2,800 years ago, the first Olympic Games were played in ancient Greece. But did you know that 1,000 years before that, there were fierce sports competitions right here in the Americas?

COMMENTARY: After starting with a series of vivid images about sports today, the introduction notes that sports have been popular around the world for thousands of years. It ends by arousing curiosity about athletic events in the Americas long before the Olympic Games in ancient Greece.

Throughout Central America talented athletes played what we know today as the great Mesoamerican ballgame. As an avid sports fan and a student athlete, I've long been fascinated with the history of sports, and I've done extensive research for this speech.

COMMENTARY: Here the speaker reveals the topic of his speech and establishes his credibility.

Today I'd like to inform you about the Mesoamerican ballgame—specifically, its history, how it was played, and its role in ancient society. Let's start with its history.

COMMENTARY: The speaker previews his main points and provides a transition from the introduction to the body.

Main point one deals with the history of the Mesoamerican ballgame, starting with where the game was played. Here, as throughout his presentation, the speaker uses well-designed visual aids to help communicate his ideas.

Take a look at this map based on the *Historical Dictionary of Mesoamerica.* It shows some of the ancient civilizations that played the ballgame on a regular basis—including the Olmec, the Maya, and the Aztec. These ancient civilizations flourished in lands that include the modern-day countries of Mexico, Honduras, Belize, El Salvador, Guatemala, and Nicaragua.

The speaker rounds out main point one by stating that the Mesoamerican ballgame is the oldest recorded team sport played with a ball anywhere in the world. He clearly identifies his source for this important piece of information.

So far, archeologists have discovered more than 1,500 ancient ballcourts, like the one you see here in modern Honduras. According to a recent article on the science and technology website *Ars Technica,* the oldest ballcourt dates back more than 3,400 years. That makes the Mesoamerican ballgame the oldest recorded team sport played with a ball anywhere in the world.

Main point two explains how the ballgame was played, beginning with the number of players on a team.

Details of the game varied by region, but some key elements were consistent. In his book *The Ball,* anthropologist John Fox explains that two teams of up to eight players squared off in a scene similar to the one depicted in this 2,000-year-old sculpture.

Continuing his skillful use of visual aids, the speaker shows a photograph of an ancient ballcourt. He then supplements the photograph with a creative drawing that further clarifies the court's size, shape, and features.

In real life, ballcourts could be as large as two football fields. Here's a ballcourt in southern Mexico. Notice the field in the middle, the open areas on the ends of the field, and the high, slanted sides. These elements were common in ancient ballcourts, which you can see clearly in this illustration. At the top and bottom of the open field were two endzones, which gave the court its distinctive "I" design. Spectators had a great view of the action from on top of the high walls.

As you can see from Video 15.6, the speaker provides an excellent explanation of the vertical hoops and their role in the ballgame. Notice how the speaker orients his slides vertically to maximize what the remote audience can see on their screens.

Most courts also contained these iconic vertical hoops, which were central to scoring points. You can get a better view of the hoops here; they were kind of like basketball hoops on their sides. Players could score through the hoops or by getting the ball in the endzone. As with most modern sports, the goal was to score more points than the other team.

The speaker shows a dramatic drawing that illustrates how players hit the ball with their hips; he follows this with photographs of ancient sculptures that illustrate the players' protective clothing. His slides are integrated smoothly into the speech and are perfectly timed with his words.

But here's the catch: Players were not allowed to use their hands or their feet. Instead, they used their arms, shoulders, thighs, and, most often, their hips, as depicted in this image. Hitting the ball with their hips was hard because it was made of solid rubber, roughly the size of a basketball, and weighed 5–10 pounds. That's why players wore protective clothing and large padded rings around their hips, which you can see in these ancient sculptures.

A transition signals that the speaker is moving into main point three, dealing with the ballgame's role in ancient Mesoamerica. He begins by noting that it was a popular form of entertainment.

The speaker continues by pointing out the game's religious purpose. Once again, he identifies the source of his information.

This and the next paragraph complete main point three by exploring the ballgame's relationship to warfare.

Throughout his presentation, the speaker's delivery is poised and confident. He talks extemporaneously, has excellent command of his ideas, gestures naturally, and maintains strong eye contact with his audience.

After reinforcing his central idea, the speaker's conclusion notes that the Mesoamerican ballgame has been taken up by modern players to honor their ancestors. The closing sentence rounds out the speech and ends on an uplifting note.

Now that we have a sense of how the game was played, let's turn to its role in ancient Mesoamerican society. Like most modern sports, it was a source of entertainment. It brought together spectators from various social classes, including rulers, warriors, and peasants. Archeologists have even discovered evidence of gambling around the game. Think of it as an early version of March Madness.

Beyond entertainment, there was a religious purpose to the game. In a 2020 article in *Science Advances,* archeologists Jeffrey Blomster and Victor Chavez explain that playing the game symbolized "the regeneration of life and the maintenance of cosmic order."

To me, the most interesting role of the game was related to warfare. *Smithsonian Magazine* explains that the game sometimes served as "a replacement for war." Because the game was thought to be connected with the cosmic order, many believed it could predict the winning and losing sides in a war. So instead of going to war, competing societies might just play the ballgame.

Sometimes, the losing team would even be put to death, as depicted in this ancient Aztec illustration. This may seem inhumane, but think about it like this: Mesoamerican societies realized that it might be better to lose the lives of some ball players than to experience the widespread devastation of war.

In conclusion, you now have a sense of how the great Mesoamerican ballgame shaped life in the Americas for thousands of years. Or should I say, continues to shape life in the Americas. Modern players have resurrected the game, which they call Ulama, and they play it to honor their ancestors. This is just one way that the great Mesoamerican ballgame lives on.

Summary

Speaking to inform occurs in a wide range of everyday situations. Improving your ability to convey knowledge effectively will be valuable to you throughout your life.

Informative speeches may be grouped into four categories—speeches about objects, speeches about processes, speeches about events, and speeches about concepts.

Objects include places, structures, animals, even people. Speeches about objects usually are organized in chronological, spatial, or topical order. A process is a series of actions that work together to produce a final result. Speeches about processes explain how something is made, how something is done, or how something works. The most common types of organization for speeches about processes are chronological and topical.

An event is anything that happens or is regarded as happening. Speeches about events are usually arranged in chronological or topical order. Concepts include beliefs, theories, ideas, and principles. Speeches about concepts are often more complex than other kinds of informative speeches, and they typically follow a topical pattern of organization.

No matter what the subject of your informative speech, be careful not to overestimate what your audience knows about it. Explain everything so thoroughly that they can't help but understand. Avoid being too technical. Make sure your ideas and your language are fully comprehensible to someone who has no specialized knowledge about the topic.

Equally important, recognize that what is fascinating to you may not be fascinating to everybody. It is your job to make your informative speech interesting and meaningful to your audience. Find ways to talk about the topic in terms of your listeners. Avoid too many abstractions. Use description, comparison, and contrast to make your audience *see* what you are talking about. Try to personalize your ideas and dramatize them in human terms. Finally, be creative in thinking of ways to communicate your ideas.

Key Terms

informative speech (266)
object (266)
process (268)
event (270)
concept (271)

description (278)
comparison (278)
contrast (279)
personalize (279)

Review Questions

After reading this chapter, you should be able to answer the following questions:

1. What are the four types of informative speeches discussed in the chapter? Give an example of a good specific purpose statement for each type.

2. Why must informative speakers be careful not to overestimate what the audience knows about the topic? What can you do to make sure your ideas don't pass over the heads of your listeners?

3. What should you do as an informative speaker to relate your topic directly to the audience?

4. What two things should you watch out for in making sure your speech is not overly technical?

5. What are three methods you can use to avoid abstractions in your informative speech?

6. What does it mean to say that informative speakers should personalize their ideas?

7. Why is it important for informative speakers to be creative in thinking about ways to communicate their ideas?

Exercises for Critical Thinking

1. Following is a list of subjects for informative speeches. Your task is twofold: (a) Select four of the topics and prepare a specific purpose statement for an informative speech about each of the four. Make sure your four specific purpose statements include at least one that deals with its topic as an object, one that deals with its topic as a process, one that deals with its topic as an event, and one that deals with its topic as a concept. (b) Explain what method of organization you would most likely use in structuring a speech about each of your specific purpose statements.

hobbies	sports	education
animals	music	media
science	cultural customs	technology

2. Analyze "Supervolcanoes: The Sleeping Giants" in the appendix of sample speeches that follows Chapter 20. Identify the specific purpose, central idea, main points, and method of organization. Evaluate the speech in light of the guidelines for informative speaking discussed in this chapter.

End Notes

[1] John R. Johnson and Nancy Szczupakiewicz, "The Public Speaking Course: Is It Preparing Students with Work-Related Public Speaking Skills?" *Communication Education,* 36 (1987), pp. 131–137; Andrew D. Wolvin and Diana Corley, "The Technical Speech Communication Course: A View from the Field," *Association for Communication Administration Bulletin,* 49 (1984), pp. 83–91.

[2] Richard E. Mayer, Sherry Fennell, Lindsay Farmer, and Julie Campbell, "A Personalization Effect in Multimedia Learning: Students Learn Better When Words Are in Conversational Style Rather Than Formal Style," *Journal of Educational Psychology,* 96 (2004), pp. 389–395.

[3] Joseph Conrad, *Youth: A Narrative, and Two Other Stories* (London: William Blackwood and Sons, 1903), p. 26.

[4] James Humes, *Roles Speakers Play* (New York: Harper and Row, 1976), p. 25.

16

Speaking to Persuade

Victoria Perez started her day on campus by stopping at her English professor's office hours. "I don't normally do this," she said, "but I'm wondering if I can have a 24-hour extension on my paper. I have two exams on the same day and I've really been overwhelmed lately." The professor hemmed and hawed. Then he said, "Okay. You've turned in all your other work just fine, so you can have an extension this one time."

With a sigh of relief, Victoria headed off for classes. Walking past the library, she ran into some friends. "Are we still playing soccer later today?" one of them asked. "I wish I could," Victoria said, "but I'm posting flyers for the food bank today. How about tomorrow?"

In the afternoon, Victoria went to her internship as social media coordinator for the local minor-league baseball team. "I've been thinking about how we can get fans closer to the players," she said at a meeting with the marketing group. "What if we get some players to wear a small camera for a day and record what they go through? We could put the best stuff online and help fans get to know the team better."

The head of marketing looked skeptical, but then replied, "Okay. Let's try it and see what happens. But first I want you to figure out the details."

If you asked Victoria how she spent her day, she might say, "I talked to my English professor. I posted flyers for the food bank. I had a staff meeting at work." In fact, she spent a large part of her day *persuading*—persuading people to do things they were reluctant to do or that had not occurred to them.

The Importance of Persuasion

persuasion

The process of creating, reinforcing, or changing people's beliefs or actions.

Persuasion is the process of creating, reinforcing, or changing people's beliefs or actions.[1] The ability to speak (and write) persuasively will benefit you in every part of your life, from personal relations to community activities to career aspirations. When economists added up the number of people—lawyers, sales representatives, public relations specialists, counselors, administrators, and others—whose jobs depend largely on persuading people to adopt their point of view, they concluded that persuasion accounts for up to 30 percent of the U.S. gross domestic product![2]

Understanding the principles of persuasion is also vital to being an informed citizen and consumer. Politicians and advertisers, salespeople and interest groups, fund-raisers and community activists—all vie for your attention, votes, money, time, and support. The more you know about persuasion, the more effectively you can use your powers of critical thinking to assess the barrage of persuasive messages you are exposed to every day.

Although persuasion has been studied for more than 2,000 years, it is still the subject of lively debate among scholars. There are a number of scientific models of the persuasive process and a wide range of respected theories about how persuasion works. In this chapter and the next, we will explore the principles of persuasion as they apply to public speaking.

When you speak to persuade, you act as an advocate. Your job is to get listeners to agree with you and, perhaps, to act on that belief. Your goal may be to defend an idea, to refute an opponent, to sell a program, or to inspire people to action. Because persuasive speakers must communicate information clearly and concisely, you will need all the skills you used in speaking to inform. But you will also need new skills that take you from giving information to affecting your listeners' attitudes, beliefs, or actions.

Ethics and Persuasion

No matter what the speaking situation, you need to make sure your goals are ethically sound and that you use ethical methods to communicate your ideas. Meeting these obligations can be especially challenging when you speak to persuade. Would you be willing to shade the truth "just a bit" if it would guarantee a successful speech? How about juggling statistics, doctoring quotations, passing off opinions as facts, or pandering to prejudice and stereotypes?

Unfortunately, there is no shortage of speakers—and other persuaders—who are willing to take ethical shortcuts to achieve their objectives. Yet, as Martin Luther King stated years ago, it is not possible to bring about a truly beneficial result by using unethical methods. Maintaining the bond of trust with listeners is also vital to a speaker's credibility. As in other kinds of public speaking, the ideal of effective persuasion is the good person speaking well.

When you work on your persuasive speech, keep in mind the guidelines for ethical speaking discussed in Chapter 2. Make sure your goals are ethically sound and that you can defend them if they are questioned or challenged. Study the topic thoroughly so you won't mislead your audience through shoddy research or muddled thinking. Learn about all sides of an issue, seek out competing viewpoints, and get your facts right.

But knowing the facts is not enough. You also need to be honest in what you say. There is no place in ethical speechmaking for deliberately false or deceptive statements. Also be on guard against more subtle forms of dishonesty such as quoting out of context, portraying a few details as the whole story, and misrepresenting the sources of facts and figures. Take care to present statistics, testimony, and other kinds of evidence fairly and accurately.

Keep in mind as well the power of language and use it responsibly. Show respect for the rights of free speech and expression, and stay away from name-calling and other forms of abusive language. Finally, check the section of Chapter 17 that discusses the role of emotional appeal (pages 329–333). Make sure that any emotional appeal you use is appropriate to the topic and that you build your speech on a firm base of facts and logic before appealing to your audience's emotions. Aim at the highest standards and construct your speech so it will be both convincing *and* ethically sound.[3]

The Psychology of Persuasion

Persuasion is a psychological process. It occurs in a situation where two or more points of view exist. The speaker supports right-to-work laws, but many listeners do not. The speaker considers genetic screening unethical, but some in the audience think it is justified in certain circumstances. The different points of view may be completely opposed, or they may simply be different in degree. Whichever the case, there must be a disagreement, or else there would be no need for persuasion.

THE CHALLENGE OF PERSUASIVE SPEAKING

Of all the kinds of public speaking, persuasion is the most complex and the most challenging. Your objective is more ambitious than in speaking to inform, and audience analysis and adaptation become much more demanding. In some persuasive speeches, you will deal with controversial topics that touch on your listeners' basic attitudes, values, and beliefs. This may increase their resistance to persuasion and make your task more difficult.

It is much easier, for example, to explain the history of the war on drugs than to persuade an audience either that marijuana should be legalized in every state or once again be outlawed across the country. In the persuasive speech, you must contend not only with your audience's knowledge about marijuana but also with their attitudes toward recreational drugs and their beliefs about the impact of marijuana use on human health and social mores.

Lines of argument that work with one part of the audience may fail with—or even upset—another part. What seems perfectly logical to some listeners may seem wildly irrational to others. No matter how expert you are on the topic, no matter how skillfully you prepare the speech, no matter how captivating your delivery—some listeners will not agree with you.

This does not mean that persuasion is impossible. It does mean that you should have a realistic sense of what you can accomplish. You can't expect a group of die-hard Democrats to become Republicans or a steak lover to turn vegetarian as a result of one speech.

In every persuasive speech, you will face some listeners who are strongly in favor of your position, some who are neutral, and some who are adamantly opposed.

FIGURE 16.1

Degrees of Persuasion

Strongly Opposed	Moderately Opposed	Slightly Opposed	Neutral	Slightly in Favor	Moderately in Favor	Strongly in Favor

Persuasion involves any movement by a listener from left to right →

If listeners are neutral or only moderately committed one way or another, you can realistically hope your speech will move at least some of them toward your side. If listeners are strongly opposed to your position, you can consider your speech a success if it leads even a few to reexamine their views.

When thinking about the range of persuasive responses, you may find it helpful to visualize listeners on a scale such as that shown in Figure 16.1. Persuasion involves any movement by a listener from left to right on the scale, no matter where the listener begins and no matter how great or small the movement.[4]

How successful you are in any particular persuasive speech will depend above all on how well you tailor your message to the values, attitudes, and beliefs of your audience. In Chapter 6, we considered the general principles of audience analysis and adaptation. Here we emphasize two additional principles that are crucial to the psychology of persuasion. The first deals with how listeners process and respond to persuasive messages. The second pertains to the target audience for persuasive speeches.

HOW LISTENERS PROCESS PERSUASIVE MESSAGES

We often think of persuasion as something a speaker does *to* an audience. In fact, persuasion is something a speaker does *with* an audience. Listeners do not just sit passively and soak in everything the speaker has to say. Instead, they engage in a mental give-and-take with the speaker.

While they listen, they assess the speaker's credibility, delivery, language, reasoning, and emotional appeals. They may respond positively at one point, negatively at another. At times they may argue, inside their own minds, with the speaker. This mental give-and-take is especially vigorous when listeners are highly involved with the topic and believe it has a direct bearing on their lives.[5]

In a sense, the psychological interaction between a speaker and audience during a persuasive speech is similar to what happens vocally during a conversation—as in this example:

Karyn: It's better to donate your time to charity than to donate your money. Plenty of charities are well supported financially, but they lack the volunteers they need.

Naomi: It's true that volunteering is important, but most of us just don't have the time. It's easier to send a donation online. I'm sure the charities would rather have me give money than do nothing at all.

Karyn: You're right about that. But you'd be surprised how easy it is to find an hour or two a week. Between classes, on the weekends, in the evenings—most people have more flexibility than they realize.

No matter what the situation, a persuasive speaker needs to adapt to the target audience. Here student Margaret Czerwienski speaks at the No Justice Walkout at Harvard University.

Vanessa Leroy/Bloomberg/Getty Images

Naomi: Perhaps, but showing up at some strange place to volunteer makes me nervous. Even if I could find the time, I get uncomfortable in new situations like that.

Karyn: I used to feel the same way, but charities are set up to help volunteers feel welcome. I got over my nervousness quickly, and now I'm excited to volunteer.

Much the same kind of interaction might occur during a persuasive speech, except that the listener would respond internally rather than out loud.

What does this mean to you as a speaker? It means you must think of your persuasive speech as a kind of mental dialogue with your audience. You must anticipate possible objections the audience will raise to your point of view and answer them in your speech. You cannot convert skeptical listeners unless you deal directly with the reasons for their skepticism.

As you prepare your persuasive speech, put yourself in the place of your audience and imagine how they will respond. Be as tough on your speech as your audience will be. Every place they will raise a question, answer it. Every place they will have a criticism, deal with it. Every place they will see a hole in your argument, fill it. Leave nothing to chance.[6]

mental dialogue with the audience
The mental give-and-take between speaker and listener during a persuasive speech.

THE TARGET AUDIENCE

Unfortunately, no matter how carefully you plot your speech, you will seldom be able to persuade all your listeners. Like most audiences, yours will probably contain some listeners who are hostile to your position, some who favor it, some who are undecided, and some who just don't care. You would like to make your speech equally appealing to everyone, but this is rarely possible. Most often you will have a particular *part* of the whole audience that you want to reach with your speech. That part is called the *target audience*.

target audience
The portion of the whole audience that the speaker most wants to persuade.

Advertising gives us an effective model. Social media platforms allow advertisers to reach particular segments of the market. As a college student, you might see an advertisement on Instagram for a ride-sharing app like Uber or Lyft. But your 50-year-old uncle might see an advertisement from a financial services company like Fidelity or Charles Schwab.

For your classroom speeches, you don't have the sophisticated analytics of a large advertising agency. But as we saw in Chapter 6, you can use questionnaires to find out where your classmates stand on your speech topic. This is your equivalent of market research. Once you know where your target audience stands, you can tailor your speech to fit their values and concerns—aim at the target, so to speak.

Here, for example, is how one student, Eveyln Xu, determined her target audience for a persuasive speech advocating lifetime GPS tracking of high-risk serial sex offenders:

> There are 22 students in my audience. My audience-analysis questionnaires show that 4 are absolutely opposed to my plan. I can't persuade them no matter what I say. My questionnaires also show that 6 already support my position. I don't need to persuade them. The other 12 students could be persuaded if they knew more about how the GPS tracking program would work and about its privacy implications.

Not only did Eveyln pinpoint her target audience, she also knew from her audience-analysis questionnaire the issues she would have to discuss to be convincing:

> The members of my target audience break down this way: 5 give "concerns over cost" as their primary concern; 5 are worried about "privacy and government surveillance"; and 2 think sex offenders will just remove the monitoring devices.

With all this information, Eveyln was able to put together a speech that focused directly on her classmates' attitudes and beliefs. As a result, she was able to convince several to support her position.

In the next chapter, we'll discuss the methods you can use to hit the target in your persuasive speeches. In the rest of this chapter, we focus on the three major kinds of persuasive speeches and how to organize them most effectively.

Persuasive Speeches on Questions of Fact

WHAT ARE QUESTIONS OF FACT?

What college basketball team has won the most games since 2000? Who was the first African American to sit on the U.S. Supreme Court? How far is it from Los Angeles to Singapore? These questions of fact can be answered absolutely. The answers are either right or wrong.

But many questions of fact cannot be answered absolutely. There is a true answer, but we don't have enough information to know what it is. Some questions like this involve prediction: Will the economy be better or worse next year? Who will win the Super Bowl this season?

Other questions deal with issues on which the facts are murky or inconclusive. Is there intelligent life in other parts of the solar system? What will happen next in the

Many persuasive speeches revolve around questions of fact. There is much debate, for example, about the impact of climate change on violent weather events around the world.

Saeed Khan/AFP/Getty Images

Middle East? No one knows the final answers to these questions, but that doesn't stop people from speculating about them or from trying to convince other people that they have the best possible answers.

ANALYZING QUESTIONS OF FACT

In some ways, a persuasive speech on a question of fact is similar to an informative speech. But the two kinds of speeches take place in different kinds of situations and for different purposes.

question of fact
A question about the truth or falsity of an assertion.

The situation for an informative speech is *nonpartisan*. The speaker acts as a lecturer or a teacher. The aim is to give information as impartially as possible, not to argue for a particular point of view.

On the other hand, the situation for a persuasive speech on a question of fact is *partisan*. The speaker acts as an advocate. The aim is not to be impartial, but to present one view of the facts as persuasively as possible. The speaker may mention competing views of the facts, but only to refute them.

For example, consider the assassination of John F. Kennedy. After more than 60 years, there is still much debate about what really happened in Dallas on November 22, 1963. Did Lee Harvey Oswald act alone, or was he part of a conspiracy? How many shots were fired at President Kennedy and from what locations? If there was a conspiracy, who was involved in it? The informative speaker would recite the known facts on both sides of these questions without drawing a conclusion about which side is correct. The persuasive speaker, however, would draw a conclusion from the known facts and try to convert listeners to his or her point of view.

If there were no possibility of dispute on questions of fact, there would be no need for courtroom trials. In a criminal trial there is usually at least one known fact—a crime has been committed. But did the defendant commit the crime? The prosecuting attorney tries to persuade the jury that the defendant is guilty. The defense attorney tries to persuade the jury that the defendant is innocent. The jury must decide which view of the facts is more persuasive.[7]

ORGANIZING SPEECHES ON QUESTIONS OF FACT

Persuasive speeches on questions of fact are usually organized *topically*. Suppose, for example, that you want to convince your classmates that an earthquake of 9.0 or above on the Richter scale will hit California within the next 10 years. Each main point in your speech will present a *reason* why someone should agree with you:

Specific Purpose: To persuade my audience that an earthquake of 9.0 or above on the Richter scale will hit California in the next 10 years.

Central Idea: There are three good reasons to believe that an earthquake of 9.0 or above on the Richter scale will hit California in the next 10 years.

Main Points:
I. California is long overdue for a major earthquake.

II. Many geological signs indicate that a major earthquake may happen soon.

III. Experts agree that an earthquake of 9.0 or above could strike California any day.

To take another example, suppose you are trying to persuade your classmates that the plays attributed to William Shakespeare were not actually written by him. Your specific purpose, central idea, and main points might be:

Specific Purpose: To persuade my audience that William Shakespeare did not write the plays attributed to him.

Central Idea: There is considerable evidence that the plays attributed to William Shakespeare were actually written by Francis Bacon or Edward de Vere.

Main Points:
I. Biographical and textual evidence suggest that William Shakespeare did not write the plays attributed to him.

II. Historical evidence suggests that Shakespeare's plays were probably written by either Sir Francis Bacon or Edward de Vere, 17th Earl of Oxford.

Notice in these examples that the speaker's purpose is limited to persuading the audience to accept a particular view of the facts. Sometimes, however, the dispute that gives rise to a persuasive speech will go beyond a question of fact and will turn on a question of value.

Persuasive Speeches on Questions of Value

WHAT ARE QUESTIONS OF VALUE?

What is the best movie of all time? Is solitary confinement morally justifiable? What are the ethical responsibilities of journalists? Such questions not only involve matters of fact, but they also demand *value judgments*—judgments based on a person's beliefs about what is right or wrong, good or bad, moral or immoral, proper or improper, fair or unfair.

Take the issue of solitary confinement. It can be discussed at a purely factual level by asking such questions as "What are the laws about solitary confinement?" or "How widespread is solitary confinement as a punishment in American prisons?" These are factual questions. The answers you reach are independent of your belief about the morality of solitary confinement.

question of value
A question about the worth, rightness, morality, and so forth of an idea or action.

But suppose you ask, "Is it morally justifiable to keep prisoners in solitary confinement for extended periods of time?" Now you are dealing with a question of value. How you answer will depend not only on your factual knowledge about solitary confinement, but also on your moral values.

ANALYZING QUESTIONS OF VALUE

Contrary to what many people think, questions of value are not simply matters of personal opinion or whim. If you say, "I enjoy bicycle riding," you do not have to give a reason why you enjoy it. You are making a statement about your personal taste. Even if bicycle riding were the most unpleasant activity ever invented, it could still be one of your favorites.

On the other hand, if you say, "Bicycle riding is the ideal form of land transportation," you are making a statement about a question of value. Whether bicycling is the ideal form of land transportation does not depend on your own likes and dislikes. To defend the statement, you cannot say, "Bicycle riding is the ideal form of land transportation because I like it."

Instead, you must *justify* your claim. The first step is to define what you mean by an "ideal form of land transportation." Do you mean a mode of transportation that gets people where they want to go as fast as possible? That is relatively inexpensive? That is fun? Nonpolluting? Beneficial for the user? In other words, you must establish your *standards* for an "ideal form of land transportation." Then you can show how bicycle riding measures up against those standards.

Whenever you give a speech on a question of value, be sure to give special thought to the standards for your value judgment.

ORGANIZING SPEECHES ON QUESTIONS OF VALUE

Persuasive speeches on questions of value are almost always organized *topically*. The most common approach is to devote your first main point to establishing the standards for your value judgment and your second main point to applying those standards to the subject of your speech.

Think back for a moment to the speech about bicycle riding as the ideal form of land transportation. If you organized this speech in topical order, your first main point would identify the standards for an ideal form of land transportation. Your second main point would show how biking measures up against those standards. Here is how your specific purpose, central idea, and main points might look:

Specific Purpose: To persuade my audience that bicycle riding is the ideal form of land transportation.

Central Idea: Bicycle riding is the ideal form of land transportation because it is faster than walking or running, is nonpolluting, and promotes the health of the rider.

Main Points:	I. An ideal form of land transportation should meet three major standards.
	A. It should be faster than running or walking.
	B. It should be nonpolluting.
	C. It should be beneficial for the person who uses it.
	II. Bicycle riding meets all these standards for an ideal form of land transportation.
	A. Bicycle riding is faster than walking or running.
	B. Bicycle riding is not a source of air, land, water, or noise pollution.
	C. Bicycle riding is extremely beneficial for the health of the rider.

When you speak on a question of value, you must make sure to justify your judgment against some identifiable standards. In the following example, notice how the speaker devotes her first main point to judging elephant trophy hunting against legal standards and her second main point to judging it against moral standards:

Specific Purpose:	To persuade my audience that elephant trophy hunting is legally and morally wrong.
Central Idea:	Elephant trophy hunting violates international accords and our duty to treat animals humanely.
Main Points:	I. Elephant trophy hunting violates international accords on species conservation.
	II. Elephant trophy hunting violates what moral philosopher Immanuel Kant says is our duty to treat animals humanely.

As you can see, speeches on questions of value may have strong implications for our actions. A person who is persuaded that elephant trophy hunting violates international accords and is morally wrong is more likely to support policies designed to ban this kind of hunting. But speeches on questions of value do not argue directly for or against particular courses of action. Once you go beyond arguing right or wrong to arguing that something should or should not be done, you move from a question of value to a question of policy.

Persuasive Speeches on Questions of Policy

WHAT ARE QUESTIONS OF POLICY?

question of policy
A question about whether a specific course of action should or should not be taken.

Questions of policy arise daily in almost everything we do. At home we debate what to do during spring vacation, whether to buy a new laptop, which movie to see on the weekend. At work we discuss whether to ask for a raise, what strategy to use in selling a product, how to improve communication between management and employees. As citizens we ponder whether to vote for or against a political candidate, what to do about national defense, how to promote economic growth.

All these are questions of policy because they deal with specific courses of action. Questions of policy inevitably involve questions of fact. (How can we decide whether to vote for a candidate unless we know the facts of her or his stand on the issues?) They may also involve questions of value. (The policy you favor on capital punishment will be affected by whether you think the death penalty is moral or immoral.) But questions of policy *always* go beyond questions of fact or value to decide whether something should or should not be done.

When put formally, questions of policy usually include the word "should," as in these examples:

> What measures should be taken to protect people's privacy online?
>
> Should the electoral college be abolished?
>
> What steps should be taken to reduce the erosion of America's coastlines?

TYPES OF SPEECHES ON QUESTIONS OF POLICY

When you speak on a question of policy, your goal may be either to gain passive agreement or to motivate immediate action from your listeners. Deciding which goal you want to achieve will affect almost every aspect of your speech.

Speeches to Gain Passive Agreement

If your goal is passive agreement, you will try to get your audience to agree with you that a certain policy is desirable, but you will not necessarily encourage the audience to do anything to enact the policy. For example, suppose you want to persuade people that the United States should abolish the electoral college and elect the president by direct popular vote. If you seek passive agreement, you will try to get your audience to concur, but you will not urge them to take any action right now to help change presidential election procedures.

Here are some specific purpose statements for policy speeches to gain passive agreement:

> To persuade my audience that there should be stricter privacy standards on companies that offer personal genetic testing.
>
> To persuade my audience that the U.S. patent system should be overhauled so as to promote innovation.
>
> To persuade my audience that our state should increase funding for all levels of public education.

speech to gain passive agreement
A persuasive speech in which the speaker's goal is to convince the audience that a given policy is desirable without encouraging the audience to take action in support of the policy.

In each case, the speaker's aim is to convince listeners that the speaker's policy is necessary and practical. The speaker is not trying to get listeners to take action in support of the policy.

Speeches to Gain Immediate Action

When your goal is immediate action, you want to do more than get your listeners to nod their heads in agreement. You want to motivate them to action—to sign a petition for abolishing the electoral college, to campaign for lower tuition, to contribute to a fund drive, and so forth.

Here are some examples of specific purpose statements for policy speeches to gain immediate action:

> To persuade my audience to donate to the Wounded Warrior Project.

To persuade my audience to vote in the upcoming state and local elections.

To persuade my audience to establish retirement accounts early in their careers.

speech to gain immediate action

A persuasive speech in which the speaker's goal is to convince the audience to take action in support of a given policy.

Some experts say you should seek action from your audience whenever possible. Although it is much easier to evoke passive agreement than to elicit action, the listener is not making much of a commitment by thinking, "Sure, I agree with you." Within a day or two that same listener may forget entirely about your speech—and about her or his agreement with it.

Action, however, reinforces belief. A great deal of research shows that if you can persuade a listener to take some kind of action—even if it is no more than signing a petition, putting a bumper sticker on a car, or attending a meeting—you have gained a more serious commitment. Once a listener acts on behalf of a speaker's position, she or he is more likely to remain committed to it.[8]

When you call for action in a persuasive speech, you should make your recommendations as specific as possible. Don't just urge listeners to "do something." Tell them exactly what to do and how to do it.

connect

View this excerpt from "Making a Difference Through the Special Olympics" in the online Media Library for this chapter (Video 16.1).

For an excellent example, watch Video 16.1. The speaker's aim was to convince her classmates to donate time to the Special Olympics. After talking about the mission of Special Olympics, the need for volunteers, and the rewarding feelings experienced by volunteers, she explained how students can get involved for whatever amount of time they are able to commit at the moment. She also brought along brochures with additional information to pass out after her speech. When you construct your persuasive speech, remember that the more specific your instructions, the more likely it is that your call to action will succeed.[9]

ANALYZING QUESTIONS OF POLICY

Regardless of whether your aim is to elicit passive agreement or to gain immediate action, you will face three basic issues whenever you discuss a question of policy—need, plan, and practicality.

Need

need

The first basic issue in analyzing a question of policy: Is there a serious problem or need that requires a change from current policy?

There is no point in arguing for a policy unless you can show a need for it:

Is there a need for more student parking on campus?

Is there a need to increase government regulation of big tech companies?

Is there a need for a national ID card in the United States?

burden of proof

The obligation facing a persuasive speaker to prove that a change from current policy is necessary.

Your first step is to convince listeners that there is a serious problem with things as they are. People are not inclined to adopt a new policy unless they are convinced that the old one is not working. This is why the *burden of proof* always rests with the speaker who advocates change. (Of course, you may be defending present policy, in which case you will argue that there is *no* need to change—that things are already working as well as can be expected.)

Plan

The second basic issue of policy speeches is plan. Once you have shown that a problem exists, you must explain your plan for solving it:

Persuasive speeches on questions of policy are given whenever people debate specific courses of action. Here New York City mayor Eric Adams speaks at a press conference announcing his choice for police commissioner.

Yuki Iwamura/AFP/Getty Images

What can we do to get more student parking on campus?

How can we regulate big tech companies to promote a fair marketplace and ensure that technological innovation continues to happen?

What information should be included on a national ID card? Who will be responsible for collecting the information and creating the cards?

Answering such questions is especially important if you call for a new policy. It's easy to complain about problems; the real challenge is developing solutions.

In most classroom speeches, you will not have time to describe your plan in detail, but you should at least identify its major features. Look, for example, at the plan section in a student speech on puppy mills (Video 16.2). First, the speaker proposes legal measures to punish dog breeders who do not take proper care of their animals. Second, he presents four steps that individual listeners can take when buying a dog to make sure they are not supporting puppy mills. The speech would have been much less persuasive if the speaker had not spelled out the major features of his plan.

Practicality

The third basic issue of policy speeches is practicality. Once you have presented a plan, you must show that it will work. Will it solve the problem? Or will it create new and more serious problems?

Building a multilevel parking garage on campus would provide more student parking, but the cost would require a sharp increase in tuition.

Because big tech companies have become so powerful, Congress should limit their influence, but regulations have the potential to slow innovation and enable foreign competitors to overtake U.S. companies.

plan
The second basic issue in analyzing a question of policy: If there is a problem with current policy, does the speaker have a plan to solve the problem?

connect
View this excerpt from "The Horrors of Puppy Mills" in the online Media Library for this chapter (Video 16.2).

practicality
The third basic issue in analyzing a question of policy: Will the speaker's plan solve the problem? Will it create new and more serious problems?

A national ID card might be an easy way for people to verify their identity for security purposes, but it could also infringe on civil liberties and give the government too much personal information about individuals.

connect

View this excerpt from "The Future of Work" in the online Media Library for this chapter (Video 16.3).

These are significant concerns. Whenever you advocate a new policy, you must be prepared to show that it is workable. No matter how serious a problem may be, listeners usually want some assurance that a speaker's plan will actually solve the problem.[10]

One way to provide this assurance is to show that a plan similar to yours has been successfully implemented elsewhere. For example, Video 16.3 shows an excerpt from a student speech calling for a four-day work week. As you view the video, notice how the speaker points to the success of a similar plan in other countries as evidence that it will work in the United States.

If you oppose a shift in policy, one of your major arguments will be that the change is impractical—that it will create more problems than it can solve. For example, critics of a plan to send astronauts to Mars might say that it is highly risky and requires technology that does not currently exist. Others might argue that the cost of the mission would be better spent on any number of causes here on Earth. If listeners accept these arguments, they will probably decide that NASA should not continue working on sending astronauts to Mars.

How much of your speech should you devote to need, to plan, and to practicality? The answer depends on your topic and your audience. For example, if your audience is not aware of the environmental problems caused by the plastic microbeads found in soaps and scrubs, you will have to give much of your time to need before covering plan and practicality. On the other hand, if your listeners already know about the problems caused by microbeads, you can quickly remind them of need and then devote most of your speech to plan and practicality.

ORGANIZING SPEECHES ON QUESTIONS OF POLICY

Effective organization is crucial when you speak on a question of policy. Although any of the basic patterns of organization explained in Chapter 9 can be used, four special patterns are especially valuable for policy speeches. They are problem-solution order, problem-cause-solution order, comparative advantages order, and Monroe's motivated sequence.

Problem-Solution Order

problem-solution order
A method of organizing persuasive speeches in which the first main point deals with the existence of a problem and the second main point presents a solution to the problem.

If you advocate a change in policy, your main points often will fall naturally into problem-solution order. In the first main point you demonstrate the need for a new policy by showing the extent and seriousness of the problem. In the second main point you explain your plan for solving the problem and show its practicality. For example:

Specific Purpose: To persuade my audience that the U.S. Congress should pass legislation that will reduce lead levels in the nation's water supply.

Central Idea: Because lead in the water supply is a serious problem in the United States, Congress should pass legislation reducing lead levels in our water.

Main Points: I. Lead in our nation's water supply is a serious problem.

    A. Lead affects the water in millions of homes and other buildings across the country.

    B. Ingesting excessive amounts of lead causes serious health problems.

    C. Currently not enough is being done to reduce lead in the water supply.

II. Solving the problem requires action by the federal government.

    A. Congress should pass legislation funding the removal of lead pipes and mandating regular water testing.

    B. Experts believe such legislation will go a long way toward solving the problem.

connect

View an excerpt from "Getting the Lead Out" in the online Media Library for this chapter (Video 16.4).

You can use the problem-solution format just as easily to organize a speech opposing a change in policy. In such a speech your job is to defend the current system and to attack your opponents' proposed policy. Thus in the first main point you might argue that there is *not* a need for change. In the second main point you might show that even if there were a serious problem, the suggested new policy would *not* solve it and would create serious problems of its own. For example:

Specific Purpose: To persuade my audience that the city council should not pass legislation merging the police and fire departments.

Central Idea: Merging the police and fire departments is neither necessary nor practical.

Main Points: I. Merging the police and fire departments is not necessary.

    A. Under the current system, the police department has developed a reputation for excellence that has made it a model for departments in other cities.

    B. The fire department is equally well respected for doing its job quickly and efficiently.

II. Besides being unnecessary, merging the police and fire departments is highly impractical.

    A. Rather than saving the city money, merging the departments would increase costs.

    B. Merging the departments would also harm morale and reduce the high level of performance we expect from our police force and firefighters.

Problem-Cause-Solution Order

For a variation on problem-solution order, you might arrange your speech in problem-cause-solution order. This produces a speech with three main points—the first identifying a problem, the second analyzing the causes of the problem, and the third presenting a solution to the problem. For example:

Specific Purpose: To persuade my audience that action is required to deal with the problem of childhood obesity.

Central Idea: Childhood obesity is a serious problem that can be controlled by changes in diet and exercise.

problem-cause-solution order

A method of organizing persuasive speeches in which the first main point identifies a problem, the second main point analyzes the causes of the problem, and the third main point presents a solution to the problem.

connect

View an excerpt from "The Epidemic of Childhood Obesity" in the online Media Library for this chapter (Video 16.5).

Main Points:	I. Childhood obesity is a major problem in the United States.
	A. Childhood obesity continues to grow at a rapid pace.
	B. Obesity is producing serious health problems among children.
	II. There are two major causes of the increase in childhood obesity.
	A. The first cause is dietary.
	B. The second cause is physical inactivity.
	III. Solving the problem requires dealing with both causes.
	A. Parents and schools must make sure that children are eating healthy foods.
	B. Parents and schools must also make sure that children get enough exercise.

Some teachers prefer this method of organization because it requires a speaker to identify the causes of the problem. This in turn makes it easier to check whether the proposed solution will get at the causes of the problem.

Comparative Advantages Order

When your audience already agrees that a problem exists, you can devote your speech to comparing the advantages and disadvantages of competing solutions. In such a situation, you might put your speech in comparative advantages order, devoting each main point to explaining why your solution is preferable to other proposed solutions.

comparative advantages order

A method of organizing persuasive speeches in which each main point explains why a speaker's solution to a problem is preferable to other proposed solutions.

Suppose you are speaking at a meeting of the city council about ways to alleviate traffic congestion in your city. Some citizens support the construction of a new highway. You, however, support a rapid bus system that can be built on already-existing roads. Using comparative advantages order, you compare the highway proposal with the bus-system proposal and show why the latter is a better choice. Your specific purpose, central idea, and main points might look like this:

Specific Purpose:	To persuade my audience that our city should build a rapid bus system instead of a new highway.
Central Idea:	A rapid bus system will be cheaper and more effective than a new highway.
Main Points:	I. Research models show that we will save $1 million if we build a rapid bus system instead of a new highway.
	II. Research models also show that a rapid bus system will reduce traffic congestion more than a new highway.

Monroe's motivated sequence

A method of organizing persuasive speeches that seeks immediate action. The five steps of the motivated sequence are attention, need, satisfaction, visualization, and action.

Monroe's Motivated Sequence

Developed in the 1930s by Alan Monroe, a professor of speech at Purdue University, Monroe's motivated sequence is tailor-made for policy speeches that seek immediate action. The sequence has five steps that follow the psychology of persuasion:

1. *Attention.* First, you gain the attention of your audience by using one or more of the methods described in Chapter 10: relating to the audience, showing the

Persuasive speeches on questions of policy are often organized in Monroe's motivated sequence. Because it follows the process of human thinking, Monroe's is especially useful for speakers who seek immediate action from their listeners.

Scott Eisen/Bloomberg/Getty Images

importance of the topic, making a startling statement, arousing curiosity or suspense, posing a question, telling a dramatic story, or using visual aids.

2. *Need.* Next, you make the audience feel a need for change. You show there is a serious problem with the existing situation. It is important to state the need clearly and to illustrate it with strong supporting materials. By the end of this step, listeners should be so concerned about the problem that they are psychologically primed to hear your solution.

3. *Satisfaction.* Having aroused a sense of need, you satisfy it by providing a solution to the problem. You present your plan and show how it will work. Be sure to offer enough details about the plan to give listeners a clear understanding of it.

4. *Visualization.* Having given your plan, you intensify desire for it by visualizing its benefits. The key to this step is using vivid imagery to show your listeners how they will profit from your policy. Make them *see* how much better conditions will be once your plan is adopted.

5. *Action.* Once the audience is convinced that your policy is beneficial, you are ready to call for action. Say exactly what you want the audience to do—and how to do it. Then conclude with a final stirring appeal that reinforces their commitment to act.

Many speakers prefer the motivated sequence because it is more detailed than problem-solution order. It follows the process of human thinking and leads the listener step by step to the desired action. One indication of its effectiveness is that it is widely used by people who make their living by persuasion, especially advertisers. The next time you watch television, pay close attention to the advertisements. You will find that many of them follow the motivated sequence.

Try using the motivated sequence when you want to spur listeners to action. You should find it easy and effective, as did one student who used it in a speech urging classmates to work for passage of a local tenants' rights bill. Here are the highlights of his speech:

Attention: Have you ever had cockroaches running through the cupboards in your apartment? Have you shivered in the cold because the furnace was broken? Or waited months for the security deposit you never got back even though you left your apartment as clean as when you moved in?

Need: Throughout this city students and other tenants are being victimized by unresponsive and unethical landlords. Just last year more than 500 complaints were filed with the city housing department, but no action has been taken against the landlords.

Satisfaction: These problems could be solved by passing a strong tenants' rights bill that defines the rights of tenants, specifies the obligations of landlords, and imposes strict penalties for violators.

Visualization: Such bills have worked in a number of college communities across the nation. If one were passed here, you would no longer have to worry about substandard conditions in your apartment. Your landlord could not violate the terms of your lease or steal your security deposit.

Action: A tenants' rights bill has been proposed to the city council. You can help get it passed by signing the petition I will pass around after my speech. I've also created an online petition that I'll send to you on email. I urge you to circulate these petitions among your friends and to support the bill when it is debated in the city council next week. If we all work together, we can get this bill through the council.

Using public speaking in your CAREER

After earning your teaching certificate, you landed a job in one of the best public schools in the city. You've excelled in the classroom, and evaluations of your teaching are consistently outstanding.

But teacher pay in the district has been frozen for five years, leading to low morale among you and your colleagues. Even with a strong economy and city revenues up, local officials have prioritized areas other than teacher salaries, including affordable housing, infrastructure, and public parks.

In one week, local officials will hold an open meeting for teachers to voice their concerns about compensation. You plan on arguing for a 10 percent pay raise for all teachers, even though that will have an impact on spending in other areas, but you're unsure of how to organize your speech. Which of the following methods of organization will be most effective, and why: problem-solution, comparative advantages, Monroe's motivated sequence?

Image Source/Getty Images

Monroe's motivated sequence is perfectly compatible with the standard method of outlining discussed in Chapter 11. The following outline shows how one speaker incorporated the sequence into a speech urging his classmates to take class notes by hand rather than on a computer.

Specific Purpose: To persuade my audience to take class notes by hand instead of on a computer.

Central Idea: You can learn more and get better grades if you take class notes by hand rather than on a computer.

Introduction

Attention:
I. Many of us use a computer to take notes in class.
II. But what if doing so actually hinders your understanding of class material?
III. Today I hope to persuade you to take notes by hand rather than on a computer.

Body

Need:
I. Using a computer to take class notes can reduce learning.
   A. We all know how distracting a computer can be in the classroom.
   B. But even when we do pay attention, using a computer encourages us to type more notes than necessary.
   C. As a result, we often lose sight of key ideas and don't connect information effectively.

Satisfaction:
II. You can avoid these problems by taking notes by hand.
   A. Research shows that taking notes by hand produces higher test scores than taking notes on a computer.
   B. Students who take notes by hand do better at remembering key ideas and synthesizing information.
   C. Taking notes by hand also facilitates creativity and critical thinking.

Visualization:
III. Taking notes by hand will improve your learning and your grades.
   A. I started taking notes by hand last semester, and I see benefits already.
   B. I concentrate better in class and my test scores have improved.
   C. You can have the same results.

Conclusion

Action:
I. So I encourage you to leave your laptop at home and put pen to paper instead.
II. This may be hard at first, but if you stick with it, you'll be glad you did.

Try using the motivated sequence when you seek immediate action from your listeners. Over the years it has worked for countless speakers—and it can work for you as well.

Sample Speech with Commentary

connect

View "Mindfulness Meditation" in the online Media Library for this chapter (Video 16.6).

The following persuasive speech deals with a question of policy and is organized according to Monroe's motivated sequence. As you read the speech, notice how the speaker relates the topic directly to her audience and uses well-chosen supporting materials as she moves through the motivated sequence. The speech also shows how a speaker's delivery can enhance the impact of his or her ideas—as you can see by watching Video 16.6.

Mindfulness Meditation

 COMMENTARY

 SPEECH

COMMENTARY	SPEECH
The first step in Monroe's motivated sequence is gaining attention, which the speaker accomplishes with a vivid scenario that gets her audience involved right at the start.	You're swamped with homework, midterms are right around the corner, and your persuasive speech is due tomorrow. We've all been there—the sleepless nights, the poor eating habits, the feelings of isolation. College life can be full of worry, stress, and anxiety. But there are ways to cope.
Here the speaker reveals the topic of her speech and cites a quotation supporting the benefits of meditation for college students.	Today I'd like to explain one of those ways: mindfulness meditation, which is a form of meditation designed to get you to focus on your mind and body in the present moment. It's a proven way to help recenter yourself and manage the challenges of college life. As stated by Aurora Reyes, a wellness director at UCLA Medical School, meditation can "relieve stress, lessen depression, lower blood pressure, and improve sleep" while boosting "mood, memory, and even social intelligence."
The speaker establishes her credibility, states her central idea, and provides a transition to the body of her speech. Notice how she relates to her audience by talking in personal terms such as "you," "we," and "your."	I've been practicing meditation for about four years, since my junior year of high school, and it has truly changed my life. I also did a great deal of research for this speech, and I hope to persuade each of you to begin daily meditation. It isn't a magic cure-all for every problem we face, but if your experience is like mine, you'll be pleasantly surprised by what it can do for you. Let's start by taking a closer look at the need to meditate.
The speaker moves into the need step of Monroe's motivated sequence. She uses statistics to document the high levels of anxiety among college students nationally.	Stress and anxiety among college students have skyrocketed in recent years. A report just last year from the American College Health Association found that 67 percent of college students experienced overwhelming anxiety in the last 12 months, while 58 percent reported above average levels of stress. These are higher numbers than the association had ever recorded.

This paragraph builds upon the previous one by turning to anxiety on the speaker's campus. She provides high-quality evidence and clearly identifies her sources. Citing her audience-analysis survey brings the issue home to her classmates.

"So what can we do?" indicates that the speaker is entering the satisfaction step of the motivated sequence, in which she explains how students can use meditation to manage stress and anxiety.

The speaker's delivery is genuine, straightforward, and highly personable. In addition to enhancing her communication, it bolsters her goodwill as a heartfelt advocate of the benefits of meditation.

The speaker continues the satisfaction step by demonstrating the basics of meditation.

You can view the speaker's demonstration on Video 16.6. As she proceeds, her nonverbal actions illustrate what she is explaining with her words.

Throughout her demonstration, the speaker continues to relate to her audience by addressing them with "you" and "your."

The speaker's extemporaneous delivery and sustained eye contact create a strong bond with her audience.

The satisfaction section ends by emphasizing that meditation is most effective when it becomes part of one's daily routine.

According to John Achter, student behavioral health coordinator for the university system, the numbers are just as high at campuses throughout our state. Even in this classroom, there is more than enough stress to go around. According to my audience-analysis questionnaire, 75 percent of you reported feeling "overwhelming anxiety" at some point last year.

So what can we do? There are many ways to deal with stress and anxiety, including counseling, medication, and therapy. But I'd like to encourage you to try mindfulness meditation. Used by itself or in conjunction with other methods, it's an effective and easy way to stay calm and controlled.

In fact, this is something people have known for a long time. According to meditation expert Giovanni Dienstmann in his book *Practical Meditation*, there is evidence of people practicing meditation more than 7,000 years ago. For most of that time, meditation was a religious practice for seeking enlightenment. Today it's something that even college students can use to manage stress and anxiety.

On my audience-analysis questionnaire, more than half of you said you'd be interested in learning how to meditate, so let's go through it. Here are the basics, as described by David Gelles, *New York Times* columnist and author of *Mindful Work*.

First, you should sit in a comfortable position and close your eyes. Then you should begin deep breathing. Inhale for about 10 seconds, hold for 5 seconds, then exhale for 10 seconds, like this.

As you continue to breathe deeply, envision yourself in a serene, peaceful place. Continue the pattern of inhaling and exhaling until your breathing settles into a comfortable rhythm, usually about a minute or two.

Once your breathing settles into a comfortable rhythm, you can relax your muscles from your head all the way to your toes. Envision your anxiety and stress melting away. Do this for 15 minutes, even 10 minutes, per day and you will soon feel more mindful and centered.

Meditation expert Giovanni Dienstmann also recommends that you strive for consistency. This means practicing your meditation around the same time every day and, whenever possible, in the same place. Think of meditation as part of your daily routine, like brushing your teeth.

Now the speaker moves into the visualization section of the motivated sequence, in which she confirms the benefits of her plan. She begins by referring to her own experience.

This paragraph goes beyond the speaker's experience to provide examples and research supporting the benefits of meditation. This kind of evidence is important when one seeks to persuade an audience to take action on a question of policy.

The speaker concludes by moving into the action section of the motivated sequence.

To help her classmates get going with meditation, she refers them to the Calm channel on YouTube.

The speaker ends with a final appeal for her classmates to test the benefits of meditation for themselves.

Once you make meditation part of your daily routine, you will soon feel the difference. Take me. I've been meditating practically every day for the past four years. My meditations are 15 minutes long and take place while I'm seated on my dorm room floor, about an hour before I go to bed. I fall asleep relaxed and wake up ready to tackle the new day.

And I am not the only one. Bill Gates, Oprah Winfrey, and Kendrick Lamar all have regular meditation routines. Besides these famous names, thousands of college students have discovered the benefits of meditation. Last year, researchers at Florida State University reviewed 25 different scholarly articles on meditation for college students. They found that mindful meditation is proven to have "a large and significant effect in decreasing college students' anxiety."

In conclusion, I encourage all of you to begin a program of mindfulness meditation. It won't get rid of all of your problems, of course. But it's been proven to help manage the stress and anxiety we all face.

If you need help getting started, you can follow the steps I laid out in this speech. Or you can go to YouTube and search "calm." There you'll find the Calm channel, which includes 10-minute meditation guides and mindfulness training.

With daily meditation, you can recenter yourself and successfully manage the challenges ahead. I encourage you to give it a try and see what kind of difference it makes in your life.

Summary

Persuasion is the process of creating, reinforcing, or changing people's beliefs or actions. When you speak to persuade, you act as an advocate. The ability to speak persuasively will benefit you in every part of your life, from personal relations to community activities to career aspirations.

How successful you are in any persuasive speech depends on how well you tailor your message to your listeners' values, attitudes, and beliefs. You should think of your speech as a mental dialogue with your audience. Identify your target audience, anticipate objections they may raise to your point of view, and answer those objections in your speech.

Persuasive speeches may center on questions of fact, value, or policy. When giving a persuasive speech about a question of fact, your role is akin to that of a lawyer in a courtroom trial. You will try to get your listeners to accept your view of the facts.

Questions of value involve a person's beliefs about what is right or wrong, good or bad, moral or immoral, ethical or unethical. When speaking about a question of value, you must justify your opinion by establishing standards for your value judgment. Speeches on questions of value do not argue directly for or against particular courses of action.

Once you go beyond arguing right or wrong to urging that something should or should not be done, you move to a question of policy. When you speak on a question of policy, your goal may be to evoke passive agreement or to spark immediate action. In either case, you will face three basic issues—need, plan, and practicality. How much of your speech you devote to each issue will depend on your topic and your audience.

There are several options for organizing speeches on questions of policy. If you advocate a change in policy, your main points will often fall naturally into problem-solution order or into problem-cause-solution order. If your audience already agrees that a problem exists, you may be able to use comparative advantages order. Whenever you seek immediate action from listeners, you should consider a more specialized organizational pattern known as Monroe's motivated sequence.

Regardless of your topic or method of organization, you need to make sure your goals are ethically sound and that you use ethical methods to persuade your audience.

Key Terms

persuasion (288)

mental dialogue with the audience (291)

target audience (291)

question of fact (293)

question of value (295)

question of policy (296)

speech to gain passive agreement (297)

speech to gain immediate action (298)

need (298)

burden of proof (298)

plan (299)

practicality (299)

problem-solution order (300)

problem-cause-solution order (301)

comparative advantages order (302)

Monroe's motivated sequence (302)

Review Questions

After reading this chapter, you should be able to answer the following questions:

1. What is the difference between an informative speech and a persuasive speech? Why is speaking to persuade more challenging than speaking to inform?

2. What does it mean to say that audiences engage in a mental dialogue with the speaker as they listen to a speech? What implications does this mental give-and-take hold for effective persuasive speaking?

3. What is the target audience for a persuasive speech?

4. What are questions of fact? How does a persuasive speech on a question of fact differ from an informative speech? Give an example of a specific purpose statement for a persuasive speech on a question of fact.

5. What are questions of value? Give an example of a specific purpose statement for a persuasive speech on a question of value.

6. What are questions of policy? Give an example of a specific purpose statement for a persuasive speech on a question of policy.

7. Explain the difference between passive agreement and immediate action as goals for persuasive speeches on questions of policy.

8. What are the three basic issues you must deal with when discussing a question of policy? What will determine the amount of attention you give to each of these issues in any particular speech?

9. What four methods of organization are used most often in persuasive speeches on questions of policy?

10. What are the five steps of Monroe's motivated sequence? Why is the motivated sequence especially useful in speeches that seek immediate action from listeners?

Exercises for Critical Thinking

1. Look back at the story of Victoria Perez at the beginning of this chapter. Like Victoria, most people do a certain amount of persuading every day in normal conversation. Keep a journal of your communication activities for an entire day, making special note of all instances in which you tried to persuade someone else to your point of view. Choose one of those instances and prepare a brief analysis of it.

   In your analysis, answer the following questions: (1) Who was the audience for your persuasive effort? (2) What were the "specific purpose" and the "central idea" of your persuasive message? (3) Did you rehearse your persuasive message ahead of time, or did it arise spontaneously from the situation? (4) Were you successful in achieving your specific purpose? (5) If you faced the same situation again, what strategic changes would you make in your persuasive effort?

2. Following are four specific purposes for persuasive speeches. In each case explain whether the speech associated with it concerns a question of fact, a question of value, or a question of policy. Then rewrite the specific purpose statement to make it appropriate for a speech about one of the other two kinds of questions. For instance, if the original purpose statement is about a question of policy, write a new specific purpose statement that deals with the same topic as either a question of fact or a question of value.

   Example:

   Original statement: To persuade my audience that it is unfair for judges to favor natural parents over adoptive parents in child custody disputes. (question of value)

   Rewritten statement: To persuade my audience that the courts should establish clear guidelines for settling disputes between adoptive parents and natural parents in child custody cases. (question of policy)

   a. To persuade my audience that refined sugar is harmful to human health.

   b. To persuade my audience that a national sales tax should be adopted to help reduce the national debt.

   c. To persuade my audience that it is unethical for doctors to receive money from pharmaceutical companies to promote their products.

   d. To persuade my audience to join Teach for America.

3. Choose a topic for a persuasive speech on a question of policy. Create two specific purpose statements about that topic—one for a speech to gain passive agreement, another for a speech to motivate immediate action. Once you have the specific purpose statements, explain how the speech seeking immediate action would differ in structure and persuasive appeals from the speech seeking passive agreement. Be specific.

4. Analyze "Getting the Lead Out" in the appendix of sample speeches that follows Chapter 20. Because this is a speech on a question of policy, pay special attention to how the speaker deals with the basic issues of need, plan, and practicality. Does the speaker present a convincing case that a serious problem exists? Does he offer a clear plan to solve the problem? Does he demonstrate that the plan is practical?

5. Select an advertisement from television or YouTube that is organized according to Monroe's motivated sequence. Prepare a brief analysis in which you (a) identify the target audience for the advertisement and (b) describe each step in the motivated sequence as it appears in the advertisement.

End Notes

[1] There are many competing definitions of persuasion. Ours is drawn from Gerald R. Miller, "On Being Persuaded: Some Basic Distinctions," in James Price Dillard and Lijiang Shen (eds.), *The SAGE Handbook of Persuasion: Developments in Theory and Practice,* 2nd ed. (Thousand Oaks, CA: Sage, 2013), pp. 70–82.

[2] Deirdre Nansen McCloskey, *Bourgeois Equality: How Ideas, Not Capital or Institutions, Enriched the World* (Chicago: University of Chicago Press, 2016), pp. 490–497.

[3] See Richard L. Johannesen, Kathleen S. Valde, and Karen E. Whedbee, *Ethics in Human Communication,* 6th ed. (Prospect Heights, IL: Waveland Press, 2008), for a full look at communication ethics.

[4] Adapted from Jean G. Jones, Andi McClanahan, and Joseph Sery, *Persuasion in Society,* 4th ed. (New York: Routledge, 2022), pp. 52–53.

[5] This view of the interaction between speaker and listener reflects cognitive processing models of persuasion in general and the elaboration likelihood model in particular. For a concise explanation of the latter, see Em Griffin, Andrew Ledbetter, and Glenn Sparks, *A First Look at Communication Theory,* 11th ed. (New York: McGraw Hill, 2022).

[6] There is a great deal of research confirming the need for persuasive speakers to answer potential objections to their arguments. See James B. Stiff and Paul A. Mongeau, *Persuasive Communication,* 3rd ed. (New York: Guilford, 2016), pp. 318–326.

[7] For an insightful look at the research on courtroom persuasion, see John C. Reinard, "Persuasion in the Legal Setting," in Dillard and Shen (eds.), *SAGE Handbook of Persuasion,* pp. 331–353.

[8] Richard M. Perloff, *The Dynamics of Persuasion: Communication and Attitudes in the Twenty-First Century,* 7th ed. (New York: Routledge, 2021), pp. 403–405.

[9] Daniel J. O'Keefe, *Persuasion: Theory and Research,* 3rd ed. (Thousand Oaks, CA: Sage, 2016), p. 216.

[10] See O'Keefe, *Persuasion: Theory and Research,* pp. 221–223.

Methods of Persuasion

Persuasion is big business. Authors and consultants promise to teach you the one key secret to persuading people to do what you want. Ryan Andrews promises to reveal the "forbidden techniques" of "how to manipulate and influence anyone in less than ten minutes." Hendrik Rodgers claims to teach you the psychology of persuasion so you can "get others to do what you want." Kevin Dutton claims to have discovered "a single, definitive formula" for "a mysterious, previously unidentified, superstrain of persuasion." These people charge thousands of dollars for their seminars and motivational speeches. Companies and individuals flock—and pay—to read and hear what they have to say.

It sounds good, but does anyone really have the "one key secret" to persuasion? Probably not. Persuasion is too complicated for that. Yet, as the number of books, seminars, and videos on the subject shows, there is a perpetual fascination with the strategies and tactics of effective persuasion.

What makes a speaker persuasive? Why do listeners accept one speaker's views and reject those of another? How can a speaker motivate listeners to act in support of a cause, a campaign, or a candidate?

People have been trying to answer these questions for thousands of years—from the ancient Greek philosopher Aristotle to modern-day communication researchers. Although many answers have been given, we can say that listeners will be persuaded by a speaker for one or more of four reasons:

Because they perceive the speaker as having high *credibility*.

Because they are won over by the speaker's *evidence*.

Because they are convinced by the speaker's *reasoning*.

Because their *emotions* are touched by the speaker's ideas or language.

In this chapter we will look at each of these. We won't discover any magical secrets that will make you an irresistible persuasive speaker. But if you learn the principles discussed in this chapter, you will greatly increase your odds of winning the minds and hearts of your listeners.

Building Credibility

Here are two sets of imaginary statements. Which one of each pair would you be more likely to believe?

> The U.S. judicial system needs major organizational changes to deal with the growing number of court cases. (Sonia Sotomayor)
> The U.S. judicial system can deal with the number of court cases without any organizational changes. (Patrick Mahomes)

> Technology is changing professional football in ways that the average fan cannot see. (Patrick Mahomes)
> Technology is not having a major impact on professional football. (Sonia Sotomayor)

Most likely you chose the first in each pair of statements. If so, you were probably influenced by your perception of the speaker. You are more likely to respect the judgment of Sotomayor, Associate Justice of the U.S. Supreme Court, when she speaks about the organization of the American judiciary. You are more likely to respect the judgment of Mahomes, quarterback of the Kansas City Chiefs, when he speaks about technology in professional football. Some instructors call this factor *source credibility*. Others refer to it as ethos, the name given by Aristotle.

FACTORS OF CREDIBILITY

Many things affect a speaker's credibility, including sociability, dynamism, physical attractiveness, and perceived similarity between speaker and audience. Above all, though, credibility is affected by two factors:

- *Competence*—how an audience regards a speaker's intelligence, expertise, and knowledge of the subject.

- *Character*—how an audience regards a speaker's sincerity, trustworthiness, and concern for the well-being of the audience.[1]

The more favorably listeners view a speaker's competence and character, the more likely they are to accept what the speaker says. No doubt you are familiar with this from your own experience. Suppose you take a course in economics. The course is taught by a distinguished professor who has published widely in prestigious journals, who sits on a major international commission, and who has won several awards for outstanding research. In class, you hang on this professor's every word. One day the professor is absent; a colleague from the Economics Department—fully qualified but not as well known—comes to lecture instead. Possibly the fill-in instructor gives the same lecture the distinguished professor would have given, but you do not pay nearly as close attention. The other instructor does not have as high credibility as the professor.

It is important to remember that credibility is an attitude. It exists not in the speaker, but in the mind of the audience. A speaker may have high credibility for

ethos
The name used by Aristotle for what modern students of communication refer to as credibility.

credibility
The audience's perception of whether a speaker is qualified to speak on a given topic. The two major factors influencing a speaker's credibility are competence and character.

one audience and low credibility for another. A speaker may also have high credibility on one topic and low credibility on another. Looking back to our imaginary statements, most people would more readily believe Patrick Mahomes speaking about professional football than Patrick Mahomes speaking about the organization of the U.S. judiciary.

TYPES OF CREDIBILITY

Not only can a speaker's credibility vary from audience to audience and topic to topic, but it can also change during the course of a speech—so much so that we can identify three types of credibility:

- *Initial credibility*—the credibility of the speaker before she or he starts to speak.
- *Derived credibility*—the credibility of the speaker produced by everything she or he says and does during the speech itself.
- *Terminal credibility*—the credibility of the speaker at the end of the speech.[2]

All three are dynamic. High initial credibility is a great advantage for any speaker, but it can be destroyed during a speech, resulting in low terminal credibility. The reverse can also occur, as in the following example:

> The head of a technology consulting firm, Maira Singh was hired by a regional restaurant chain to modernize their point-of-sale system. She and her team selected the industry-standard POS system, promising to customize it exactly as the restaurant chain needed. Maira assumed there would be glitches, but they turned out to be much worse than anything she had imagined. It took nine months to get the system working properly.
>
> Two years later, the restaurant chain wanted to take advantage of a recent industry trend toward touchless ordering, which involves customers scanning a QR code, ordering, and paying directly from their mobile device. Despite the problems with the previous POS system, Maira was excited about what her team could do with a touchless system, so she decided to bid on the project.
>
> Aware of her low initial credibility with the restaurant chain's management, Maira began her bid presentation by reminding everyone that she hoped to make their business run smoothly. She then acknowledged that she had told them the same thing about the POS system—an admission that drew a laugh and helped everyone relax. Finally, she explained her success implementing touchless systems at other businesses, all of which were thrilled with the results.
>
> A day after the meeting, Maira got a call that she had won the contract. The management team was impressed with her presentation and confident in her abilities. She had achieved high terminal credibility.

In every speech you give you will have some degree of initial credibility, which will be strengthened or weakened by your message and how you deliver it. And your terminal credibility from one speech will affect your initial credibility for the next one. If your audience sees you as sincere and competent, they will be much more receptive to your ideas.

ENHANCING YOUR CREDIBILITY

How can you build your credibility in your speeches? At one level, the answer is frustratingly general. Since everything you say and do in a speech will affect your

initial credibility
The credibility of a speaker before she or he starts to speak.

derived credibility
The credibility of a speaker produced by everything she or he says and does during the speech.

terminal credibility
The credibility of a speaker at the end of the speech.

credibility, you should say and do *everything* in a way that will make you appear capable and trustworthy. In other words—give a brilliant speech and you will achieve high credibility!

The advice is sound, but not all that helpful. There are, however, some specific ways you can boost your credibility while speaking. They include explaining your competence, establishing common ground with the audience, and speaking with genuine conviction.

Explain Your Competence

One way to enhance your credibility is to advertise your expertise on the speech topic. Did you investigate the topic thoroughly? Then say so. Do you have experience that gives you special knowledge or insight? Again, say so.

Here is how two students revealed their qualifications. The first stressed her study and research:

> I first learned about eyewitness misidentification in a criminal justice class I took last year. That class opened my eyes to the many problems that plague our justice system. . . .
>
> After conducting extensive research for this speech, I've learned that eyewitness misidentification is a problem that we can fix, or at least minimize, through a few basic policy changes.

The second student emphasized her background and personal experience:

> For the past year, I've been volunteering at the Literacy Network—a local, Madison-based, nonprofit organization that helps adults and families with reading, writing, and speaking skills. I've seen the problems people face because of low literacy, and I've also seen how improved literacy can change people's lives for the better.

Both speakers greatly increased their persuasiveness by establishing their credibility.

Establish Common Ground with Your Audience

Another way to bolster your credibility is to establish common ground with your audience. You do not persuade listeners by assaulting their values and rejecting their opinions. As the old saying goes, "You catch more flies with honey than with vinegar." The same is true of persuasion. Show respect for your listeners. You can make your speech more appealing by identifying with your audience—by showing how your point of view is consistent with who they are and what they believe.

Creating common ground is especially important at the start of a persuasive speech. Begin by identifying with your listeners. Show that you share their values, attitudes, and experiences. Get them nodding their heads in agreement, and they will be much more receptive to your ultimate proposal. Here is how a businesswoman from Massachusetts, hoping to sell her product to an audience in Colorado, began her persuasive speech:

> I have never been in Colorado before, but I really looked forward to making this trip. A lot of my ancestors left Massachusetts and came to Colorado nearly 150 years ago. Sometimes I have wondered why they did it. They came in covered wagons, carrying all their possessions, and many of

connect

View these excerpts from "Eyewitness Misidentification" and "Changing Lives Through the Literacy Network" in the online Media Library for this chapter (Video 17.1).

creating common ground
A technique in which a speaker connects himself or herself with the values, attitudes, or experiences of the audience.

A speaker's credibility has a powerful impact on how his or her speech is received. One way to boost your credibility is to deliver your speeches expressively and with strong eye contact.

Ludovic Marin/AFP/Getty Images

them died on the journey. The ones who got through raised their houses and raised their families. Now that I've seen Colorado, I understand why they tried so hard!

The audience laughed and applauded, and the speaker was off to a good start.

Now look at a different approach, used in a classroom speech calling for the elimination of the school's football program—an unpopular point of view with the speaker's classmates. He began by saying:

> Gameday. The crowds, the enthusiasm, the TV cameras, the action on the field. I love the sights and sounds of college football. I know many of you do, too; I've seen you at the games! Football is a big part of our school, and it's hard to imagine this place without a football program.
>
> But it might be time to start imagining just that. College football is not what it used to be, here and elsewhere. The amount of money we pay our coaches, the cost of the facilities, the way it detracts from academics, the culture it creates on campus, and the long-term health effects on our players—these are just some of the ways that college football has gotten out of hand.
>
> As much as it pains me to say, it's time for us to reassess football on campus. Today, I hope to persuade you that for the sake of our school and our education, we should reconsider the future of our football program.

By stressing common perceptions of the problem, the student hoped to get off on the right foot with his audience. Once that was done, he moved gradually to his more controversial ideas.

Deliver Your Speeches Fluently, Expressively, and with Conviction

There is a great deal of research to show that a speaker's credibility is strongly affected by his or her delivery. Moderately fast speakers, for example, are usually seen as more intelligent and confident than slower speakers. So too are speakers who use vocal variety to communicate their ideas in a lively, animated way. On the other hand, speakers

connect

View this excerpt from "Football and Our Future" in the online Media Library for this chapter (Video 17.2).

who consistently lose their place, hesitate frequently, or pepper their talk with "uh," "er," and "um" are seen as less competent than speakers who are poised and dynamic.[3]

All of this argues for practicing your persuasive speech fully ahead of time so you can deliver it fluently and expressively. In addition to being better prepared, you will take a major step toward enhancing your credibility. (Review Chapter 13 if you have questions about speech delivery.)

Speaking techniques aside, the most important way to strengthen your credibility is to deliver your speeches with genuine conviction. President Harry Truman once said that in speaking, "sincerity, honesty, and a straightforward manner are more important than special talent or polish." If you wish to convince others, you must first convince yourself. If you want others to believe and care about your ideas, you must believe and care about them yourself. Your spirit, enthusiasm, and conviction will carry over to your listeners.

Using Evidence

Evidence consists of supporting materials—examples, statistics, testimony—used to prove or disprove something. As we saw in Chapter 8, most people are skeptical. They are suspicious of unsupported generalizations. They want speakers to justify their claims. If you hope to be persuasive, you must support your views with evidence. Whenever you say something that is open to question, you should give evidence to prove you are right.

Evidence is particularly important in classroom speeches because few students are recognized as experts on their speech topics. Research has shown that speakers with very high initial credibility do not need to use as much evidence as do speakers with lower credibility. For most speakers, though, strong evidence is absolutely necessary. It can enhance your credibility, increase both the immediate and long-term persuasiveness of your message, and help "inoculate" listeners against counterpersuasion.[4]

Evidence is also crucial whenever your target audience opposes your point of view. As we saw in Chapter 16, listeners in such a situation will mentally argue with you—asking questions, raising objections, and creating counterarguments to "answer" what you say. The success of your speech will depend partly on how well you anticipate these internal responses and give evidence to refute them.

You may want to review Chapter 8, which shows how to use supporting materials. The following case study illustrates how they work as evidence in a persuasive speech.

HOW EVIDENCE WORKS: A CASE STUDY

Let's say one of your classmates is talking about shortcomings in the U.S. mental-health system. Instead of just telling you what she thinks, the speaker offers strong evidence to prove her point. Notice how she carries on a mental dialogue with her listeners. She imagines what they might be thinking, anticipates their questions and objections, and gives evidence to answer the questions and resolve the objections.

She begins this way:

> Right now in our city, there is a homeless man muttering to himself on a street corner. An elderly woman isolated from the rest of the world. A teenager cutting her arms and legs. Some call them crazy. But to me, these are people who need help—help that they're not receiving because of our nation's inadequate mental-health services.

evidence
Supporting materials used to prove or disprove something.

How do you react? If you already know about the deficiencies in mental-health services, you probably nod your head in agreement. But what if you don't know? Or what if you're skeptical? Perhaps you think taxpayer dollars could be better spent elsewhere. If so, a few anecdotes probably won't persuade you. Mentally you say to the speaker, "These are sad stories, but maybe they're isolated cases. Do we really have a national problem?"

Anticipating just such a response, the speaker gives evidence to support her point:

> According to a recent story in *U.S. News and World Report,* more than 120 million Americans—37 percent of the population—live in areas where mental-health professionals are in short supply. In fact, we need an estimated 6,400 new mental-health providers to fill the gaps in coverage.

"Okay, that's a big number," you may think. "But people with mental-health issues receive care in other ways. Rural areas with few options for care don't tell the whole story." The speaker answers:

> What happens to the people who can't receive treatment? According to Dr. Christine Montross, a psychiatrist at Brown University, many end up behind bars. There are around 350,000 people currently in prison who have severe mental illness. That is 10 times the number of people in state psychiatric hospitals. Our prisons are now more responsible for mental-health care than our mental-health facilities.

"That's an interesting point," you say to yourself. "But is that the extent of the problem?" Keeping one step ahead of you, the speaker continues:

> Nor is the mental-health crisis isolated to our prisons. Consider the following statistics from the National Alliance on Mental Illness. Untreated mental illnesses cost the United States almost $300 billion a year in lost productivity. Adults with serious, but treatable, mental illness die an average of 25 years earlier than the rest of the population. And veterans with mental-health issues are committing suicide at alarming rates—an average of 20 every single day.

Now are you convinced? Chances are you will at least think about the lack of mental-health care as a serious problem. You may even decide that increasing funding for mental-health services would be a good investment of tax dollars. If so, you will have changed your mind in part because the speaker supported each of her claims with evidence.

TIPS FOR USING EVIDENCE

Any of the supporting materials discussed in Chapter 8—examples, statistics, testimony—can work as evidence in a persuasive speech. As we saw in that chapter, there are guidelines for using each type of supporting material regardless of the kind of speech you are giving. Here we look at four special tips for using evidence in a persuasive speech.[5]

Use Specific Evidence

No matter what kind of evidence you employ—statistics, examples, or testimony—it will be more persuasive if you state it in specific rather than general terms. In the

Persuasive speeches need strong evidence to convince skeptical listeners. Research shows that evidence will be most convincing when it is stated in specific rather than general terms.

Somyot Techapuwapat/Getty Images

speech about mental illness, for example, the speaker did not say, "Lack of adequate mental-health care costs the U.S. economy lots of money." That would have left the audience wondering how much "lots" amounts to. By saying, "untreated mental illnesses cost the United States almost $300 billion a year in lost productivity," the speaker made her point much more persuasively. She also enhanced her credibility by showing that she had a firm grasp of the facts.

Use Novel Evidence

Evidence is more likely to be persuasive if it is new to the audience. You will gain little by citing facts and figures that are already well known to your listeners. If they have not persuaded your listeners already, they will not do so now. You must go beyond what the audience already knows and present striking new evidence that will get them to say, "Hmmm, I didn't know *that*. Maybe I should rethink the issue." Finding such evidence usually requires hard digging and resourceful research, but the rewards are worth the effort.

Use Evidence from Credible Sources

Careful listeners find evidence from competent, credible sources more persuasive than evidence from less qualified sources. Above all, they are suspicious of evidence from sources that appear to be biased or self-interested. In assessing the current state of airline safety, for example, they are more likely to be persuaded by testimony from impartial aviation experts than from the president of American Airlines. If you wish to be persuasive, rely on evidence from objective, nonpartisan sources.

Make Clear the Point of Your Evidence

When speaking to persuade, you use evidence to prove a point. Yet you would be surprised how many novice speakers present their evidence without making clear the point it is supposed to prove. A number of studies have shown that you cannot count on listeners to draw, on their own, the conclusion you want them to reach. When using evidence, be sure listeners understand the point you are trying to make.

Notice, for example, how the speaker in Video 17.3 drives home the point of his evidence about the rate of motorcycle fatalities in comparison to automobile fatalities:

> According to the Governors Highway Safety Association, last year there were more than 5,000 motorcycle deaths in the United States. That's a jump of 9 percent from the previous year. If 5,000 people dead doesn't sound like a lot, consider this: Over the past 15 years, motorcycle deaths have doubled, while automobile deaths have dropped by 23 percent. Here in Wisconsin alone, 114 people died last year. That's a 34 percent increase from the year before.
>
> Clearly, we can do more to solve the problem. Here in Wisconsin, there's an easy solution: We can save lives simply by requiring that all motorcyclists wear a helmet.

connect
View this excerpt from "Saving Lives with Motorcycle Helmets" in the online Media Library for this chapter (Video 17.3).

Evidence is one element of what Aristotle referred to as logos—the logical appeal of a speaker. The other major element of logos is reasoning, which works in combination with evidence to help make a speaker's claims persuasive.

Reasoning

The story is told about Hack Wilson, a hard-hitting outfielder for the Brooklyn Dodgers baseball team in the 1930s.[6] Wilson was a great player, but he had a fondness for the good life. His drinking exploits were legendary. He was known to spend the entire night on the town, stagger into the team's hotel at the break of dawn, grab a couple hours sleep, and get to the ballpark just in time for the afternoon game.

This greatly distressed Max Carey, Wilson's manager. At the next team meeting, Carey spent much time explaining the evils of drink. To prove his

logos
The name used by Aristotle for the logical appeal of a speaker. The two major elements of logos are evidence and reasoning.

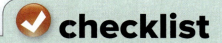

checklist

Evidence

YES	NO	
☐	☐	1. Are all my major claims supported by evidence?
☐	☐	2. Do I use sufficient evidence to convince my audience of my claims?
☐	☐	3. Is my evidence stated in specific rather than general terms?
☐	☐	4. Do I use evidence that is new to my audience?
☐	☐	5. Is my evidence from credible, unbiased sources?
☐	☐	6. Do I identify the sources of my evidence?
☐	☐	7. Is my evidence clearly linked to each point that it is meant to prove?
☐	☐	8. Do I provide evidence to answer possible objections the audience may have to my position?

point, he stood beside a table on which he had placed two glasses and a plate of live angleworms. One glass was filled with water, the other with gin—Wilson's favorite beverage. With a flourish Carey dropped a worm into the glass of water. It wriggled happily. Next Carey plunged the same worm into the gin. It promptly stiffened and expired.

A murmur ran through the room, and some players were obviously impressed. But not Wilson. He didn't even seem interested. Carey waited a little, hoping for some delayed reaction from his wayward slugger. When none came, he prodded, "Do you follow my reasoning, Wilson?"

"Sure, skipper," answered Wilson. "It proves that if you drink gin, you'll never get worms!"

And what does this story prove? No matter how strong your evidence, you will not be persuasive unless listeners grasp your reasoning.

Reasoning is the process of drawing a conclusion based on evidence. Sometimes we reason well—as when we conclude that ice particles forming on the trees may mean the roads will be slippery. Other times we reason less effectively—as when we conclude that spilling salt will bring bad luck. Most superstitions are actually no more than instances of faulty reasoning.

Reasoning in public speaking is an extension of reasoning in other aspects of life. As a public speaker, you have two major concerns with respect to reasoning. First, you must make sure your own reasoning is sound. Second, you must try to get listeners to agree with your reasoning. Let us look, then, at four basic methods of reasoning and how to use them in your speeches.

reasoning

The process of drawing a conclusion on the basis of evidence.

REASONING FROM SPECIFIC INSTANCES

When you reason from specific instances, you progress from a number of particular facts to a general conclusion.[7] For example:

Fact 1: My physical education course last term was easy.

Fact 2: My roommate's physical education course was easy.

Fact 3: My brother's physical education course was easy.

Conclusion: Physical education courses are easy.

reasoning from specific instances

Reasoning that moves from particular facts to a general conclusion.

As this example suggests, we use reasoning from specific instances daily, although we probably don't realize it. Think for a moment of all the general conclusions that arise in conversation: Politicians are corrupt. Professors are bookish. Dorm food is awful. Where do such conclusions come from? They come from observing particular politicians, professors, dormitories, and so on.

The same thing happens in public speaking. The speaker who concludes that unethical banking practices are common in the United States because several major banks have been guilty of fraud in recent years is reasoning from specific instances. So is the speaker who argues that anti-Semitism is increasing on college campuses because there have been a number of attacks on Jewish students and symbols at schools across the nation.

Such conclusions are never foolproof. No matter how many specific instances you give (and you can give only a few in a speech), it is always possible that an exception exists. Throughout the ages people observed countless white swans in

Reasoning is an important part of persuasive speaking. Depending on the situation, a speaker may reason from specific instances, from principle, analogically, or causally.

Olivier Douliery/AFP/Getty Images

Europe without seeing any of a different color. It seemed an undeniable fact that all swans were white. Then, in the 19th century, black swans were discovered in Australia![8]

When you reason from specific instances, beware of jumping to conclusions on the basis of insufficient evidence. Make sure your sample of specific instances is large enough to justify your conclusion.

Also make sure the instances you present are fair, unbiased, and representative. (Are three physical education courses *enough* to conclude that physical education courses in general are easy? Are the three courses *typical* of most physical education courses?)

Finally, reinforce your argument with statistics or testimony. Because you can never give enough specific instances in a speech to make your conclusion irrefutable, you should supplement them with testimony or statistics demonstrating that the instances are representative.

REASONING FROM PRINCIPLE

Reasoning from principle is the opposite of reasoning from specific instances. It moves from the general to the specific.[9] When you reason from principle, you progress from a general principle to a specific conclusion. We are all familiar with this kind of reasoning from statements such as the following:

1. All people are mortal.
2. Socrates is a person.
3. Therefore, Socrates is mortal.

This is a classic example of reasoning from principle. You begin with a general statement ("All people are mortal"), move to a minor premise ("Socrates is a person"), and end with a specific conclusion ("Socrates is mortal").

Speakers often use reasoning from principle when trying to persuade an audience. One of the clearest examples from American history is Susan B. Anthony's

reasoning from principle
Reasoning that moves from a general principle to a specific conclusion.

famous speech "Is It a Crime for a U.S. Citizen to Vote?" Delivered on numerous occasions in 1872 and 1873, at a time when women were legally barred from voting, Anthony's speech reasoned along the following lines:

1. The United States Constitution guarantees all U.S. citizens the right to vote.
2. Women are U.S. citizens.
3. Therefore, the United States Constitution guarantees women the right to vote.

This argument progresses from a general principle ("The United States Constitution guarantees all U.S. citizens the right to vote") through a minor premise ("Women are U.S. citizens") to a conclusion ("Therefore, the United States Constitution guarantees women the right to vote").

When you use reasoning from principle in a speech, pay special attention to your general principle. Will listeners accept it without evidence? If not, give evidence to support it before moving to your minor premise. You may also need to support your minor premise with evidence. When both the general principle and the minor premise are soundly based, your audience will be more likely to accept your conclusion.

CAUSAL REASONING

There is a patch of ice on the sidewalk. You slip, fall, and break your arm. You reason as follows: "*Because* that patch of ice was there, I fell and broke my arm." This is an example of causal reasoning, in which someone tries to establish the relationship between causes and effects.

As with reasoning from specific instances, we use causal reasoning daily. Something happens and we ask what caused it to happen. We want to know the causes of chronic fatigue syndrome, of the basketball team's latest defeat, of our roommate's peculiar habits. We also wonder about effects. We speculate about the consequences of chronic fatigue syndrome, of the star point guard's leg injury, of telling our roommate that a change is needed.

causal reasoning
Reasoning that seeks to establish the relationship between causes and effects.

As any scientist (or detective) will tell you, causal reasoning can be tricky. The relationship between causes and effects is not always clear. For example, the fact that one event happens after another does not mean that the first is the cause of the second. The closeness in time of the two events may be entirely coincidental. If a black cat crosses your path and five minutes later you fall and break your arm, you needn't blame your accident on the poor cat.

You also need to beware of assuming that events have only one cause. In fact, most events have several causes. What causes the economy to boom or bust? Interest rates? Gas prices? Tax policy? Labor costs? Consumer confidence? World affairs? *All* these factors—and others—affect the economy. When you use causal reasoning, be wary of the temptation to attribute complex events to single causes.

ANALOGICAL REASONING

When arguing from analogy, a speaker compares two similar cases and infers that what is true for one case is also true for the other: For example:

> If you're good at tennis, you will probably be good at Ping-Pong.

Although playing Ping-Pong is not exactly the same as playing tennis, the two are close enough that the speaker is on firm ground in concluding that being skilled at one increases the odds of being skilled at the other.

Analogical reasoning is used frequently in persuasive speeches—especially when the speaker is dealing with a question of policy. When arguing for a new policy, you should find out whether it has been tried elsewhere. You may be able to claim that your policy will work because it has worked in like circumstances. Here is how one speaker used reasoning from analogy to support his claim that controlling handguns will reduce violent crime in the United States:

> Will my policy work? The experience of foreign countries suggests it will. In England, guns are tightly regulated; even the police are unarmed, and the murder rate is trivial by American standards. Japan has even fewer guns than England, and its crime rate is lower than England's. On the basis of these comparisons, we can conclude that restricting the ownership of guns will reduce crime and murder rates in America.

By the same token, if you argue against a change in policy, you should check whether the proposed policy—or something like it—has been implemented elsewhere. Here, too, you may be able to support your case by reasoning from analogy—as did one speaker who opposed gun control:

> Advocates of gun control point to foreign countries such as England and Japan to prove their case. But the key to low personal violence in these and other countries is the peaceful character of the people, not gun control laws. Switzerland, for example, has a militia system; more than 1 million automatic rifles and military pistols are sitting at this moment in Swiss homes. Yet Switzerland's murder rate is only one-seventh of ours. In other words, cultural factors are more important than gun control when it comes to violent crime.

As these examples illustrate, argument from analogy can be used on both sides of an issue. You are more likely to persuade your audience if the analogy shows a truly parallel situation.

FALLACIES

A fallacy is an error in reasoning. As a speaker, you need to avoid fallacies in your speeches. As a listener, you need to be alert to fallacies in the speeches you hear.

Logicians have identified more than 125 different fallacies. Here we look at 10 that you should guard against.

fallacy
An error in reasoning.

Hasty Generalization

Hasty generalization is the most common fallacy in reasoning from specific instances. It occurs when a speaker jumps to a conclusion on the basis of too few cases or on the basis of atypical cases. For example:

> College dropouts always make excellent business leaders. Just look at Mark Zuckerberg, Bill Gates, and Steve Jobs. They all dropped out and went on to create powerful companies.

hasty generalization
A fallacy in which a speaker jumps to a general conclusion on the basis of insufficient evidence.

Zuckerberg, Gates, and Jobs are widely regarded as successful corporate executives, but are these examples enough to conclude that college dropouts *always* make excellent business leaders? In fact, they are not. There are countless college dropouts

In addition to using evidence to support their ideas, effective persuasive speakers rely on research to help them avoid fallacies that may undermine their credibility and persuasiveness.

Rido/Shutterstock

who did not go on to lead successful companies. In fact, the vast majority of business leaders did graduate from college. An accurate statement would be:

> Some college dropouts have gone on to make excellent business leaders—including Mark Zuckerberg, Bill Gates, and Steve Jobs.

This statement is factually correct and avoids the fallacy of hasty generalization.

False Cause

The fallacy of false cause is often known by its Latin name, *post hoc, ergo propter hoc,* which means "after this, therefore because of this." In other words, the fact that one event occurs after another does not mean that the first is the cause of the second. The closeness in time of the two events may be entirely coincidental—as in this case:

false cause
A fallacy in which a speaker mistakenly assumes that because one event follows another, the first event is the cause of the second.

> When a team from the NFC wins the Super Bowl, economic growth during the next year is stronger than when a team from the AFC wins the Super Bowl. Therefore, if we want economic growth, we should root for a team from the NFC to win this year's Super Bowl.

There may be a slight correlation between economic growth and which conference wins the Super Bowl, but there is no *causal* connection between the two events. Whether the American economy rises or falls is not dependent on the outcome of the Super Bowl.

Invalid Analogy

As we saw earlier, when reasoning from analogy, a speaker concludes that what is true in one case is also true in another. An invalid analogy occurs when the two cases being compared are not essentially alike. For example:

> Employees are like nails. Just as nails must be hit on the head to get them to work, so must employees.

This statement is obviously fallacious. No one in his or her right mind can seriously think that employees, which are human beings, can be compared with inanimate objects such as nails.

But what about the following statement:

> In Great Britain, the general election campaign for prime minister lasts about a month. Surely we can do the same with the U.S. presidential election.

At first glance, this analogy may seem perfectly sound. But are the British and American political systems enough alike to warrant the conclusion? Not really. The United States is much larger than Great Britain and its party system operates much differently. As a result, the factors that allow Great Britain to conduct campaigns for prime minister in a month are not present in the United States. The analogy is not valid.

As this example suggests, determining whether an analogy is valid or invalid is not always easy, but doing so is important for speakers and listeners alike.

invalid analogy
An analogy in which the two cases being compared are not essentially alike.

Bandwagon

How often have you heard someone say, "It's a great idea—everyone agrees with it"? This is a classic example of the bandwagon fallacy, which assumes that because something is popular, it is therefore good, correct, or desirable.

Much advertising is based on the bandwagon fallacy. The fact that more people use Tylenol than Advil does not prove that Tylenol is a better painkiller. Tylenol's popularity could be due to clever marketing. The question of which product does a better job reducing pain is a medical issue that has nothing to do with popularity.

The bandwagon fallacy is also evident in political speeches. Consider the following statement:

> The governor must be correct in his approach to social policy; after all, the polls show that 60 percent of the people support him.

bandwagon
A fallacy which assumes that because something is popular, it is therefore good, correct, or desirable.

This statement is fallacious because popular opinion cannot be taken as proof that an idea is right or wrong. Remember, "everyone" used to believe that the world is flat and that space flight is impossible.

Red Herring

The name of this fallacy comes from an old trick used by farmers in England to keep fox hunters and their hounds from galloping through the crops. By dragging a smoked herring with a strong odor along the edge of their fields, the farmers could throw the dogs off track by destroying the scent of the fox.

A speaker who uses a red herring introduces an irrelevant issue to divert attention from the subject under discussion. For instance:

> How dare my opponents accuse me of political corruption at a time when we are working to improve the quality of life for all people in the United States.

red herring
A fallacy that introduces an irrelevant issue to divert attention from the subject under discussion.

What does the speaker's concern about the quality of life in the United States have to do with whether he or she is guilty of political corruption? Nothing! It is a red herring used to divert attention away from the real issue.

Ad Hominem

Latin for "against the man," *ad hominem* refers to the fallacy of attacking the person rather than dealing with the real issue in dispute. For instance:

> The head of the commerce commission has a number of interesting economic proposals, but let's not forget that she comes from a very wealthy family.

By impugning the commissioner's family background rather than dealing with the substance of her economic proposals, the speaker is engaging in an *ad hominem* attack.

Sometimes, of course, a person's character or integrity can be a legitimate issue—as in the case of a police chief who violates the law or a corporate president who swindles stockholders. In such cases, a speaker might well raise questions about the person without being guilty of the *ad hominem* fallacy.

Either-Or

Sometimes referred to as a false dilemma, the either-or fallacy forces listeners to choose between two alternatives when more than two alternatives exist. For example:

> The government must either raise taxes or eliminate services for the poor.

This statement oversimplifies a complex issue by reducing it to a simple either-or choice. Is it true that the *only* choices are to raise taxes or to eliminate services for the poor? A careful listener might ask, "What about cutting the administrative cost of government or eliminating pork-barrel projects instead?"

You will be more persuasive as a speaker and more perceptive as a listener if you are alert to the either-or fallacy.

Slippery Slope

The slippery slope fallacy takes its name from the image of a boulder rolling uncontrollably down a steep hill. Once the boulder gets started, it can't be stopped until it reaches the bottom.

A speaker who commits the slippery slope fallacy assumes that taking a first step will lead inevitably to a second step and so on down the slope to disaster—as in the following example:

> Now that everyone is texting, posting on social media, and sending video messages, it's only a matter of time before people forget how to write complete sentences and the whole English language falls apart.

If a speaker claims that taking a first step will lead inevitably to a series of disastrous later steps, he or she needs to provide evidence or reasoning to support the claim. To assume that all the later steps will occur without proving that they will is to commit the slippery slope fallacy.

Appeal to Tradition

Appeal to tradition is fallacious when it assumes that something old is *automatically* better than something new. For example:

> I don't see any reason to abolish the electoral college. It has been around since the ratification of the U.S. Constitution in 1789, and we should keep it as long as the United States continues to exist.

---

ad hominem
A fallacy that attacks the person rather than dealing with the real issue in dispute.

either-or
A fallacy that forces listeners to choose between two alternatives when more than two alternatives exist.

slippery slope
A fallacy which assumes that taking a first step will lead to subsequent steps that cannot be prevented.

appeal to tradition
A fallacy which assumes that something old is automatically better than something new.

There are good arguments on both sides of the debate over abolishing the electoral college. However, to conclude that the electoral college should be kept forever solely because it has always been a part of the U.S. Constitution commits the fallacy of appeal to tradition.

Just because a practice, an institution, or an idea is old does not automatically make it better. Its value should be based on its contributions to society, not on its age. If tradition were the sole measure of value, we would still have slavery, women would not be able to vote, and people would undergo surgery without anesthesia.

Appeal to Novelty

The fallacy of appeal to novelty is the opposite of appeal to tradition. Appeal to novelty assumes that because something is new, it is therefore superior to something that is older. For example:

> Our church should adopt the updated New International Version of the Bible because it is 400 years newer than the King James Version.

The fact that the New International Version of the Bible is newer than the King James Version (completed in 1611) does not *automatically* make it better. There are many reasons why a church might prefer the New International Version, but the speaker should *explain* those reasons, rather than assuming that one version is better than another simply because it is new.

Advertisers often commit the fallacy of appeal to novelty. They tout their latest products as "new and improved," yet we know from experience that new does not necessarily mean improved. As always, we need to look carefully at the claim and make sure it is based on sound reasoning.[10]

appeal to novelty
A fallacy which assumes that something new is automatically better than something old.

Appealing to Emotions

Effective persuasion often requires emotional appeal. As the Roman rhetorician Quintilian stated, "It is feeling and force of imagination that make us eloquent."[11] By adding "feeling" and the "force of imagination" to your logical arguments, you can become a more compelling persuasive speaker.

WHAT ARE EMOTIONAL APPEALS?

Emotional appeals—what Aristotle referred to as pathos—are intended to make listeners feel sad, angry, guilty, afraid, happy, proud, sympathetic, reverent, or the like. These are often appropriate reactions when the question is one of value or policy. As George Campbell wrote in his *Philosophy of Rhetoric,* "When persuasion is the end, passion also must be engaged."[12]

Following is a list of some of the emotions evoked most often by public speakers. After each emotion are a few examples of subjects that might stir that emotion:

- *Fear*—of serious illness, of natural disasters, of sexual assault, of personal rejection, of economic hardship.
- *Compassion*—for war refugees, for battered women, for neglected animals, for starving children, for victims of cancer.

pathos
The name used by Aristotle for what modern students of communication refer to as emotional appeal.

- *Pride*—in one's country, in one's family, in one's school, in one's ethnic heritage, in one's personal accomplishments.

- *Anger*—at terrorists and their supporters, at business leaders who act unethically, at members of Congress who abuse the public trust, at landlords who exploit student tenants, at vandals and thieves.

- *Guilt*—about not helping people less fortunate than ourselves, about not considering the rights of others, about not doing one's best.

- *Reverence*—for an admired person, for traditions and institutions, for one's deity.

There are many other emotions and many other subjects that might stir them. However, this brief sample should give you an idea of the kinds of emotional appeals you might use to enhance the message of your persuasive speech.

GENERATING EMOTIONAL APPEAL

Use Emotional Language

As we saw in Chapter 12, using emotion-laden words is one way to generate emotional appeal. Here, for instance, is part of the conclusion from a student speech about the challenges and rewards of working as a volunteer teacher:

> The <u>promise of America sparkles</u> in the <u>eyes of every child</u>. Their <u>dreams</u> are the <u>glittering dreams</u> of <u>America</u>. When those <u>dreams</u> are <u>dashed</u>, when <u>innocent hopes</u> are <u>betrayed</u>, so are the <u>dreams and hopes</u> of the <u>entire nation</u>. It is our <u>duty</u>—to me, it is a <u>sacred duty</u>—to give <u>all children</u> the chance to <u>learn and grow</u>, to share <u>equally</u> in the <u>American dream</u> of <u>freedom, justice, and opportunity</u>.

Using public speaking in your CAREER

As the service manager for a local home improvement company, you have been pleased to see your company expand its size and scope, but you don't want that growth to come at the expense of customer service. In particular, you're worried about losing touch with one of the company's key demographics—women, who make up 55 percent of your customer base. To prevent this from happening, you have developed a plan for a range of personalized services targeted at women, including one-on-one teaching of do-it-yourself skills and free in-home consultations.

When you present your plan at a meeting of the company's management team, you listen as one executive argues in opposition. Among his points are the following: (1) If your plan is adopted, customers will expect more and more special services and eventually will demand free installation of flooring and carpeting. (2) Because a majority of the management team opposes your plan, it must not be a good idea. (3) One of your competitors tried a customer service plan specifically for women, but it did not succeed; therefore, your plan is doomed to failure.

In your response to the executive, you will point out the fallacy in each of his points. What are those fallacies?

Antonio Diaz/123RF

Emotional appeals often make a speech more compelling, as in these remarks by Jonathan Van Ness at the Point Honors Gala for outstanding student scholars.
Cindy Ord/Getty Images

The underlined words and phrases have strong emotional power, and in this case they produced the desired effect. Be aware, however, that packing too many emotionally charged words into one part of a speech can call attention to the emotional language itself and undermine its impact. The emotion rests in your audience, not in your words. Even the coldest facts can touch off an emotional response if they strike the right chords in a listener.

Develop Vivid Examples

Often a better approach than relying on emotionally charged language is to let emotional appeal grow naturally out of the content of your speech. The most effective way to do this is with vivid, richly textured examples that pull listeners into the speech.

Here is how one speaker used a vivid example for emotional appeal. She was speaking about the malaria epidemic in Africa. Here is what she might have said, stripping the content of emotional appeal:

> Malaria is one of the biggest problems facing Africa. Many die from it every day. If the rest of the world doesn't help, the malaria epidemic will only get worse.

What she actually said went something like this:

> Nathan was only five years old when the fever struck him. At first, no one knew what was wrong. No one knew that parasites inside his body had infected his red blood cells. No one knew those cells were clumping together, choking the flow of blood through his body and damaging his vital organs. No one knew his kidneys would soon fail and seizures would begin. No one knew he would wind up in a coma.
>
> The parasites in Nathan's body came from a mosquito bite, a bite that gave him malaria. And Nathan is not alone. The World Health Organization tells us the horrible truth: In Africa, a child dies from malaria every 30 seconds.

connect

View this excerpt from "The Tragedy of Malaria" in the online Media Library for this chapter (Video 17.4).

People who listen to a speech like that will not soon forget it. They may well be moved to action—as the speaker intends. The first speech, however, is not nearly as compelling. Listeners may well nod their heads, think to themselves "good idea"—and then forget about it. The story of Nathan and his tragic fate gives the second speech emotional impact and brings it home to listeners in personal terms.

Speak with Sincerity and Conviction

Ronald Reagan was one of the most effective speakers in U.S. history. Even people who disagreed with his political views often found him irresistible. Why? Partly because he seemed to speak with great sincerity and conviction.

What was true for Reagan is true for you as well. The strongest source of emotional power is your conviction and sincerity. All your emotion-laden words and examples are but empty trappings unless *you* feel the emotion yourself. And if you do, your emotion will communicate itself to the audience through everything you say and do—not only through your words, but also through your tone of voice, rate of speech, gestures, and facial expressions.

ETHICS AND EMOTIONAL APPEAL

Much has been written about the ethics of emotional appeal in speechmaking. Some people have taken the extreme position that ethical speakers should avoid emotional appeal entirely. To support this view, they point to speakers who have used emotional appeal to fan the flames of hatred, bigotry, and fanaticism.

There is no question that emotional appeals can be abused by unscrupulous speakers for detestable causes. But emotional appeals can also be wielded by honorable speakers for noble causes—by Winston Churchill to rouse the world against Adolf Hitler and the forces of Nazism, by Martin Luther King to call for racial justice. Few people would question the ethics of emotional appeal in these instances.

Nor is it always possible to draw a sharp line between reason and emotional appeal. Think back to the story of Nathan, the five-year-old boy who was infected

Emotional language and vivid examples can help generate emotional appeal, but neither will be effective unless the speaker talks with genuine sincerity and conviction.

Annette Riedl/picture alliance/Getty Images

with malaria. The story certainly has strong emotional appeal. But is there anything unreasonable about it? Or is it irrational for listeners to respond to it by donating to antimalarial causes? By the same token, is it illogical to be compassionate for victims of natural disasters? Angered by corporate wrongdoing? Fearful about cutbacks in student aid? Reason and emotion often work hand in hand.

One key to using emotional appeal ethically is to make sure it is appropriate to the speech topic. If you want to move listeners to act on a question of policy, emotional appeals are not only legitimate but perhaps necessary. If you want listeners to do something as a result of your speech, you will probably need to appeal to their hearts as well as to their heads.

On the other hand, emotional appeals are usually inappropriate in a persuasive speech on a question of fact. Here you should deal only in specific information and logic. Suppose someone charges your state governor with illegal campaign activities. If you respond by saying "I'm sure the charge is false because I have always admired the governor," or "I'm sure the charge is true because I have always disliked the governor," then you are guilty of applying emotional criteria to a purely factual question.

Even when trying to move listeners to action, you should never substitute emotional appeals for evidence and reasoning. You should *always* build your persuasive speech on a firm foundation of facts and logic. This is important not just for ethical reasons, but for practical ones as well. Unless you prove your case, careful listeners will not be stirred by your emotional appeals. You need to build a good case based on reason *and* kindle the emotions of your audience.[13]

When you use emotional appeal, keep in mind the guidelines for ethical speechmaking discussed in Chapter 2. Make sure your goals are ethically sound, that you are honest in what you say, and that you avoid name-calling and other forms of abusive language. In using emotional appeal, as in other respects, your classroom speeches will offer a good testing ground for questions of ethical responsibility.

Sample Speech with Commentary

The following persuasive speech on a question of policy is organized in problem-solution order. As you read the speech, notice how it employs the methods of persuasion discussed in this chapter. Pay special attention to the speaker's evidence, which she uses not only to establish the existence of a serious problem, but also to explain her plan and to document its practicality.

The speech also shows how visual aids can be used in a persuasive presentation to help clarify and document a speaker's arguments—as you can see by watching Video 17.5.

View "Eyewitness Misidentification" in the online Media Library for this chapter (Video 17.5).

Eyewitness Misidentification

COMMENTARY	SPEECH
The speaker opens with a realistic scenario that gains attention and draws the audience into the speech.	We've all seen it on cop shows. An eyewitness to a crime is brought to a police station, shown a lineup of suspects or a batch of photographs, and asked to pick out the perpetrator. Easy to do, right? After all, the eyewitness saw the crime with his or her own eyes.

As it turns out, not so easy. Over the past 30 years, psychologists and criminologists have been studying how eyewitness identifications can go horribly wrong. The Innocence Project, a national organization that works to free people who have been wrongly convicted, has found that eyewitnesses mistakenly identified suspects in 70 percent of convictions that were later overturned by DNA evidence. In fact, eyewitness identification can be so problematic that experts have come up with a new term for it—eyewitness *mis*identification.

I first learned about eyewitness misidentification in a criminal justice class I took last year. That class opened my eyes to the many problems that plague our justice system, and eyewitness misidentification is just one of them. But it's a huge one, and it's responsible for wrongfully incarcerating tens of thousands of people, according to the Innocence Project.

After conducting extensive research for this speech, I've learned that eyewitness misidentification is a problem we can fix, or at least minimize, through a few basic policy changes. Today, I want to persuade you that police departments across the country need to enact strong eyewitness identification guidelines. Doing so is essential to keeping innocent people out of prison and guilty people off the street. Let's start by looking more closely at the problem of eyewitness misidentification.

The problem of eyewitness misidentification is rooted in human psychology. Imagine that you're an eyewitness to a violent crime. Because it's violent, the situation is tense and you're naturally scared. Even if you get a good look at the suspect, your brain and body are on edge. Then the police bring you to the station for a lineup. Can you accurately pinpoint the perpetrator?

According to my audience-analysis survey, more than 80 percent of you think you could. Yet researchers have identified three factors that consistently undermine the reliability of eyewitness testimony.

First, when viewing a traumatic event like a violent crime, our perceptions often don't line up with reality. Doctor Thomas Albright of the Salk Institute for Biological Studies explains that with unexpected events like crimes, our eyes work quickly to take in what we see. But we can't keep up, so our brains fill in details that simply might be wrong.

Second, in addition to problems with perception, there are problems associated with memory. Most people think our memory simply records events, but that's not true. Writing for the Association for Psychological Science, Professor Stephen Chew explains that "stress and terror can actually inhibit memory formation, and memories continue to be constructed after the originating event on the basis of information learned afterward."

The speaker moves from her opening scenario to show that, contrary to conventional wisdom, eyewitness identification is so unreliable that experts often refer to it as eyewitness *mis*identification.

The speaker establishes her credibility by stating that she learned about the problem of eyewitness misidentification in a criminal justice class.

After further bolstering her credibility by referring to her research on the topic, the speaker states her central idea and provides a transition from the introduction to the body.

This speech is organized in problem-solution order. The speaker begins the problem section by asking her audience to imagine themselves witnessing a violent crime and being asked to identify the perpetrator. Would they be able to do so accurately?

Referring to her audience-analysis survey relates the topic directly to the speaker's classmates.

The speaker explores three factors that undermine the reliability of eyewitness testimony. The first deals with problems in perception.

The second factor deals with problems in memory. The speaker explains her ideas clearly, supports them with credible evidence, and identifies the source of her evidence.

Here the speaker completes her discussion of how problems with memory can lead to errors in eyewitness identification.

This paragraph focuses on own-race bias and how it contributes to errors in eyewitness identification. The speaker explains the issue convincingly, and she again supports her position with expert testimony.

The speaker ends the problem section by personalizing the consequences of eyewitness misidentification with the example of James Watson, who spent nearly 40 years in jail before being exonerated by DNA evidence.

The speaker transitions into the solution section, in which she presents four guidelines for reducing the problem of eyewitness misidentification.

As the speaker proceeds, she uses a signpost to introduce each guideline.

As you can see from Video 17.5, the speaker highlights each guideline with a PowerPoint slide.

The speaker uses her voice, gestures, and eye contact to emphasize key points and to enhance communication with her audience.

This means a lineup that occurs long after a crime is committed is much less reliable than one shortly after the crime. Worse still, as police and attorneys ask more and more questions, our memories can actually change over time, leading to faulty identifications.

Third, there's the problem of what legal scholar Bryan Ryan of Washington University Law School calls own-race bias and cross-race effect. Simply put, it's easier to recognize distinguishing characteristics of someone of your own race than someone of a different race. A white person trying to pick out a person of color from a lineup, or vice-versa, is prone to much greater bias and error than someone trying to pick out a person of his or her own race.

Time and time again, these problems of perception, memory, and own-race bias lead to the wrong person being put behind bars—the wrong person like James Watson, who spent 38 years in a Massachusetts prison for murder. As the University of Michigan National Registry of Exonerations explains, his conviction stemmed from a mistaken cross-race identification that emerged long after the crime and only after extensive police prodding. Watson was finally set free in 2020 after DNA exonerated him.

We can't allow tens of thousands of people like James Watson to waste another day behind bars. That's why police departments across the country need to adopt strong eyewitness identification guidelines. Here are four key guidelines I propose that are based on scientific research and are supported by psychologists, criminologists, and the Innocence Project.

One, all police lineups should be double-blind. This means that neither the person administering the lineup nor the eyewitness should know ahead of time who the primary suspect is. We don't want the lineup administrator to give off any clues that could bias the eyewitness.

Two, the lineup administrator needs to provide careful instructions. The eyewitness needs to be told not to feel pressure to make a choice, and that the suspect may not actually be in the lineup. This will free the eyewitness to make a choice—or not—on their own terms.

Three, the lineup needs to be carefully composed so as not to bias the eyewitness. The people in the lineup—often known as "fillers"—should resemble the suspect as much as possible. For instance, instead of having a lineup where only the suspect has facial hair, everyone in the lineup should have facial hair.

Throughout her speech, the speaker does an excellent job of explaining complex ideas plainly and concisely. She provides enough detail about each guideline for the audience to understand it, but not so much as to bog down her momentum.

And four, immediately after making an identification, the eyewitness should provide a confidence statement. This statement indicates how confident the eyewitness is about the person he or she identified—40 percent confident, 80 percent, 100 percent, whatever the figure is. This should happen immediately after the lineup, and it should be available to prosecutors and defense attorneys when the case goes to trial.

The speaker wraps up her solution section by affirming the practicality of her guidelines. The quotation from Professor Smalarz stresses the importance of having all the states implement all four guidelines to prevent further miscarriages of justice.

These four guidelines are so important that they've been endorsed by the National Academy of Sciences and the U.S. Department of Justice. States, however, have been slow to implement them. According to Laura Smalarz, professor of psychology at Arizona State University, 24 states have adopted at least one of the guidelines. But as Professor Smalarz says, we need *all* the states to adopt *all* the guidelines if we are to "prevent additional miscarriages of justice."

The speaker signals the beginning of her conclusion and summarizes her main points. Her final words end the speech on a forceful note.

In conclusion, I hope you see how serious the problem of eyewitness misidentification is and how it can be brought under control. Doing so will not eliminate all the problems in our justice system, but it will make the system more just for thousands of people.

Summary

Listeners accept a speaker's ideas for one or more of four reasons—because they perceive the speaker as having high credibility, because they are won over by the speaker's evidence, because they are convinced by the speaker's reasoning, and because they are moved by the speaker's emotional appeals.

Credibility is affected by many factors, but the two most important are competence and character. The more favorably listeners view a speaker's competence and character, the more likely they are to accept her or his ideas. Although credibility is partly a matter of reputation, you can enhance your credibility during a speech by establishing common ground with your listeners, by letting them know why you are qualified to speak on the topic, and by presenting your ideas fluently and expressively.

If you hope to be persuasive, you must also support your views with evidence—examples, statistics, and testimony. Regardless of what kind of evidence you use, it will be more persuasive if it is new to the audience, is stated in specific rather than general terms, and is from credible sources. Your evidence will also be more persuasive if you state explicitly the point it is supposed to prove.

No matter how strong your evidence, you will not be persuasive unless listeners agree with your reasoning. In reasoning from specific instances, you move from a number of particular facts to a general conclusion. Reasoning from principle is the reverse—you move from a general principle to a particular conclusion. When you use causal reasoning, you try to establish a relationship between causes and effects. In analogical reasoning, you compare two cases and infer that what is true for one is also true for the other.

Whatever kind of reasoning you use, avoid fallacies such as hasty generalization, false cause, invalid analogy, appeal to tradition, and appeal to novelty. You should also be on guard against the red herring, slippery slope, bandwagon, *ad hominem,* and either-or fallacies.

Finally, you can persuade your listeners by appealing to their emotions. One way to generate emotional appeal is by using emotion-laden language. Another is to develop vivid, richly textured examples. Neither, however, will be effective unless you feel the emotion yourself and communicate it by speaking with sincerity and conviction.

As with other methods of persuasion, your use of emotional appeal should be guided by a firm ethical rudder. Although emotional appeals are usually inappropriate in speeches on questions of fact, they are legitimate—and often necessary—in speeches that seek immediate action on questions of policy. Even when trying to move listeners to action, however, you should never substitute emotional appeals for evidence and reasoning.

Key Terms

ethos (314)
credibility (314)
initial credibility (315)
derived credibility (315)
terminal credibility (315)
creating common ground (316)
evidence (318)
logos (321)
reasoning (322)
reasoning from specific instances (322)
reasoning from principle (323)
causal reasoning (324)
analogical reasoning (325)

fallacy (325)
hasty generalization (325)
false cause (326)
invalid analogy (327)
bandwagon (327)
red herring (327)
ad hominem (328)
either-or (328)
slippery slope (328)
appeal to tradition (328)
appeal to novelty (329)
pathos (329)

Review Questions

After reading this chapter, you should be able to answer the following questions:

1. What is credibility? What two factors exert the most influence on an audience's perception of a speaker's credibility?

2. What are the differences among initial credibility, derived credibility, and terminal credibility?

3. What are three ways you can enhance your credibility during your speeches?

4. What is evidence? Why do persuasive speakers need to use evidence?

5. What are four tips for using evidence effectively in a persuasive speech?

6. What is reasoning from specific instances? Why is it important to supplement reasoning from specific instances with testimony or statistics?

7. What is reasoning from principle? How is it different from reasoning from specific instances?

8. What is causal reasoning? Why is the relationship between causes and effects not always clear?

9. What is analogical reasoning? Why is analogical reasoning frequently used in persuasive speeches on questions of policy?

10. What are the ten logical fallacies discussed in this chapter?

11. What is the role of emotional appeal in persuasive speaking? Identify three methods you can use to generate emotional appeal in your speeches.

Exercises for Critical Thinking

1. Research has shown that a speaker's initial credibility can have great impact on how the speaker's ideas are received by listeners. Research has also shown that a speaker's credibility will vary from topic to topic and audience to audience. In the left-hand column below is a list of well-known public figures. In the right-hand column is a list of potential speech topics. Assume that each speaker will be addressing your speech class.

   For each speaker, identify the topic in the right-hand column on which she or he would have the highest initial credibility for your class. Then explain how the speaker's initial credibility might be affected if the speaker were discussing the topic in the right-hand column directly across from her or his name.

Speaker	Topic
Jennifer Lopez	Horror and Modern Fiction
Tim Cook	My Life in Tennis
Oprah Winfrey	Trends in Pop Music
Stephen King	The Art of Interviewing
Roger Federer	The Future of Smartphones

2. Identify the kind of reasoning used in each of the following statements. What weaknesses, if any, can you find in the reasoning of each?

   a. The U.S. Constitution prohibits cruel and unusual punishment. Life sentencing for juvenile offenders is cruel and unusual punishment. Therefore, life sentencing for juvenile offenders is contrary to the U.S. Constitution.

   b. We can see from its work all around the world that Women for Women International is a worthy charitable organization. It has helped women in Rwanda operate sewing machines and make clothing. It has given women in Kosovo the skills to operate businesses in their communities. It has shown women in the Democratic Republic of Congo how to create and market ceramics.

   c. According to a study by the National Institutes of Health, children with gluten sensitivity are three times more likely to develop scoliosis than children without gluten sensitivity. We can see, then, that gluten sensitivity is the cause of scoliosis.

   d. Portugal decriminalized the use of drugs two decades ago, and now drug-related deaths are extremely rare. If decriminalization can work in Portugal, it can work in the United States.

3. Over the years there has been much debate about the role of emotional appeal in public speaking. Do you believe it is ethical for public speakers to use emotional appeals when seeking to persuade an audience? Do you feel there are certain kinds of emotions to which an ethical speaker should not appeal? Why or why not? Be prepared to explain your ideas in class.

4. Analyze "Changing Lives Through the Literacy Network" in the appendix of sample speeches that follows Chapter 20. Pay special attention to the speaker's credibility, evidence, reasoning, and emotional appeal. In addition to reading the text, view the speech on Video 17.6 so you can assess the speaker's delivery and its impact on her persuasiveness.

connect·

View "Changing Lives Through the Literacy Network" in the online Media Library for this chapter (Video 17.6).

End Notes

[1] The dimensions of credibility have been much studied by social scientists. Excellent research reviews can be found in Daniel J. O'Keefe, *Persuasion: Theory and Research,* 3rd ed. (Thousand Oaks, CA: Sage, 2016), pp. 188–213; and James B. Stiff and Paul A. Mongeau, *Persuasive Communication,* 3rd ed. (New York: Guilford, 2016), pp. 137–163.

[2] James C. McCroskey, *An Introduction to Rhetorical Communication,* 9th ed. (Boston, MA: Allyn and Bacon, 2006), pp. 84–96.

[3] O'Keefe, *Persuasion: Theory and Research,* p. 191.

[4] See Richard M. Perloff, *The Dynamics of Persuasion: Communication and Attitudes in the Twenty-First Century,* 7th ed. (New York: Routledge, 2021), pp. 209–212.

[5] On the efficacy of these tips, see Perloff, *Dynamics of Persuasion,* pp. 302–304.

[6] Adapted from James C. Humes, *A Speaker's Treasury of Anecdotes about the Famous* (New York: Harper and Row, 1978), p. 131.

[7] In classical systems of logic, reasoning from particular facts to a general conclusion was known as induction. Contemporary logicians, however, have redefined induction as any instance of reasoning in which the conclusion follows from its premises with probability, regardless of whether the reasoning moves from specific instances to a general conclusion or from a general premise to a specific conclusion. In this scheme, reasoning from specific instances is one kind of inductive argument—as are causal reasoning and analogical reasoning. See, for example, Frank Boardman, Nancy Cavender, and Howard Kahane, *Logic and Contemporary Rhetoric: The Use of Reason in Everyday Life,* 13th ed. (Wadsworth, Cengage Learning, 2018).

[8] Lionel Ruby, *The Art of Making Sense* (Philadelphia: Lippincott, 1954), p. 261.

[9] In classical systems of logic, reasoning from a general premise to a specific conclusion was known as deduction. But just as contemporary logicians have redefined induction (see note 7), they have redefined deduction as any instance of reasoning in which the conclusion follows from its premises with certainty. Some deductive arguments move from general premises to a specific conclusion, but others move from specific premises to a general conclusion. Many speech textbooks confuse reasoning from principle, which is one form of deduction, with deductive reasoning in general.

[10] For more on fallacies and argumentation in general, see Douglas Walton, *Methods of Argumentation* (New York: Cambridge University Press, 2013).

[11] H. E. Butler (trans.), *The Institutio Oratoria of Quintilian* (Cambridge, MA: Harvard University Press, 1961), IV, p. 141.

[12] George Campbell, *The Philosophy of Rhetoric,* ed. Lloyd F. Bitzer (Carbondale: Southern Illinois University Press, 1988), p. 77.

[13] Research on fear appeals, for example, has demonstrated that messages devoted exclusively to arousing fear in the audience are usually less effective than messages that combine fear appeals with reasonable explanations of how to eliminate or cope with the source of fear. For a review of that research, see Perloff, *Dynamics of Persuasion,* pp. 339–355.

18 Speaking on Special Occasions

Speeches of Introduction

Speeches of Presentation

Speeches of Acceptance

Commemorative Speeches

Special occasions are the punctuation marks of day-to-day life, the high points that stand out above ordinary routine. Christenings, weddings, funerals, graduations, award ceremonies, inaugurals, retirement dinners—all these are occasions, and they are very special to the people who take part in them. Nearly always they are occasions for speechmaking. A close friend proposes a toast to the newly married couple; the sales manager presents an award to the sales representative of the year; a family member delivers a moving eulogy to the deceased. These speeches help give the occasion its "specialness." They are part of the ceremonial aura that marks the event.

Speeches for special occasions are different from the speeches we have considered so far in this book. They may convey information or persuade, but that is not their primary purpose. Rather, they aim to fit the special needs of a special occasion. In this chapter we look at the most common special occasions and the kinds of speeches appropriate for each.

Speeches of Introduction

"Distinguished guests, the President of the United States." If you are ever in a situation in which you have to introduce the president, you will need no more than the eight words that begin this paragraph. The president is so well known that any further remarks would be inappropriate and almost foolish.

Most of the time, however, a speech of introduction will be neither this brief nor this ritualized. If you are introducing another speaker, you will need to accomplish three purposes in your introduction:

Build enthusiasm for the upcoming speaker.

Build enthusiasm for the speaker's topic.

Establish a welcoming climate that will boost the speaker's credibility.

A good speech of introduction can be a delight to hear and can ease the task of the main speaker. Usually you will say something about the speaker and the topic—in that order. Following are some guidelines for speeches of introduction.

Be Brief

During World War I, Lord Balfour, Great Britain's foreign secretary, was to be the main speaker at a rally in the United States. But the speaker introducing him gave a 45-minute oration on the causes of the war. Then, almost as an afterthought, he said, "Now Lord Balfour will give his address." Lord Balfour rose and said, "I'm supposed to give my address in the brief time remaining. Here it is: 10 Carleton Gardens, London, England."[1]

Everyone who has ever sat through a long-winded introduction knows how dreary it can be. The purpose of a speech of introduction is to focus attention on the main speaker, not on the person making the introduction. A speech of introduction will usually be no more than two to three minutes long, and may be shorter if the speaker is already well known to the audience.

Make Sure Your Remarks Are Completely Accurate

Many an introducer has embarrassed himself or herself, as well as the main speaker, by garbling basic facts. Always check with the speaker ahead of time to make sure your introduction is accurate in every respect.

Above all, get the speaker's name right. If the speaker's name is at all difficult—especially if it involves a foreign pronunciation—practice saying it in advance. However, don't practice so much that you frighten yourself about getting it wrong. This was the plight of an announcer whose gaffe is now a classic: "Ladies and gentlemen, the President of the United States—Hoobert Heever!"

Adapt Your Remarks to the Occasion

In preparing your introduction, you may be constrained by the nature of the occasion. Formal occasions require formal speeches of introduction. If you were presenting a guest speaker at an informal business meeting, you might be much more casual than at a formal banquet.

Adapt Your Remarks to the Main Speaker

No matter how well it is received by the audience, a speech of introduction that leaves the main speaker feeling uncomfortable has failed in part of its purpose. How can you make a main speaker uncomfortable? One way is to overpraise the person—especially for his or her speaking skills. Never say, "Our speaker will keep you on the edge of your seat from beginning to end!" You create a set of expectations that are almost impossible to fulfill.

Another way to create discomfort is by revealing embarrassing details of the speaker's personal life or by making remarks that are in poor taste. An introducer may think this line is funny: "Why, I've known Anita Fratello since she was 10 years old and weighed so much that everybody called her Blimpo!" To the speaker, however, the statement will probably not be a bit funny and may be painful.

Adapt Your Remarks to the Audience

Just as you adapt other speeches to particular audiences, so you need to adapt a speech of introduction to the audience you are facing. Your aim is to make *this* audience want to hear *this* speaker on *this* subject. If the speaker is not well known to the audience, you will need to establish her or his credibility by recounting some of the speaker's main achievements and explaining why she or he is qualified to speak on the topic at hand. But if the speaker is already personally known to the audience, it would be absurd to act as if the audience had never heard of the person.

Also, you will want to tell each audience what *it* wants to hear—to give the kind of information that is interesting and accessible to the members of that audience. If you were introducing the same speaker to two different groups, some of the information in the speeches of introduction might be the same, but it would be slanted differently.

Suppose, for example, that tennis legend Serena Williams is going to address two groups—an elementary-school assembly and the annual meeting of the United States Tennis Association. The introduction to the school assembly might go like this:

> Children, today we have a very special guest. She is the most famous women's tennis player in the world. Many of you have probably seen her on TV. She started playing tennis when she was four years old—younger than all of you. Today, she's going to talk to us about her life in tennis and how you, too, can become great at whatever you love if you are willing to work hard enough. Let's give a big round of applause to Serena Williams.

But the introduction to the United States Tennis Association would be along these lines:

> Ladies and gentlemen, it is my privilege to introduce to you a tennis legend. We watched her play for over twenty-five years. Few of us can forget her early matches against Steffi Graf, her seven Wimbledon championships, her twenty-three Grand Slam singles titles, or her four Olympic gold medals.
>
> The story of how she climbed to the top of our sport is well known. After starting the game at age four, she turned professional when she was fourteen and, along with her older sister Venus, quickly emerged as a rare talent and a fierce competitor.
>
> But nothing comes without struggle. In addition to the on-court competition, she dealt with off-court issues such as mental fatigue, health scares that nearly ended her career, and debates over women, race, and body image. And, of course, she's a mother as well. Today, she's going to talk to us about playing through the struggles of life and remaining resilient in the face of adversity. I also hope she'll give us some pointers on perfecting our backhands!
>
> Please give a warm welcome to Serena Williams.

Try to Create a Sense of Anticipation and Drama

You may have noticed one detail shared by the two speeches introducing Serena Williams: In both cases the speaker's name was saved for last. This is a convention in speeches of introduction. While there may occasionally be a good reason to break the convention, usually you will avoid mentioning the speaker's name until the final moment—even when the audience knows exactly whom you are discussing. By doing this you build a sense of drama, and the speaker's name comes as the climax of your introduction.

Often you will find yourself in the situation of introducing someone who is fairly well known to the audience—a classmate, a colleague at a business meeting, a neighbor in a community group. Then you should try to be creative and cast the speaker in a new light. Talk to the speaker beforehand and see if you can learn some interesting facts that are not generally known—especially facts that relate to the speaker's topic.

Above all, if you expect to be creative and dramatic, be sure to practice your speech of introduction thoroughly. You should be able to deliver it extemporaneously, with sincerity and enthusiasm.

Speeches of Presentation

Speeches of presentation are given when someone receives a gift, an award, or some other form of public recognition. Usually such speeches are brief. They may be no more than a mere announcement ("And the winner is . . .") or be up to four or five minutes in length.

PRESENTING THE NATIONAL TEACHER OF THE YEAR AWARD

Miguel Cardona

It's an honor to celebrate your achievements, especially over the past two years, which have marked the most challenging period in our education history. Congratulations . . . to all state teachers of the year for this well-deserved recognition.

Juliana is an educator with a passion near to my heart. As a first-generation bilingual immigrant, Juliana works to help her students feel proud of their cultures and who they are. She works in special-education classrooms and as an elementary school instructional strategist. I'm heartened that Juliana is the first Latina national teacher of the year in more than 15 years.

Juliana, thank you for using your platform to advocate for a joyful and just education for all students—one that is inclusive, affirming, and celebrates the wonder of learning. . . .

Your contributions to our children's success and our nation's future can't be overstated. You are our country's greatest child advocate. And, as you know, this is our moment. This is our moment. There's no more important time to represent the profession as teachers of the year than now. . . .

With each new group of honorees, we pay tribute to the countless dedicated and passionate educators in classrooms across America—teachers who are pouring their hearts into their work, inspiring their students, and collaborating with their colleagues and neighbors to make their school communities vibrant places to learn.

I've always said it shouldn't take a pandemic for us to realize how important teachers are to this country. We know that great teachers are life-changing. They literally shape the lives of those in their reach. . . .

I'm excited now to turn the stage over to our 2021 National Teacher of the Year, Juliana Urtubey.

Whether given on the world stage or in one's local community, speeches for special occasions should seek to invest the occasion with dignity, meaning, and honest emotion.
The Asahi Shimbun/Getty Images

The main purpose of a speech of presentation is to tell the audience why the recipient is receiving the award: to point out his or her contributions, achievements, and so forth. Do not deal with everything the person has ever done. Focus on achievements related to the award, and discuss these achievements in a way that will make them meaningful to the audience.

Depending on the audience and the occasion, you may also need to discuss two other matters in a speech of presentation. First, if the audience is not familiar with the award, you should explain it briefly. Second, if the award was won in a public competition and the audience knows who the losers are, you might take a moment to praise the losers.

speech of presentation
A speech that presents someone a gift, an award, or some other form of public recognition.

On page 344 is a sample speech of presentation. It was presented by U.S. Secretary of Education Miguel Cardona when giving the 2021 National Teacher of the Year award to Juliana Urtubey, a special education teacher at Kermit R. Booker Sr. Innovative Elementary School in Las Vegas, Nevada. Because the Teacher of the Year ceremony recognizes exemplary teachers from every state, Cardona acknowledged the larger group before turning to the national honoree. His speech focused on Urtubey's commitment to educational excellence and equity.

Speeches of Acceptance

The purpose of an acceptance speech is to give thanks for a gift or an award. When giving such a speech, you thank the people who are bestowing the award and recognize the people who helped you gain it.

The acceptance speech on page 346 is the companion piece to the speech of presentation by Miguel Cardona. It was delivered by Juliana Urtubey in accepting the National Teacher of the Year Award, and it exemplifies the major traits of a good acceptance speech—brevity, humility, and graciousness.[2]

acceptance speech
A speech that gives thanks for a gift, an award, or some other form of public recognition.

Commemorative Speeches

commemorative speech
A speech that pays tribute to a person, a group of people, an institution, or an idea.

Commemorative speeches are speeches of praise or celebration. Eulogies, Fourth of July speeches, and dedications are examples of commemorative speeches. Your aim in such speeches is to pay tribute to a person, a group of people, an institution, or an idea.

As in an informative speech, you probably will have to give the audience information about your subject. After all, the audience must know *why* your subject is praiseworthy. As in other speeches, you may draw on examples, testimony, even statistics to illustrate the achievements of your subject.

Your fundamental purpose in a commemorative speech, however, is not to inform your listeners but to *inspire* them—to arouse and heighten their appreciation of or admiration for the person, institution, or idea you are praising. If you are paying tribute to a person, for example, you should not simply recount the details of the person's life. Rather, you should penetrate to the *essence* of your subject and generate in your audience a deep sense of respect.

When speaking to commemorate, you want to express feelings, to stir sentiments— joy and hope when a new building is dedicated, anticipation and good wishes at a commencement celebration, lament and consolation at a funeral, admiration and respect at a testimonial dinner. A commemorative speech is like an impressionist painting—"a picture with warm colors and texture capturing a mood or a moment."[3]

But while the painter works with brush and colors, the commemorative speaker works with language. Of all the kinds of speeches, none depends more on the creative and subtle use of language. Some of the most memorable speeches in history, including Abraham Lincoln's "Gettysburg Address," have been commemorative. We continue to find such speeches meaningful and inspiring largely because of their eloquent use of language.

One of the most effective commemorative speakers in American history was President Ronald Reagan. After the explosion of the space shuttle *Challenger* in 1986, Reagan delivered a nationally televised eulogy to the astronauts killed in the blast. Following are two versions of Reagan's closing lines. The first is what he *might* have said, stripping the text of its warm emotional content and poignant language:

> Like Francis Drake, the great explorer of the oceans, the *Challenger* astronauts gave their lives for a cause to which they were fully dedicated. We are honored by them, and we will not forget them. We will always remember seeing them for the last time this morning as they prepared for their flight.

Here is what Reagan *actually* said:

> There's a coincidence today. On this day 390 years ago, the great explorer Francis Drake died aboard ship off the coast of Panama. In his lifetime the great frontiers were the oceans, and an historian later said, "He lived by the sea, died on it, was buried in it." Well, today we can say of the *Challenger* crew: Their dedication was, like Drake's, complete.
>
> The crew of the space shuttle *Challenger* honored us by the manner in which they lived their lives. We will never forget them, nor the last time we saw them, this morning, as they prepared for their journey and waved goodbye and "slipped the surly bonds of earth" to "touch the face of God."[4]

The final words—"'slipped the surly bonds of earth' to 'touch the face of God'"—are especially effective. Drawn from a sonnet called "High Flight" that many pilots keep with them, they ennoble the deaths of the astronauts and end the speech on an eloquent, moving, and poetic note.

When speaking to commemorate, your success will depend on your ability to put into language the thoughts and emotions appropriate to the occasion. It is easy—too easy—to fall back on clichés and trite sentiments. Your challenge will be to use language imaginatively to invest the occasion with dignity, meaning, and honest emotion.

In doing so, you may want to utilize the special resources of language discussed in Chapter 12. Metaphor, simile, parallelism, repetition, antithesis, alliteration—all are appropriate for commemorative speeches. Some highly acclaimed commemorative speeches—including Martin Luther King's "I Have a Dream" and John Kennedy's inaugural address—are distinguished by their creative use of such devices.

Confronted with the evocative speeches of a Kennedy or a King, you may decide that the speech of commemoration is far beyond your abilities. But other students have delivered excellent commemorative speeches—not immortal, perhaps, but nonetheless dignified and moving.

Look, for example, at "Make a Wish" in the appendix of sample speeches that follows Chapter 20. The speaker's aim was to pay tribute to one of the most respected charities in the United States. Although the speaker provides basic information about the Make-A-Wish foundation and its programs, she does not present a history of the organization. Instead, she focuses on its generosity, selflessness, and healing. She gives enough detail to let us see why Make-A-Wish is commendable, but not so much as to slow the pace of the speech.

The speaker also uses several of the language devices discussed in Chapter 12 to provide the kind of formal tone appropriate for a commemorative speech. You can see this in the following passage, about the volunteers who help Make-A-Wish fulfill the dreams of children in need:

> The volunteers aren't just politicians and superstars. They're the people behind the scenes orchestrating the visits and vacations. They're the counselors who help these kids identify their most heartfelt wishes. They're the office workers who enter data, answer phones, and finalize details. Make-A-Wish has 25,000 active volunteers who give their time to help kids like my sister. That's selflessness.

These lines have an elegance that comes not only from their ideas but also from their use of parallelism, repetition, and vivid language. Consider, in contrast, how much less effective the passage would have been if the speaker had said:

> Make-A-Wish depends on the selflessness of many volunteers, including support staff and counselors, plus office workers and others.

These lines convey the same ideas, but not with the same effect.

For another example, consider the student commemorative speech printed on page 349. The subject is Ida B. Wells, a pioneering civil rights activist who spoke, wrote, and fought against the injustices of her time. Notice the crispness and clarity of the speaker's language and how she begins and ends each main point in parallel fashion. The speaker tells us enough about Wells to know why she is praiseworthy without getting bogged down with details more appropriate for an informative speech.

connect

View "Make a Wish" in the online Media Library for this chapter (Video 18.1).

connect

View "Ida B. Wells" in the online Media Library for this chapter (Video 18.2).

Speeches for special occasions are part of the ceremonial aura that makes an event special. Here Jin Young Ko addresses the crowd after winning the Cambia Portland Classic golf tournament.

Brian Murphy/Icon Sportswire/Getty Images

IDA B. WELLS

Frederick Douglass, Rosa Parks, Dr. Martin Luther King. All three were champions of civil rights and racial justice. But there's another name that should ring just as loudly as these famous figures; another name that should roll off the tongue of every student in this country: Ida B. Wells.

Wells stares at us out of the past—her eyes strong, her face resolute, her mind made up. Although Wells lived long ago—from 1862 to 1931—her contributions to society persist. Today, I commemorate her for those contributions: for the courage to stand up, for the courage to speak up, for the courage to stay up.

Ida B. Wells had the courage to stand up—to stand up for herself and for equality under the law. Born in muggy Mississippi in the dark days of the Civil War, Wells faced segregation every day, but she refused to accept it.

In 1883 she bought a first-class ticket for a train ride from Memphis to Nashville. Even though she paid just as much as the white, first-class passengers, and had already taken her seat, crew members told her to move to the crowded, run-down smoking car reserved for Black people. When she refused and stayed in her seat, she was dragged away and forcibly removed from the train.

Seventy years before Rosa Parks ignited the civil rights movement by refusing to give up her bus seat, Wells stood up for equality—also by staying seated.

Ida B. Wells also had the courage to speak up—to speak up for her friends and for justice. With powerful pen and soaring voice, she denounced the injustices of segregation. Her primary platform was the *Memphis Free Speech and Headlight*, the newspaper of which she was editor and part-owner.

In 1892, while Wells was living in Memphis, three of her friends were lynched by a white mob. In her paper, she condemned the lynching and the mob who carried it out. Afraid of the power of her pen, another mob destroyed her newspaper office in an effort to silence her. It didn't work.

Like the great abolitionist speaker and writer Frederick Douglass, Wells lent her voice to the cause of justice regardless of opposition.

Finally, Ida B. Wells had the courage to stay up—to stay up and keep fighting for future generations. Because of her commitment to equality and justice, she created organizations that would long outlive her.

To champion the right of women to vote, she helped create the first suffrage organization for African-American women. To unite African-American women in common purpose, she helped create the National Association of Colored Women's Clubs. To advance civil rights for all African Americans, she helped create an organization I'm sure you've heard of—the NAACP.

Just as Dr. Martin Luther King created civil rights organizations that would continue long after his death, Wells brought people together for lasting change.

Ida B. Wells. I hope it's a name you will remember alongside Frederick Douglass, Rosa Parks, and Dr. Martin Luther King. For her courage to stand up for equality, for her courage to speak up for justice, for her courage to stay up for all of us, Wells deserves recognition and respect. As she stares at us out of the past, her undaunted gaze serves as a reminder that the quest for justice cannot be abandoned.

Summary

In this chapter we have considered speeches of introduction, speeches of presentation, speeches of acceptance, and commemorative speeches.

Your job in a speech of introduction is to build enthusiasm for the main speaker and to establish a welcoming climate. Keep your remarks brief, make sure they are accurate, and adapt them to the audience, the occasion, and the main speaker.

Speeches of presentation are given when someone receives a gift or an award. The main theme of such a speech is to acknowledge the achievements of the recipient. The purpose of an acceptance speech is to give thanks for a gift or an award. When delivering such a speech, you should thank the people who are bestowing the award and recognize the contributions of people who helped you gain it. Be brief, humble, and gracious.

Commemorative speeches are speeches of praise or celebration. Your aim in such a speech is to pay tribute to a person, a group of people, an institution, or an idea. A commemorative speech should inspire the audience, and its success will depend largely on how well you put into language the thoughts and feelings appropriate to the occasion.

Key Terms

speech of introduction (340)

speech of presentation (345)

acceptance speech (346)

commemorative speech (346)

Review Questions

After reading this chapter, you should be able to answer the following questions:

1. What are the three purposes of a speech of introduction? What guidelines should you follow in preparing such a speech?

2. What is the main theme of a speech of presentation? Depending on the audience and occasion, what two other themes might you include in such a speech?

3. What are the three major traits of a good acceptance speech?

4. What is the fundamental purpose of a commemorative speech? Why does a successful commemorative speech depend so much on the creative and subtle use of language?

Exercises for Critical Thinking

1. Attend a speech sponsored by a campus organization. Pay special attention to the speech introducing the main speaker. How well does it fit the guidelines discussed in this chapter?

2. Observe several speeches of presentation and acceptance—at a campus awards ceremony or on a show such as the Academy Awards, Grammy Awards, or Emmy Awards. Which speeches do you find most effective? Least effective? Why?

3. Eulogies are among the most common types of commemorative speeches. Imagine that you have been asked by family members to deliver a eulogy at the funeral for one of your grandparents. What would be your primary purpose in delivering a speech on such an occasion? What praiseworthy characteristics would you focus on in eulogizing your grandparent? How might you adapt your remarks to other family members in attendance?

4. Analyze "Ida B. Wells" (page 349) in light of the criteria for commemorative speaking presented in this chapter.

End Notes

[1] James C. Humes, *Roles Speakers Play* (New York: Harper and Row, 1976), p. 8.

[2] Printed with permission of Juliana Urtubey.

[3] Humes, *Roles Speakers Play,* pp. 33–34, 36.

[4] Ronald Reagan, "Address on the *Challenger* Explosion," in Stephen E. Lucas and Martin J. Medhurst (eds.), *Words of a Century: The Top 100 American Speeches, 1900–1999* (New York: Oxford University Press, 2009), pp. 611–612.

19 Presenting Your Speech Online

Before the COVID-19 pandemic, online public speaking was something of a novelty. A few people had delivered online speeches in virtual college courses. Others had gained experience through virtual job interviews or remote meetings. But online speaking was far from common.

Then everything changed. During the pandemic we watched teachers deliver lessons online, we met in groups with classmates spread across the country, and we learned the good, the bad, and the ugly of Zoom. Church services, city council meetings, sales presentations, weddings, funerals, and so much more—all went virtual and immersed us in the world of online public speaking.

In this world we started to notice what worked and what didn't work. Some speakers sat in front of windows, which washed them out and made them difficult to see clearly. Others rambled on with little concern for the pacing of their speech or keeping the audience engaged. Still others spoke from kitchens with dirty dishes piled high, making them seem unprofessional and unprepared.

The result of it all was a valuable lesson: Delivering an online speech is difficult. In fact, it's usually more difficult than delivering an in-person speech. Why? In an online speech, you have to do everything you would do in an in-person speech—and more.

Regardless of how many online speeches you delivered or listened to during the pandemic, you will almost surely be giving more in the years to come. This chapter will help you take much of what you have already noticed about online speaking and turn it to your advantage.

The Special Nature of the Online Environment

When you deliver a traditional speech, you're in the same room as your audience. You can see how many people are present. You can look them in the eye to keep them engaged. You have multiple forms of feedback to assess how fully they are paying attention and how well they are grasping your message.

online environment
The elements of Internet communication that influence an online speech, including the remote audience, factors of technology, and unique forms of interference.

In the online environment, you have a fundamentally different relationship with your audience. Because you're not in the same room with them, gauging their responses can be difficult. You might not know if they begin staring out the window, checking Instagram, or reading news online. Even if you can see the audience on your computer screen, you don't have the same relationship with them that you would if you were personally present in the room.

In fact, almost every aspect of the speech communication process can be affected by the online environment. Think, for example, about the kinds of interference you might face online. Interference can come from the physical spaces where your listeners are located—someone unexpectedly entering the room or a noise in the hallway outside. But interference can also come from the technology connecting you with your audience. A glitch might cause the connection to freeze or drop. Bandwidth congestion might lead to lagging video or buffering issues. Someone's computer might decide to update itself in the middle of your presentation.

Then there is the temptation to multitask, which is often irresistible in the online environment. Who among us hasn't responded to email, browsed shopping sites, or checked sports scores while listening to an online presentation?

These are just some of the challenges facing online public speakers. As with other aspects of life, there is no substitute for experience when it comes to giving speeches online. But if you follow the principles discussed in this chapter, you'll get started in the right direction. We'll begin by looking at two types of online speeches.

Kinds of Online Speeches

recorded online speech
A speech that is delivered, recorded, then uploaded to the Internet.

There are two major kinds of online speeches. One is *recorded* online speeches that are designed primarily for viewing on the Internet. TED Talks are an example. The speakers spend months creating their presentations with the help of TED advisers. On speech day, they address an in-person audience, but that audience is largely a formality. The target audience is composed of the millions of people who will access the talks after they are edited and uploaded to YouTube.

Recorded online speeches can also be found in blended or online public speaking classes. Students make their presentations at their dorm, home, or apartment and upload them to a server where their instructor and fellow students can view the speeches later.

real-time online speech
A speech that has been created specifically for an audience that will view it online as it is being delivered.

The second major kind of online speech is a *real-time* online speech created for an audience that will view it online as it is being delivered, often using software designed specifically for that purpose. Sometimes the audience is in a classroom or office, but it can also be spread across several locations in multiple time zones. The speaker is seated or standing and talks into a webcam that is located a couple feet away. The entire speech—content, delivery, visual aids—is communicated live via the webcam.

Unlike a recorded online speech, a real-time online presentation is seen by the remote audience as it is being delivered. To be successful, every aspect of such a speech must be strategically adapted to the online environment.
Luis Alvarez/Getty Images

The distinctions between recorded and real-time online speeches are not absolute, but they are essential to keep in mind whenever you present an online speech. If you are recording and uploading a traditional speech for remote viewing—as in an online speech class—you will prepare and present the speech largely as if you were speaking in the classroom.

On the other hand, if you are talking in real time to a remote audience via a webcam, they will expect a speech that is created specifically for the online environment. Such a presentation will have all the usual elements of a public speech—introduction, body, conclusion—with clear main points, strong supporting materials, and engaging delivery. To be successful, however, every aspect of it will have to be adapted to the fact that you are not physically present with the audience and are communicating through a webcam while the audience views the speech on a computer monitor or a video screen.[1]

Guidelines for Online Speaking

If you follow the principles discussed in previous chapters, you will be well prepared for most aspects of giving an online speech. Yet, as we noted earlier, you need to adapt those principles to the special nature of online communication. In this section of the chapter, we explore general guidelines for online speaking. In the next section, we focus specifically on optimizing the use of visual aids in online speeches.

CONTROL THE VISUAL ENVIRONMENT

The Internet is often informal. We FaceTime with family members, post photos of our social lives to Instagram, and record dances for TikTok. Online speeches, however, should *not* be informal. They should be as polished and professional as in-person speeches. This requires, among other things, making the visual environment—what the

visual environment
The on-screen elements seen by the audience during an online speech.

audience sees on-screen—work for you rather than against you. Major elements of the visual environment are setting, lighting, framing, eye contact, and personal appearance.

Setting

One way to control the visual environment is to choose a setting that will communicate the level of professionalism needed for your speech. Find a quiet room where you will not be interrupted by traffic noise or by people coming and going. Make sure there are no posters, paintings, or knickknacks behind you that will deflect attention from your message. The same is true of clutter—cups, dishes, pens, paper, erasers, staplers, and so forth.

Programs like Zoom allow you to replace your actual background with a virtual one. This can be helpful in obscuring your surroundings, but it can also be distracting, depending on what background you choose. In addition, when the program inserts the virtual background, it sometimes results in artifacting—small digital glitches that dance around the edges of the speaker and render the setting obviously artificial. Your best bet is usually to avoid virtual backgrounds and, if possible, to find an uncluttered location with a plain backdrop.

Lighting

Also pay attention to lighting. You don't want the room to seem too dark; neither do you want so much light that it washes you out. Avoid having windows in the background because they will illuminate what is behind you while darkening your face. In general, you want a light source that will present you clearly and pleasingly.

If you expect to give a lot of online presentations in your speech class and beyond, you might consider purchasing an inexpensive portable ring light. A favorite among YouTube creators, the ring light is easy to position behind your webcam and does a good job casting light evenly on you without producing significant shadows.

Framing

Another aspect of the visual environment is knowing how to frame what the audience will see. If you're presenting a recorded online speech for class, your teacher will usually provide instructions about how the shot should be framed. Most instructors want to see the speaker's body from the knees up so as to observe posture, gestures, and how the speaker handles their notes. In Figure 19.1 (page 357), you can see this kind of framing for an online recorded speech.

If you're giving a real-time online speech, questions of framing will revolve mainly around how far you sit or stand from the webcam. If you're too far away, you'll seem small and removed from your listeners. If you're too close, you'll look like a selfie. A good rule of thumb is to sit or stand two to four feet from the webcam so you fill most of the frame and the audience can see you from the chest up—as shown in Figure 19.2 (page 357).

Eye Contact

As with in-person speeches, eye contact is essential for effective online speeches. If you're giving a recorded online speech, there are two general approaches to eye contact. One involves making eye contact with an audience you've assembled for the purpose of listening to your speech. This assembled audience might consist of a few friends or family members, and you will make eye contact with them throughout the speech.

FIGURE 19.1

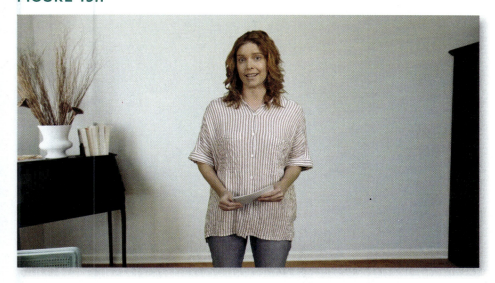

The other approach to eye contact in recorded online speeches is to treat the webcam as what virtual presentation expert Patti Sanchez calls "the eye of the audience."[2]

In this situation, there is no in-person audience assembled for the speech. Instead, you look directly at the webcam and deliver the speech to your instructor and classmates who will view it later. This was the case for the speaker in Figure 19.1.

If you're giving a real-time online speech, you will also treat the webcam as the eye of the audience. As you speak, remember that the webcam is located in the bezel above the screen. To make eye contact with the audience, you need to look there, not at the screen, as shown in Figure 19.3 (page 358).

Also pay attention to the height of the webcam. If you're speaking from a laptop, avoid tilting the webcam up at your face. Instead, put the laptop on a stand or a stack of books so the webcam is aimed directly at you or is tilting slightly down toward you. The goal is to have the audience view you from a straight-on or downward angle, both of which are more flattering than an upward angle.[3]

FIGURE 19.2

Ineffective   Ineffective   More Effective

Djomas/Shutterstock

FIGURE 19.3

Michael Trevis, photographer/McGraw Hill

Personal Appearance

Controlling the visual environment also means taking your personal appearance seriously. Dress in a professional manner that will project well on-screen. Stick with solid colors, but avoid white (which is too bright on-screen) and greens and purples (which may not register accurately). Also stay away from busy patterns and glitzy prints. The more professional you look, the more professional you will feel—and the more professional you will appear to your audience.

Figure 19.4 (below) provides examples of less effective and more effective attempts to control the visual environment. In the first figure, the speaker hasn't found an appealing backdrop, hasn't properly framed herself on-screen, and hasn't dressed as she would for an in-person speech. In the second figure, the speaker has overcome all these problems. There is nothing to distract the audience's attention.

FIGURE 19.4

Ineffective　　　　　**More Effective**

ADAPT YOUR NONVERBAL COMMUNICATION

Your nonverbal communication is magnified dramatically when you speak via a camera of any kind. Gestures, facial expressions, eye movements—all become more noticeable, and potentially distracting.

This is something newscasters have long known. Their on-camera techniques can be especially useful if you are giving an online presentation. Because much of your speech will involve sitting or standing in front of the webcam, your posture will need to be straight, but not rigid. Your goal is to appear professional, relaxed, and confident.

Well-planned and deliberate hand gestures are also important. Too many hand movements in any kind of online speech can be distracting; they can also make you seem nervous and fidgety. Concentrate on using gestures that are natural but controlled. As one specialist in online presentations states, "The more defined your hands appear, the more defined your message will appear to your audience."[4]

Also be aware that the webcam will magnify every eye movement when you are looking directly at it. Avoid glancing up at the ceiling or out the window, and make sure your eyes do not dart back and forth. This will help your eye movements seem deliberate, controlled, and confident.

Another aspect of nonverbal communication is sound—what you communicate through your volume, rate, and tone of voice. Because you are dependent on the quality of your microphone—as well as on your audience's acoustic environment—experts in online speaking recommend that you give special attention to enunciating your words concisely and projecting them clearly.

Even people who speak effectively to live audiences can come across as flat and dull when communicating through a computer screen. The more experience you gain with online speeches, the more effective you will become. Still, you want to work consciously on using your voice to convey dynamism and enthusiasm when speaking in the online environment.

If you have to speak online frequently—whether for school or work—you might want to invest in a stand-alone microphone that can make your voice sound richer and more robust. It's an excellent way to strengthen your vocal presence whether you are giving a formal speech or participating in an informal meeting.[5]

KNOW YOUR TECHNOLOGY

Unlike when you speak to an in-person audience, an online speech *requires* the use of technology. In most speech classes, the instructor will stipulate the technology to use. Zoom is now the standard program for online speaking. Other programs include GoReact, Microsoft Teams, Skype, and Adobe Connect.

Regardless of the specific program you use, give yourself plenty of time to master it. One of the quickest ways to destroy your credibility is to fuss and fumble when operating the software. For recorded online speeches, you'll need to ensure that your webcam properly integrates with the software, that your microphone captures your voice at an acceptable level, and that your computer records the speech in a file format you can easily share with your class.

For real-time online speeches, you'll need to know how to operate the program seamlessly on the day of your speech. This means ensuring that your camera and microphone are working properly and that you know the software commands to be used during the speech. If your speech includes visual aids, you should know how to switch smoothly between showing yourself and showing your visual aids.

As with any other kind of speech, online presentations need careful planning and preparation. Feedback from friends, family, or colleagues can help you avoid pitfalls and smooth out rough spots.

Izusek/Getty Images

If you need help learning the technology for your online speech, you can find numerous tutorials online for Zoom, GoReact, Microsoft Teams, Skype, and others. Also check with your instructor about any resources she or he may recommend.

DON'T FORGET YOUR AUDIENCE

This might seem like strange advice given the fact that we have referred many times to the audience throughout this chapter. Yet we know from experience that it can be difficult for speakers to keep their audience as clearly in mind when speaking online as when speaking to a group of people sitting right in front of them.

This is often a special challenge for students enrolled in an online speech class. They may never be in the same location as their classmates and may deliver all their speeches without an audience being physically present. As a result, it's easy for them to think that they don't have an audience at all. But if you are in such a class, you *do* have an audience—your classmates and your instructor. Even though they will view your speeches remotely, your aim is still to communicate with them, just as you would if you were speaking in a classroom.

When preparing your speeches, follow the principles of audience analysis and adaptation discussed in Chapter 6. Consider conducting an online audience analysis survey using SurveyMonkey or a similar program. This will give you a picture of your listeners' interest in, knowledge about, and attitudes toward your speech topic.

Also keep in mind the notion of public speaking as a mental dialogue between speaker and audience, which we discussed in Chapter 16 (see pages 290–291). Try to anticipate how your listeners will respond to your ideas. Think about how you can structure your speech, phrase your remarks, and use supporting materials to make your audience care about what you have to say.

In short, you may be presenting your speech for remote viewing, but you still need to keep the *public* in public speaking.[6]

PRACTICE, PRACTICE, PRACTICE

No matter what kind of online speech you give, the audience will assess your perfor-mance somewhat differently than if they were watching an in-person speech. We are accustomed to seeing highly polished performances on TED Talks, newscasts, and other programs, and we have come to expect polished performances in other video speech presentations, too.

Because the camera is less forgiving than the naked eye, you will need more rehearsal time for an online speech than for an in-person presentation. In Chapter 13, we looked at a five-step method for rehearsing speech delivery. All of those steps apply to online speeches. In addition, give special attention to the following tips:

When practicing any kind of online speech, record your rehearsals so you can gauge what the audience will see on their end. Watch the video and check your fram-ing, listen to your voice, gauge your eye contact, assess your visual aids, and, above all, try to see yourself through your audience's eyes. Make the necessary adjustments and record the speech again until you're happy with the final result.

If you're giving a real-time online speech, be sure to practice with the computer and the presentation software you will use on the day of your speech. Take time to master all the computer commands so you can execute them flawlessly. Stand or sit as close to the webcam when you practice as you will during the speech itself, so you can assess how you will come across to the audience. Don't be shy about asking friends or family to give you feedback and suggestions.

How much rehearsal is required for an online speech? One expert recommends at least 50 percent more rehearsal time than for an in-person presentation.[7] When it comes to online speaking, don't skimp on your practice sessions.

checklist

Presenting an Online Speech

YES	NO	
☐	☐	1. Have I considered the special nature of the online speech environment?
☐	☐	2. Do I understand the differences between recorded and real-time online speeches?
☐	☐	3. Do I control the visual environment of my presentation so it will work to my advantage?
☐	☐	4. Have I adapted my nonverbal communication so it will be effective when viewed online?
☐	☐	5. Have I mastered the technology necessary for my online speech?
☐	☐	6. Have I carefully considered my online audience and adapted my speech to them?
☐	☐	7. Have I optimized my visual aids for the online environment?
☐	☐	8. Have I taken all the steps necessary to practice my online speech?
☐	☐	9. Do I have a backup plan in case I encounter technical problems?

Optimizing Visual Aids in Online Speeches

If you're delivering a brief online speech, you likely won't need to include visual aids. But as your speech reaches three minutes or more, the more valuable visual aids become to sharpen your message and keep your audience engaged.

Chapter 14 discusses several kinds of visual aids and guidelines for using them. Those guidelines include:

- Keep your visual aids simple so they communicate your point but don't confuse or distract the audience.
- Make your visual aids large enough for the audience to see clearly.
- Use a limited amount of text so the audience can process the information quickly.
- Use fonts, colors, and images in a way that creates dynamic, audience-friendly visual aids.
- Display your visual aids only while you are discussing them.
- Practice with your visual aids so your words, text, and graphics are skillfully coordinated.

Here we discuss special considerations for using visual aids in real-time and recorded online speeches.

VISUAL AIDS IN REAL-TIME ONLINE SPEECHES

Programs like Zoom, Skype, and Microsoft Teams allow you to share your screen so the audience can see what is on your computer—a PowerPoint presentation, for instance. In many programs, sharing your screen will replace video of you with video of your slides, allowing the audience to view your visual aids while you continue to talk over them.

When planning to share your screen, it's important to strike the right balance between displaying yourself and showing your visual aids. Stay on-screen early in the speech to create a visual connection with the audience. Once you've established that

FIGURE 19.5

Credit: Dorling Kindersley/Getty Images

connection, you can alternate between shots of yourself and shots of your visual aids. This will return the focus to you and your message at appropriate times.

For an example of how to alternate between the speaker and visual aids in a real-time online speech, look at the speech excerpt in Video 19.1. The speaker is seeking to persuade her classmates to donate to the organization charity: water. As you watch, notice that the speaker's visual aids fill the entire screen so the audience can see them clearly. When the speaker is not discussing the visual aids, she switches back to showing just herself. This gives the speech visual variety, alters the pacing, and heightens audience interest. (Text and video of the full speech appear at the end of this chapter.)

VISUAL AIDS IN RECORDED ONLINE SPEECHES

When giving a recorded online speech, you have a couple options for incorporating visual aids. If you're addressing an assembled audience of a few friends or family members, you can display visual aids as you would in the classroom—usually on a monitor or a TV screen.

If you're recording the speech for an audience that will watch it remotely after it has been uploaded to the Internet, you can use a software program such as GoReact, which is included on the Connect website that accompanies this book. GoReact divides the audience's video player into two sections. You will appear in one section while your visual aids appear in the other. This allows the audience to see both you and your aids at the same time—as illustrated in Figure 19.5 (page 362). This is often referred to as the "concurrent view" of online presentations.[8]

To see how the concurrent view works in action, watch Video 19.2, which presents a portion of a student speech titled "The Great Mesoamerican Ballgame." As you will see, the speaker appears on one part of the screen. The other part is reserved for his visual aids, which he controls with a remote, much as he would if he were speaking to an in-person audience. When he is not showing a visual aid, the other part of the screen displays an unobtrusive background of the speaker's choosing.

Many instructors prefer this concurrent view because it keeps the speaker on-screen during the entire speech, just as he would be visible throughout an in-person presentation.

connect

View an excerpt from "charity: water" in the online Media Library for this chapter (Video 19.1).

concurrent view
A visual layout for online speeches that displays the speaker and visual aids side-by-side.

connect

View an excerpt from "The Great Mesoamerican Ballgame" in the online Media Library for this chapter (Video 19.2).

FIGURE 19.6

Whether you are presenting an online speech for class or for another situation, you need to support your ideas with clear, convincing supporting materials and to develop a backup plan in case you face technological glitches.

FG Trade/E+/Getty Images

If you use the concurrent view, be sure to format your slides in "portrait" orientation, which is an option in all the major presentation technology programs, including PowerPoint, Keynote, and Google Slides. This will allow your slides to fill the entire vertical space on the left-hand side of the screen. Otherwise, they will be much smaller and will appear with wide black bands above and below them—as shown in Figure 19.6 (page 363).

As you watch Video 19.2, notice that the speaker has rehearsed so thoroughly that he can present his visual aids in perfect coordination with his words. There are no gaps in content or errors in using the remote. Notice, too, how he treats the webcam as the eye of the audience, which allows him to maintain eye contact from beginning to end. Finally, pay attention to how he removes each slide from view when he is finished discussing it. This keeps the audience focused on the speaker and his message rather than allowing its attention to linger on the preceding slide.

All of these practices are part of using visual aids effectively in any type of speech, but they are especially important in online speeches. Because such speeches depend entirely on what appears on-screen, you want to make sure that your visual aids are suitably adapted for the screen.

Have a Backup Plan

No matter how much time you put into preparing your visual aids and other aspects of your speech, you can still be undermined by technological glitches at the audience's end. This is why experts recommend that you always have a backup plan.

For a recorded online speech, the best backup plan is to give yourself plenty of time before a speech is due to overcome problems with your equipment, Internet connection, and preferred platform. Don't wait until the last minute to record your speech or to upload it. If worse comes to worst, you might need to borrow a different computer, find a better Internet connection, or upload your speech to a different platform.

For a real-time online presentation, your backup plan might include one or more of the following:

- Distribute an outline of your speech via email.
- Move the speech to an audio-only conference call.
- Share the text of your speech through a document collaboration program such as Google Docs and invite your audience to comment on the text.
- Turn your real-time online speech into a recorded speech, capturing it first on your computer, then uploading it to a video-sharing website such as YouTube for your audience to view later.
- Reschedule the speech once the technical problems are resolved.

Because we have all been sabotaged by technology at one time or another, audiences usually have sympathy for a speaker who encounters such problems. Having a backup plan will make you look conscientious and considerate.

Sample Speech with Commentary

In earlier chapters of the book, you will find two recorded online speeches: "Twists and Turns" (Video 4.3), which appears at the end of Chapter 4, and "The Great Mesoamerican Ballgame" (Video 15.6), which we previously discussed and appears in full at the end of Chapter 15. Both speeches illustrate the guidelines for recorded online speaking discussed in this chapter.

The following speech demonstrates how to apply the principles of online speaking in a real-time presentation. The speaker's assignment was to present a real-time online speech of four to five minutes persuading the audience to support a charity of the speaker's choice. The speech follows the criteria for persuasive speaking discussed in Chapters 16 and 17, but it is adapted to meet the challenges of the online environment.

In addition to reading the speech, you can view it on Video 19.3. As you watch, notice how the speaker has full command of the technology and uses it to integrate visual aids into her presentation. The background for the speech is uncluttered, the speaker's delivery is well adapted to the online setting, and she communicates in a poised and professional manner.

connect·

View "charity: water" in the online Media Library for this chapter (Video 19.3).

charity: water

 COMMENTARY   **SPEECH**

Hi, everyone. Can you see me and hear me okay? Great.

> The speaker begins by making sure the audience can see her and hear her. This is usually a good idea at the start of a real-time online speech.

Like many speeches that seek direct action, this one follows Monroe's motivated sequence, beginning with the attention section. The speaker's contrast between a water bottle, which she holds in her hand, and the water inside is especially effective.

The speaker introduces charity: water, which she will ask listeners to support as the speech proceeds.

The speaker relates to the audience as fellow college students, and she creates goodwill by emphasizing the financial responsibility of charity: water.

Here the speaker moves into the need section of Monroe's motivated sequence. She supports her argument with credible, well-chosen statistics. She varies the visual environment with a slide that shows her statistics.

To keep the visual environment dynamic, the speaker switches back to showing herself. As you can see from the video, she has an engaging delivery and maintains strong eye contact through the webcam.

Now the speaker moves to the satisfaction section of Monroe's motivated sequence. She explains how charity: water helps people in poor communities build projects that improve the quality of their drinking water.

If you're like me, a water bottle like this is never too far away. But there are millions of people who don't have such a luxury. Not the bottle—they don't have the luxury of the water inside. In fact, there's a worldwide water crisis. The World Health Organization estimates that over two billion people—30 percent of the world's population—lack regular access to clean, safe drinking water.

One way to address this crisis is to support organizations that help communities access clean water. I'm here to encourage you to support one of those organizations—charity: water, a highly regarded charity that helps people in some of the poorest places around the world access clean water.

Now, I know we're all college students, and we don't have lots of extra money. But one of the best things about charity: water is that every penny you contribute goes directly to helping people in need. Let's start with some basic facts about water.

The sad truth is that far too many people don't have access to clean, safe drinking water. Here's the most recent data from the World Health Organization. More than 2 billion people drink water from a source contaminated with feces. Of that number, around 900 million don't have access to a managed source of drinking water. And of that number, some 160 million have to collect their own water from untreated lakes, rivers, and ponds.

These numbers come with some horrific results. Contaminated water is linked to the spread of cholera, dysentery, typhoid, hepatitis, and polio. The WHO estimates that every year 850,000 people die just from diarrhea caused by unsafe drinking water. About 360,000 of those people are children under the age of five.

It's because of these heartbreaking numbers that we ought to support charity: water. Charity: water works with community partners to build sustainable water projects in some of the world's poorest communities. The key to their work is connecting with organizations, groups, and individuals that can build and manage their own water projects. With charity: water's help, communities can drill wells, set up rain-holding tanks, and install purification systems.

Having explained her plan, the speaker enters the visualization section. In this paragraph, she uses a combination of statistics, brief examples, and visual aids to show that charity: water achieves concrete results. When the paragraph is over, she returns to showing herself on-screen.

The next two paragraphs continue the visualization section by showing that charity: water is highly responsible in using the money donated to it. This is always an important issue to address when asking people to donate to a charity.

Knowing that listeners need evidence, the speaker cites third-party organizations that have verified charity: water's accountability.

Now the speaker moves into her action section, in which she urges the audience to donate to charity: water.

The speaker's conclusion, like the rest of her presentation, is strengthened by her delivery, which is sincere, personable, and heartfelt.

Most important, charity: water works. As its website explains, it has helped with 23,000 water projects in 24 countries, serving an estimated 7 million people. In Honduras, charity: water helped install a water pump so villagers didn't have to get water from the nearby river. In Rwanda, it helped dig a well so people didn't have to drink water from a stagnant pond. In India, it helped construct a water system to pipe clean water into town from a nearby mountain.

Not only does charity: water complete these projects, but it does so while being financially responsible. Usually, when you donate to a charity, a percentage of your money goes to overhead costs and administrative work. But with charity: water, private donors pay for all these costs. This means every penny you give goes to helping people in need.

But you don't have to take my word for it. The charity-evaluation website Charity Navigator gives charity: water a four-star rating, the highest possible. Likewise, Give.org reports that charity: water meets or exceeds all twenty of its standards for accountability.

These are just some of the reasons we should support charity: water. Even though we're college students and don't have bundles of cash lying around, we can still make a difference.

So go to charity: water's website and give five bucks, ten bucks, or twenty bucks—the same amount you might spend at Starbucks or hanging out with friends this weekend. Every penny you donate will give the gift of clean water that we take for granted. Thank you.

Summary

There are two major types of online speeches. A recorded online speech is delivered, recorded, and then uploaded to the Internet for later viewing. Examples are TED Talks and presentations in online or blended speech classes. A real-time online speech is created for an audience that will view the speech on the Internet as it is being delivered—as, for instance, in a job interview, a training session, or a sales presentation.

Both types of speeches must be adapted to the online environment, and both can be more challenging and time-consuming to prepare than speeches for in-person audiences. Challenges include controlling the visual environment, adapting your nonverbal communication, knowing your technology, adapting to the online audience, and rehearsing specifically for online viewing.

Learning to use visual aids effectively in the online environment can make your speeches more dynamic and engaging. You can enhance the pacing and visual variety of a real-time online speech by switching back and forth between showing yourself and your visual aids. In recorded online speeches, certain software programs allow you to display yourself alongside your visual aids, much as you would in an in-person speech.

No matter which kind of online presentation you are going to give, you'll need a backup plan in case you run into technological glitches on speech day. Always keep in mind that your online speech will require everything needed for an in-person speech—and more.

Key Terms

online environment (354)

recorded online speech (354)

real-time online speech (354)

visual environment (355)

concurrent view (363)

Review Questions

After reading this chapter, you should be able to answer the following questions:

1. How does public speaking in the online environment differ from public speaking to in-person audiences?
2. What are the two major kinds of online speeches? Explain the differences between them.
3. What guidelines are given in the chapter for effective online speaking?
4. What steps can you take to control the visual environment in an online speech?
5. What steps can you take to adapt your nonverbal communication when speaking in the online environment?
6. How can you optimize visual aids for real-time and recorded online speeches?
7. Why is it important for online speakers to have a backup plan?

Exercises for Critical Thinking

1. View a TED Talk on www.TED.com. Select a speech on a topic that interests you. As you watch the speech, answer the following questions: (1) How does the speaker organize his or her talk for effective communication? (2) How does the speaker control the online environment? (3) How effective is the speaker's delivery on your computer screen?
2. Plan to use visual aids in an online speech following the tips presented in this chapter. Rehearse the speech with your visual aids using your online presentation software program. After the speech, analyze how effectively you used the aids and what changes you would make if you were to deliver the speech again.

3. If you're planning on delivering a real-time online speech, analyze "charity: water," which appears at the end of this chapter (pages 365–367). View the speech on Video 19.3 so you can see the speaker's delivery and use of visual aids. Evaluate the speech in light of the guidelines for online speaking discussed in this chapter.

4. If you're planning on delivering a recorded online speech, analyze "The Great Mesoamerican Ballgame," which appears at the end of Chapter 15 (pages 281–283). View the speech on Video 19.4 so you can see the speaker's delivery and use of visual aids. Evaluate the speech in light of the guidelines for online speaking discussed in this chapter.

connect

View "The Great Mesoamerican Ballgame" in the online Media Library for this chapter (Video 19.4).

End Notes

[1] The distinctions between real-time and recorded online speeches correspond with what are sometimes called synchronous and asynchronous online speeches.

[2] Patti Sanchez, *Presenting Virtually: Communicate and Connect with Online Audiences* (Santa Clara, CA: Duarte Press, 2021), p. 144.

[3] For additional insight on creating an effective audience connection via a webcam, see Pat Lore, *Be Authentic on Video: The Playbook* (Headline Productions, 2021), pp. 65–70.

[4] Timothy J. Koegel, *The Exceptional Presenter Goes Virtual* (Austin, TX: Greenleaf Book Group, 2010), p. 117.

[5] Mike Acker, *Speak and Meet Virtually: Go from Zoom Fatigue, Online Meeting Boredom, and Impersonal Presentations to Engaging, Efficient, and Empowering Web Conferencing* (Advantage-Publishing.Com, 2021), pp. 177–193, offers a number of helpful suggestions on this and other aspects of effective online speaking.

[6] We are indebted to Jennifer Cochrane for making this point in a review of the chapter.

[7] Sanchez, *Presenting Virtually*, p. 102.

[8] Sanchez, *Presenting Virtually*, p. 108.

20 Speaking in Small Groups

What Is a Small Group?

Leadership in Small Groups

Responsibilities in a Small Group

The Reflective-Thinking Method

Presenting the Recommendations of the Group

The president of a medical-device company asked Noah Cox, the new head of the human resources department, to organize an October retreat for the company's sales division. Noah went to work on setting a date, finding a place to stay, and creating an agenda for the retreat.

Noah was very pleased with his plan. He thought he had taken everyone's needs into account. But when he explained his plan at the company's next staff meeting, no one seemed happy.

"The date you set for the retreat is over Halloween," said the marketing manager. "I know you don't have children, but no one with kids is going to want to be away at that time."

The administrative assistant responded next. "Do you realize," he said, "that the hotel you booked is the same one we used for a retreat five years ago? It was a disaster! The food was awful, the meeting rooms were uncomfortable, and the tech support was nonexistent."

Next a junior member of the sales team said, "I see that all the sessions involve executives. Did you mean to exclude the younger team members? We're the ones on the ground at the hospitals."

Finally, the vice president of product development said, "I wish you had checked with me at some point. I could have warned you about the hotel, the conflict with Halloween, and the need to include junior staff."

What went wrong? Noah did not have enough time or resources on his own to create a successful retreat. If a group, instead of a single person, had been assigned to plan the retreat, the problems might have been averted. One person could have taken charge of looking into the best dates, another of finding accommodations, a third of coordinating with other staff members about who should be included in the retreat, and so forth. The plan would have taken *all* factors into account.

Of course, you may have heard the old saying, "A camel is a horse designed by a committee." If you have ever been part of a group that seemed to get nothing done, you may be inclined to say, "Oh, let one person decide and get it over with." The problem in such cases, however, is not that there is a group, but that the group is not functioning properly. A great deal of research shows that if members of a group work well together, they can usually resolve a problem better than a single person.[1]

This chapter deals with speaking in a particular kind of group—the problem-solving small group.

What Is a Small Group?

As its name implies, a small group has a limited number of members. The minimum number is three. (A group of two persons is called a dyad, and it operates quite differently from a group of three or more.) There is some difference of opinion about the maximum number of people who constitute a small group. Most experts set the maximum number at 7 or 8; some go as high as 12. The important point is that the group must be small enough to allow free discussion among all members. In small-group communication, all participants are potentially speakers *and* listeners.

Members of a small group assemble for a specific purpose. Several shoppers milling around the clothing section of a department store are not a small group, even if they speak to one another or comment about high prices and poor service. But if those same shoppers decided to meet together and prepare a formal complaint to the store manager about high prices and poor service, they would then constitute a small group.

A *problem-solving small group* is formed to solve a particular problem. Such groups exist in every area of life. Business groups consider ways of increasing sales. Church groups discuss how to raise funds and provide for people in need. Groups of parents work on improving day-care facilities. You will almost surely be a member of many problem-solving small groups during your life.

Although speaking in a small group is not the same as public speaking, it involves similar skills. Members of a small group influence one another through communication. As a participant in a small group, you might influence your colleagues by giving them important information, by encouraging them to speak, by convincing them to change their minds, even by getting them to end a meeting of the group. All other members of the group have the same opportunity to influence you through effective communication.[2]

Leadership in Small Groups

We have said that small groups often make better decisions than do individuals. To do so, however, they need effective leadership.

KINDS OF LEADERSHIP

Sometimes there is *no specific leader*. In such a situation, members of effective groups tend to have equal influence. When a need for leadership arises, any of the members can—and one probably will—provide the necessary leadership. A typical instance might be a class project, in which you and several classmates are working together.

Small groups require effective leadership to accomplish their goals. Some groups have a designated leader, while others have an implied leader or an emergent leader.

Fizkes/Shutterstock

From time to time, each of you will help the group move toward its goal by suggesting when and where to meet, by outlining the strengths and weaknesses of a certain viewpoint, by resolving disagreements among other members, and so forth.

A group may have an *implied leader*. For example, if a business meeting includes one vice president and several subordinates, the vice president becomes the implied leader. The same is true if one member of the group is a specialist in the topic at hand and the others are not. Members will likely defer to the person with the highest rank or greatest expertise.

Even when a group starts out leaderless, there may be an *emergent leader*. This is a person who, by ability or by force of personality, or just by talking the most, takes a leadership role. The emergence of a leader may or may not be desirable. If the group is stalemated or has dissolved into bickering or making jokes, an emergent leader can put it back on track. There is a danger, however, that the emergent leader may not be the most effective leader but merely the most assertive personality.

Finally, there may be a *designated leader*—a person elected or appointed as leader when the group is formed. A group that meets for only one session should almost always have a designated leader who takes care of the procedural tasks and serves as spokesperson. Likewise, a formal committee will usually have a designated chairperson. The chair can perform leadership functions or delegate them, but he or she remains in charge.

A group may or may not need a specific leader, but it always needs *leadership*. When all members of the group are skilled communicators, they can take turns at providing leadership even if the group has a designated or implied leader. As you develop group communication skills, you should be prepared to assume a leadership role when necessary.[3]

implied leader
A group member to whom other members defer because of her or his rank, expertise, or other quality.

emergent leader
A group member who emerges as a leader during the group's deliberations.

designated leader
A person who is elected or appointed as leader when the group is formed.

FUNCTIONS OF LEADERSHIP

An effective leader helps the group reach its goals by fulfilling three overlapping sets of needs—procedural needs, task needs, and maintenance needs.

Procedural Needs

Procedural needs can be thought of as the "housekeeping" requirements of the group. They include:

procedural needs
Routine "housekeeping" actions necessary for the efficient conduct of business in a small group.

Deciding when and where the group will meet.

If the group will meet in person, reserving the room, checking the number of chairs, making sure the heat or air conditioning is turned on.

If the group will meet virtually, selecting the meeting software, sending an invitation link, circulating instructions to participants.

Setting the agenda of each meeting.

Taking notes during the meeting.

Preparing and distributing any handouts needed for the meeting.

Summarizing the group's progress at the end of the meeting.

If there is a designated leader, he or she can attend to these needs or assign one or more group members to do so. Otherwise, members of the group must split the procedural responsibilities.

Task Needs

Task needs are substantive actions necessary to help the group complete the particular task at hand. They include:

task needs
Substantive actions necessary to help a small group complete its assigned task.

Analyzing the issues facing the group.

Distributing the workload among the members.

Collecting information.

Soliciting the views of other members.

Keeping the group from going off on a tangent.

Playing devil's advocate for unpopular ideas.

Formulating criteria for judging the most effective solution.

Helping the group reach consensus on its final recommendations.

All members should help the group satisfy its task needs. The best small groups are those in which each person contributes fully to accomplishing the group's objective.

Maintenance Needs

Maintenance needs involve interpersonal relations in the group. They include such factors as:

maintenance needs
Communicative actions necessary to maintain interpersonal relations in a small group.

How well members get along with one another.

How willing members are to contribute to the group.

Whether members are supportive of one another.

Whether members feel satisfied with the group's accomplishments.

Whether members feel good about their roles in the group.

If interpersonal problems dominate discussion, the group will have a difficult time working together and reaching a decision. A leader can do much to create and sustain supportive communication in the group. By helping group members handle conflict, by working out differences of opinion, by reducing interpersonal tension, by encouraging participation from all members, by being alert to personal feelings, and by promoting solidarity within the group, a leader can make a tremendous contribution toward helping the group achieve its goals.

Responsibilities in a Small Group

Every member of a small group must assume certain responsibilities, which can be divided into five major categories: (1) commit yourself to the goals of your group; (2) fulfill individual assignments; (3) avoid interpersonal conflicts; (4) encourage full participation; (5) keep the discussion on track. Some of these responsibilities involve leadership roles, but all five are so important that each participant should take them as personal obligations, regardless of the group's leadership.

COMMIT YOURSELF TO THE GOALS OF YOUR GROUP

For a group to succeed, members must align their personal goals with the group's goal. This sounds obvious, but it is not always easy. When you are working with other students on a class project, the group goal—and most likely the goal of each member—is to get a good grade. There is a strong incentive for members to cooperate and commit themselves to completing the task.

Problems arise when one or more members have personal goals that conflict with the group's goal. Here is the kind of situation that can occur:

> Tiffany Varga is a member of the committee to buy new equipment for the local art museum's cafeteria. Because the budget is very tight, the committee's goal is to get the best equipment for the lowest price. But unknown to the other members of the group, Tiffany's son-in-law is a salesman for a distributor of high-priced kitchen appliances. Privately, Tiffany has reasoned that if she can sway the committee toward that company, her son-in-law will get a large commission. Tiffany does not mention this fact to the group. Instead, she argues that quality—not price—should be the determining factor in the purchase. The group process breaks down because Tiffany will not surrender her private goal.

This is an extreme example, but there can be more subtle kinds of private goals, as in the following case:

> Carlos and Bianca are part of a group, and Carlos would like to be on closer terms with Bianca. To impress her, he may agree with everything she says, regardless of whether he really shares her views. Consequently,

Carlos's expressed views are not his actual views. In short, Carlos has a *hidden agenda* in the group meeting. The group's agenda is to solve the problem, but Carlos's agenda is to go out with Bianca.

hidden agenda

A set of unstated individual goals that may conflict with the goals of the group as a whole.

Group members may have all sorts of *hidden agendas*. One may be experiencing personal problems—lowered grades, a breakup with a friend, or just a bad day. Another may have a commitment to a different group whose goals conflict with those of the present group. A third may want to take charge of the group for reasons of personal power, regardless of the group's task.

Remember that what one member of a group does affects all the other members. You should not try to advance your own interests or boost your own ego at the expense of the group and its goals. Beware of hidden agendas—whether yours or someone else's—and participate with a positive spirit.

FULFILL INDIVIDUAL ASSIGNMENTS

As mentioned earlier, one of the advantages of the group process is that it divides the workload among several people. But unless every member fulfills his or her assignments, the group's entire project may fail—as in the following example:

> A number of years ago, one student group decided to raise money for the local children's hospital by hosting a silent auction. After the fund-raiser had been approved, assignments were given out. Carina would contact local businesses about donating items to be auctioned. Megan would set up the room with tables and chairs. Alejandro would prepare light refreshments. Samantha would handle decorations. Derrick would publicize the auction.
>
> Everybody completed their assignments except Derrick, who was busy writing a term paper. He figured he would send an email announcement and post the information to social media in the days leading up to the auction. But he neglected to do any of those things. Realizing this on the morning of the event, he hurriedly posted the information to social media, and even got some accounts to repost the details, but it was too little, too late. Only a handful of people showed up to the auction, and they were all friends of other group members.

No matter what other assignments they may have, *all* members of a group have one very critical assignment—listening. First, it helps you understand what is happening in the group. And unlike a public speaking situation, you can stop the speaker and ask for clarification at any point. Second, listening helps you evaluate the merits of the speaker's position. Third, listening provides support for the speaker and helps create a positive climate for discussion. Without effective listening, no group is going to make much progress.

AVOID INTERPERSONAL CONFLICTS

If groups were made up of robots, there would be no interpersonal conflicts. But groups are made up of people with likes and dislikes, animosities and biases, and very different personalities. It is vital to the group process that disagreements be kept on a task level, rather than on a personal level.

Suppose you disagree with another member's idea. Disagreement on the personal level could sound like this: "That's the most stupid idea I ever heard of! Do you realize how much money it would cost to do that?" But on the task level, disagreement is aimed at the *idea*, not the person: "Potentially that's a very good solution, but I'm not sure we have enough money to accomplish it."

No matter what the group, personal antagonism leaves a bad taste in everyone's mouth and harms the performance of the group. It's essential that someone take a leadership role and bring the discussion back to the relevant issues. Let's say you are part of a committee charged with setting up a speakers' series on your campus. The discussion might go like this:

Jacob:	We should ask Alvin Johnson to speak. He's one of the university's biggest supporters.
Minh:	Are you crazy? He's a gun lobbyist. He's opposed just about every measure to limit gun violence.
Jacob:	That's even more of a reason to invite him. If you had your way, none of us would be allowed to own guns, not even for hunting.
Minh:	You're just another gun nut. It's people like you who stop every reasonable effort to get guns off the streets.
Leader:	Just a minute. This might make a good subject for our speakers' series. We can ask Mr. Johnson and a gun-control advocate to debate each other.

This is not to say that members of a group should never disagree. In fact, a serious problem occurs when members get along so well and are so concerned about maintaining the harmony of the group that they will not disagree with one another about anything. When this happens, there is no chance to reach the best decision by exploring an array of perspectives, opinions, and information. The aim is not for groups to avoid conflict but to keep it at the task level so it will not degenerate into personal feuding.[4]

ENCOURAGE FULL PARTICIPATION

If a group is to work effectively, all members must contribute fully and share their ideas with one another. Every member of a group should take responsibility for encouraging other members to participate. You can do this, first of all, by listening attentively. After all, how would you like to speak in a group where everybody else appears bored or distracted?

If there are one or two quiet members in the group, you can draw them into the discussion by asking their opinions and showing interest in their ideas. When a member speaks, you can say, "I never knew that; can you tell us more about it?" Conversely, try to avoid negative comments that will squelch a speaker before he or she has finished—comments like "Oh, no, that never works" or "What a terrible idea." Supportive comments create goodwill among group members and make everyone feel free to discuss their ideas without ridicule or embarrassment.

If you are shy or afraid your ideas will be taken too critically, you may be unwilling to participate at first. To overcome your diffidence, remember that your contribution is necessary to the group. At the very least, you can help provide a supportive environment for discussion by listening, reacting, and encouraging the free exchange of ideas.[5]

KEEP THE DISCUSSION ON TRACK

In some groups the discussion proceeds like a stream-of-consciousness exercise. Here is a hypothetical example in which a town planning board is considering installing a new traffic light at a busy intersection:

Aaron:	You know, we're going to have trouble getting cars to come to a full stop even if we do put in a traffic light.
Dawn:	Tell me about it! I came through there yesterday and hit my brakes, and the car just kept going. Maybe I need the brakes adjusted, though.
Sharif:	Get ready to pay through the nose. I had a brake job on my car last week, and it was nearly twice as much as last time.
Austin:	That's nothing. Have you looked at lawnmowers lately? And if you think lawnmowers are high. . . .
Camila:	Who mows lawns? I had my yard planted with ground cover and put gravel over the rest. It's . . .
Leader:	Excuse me, folks, but weren't we talking about the traffic light?

Every member has a responsibility to keep the discussion on track and to intervene if the group wanders too far afield. There is nothing wrong with a little casual conversation, but it shouldn't be allowed to get out of hand. When working in a problem-solving group, make sure the group's ultimate goal is always in the forefront. Do your best to see that discussion proceeds in an orderly fashion from one point to the next and that the group does not get bogged down in side issues.

On the other hand, you need to guard against the tendency to progress to a solution too quickly, without thoroughly exploring the problem. If you feel your group is taking the easy way out and jumping at an easy solution, try to make the other members aware of your concern. By suggesting that they talk about the problem in more detail, you may bring out vital information or ideas.

There are systematic ways to keep the discussion on track and to avoid hasty group decisions. Research shows that if your group follows a tested method of decision making, it will have a better chance of reaching a satisfactory outcome.[6] We turn, therefore, to the most common decision-making technique for small groups—the reflective-thinking method.

The Reflective-Thinking Method

reflective-thinking method

A five-step method for directing discussion in a problem-solving small group.

The reflective-thinking method is derived from the writings of the American philosopher John Dewey. It offers a step-by-step process for discussion in problem-solving groups and consists of five steps: (1) defining the problem; (2) analyzing the problem; (3) establishing criteria for solving the problem; (4) generating potential solutions; (5) selecting the best solution. As we look at these steps, we'll illustrate each by following a single group through the entire reflective-thinking process.

DEFINE THE PROBLEM

Before a problem-solving group can make progress, it must know exactly what problem it is trying to solve. Defining the problem for group discussion is akin to settling

In effective groups, all members participate fully and interact positively with each other. They also feel that their contributions are respected and valued by the full group.

JohnnyGreig/E+/Getty Images

on a specific purpose for a speech. Unless it is done properly, everything that follows will suffer.

The best way to define the problem is to phrase it as a question of policy. As we saw in Chapter 16, questions of policy inquire about the necessity or practicality of specific courses of action. They typically include the word "should." For example:

question of policy
A question about whether a specific course of action should or should not be taken.

> What measures should our school take to protect free speech on campus?
>
> What should the federal government do to deal with income inequality?
>
> What policy should the United States adopt with respect to the exploitation of child labor in other countries around the world?

When phrasing the question for discussion, your group should follow several guidelines. First, make sure the question is as clear and specific as possible. For example:

Ineffective: What should be done about on-campus security?

More Effective: What measures should our school take to improve on-campus security for students?

Second, phrase the question to allow for a wide variety of answers. Be especially wary of questions that can be answered with a simple yes or no. For example:

Ineffective: Should the city build a new elementary school?

More Effective: What steps should the city take to deal with increasing enrollment in the elementary schools?

Third, avoid biased or slanted questions. For example:

Ineffective: How can we keep predatory student-loan vendors from ripping off students?

More Effective: What changes, if any, should be made in the practices of student-loan vendors?

Fourth, make sure you pose a single question. For example:

Ineffective: What revisions should the college consider in its admissions requirements and in its graduation requirements?

More Effective: What revisions should the college consider in its admissions requirements?

More Effective: What revisions should the college consider in its graduation requirements?

To clarify this first step of the reflective-thinking method, let's see how our model problem-solving group defined the problem:

> As a class project, the group set out to discuss the problem of rising costs for attending college. Following the reflective-thinking method, they began by defining the problem. After several false starts, they phrased the problem this way: "What steps should our school take to reduce student costs for attending college?"

ANALYZE THE PROBLEM

After the problem has been defined, the group begins to analyze it. Too often, groups (like individuals) start mapping out solutions before they have a firm grasp of what is wrong. This is like a doctor prescribing treatment before fully diagnosing the patient's ailment. If your group investigates the problem as thoroughly as possible, you will be in a much better position to devise a workable solution.

In analyzing the problem, pay particular attention to two questions. First, how severe is the problem? Investigate its scope. Determine how many people it affects. Assess what might happen if it is not resolved. Second, what are the causes of the problem? Check the history of the problem and learn what factors contributed to it.

As you might imagine, analyzing the problem requires research. Effective group decisions depend on having the best information available. You can get this information in the same way you gather materials for a speech. Sometimes you can rely on your own knowledge and experience. More often, you need to get information from other sources—by looking on the Internet, by interviewing someone with expertise on the topic, or by working in the library (see Chapter 7). When meeting with your group, make sure you have done the research assigned to you so you can offer complete and unbiased information.

Let's return now to our sample group and see how it analyzed the problem of rapidly escalating student costs for attending college:

> The group talked first about the severity of the problem. Tuition had risen dramatically, as had outlays for books and incidentals. One member found statistics showing that the cost of attending college had more than

The goal of a problem-solving small group is to make sound recommendations. Doing so requires thorough research about the nature of the problem and the practicality of potential solutions.

Weedezign/Alamy Stock Photo

doubled in the past 10 years. Another provided evidence that average annual costs were now more than $25,000 for students at in-state public colleges and universities, and roughly $50,000 for students at private schools.

To determine the causes of the problem, the group researched articles about the rise in student costs for attending college across the nation. They also interviewed an economics professor and the head of the student aid program on campus. After studying the matter thoroughly, the group identified several major causes, including administrative costs, faculty salaries, the price of textbooks, and increased living expenses.

ESTABLISH CRITERIA FOR SOLUTIONS

If you planned to buy a car, how would you proceed? You would probably not just walk into a showroom and buy whatever appealed to you on the spur of the moment. You would most likely decide ahead of time what kind of car you wanted, what options it should have, and how much money you could spend. That is, you would establish *criteria* to guide you in deciding exactly which car to buy.

criteria
Standards on which a judgment or decision can be based.

You should do the same thing in group discussion. Once your group has analyzed the problem, you should not jump immediately to proposing solutions. Instead, you should establish criteria—standards—for responsible solutions. You should work out (and write down) exactly what your solutions must achieve and any factors that might limit your choice of solutions.

To get a better idea of how this stage of the reflective-thinking method works, let's look at the cost-cutting group we have been following:

After some discussion, the group established these criteria for possible solutions: (1) The solution should significantly reduce students' costs. (2) The solution should come into force at the start of the next school year. (3) The solution should not hurt the prestige of the college. (4) The cost of the solution should be minimal and should be paid by the administration. (5) The human resources needed to implement the solution should come from administrative personnel already working on the school's staff. (6) The solution should involve only actions controlled by the college—not matters controlled by outside individuals or agencies.

GENERATE POTENTIAL SOLUTIONS

Once your group has the criteria firmly in mind, you are ready to discuss solutions. Your goal at this stage is to come up with the widest possible range of potential solutions—not to judge the solutions. One member of the group should be responsible for writing down all the solutions proposed at this time.

brainstorming
A method of generating ideas by free association of words and thoughts.

Many groups find the technique of brainstorming helpful in this stage. In Chapter 5, we discussed how brainstorming can work for an individual in choosing a speech topic. Here brainstorming is expanded to the whole group.

The best approach is to begin by having each member of the group write down all the possible solutions he or she can think of. One person should then consolidate the individual lists into a master list. The group should discuss the master list to make sure potential solutions have not been overlooked.

At this stage, members often "piggyback" new ideas onto ideas on the master list. For example, if one suggestion is "Establish food co-ops," a group member might say, "Yes, and we could establish clothing co-ops, too." One member should write down these new ideas and add them to the master list. The brainstorming process continues until the group can't think of any more solutions.

Brainstorming in this fashion has two advantages. First, it encourages creativity. Research shows that beginning with written lists usually produces more and higher-quality ideas than relying solely on oral discussion.[7] Second, this method of brainstorming encourages equal participation. Having each member create his or her own list makes it less likely that one or two members will dominate the process or that anyone will hold back ideas for fear of being hooted down.

Let's see how our cost-cutting group handled this stage:

> By brainstorming, the group came up with the following possible solutions: (1) reduce the number of required books for each course; (2) cut some of the "fat" from the administrative staff; (3) make all professors teach more courses; (4) approach landlords about stabilizing rent and utility costs; (5) establish food and clothing co-ops; (6) increase financial aid; (7) decrease the amount of money available for faculty research; (8) boycott businesses around the campus where price markups are highest; (9) increase out-of-state tuition; (10) decrease dormitory expenses; (11) organize fund-raising programs with the student government; (12) redirect some money from construction of new buildings to student aid. This was a good yield from a brainstorming session—twelve solid suggestions.

SELECT THE BEST SOLUTION

After all potential solutions have been listed, it is time to evaluate them. The best way to proceed is to discuss each solution with regard to the criteria established earlier, then move to the next solution, and so on. This orderly process ensures that all potential solutions receive equal consideration.

As each potential solution is discussed, the group should try to reach consensus. A consensus decision is one that all members accept, even though the decision may not be ideal in the eyes of every member. Because it usually results in superior decisions as well as in a high degree of unity within the group, consensus is the ideal of group decision making. It comes about when members have been so cooperative that they reach a common decision through reasoning, honest exchange of ideas, and full examination of the issues.

Like most ideals, consensus can be difficult to achieve. If there are different viewpoints, members of the group will often try to find the easiest way to resolve the differences. Sometimes a member will call for a vote, which is very agreeable to those holding a majority opinion but not so pleasant for those in the minority. Resorting to a vote does resolve the immediate conflict, but it may not result in the best solution. Moreover, it weakens unity in the group by fostering factions and perhaps by creating bitterness among the members who lose the vote. A group should vote only when it has failed in every other attempt to agree on a solution.[8]

What kind of final decision did our model cost-cutting group reach? Let's see:

> The cost-cutting group had twelve possible solutions to evaluate. Three were rejected because they violated the group's criterion that an acceptable solution must involve only actions controlled directly by the college.

consensus
A group decision that is acceptable to all members of the group.

✔ checklist

Reflective-Thinking Method

YES	NO	
☐	☐	1. Did the group clearly define the problem for discussion?
☐	☐	2. Did the group phrase the question for discussion as a question of policy?
☐	☐	3. Did the group phrase the question for discussion as clearly as possible?
☐	☐	4. Did the group phrase the question for discussion so as to allow for a wide variety of answers?
☐	☐	5. Did the group phrase the question for discussion in an unbiased manner?
☐	☐	6. Did the group phrase the question for discussion as a single question?
☐	☐	7. Did the group analyze the problem thoroughly before attempting to map out solutions?
☐	☐	8. Did the group establish criteria for an ideal solution to the problem before discussing specific solutions?
☐	☐	9. Did the group brainstorm to generate a wide range of potential solutions to the problem?
☐	☐	10. Did the group evaluate each potential solution in light of the criteria for an ideal solution?
☐	☐	11. Did the group make a determined effort to reach consensus with regard to the best solution?
☐	☐	12. Did the group achieve consensus?

Three more solutions were rejected because they were economically impractical. Increasing financial aid would hurt many students because the funds would have to come from student fees. Raising out-of-state tuition would drive away too many out-of-state students. And decreasing dorm costs would make it impossible to provide minimally acceptable services.

The proposal to reduce funds for faculty research was also rejected since most research money comes from government, corporations, and foundations. Finally, the suggestion to reduce administrative "fat" was rejected as too costly because a group would have to be established to audit all administrative duties.

After refining the suggestions, the group finally reached consensus on a solution that included the following provisions: (1) A student should not have to spend more than $200 on required books for any single course. (2) The university should authorize the student government to organize food, book, and clothing co-ops. (3) The student government should conduct five fund-raising projects each academic year. (4) Each professor should teach one more class a year.

Once consensus has been reached, the group is ready to present its findings.

Presenting the Recommendations of the Group

The work of a problem-solving group does not end with the last stage of the reflective-thinking process. Once a group has agreed on its recommendations, it usually needs to present them to somebody. A business group might report to the president of the company or to the board of directors. A presidential commission reports to the president and to the nation at large. A classroom group reports to the instructor and to the rest of the class. The purpose of such reports is to present the group's recommendations clearly and convincingly.

Sometimes a group will prepare a formal written report. Often, however, the written report is supplemented with—or replaced by—an oral report, a symposium, or a panel discussion.

ORAL REPORT

oral report
A speech presenting the findings, conclusions, or decisions of a small group.

An oral report is much the same in content as a written report. If the group has a designated leader, she or he will probably deliver the report. Otherwise, the group will select one person for the job.

If you are picked to present your group's report, you should approach it as you would any other speech. Your task is to explain the group's purpose, procedures, and recommendations. Your report should have three main sections. The introduction will state the purpose of the report and preview its main points. The body will spell out the problem addressed by your group, the criteria set for a solution, and the solution being recommended. The conclusion will summarize the main points and, in some cases, urge that the group's recommendations be adopted.

As with any other speech, you should adapt your report to the audience. Use supporting materials to clarify and strengthen your ideas, and consider whether visual aids will enhance your message. Make sure your language is accurate, clear, vivid, and appropriate. Rehearse the report so you can deliver it fluently and decisively. Afterward, you—and possibly other members of the group—may be called on to answer questions from the audience.

SYMPOSIUM

A symposium consists of a moderator and several speakers seated together in front of an audience. If the group presenting the symposium has a designated leader, she or he will typically be the moderator. The moderator's job is to introduce the topic and the speakers. Each speaker delivers a prepared speech on a different aspect of the topic. After the speeches, there may be a question-and-answer session.

symposium
A public presentation in which several people present prepared speeches on different aspects of the same topic.

The symposium is often used for group reports in speech classes. One way to organize it is to have each member of the group present a brief talk sketching the group's work and decisions during one stage of the reflective-thinking process. Another way is to have each speaker deal with a major issue relating to the discussion topic. A group dealing with capital punishment, for example, might have one speaker present the group's conclusion on the issue of whether capital punishment is an effective deterrent to crime, another speaker present the group's position on the morality of capital punishment, and so forth.

All the speeches should be carefully planned. They should also be coordinated with one another to make sure the symposium reports on all important aspects of the group's project.

PANEL DISCUSSION

A panel discussion is essentially a conversation in front of an audience. The panel should have a moderator who introduces the topic and the panelists. Once the discussion is under way, the moderator may interject questions and comments as needed to focus the discussion. The panelists speak briefly, informally, and impromptu. They talk to each other, but loudly enough for the audience to hear. As with a symposium, a panel discussion may be followed by a question-and-answer session.

panel discussion
A structured conversation on a given topic among several people in front of an audience.

Because of its spontaneity, a panel discussion can be exciting for participants and audience alike. But, unfortunately, that spontaneity inhibits systematic presentation of a group's recommendations. Thus the panel discussion is seldom used by problem-solving groups, although it can work well for information-gathering groups.

If you are a participant in a panel discussion, beware of the common fallacy that no serious preparation is required. Although you will speak impromptu, you need to study the topic ahead of time, analyze the major issues, and map out the points you want to make. An effective panel discussion also requires planning by the moderator and panelists to decide what issues will be discussed and in what order. Finally, all panelists must be willing to share talking time, so the discussion is not monopolized by one or two people.

Whatever method your group uses to present its findings, you will benefit from the public speaking guidelines given throughout this book. The techniques of effective speech remain the same whether you are one person addressing an audience, part of a small group of people working to solve a problem, or a participant in a symposium or a panel discussion.

Summary

A small group consists of three to twelve people assembled for a specific purpose. A problem-solving small group is formed to solve a particular problem. When such a group has effective leadership, it usually makes better decisions than individuals do by themselves.

Most groups have a designated leader, an implied leader, or an emergent leader. Some groups have no specific leader, in which case all members of the group must assume leadership responsibilities. An effective leader helps a group reach its goals by fulfilling procedural needs, task needs, and maintenance needs.

Apart from leadership, all members of a group have five basic responsibilities. You should commit yourself to the goals of your group, fulfill your individual assignments, avoid interpersonal conflict within the group, encourage full participation by all members, and help keep the group on track.

Your group will also be more successful if it follows the reflective-thinking method, which offers a step-by-step process for decision making in problem-solving groups. The method consists of five steps: (1) defining the problem as clearly and specifically as possible; (2) analyzing the problem to determine its severity and causes; (3) establishing criteria for evaluating solutions; (4) generating a wide range of potential solutions; (5) selecting the best solution(s).

Once your group has agreed on its recommendations, it usually has to make an oral report or participate in a symposium or a panel discussion. Whichever kind of oral presentation your group gives will call for skills of effective speechmaking.

Key Terms

dyad (372)

small group (372)

problem-solving small group (372)

leadership (372)

implied leader (373)

emergent leader (373)

designated leader (373)

procedural needs (374)

task needs (374)

maintenance needs (374)

hidden agenda (376)

reflective-thinking method (378)

question of policy (379)

criteria (381)

brainstorming (382)

consensus (383)

oral report (384)

symposium (385)

panel discussion (385)

Review Questions

After reading this chapter, you should be able to answer the following questions:

1. What is a small group? What is a problem-solving small group?

2. What are the four kinds of leadership that may occur in a small group? Explain the three kinds of needs fulfilled by leadership in a small group.

3. What are the five major responsibilities of every participant in a small group?

4. What are the stages of the reflective-thinking method? Explain the major tasks of a group at each stage.

5. What are the three methods for presenting orally the recommendations of a problem-solving group?

Exercises for Critical Thinking

1. Identify the flaw(s) in each of the following questions for a problem-solving group discussion. Rewrite each question so it conforms to the criteria discussed in the chapter for effective discussion questions.

   a. What should be done to control the utterly ridiculous amount of money paid to college football coaches?

   b. What should be done about child abuse?

   c. What should our state government do to reduce homelessness and to combat drunk driving?

   d. Should the federal government increase funding for the nation's cyber defenses?

2. If possible, arrange to observe a problem-solving small group in action. You might attend a meeting of your city council, the school board, the zoning commission, a local business, or a church committee. To what extent does the discussion measure up to the criteria for effective discussion presented in this chapter? What kind of leadership does the group have, and how well does the leader(s) fulfill the group's procedural needs, task needs, and maintenance needs? How do the other members meet their responsibilities? What aspects of the meeting are handled most effectively? Which are handled least effectively?

3. Identify a relatively important decision you have made in the last year or two. Try to reconstruct how you reached that decision. Now suppose you could remake the decision following the reflective-thinking method. Map out what you would do at each stage of the method. Do you still reach the same decision? If not, do you believe the reflective-thinking method would have led you to a better decision in the first place?

4. Attend a symposium or panel discussion sponsored by a campus organization. Prepare a brief analysis of the proceedings. First, study the role of the moderator. How does she or he introduce the topic and participants? What role does the moderator play thereafter? Does she or he help guide and focus the panel discussion? Does she or he summarize and conclude the proceedings at the end?

   Second, observe the participants. Are the speeches in the symposium well prepared and presented? Which speaker(s) do you find most effective? Least effective? Why? Do participants in the panel discussion share talking time? Does their discussion appear well planned to cover major aspects of the topic? Which panelist(s) do you find most effective? Least effective? Why?

End Notes

[1]Gloria J. Galanes and Katherine Adams, *Effective Group Discussion: Theory and Practice,* 15th ed. (New York: McGraw-Hill, 2019).

[2]See Kyle R. Andrews, Franklin J. Boster, and Christopher J. Carpenter, "Persuading in the Small Group Context," in James Price Dillard and Lijiang Shen (eds.), *The SAGE Handbook of Persuasion: Developments in Theory and Practice,* 2nd ed. (Thousand Oaks, CA: Sage, 2013), pp. 354–370, for a review of scholarship on this subject.

[3]For more on the many dimensions of group leadership, see John W. Gastil, *The Group in Society* (Thousand Oaks, CA: Sage 2010), pp. 139–166.

[4]Consult J. Dan Rothwell, *In Mixed Company: Communicating in Small Groups and Teams,* 11th ed. (New York: Oxford University Press, 2021), for more detail on dealing with conflict in small groups.

[5]For a concise, practical look at the roles and responsibilities of group participants, see Susan A. Wheelan, Maria Akerlund, and Christian Jacobsson, *Creating Effective Teams: A Guide for Members and Leaders,* 6th ed. (Thousand Oaks, CA: Sage, 2020).

[6]Charles Pavitt and Kelly K. Johnson, "Scheidel and Crowell Revisited: A Descriptive Study of Group Proposal Sequencing," *Communication Monographs,* 69 (2002), pp. 19–32.

[7]For research on this subject, see Michele H. Jackson and Marshall Scott Poole, "Idea-Generation in Naturally Occurring Contexts: Complex Appropriation of Simple Group Procedure," *Human Communication Research,* 29 (2003), pp. 560–591.

[8]Scholars often point to the linkages between small groups and democratic norms. See, for example, John Gastil, *Democracy in Small Groups: Participation, Decision Making, and Communication,* 2nd ed. (John Gastil, 2014).

Appendix

Speeches for Analysis and Discussion

Adam Blasberg/Getty Images

One of the biggest challenges facing a public speaker is discussing a technical topic with a general audience. The speaker must find a way to communicate complex ideas so they will be clear and meaningful to people who are not experts in the subject—and who may know little about it in advance of the speech.

The following informative presentation on supervolcanoes shows how a speaker can accomplish this. In addition to reading the speech, you can watch it on Video A.1. As you do so, notice how clearly it is organized, how each point is explained in straightforward, nontechnical language, and how the speaker uses well-designed visual aids to illustrate the power and impact of supervolcanoes.

The speech also provides an excellent example of extemporaneous delivery. The speaker maintains strong eye contact with her listeners, gestures naturally and spontaneously, and uses her voice expressively and engagingly.

connect

View "Supervolcanoes: The Sleeping Giants" in the online Media Library for this appendix (Video A.1).

1 Hurricanes. Earthquakes. Tornados. Tsunamis. We're familiar with these natural disasters. But for all the death and destruction they cause, they're minuscule compared to the full force of planet Earth. Beneath our feet are what *National Geographic* calls "sleeping giants" that "stir occasionally" but will someday wake up and roar with "unprecedented force."

2 What are these sleeping giants? In a word: supervolcanoes. Supervolcanoes don't erupt often, but when they do, they transform our world. As a geoscience major, I've been fascinated by supervolcanoes for a long time, but I know even more about them after doing research for this speech.

3 Today, we'll first examine the mechanics of supervolcanoes. Second, we'll examine the way they shape our world. And third, we'll look at a supervolcano that's located right here in the United States. Let's begin with the mechanics.

4 Supervolcanoes are the result of massive magma pools beneath the earth's surface. Magma consists primarily of molten rock. As a 2014 article in the journal *Nature Geoscience* explains, magma seeps from deep in the earth into giant chambers in the earth's crust, where it cools and hardens. Over time, more magma seeps into the chamber and pushes it toward the surface. Over tens of thousands or even millions of years, enough pressure builds up to produce a supervolcano.

5 Scientists have created a scale to measure volcanic eruptions. It's called the Volcanic Explosivity Index, or VEI, and it's based on the amount of debris released into the atmosphere by an eruption. As seen on this chart from the U.S. Geological Survey, the VEI consists of an eight-step scale; each step is 10 times more powerful than the preceding step.

6 A supervolcano is up here at the top—VEI 8. For comparison, the famous eruption of Mt. Vesuvius that buried the ancient Roman city of Pompeii in 79 A.D. is down here at VEI 5. A supervolcano eruption would be at least 250 times more powerful than Mt. Vesuvius. According to science writer Amanda DeMatto, a supervolcano eruption is like 1,000 atomic bombs going off—every second.

7 Now that we understand some of the basics of supervolcanoes, let's take a look at the ways they've shaped our world. According to the BBC, scientists have identified more than 15 supervolcanoes. As you can see from this map, most are located in East Asia, North America, and South America.

8 The tell-tale sign of an ancient supervolcano is a giant crater known as a caldera. The photo you see here is a caldera that is now Lake Toba, in Indonesia. The largest volcanic lake in the world, it was created by a supervolcano eruption 75,000 years ago. This aerial view from a NASA satellite gives you a sense of the Toba caldera, which is 18 miles wide and 60 miles long.

9 But supervolcanoes don't affect just the immediate area. According to a report on NPR, the amount of ash propelled into the atmosphere by a supervolcano can darken the sky around the world for so long that temperatures decrease by an average of 20 degrees Fahrenheit. A 2017 study in *Nature Communications* states that supervolcano eruptions can produce earthquakes, landslides, and tsunamis that last for tens of thousands of years.

10 Fortunately, the likelihood of any of us being around for a supereruption is almost nonexistent. The last one occurred in New Zealand 26,500 years ago.

11 But there is a supervolcano right here in the United States. It's responsible for this, which I visited last summer. This is Old Faithful, one of 500 geysers in Yellowstone National Park. The park is also home to hundreds of hydrothermal pools, like the one you see here, which is larger than a football field. The geysers and hydrothermal pools are some of the beautiful sites above ground at Yellowstone. But things are quite different under the surface.

12 What's down there? First, there's a large magma chamber, as shown here in a drawing from *National Geographic*. This chamber contains enough magma to fill the Grand Canyon 11 times over. But second, even though this chamber is huge, it's dwarfed in comparison to a giant magma plume that extends more than 20 miles into the earth. When Yellowstone erupts again, all this magma will be devastating.

13 I say when it erupts again because it has erupted three times already— 2.1 million years ago in a large eruption, 1.3 million years ago in a smaller eruption, and 640,000 years ago in a truly massive eruption. According to the U.S. Geological Survey website, this last eruption covered more than half the United States in a layer of ash up to 40 feet deep from California to the Mississippi River. Geologists agree it's only a matter of time until Yellowstone erupts again.

14 In this speech, I've tried to inform you about the sleeping giants beneath our feet. Right now, magma is dripping ever so slowly into giant chambers in the earth. One day, perhaps thousands of years from now, another supervolcano will explode again, changing our world forever. But this is no reason for us to be alarmed today. In fact, to me, it's cause for awe at these sleeping giants and what they can do.

USING A TOURNIQUET TO SAVE A LIFE

Would you know how to apply a tourniquet if one were necessary in an emergency situation? The following demonstration speech shows the correct procedure. As you can judge from reading the speech, it explains each step clearly and concisely.

To get a full sense of it, however, you should watch Video A.2 so you can see how the speaker coordinates his actions with his words, all while maintaining eye contact with his audience. Despite his nerves, he comes across as credible and confident, and his voice conveys a strong sense of communication.

When done well, a demonstration speech looks perfectly natural, but it requires a great deal of planning and rehearsal. If you are going to present such a speech, be sure to give yourself plenty of time to make it as effective as possible.

connect

View "Using a Tourniquet to Save a Life" in the online Media Library for this appendix (Video A.2).

1 It's a bright spring day. You're walking up Bascom Hill on your way to class. Suddenly gunshots ring out. Then screams. You realize students nearby have been shot. The lone gunman flees the scene, and you rush in to help the victims. What can you do?

2 Attacks like these happen far too frequently these days, but I'm not here to scare you. I'm here to equip you with knowledge that you can use to save someone from bleeding to death. It all has to do with this simple strap. Actually, it's more than just a strap—it's a tourniquet. As the *Journal of Emergency Medical Services* explains, a tourniquet "can be applied quickly, with minimal personnel and no other equipment." Today, I'd like to demonstrate how you can apply it in emergency situations.

3 As you know from my intro speech, I was in the Marine Corps for five years. That's where I first learned how to apply a tourniquet. Researching this speech gave me even more helpful information. I'll start by discussing when a tourniquet should be used. Then I'll demonstrate how to apply a standard Combat Application Tourniquet. Finally, I'll show you what you do if you don't have a Combat Application Tourniquet and have to improvise. Let's start off with when to use a tourniquet.

4 Tourniquets are useful in situations where somebody is hemorrhaging or bleeding heavily from a limb. This could include somebody who has been shot, stabbed, or in a serious accident. An article last year in *Prehospital Emergency Care* explains that in these situations, tourniquets are "a useful method to forestall the catastrophic effects" of rapid blood loss.

5 To assess whether a person needs a tourniquet, look for severe or rapid blood loss from the victim's arms or legs. If you see rapid blood loss, a tourniquet is a good idea. However, if you do not see rapid blood loss, or if the blood loss is happening from the torso, then a tourniquet probably won't help.

6 Now that we know when to use a tourniquet, let's look at how to apply one. I'll be using this Combat Application Tourniquet—or CAT—the same tourniquet used by military, law enforcement, fire-fighters, and paramedics. It's standard in many first-aid kits. For this demonstration, let's imagine that the wound we're treating is on the leg, right here.

7 Now let's use the five steps laid out by the National Institutes of Health— the same steps I learned in the Marine Corps. First, remove all clothing from the wound to prevent the tourniquet from slipping. Second, undo the band and place the tourniquet two to four inches above the wound—like this. Third, tighten the band snug to the skin. Fourth, twist the tension rod clockwise until you cannot twist it any further. Fifth, lock the rod into place, and place the white band over it.

8 If possible, write down the time of application on the white band with a pencil or pen or anything that will write, like lipstick. It's crucial to record or remember the time. As University of Texas health sciences professor Robert Sippel states, if a tourniquet is left on for more than two hours, it could result in permanent nerve damage to the limb. Once the tourniquet is applied, wait with the injured person until emergency personnel arrive.

9 Now what if you don't have a CAT available? In that case, it's easy to improvise. The best way to improvise is with a belt, a scarf, or even a T-shirt. Without a CAT rod, you can use a pen, pencil, or even a stick.

10 For this demonstration, I'm going to use a scarf and a pencil. First, tie the scarf into a loose knot around the limb. Then insert the pencil into the knot, tighten the knot, and twist the pencil until you cannot twist it any further. Hold in place until emergency personnel arrive.

11 In conclusion, whether it's a traditional CAT or something improvised, tourniquets can be a life-saver. Today I've showed you when to apply a tourniquet and how to apply one. I hope you're never in a situation where a tourniquet is needed, but if you are, you now know what to do.

LADY LIBERTY

As America's most famous structural symbol, the Statue of Liberty is an excellent topic for an informative speech—but only if the speaker goes beyond clichés and common knowledge so listeners will learn something new and interesting. The following speech does just that as it explores the statue's symbolism, history, and architecture.

As you read the speech, notice how it applies the principles of effective informative speaking explored in Chapter 15. It is sharply organized, employs well-chosen supporting materials, and explains technical ideas in clear, nontechnical language.

It is also dynamically delivered and utilizes a number of superb visual aids to enhance interest and communication. Most notable is the creative use of PowerPoint in paragraph 12 to visualize for listeners the iron skeleton that supports the Statue of Liberty's thin copper exterior. You can view all these aspects of the speech on Video A.3.

connect
View "Lady Liberty" in the online Media Library for this appendix (Video A.3).

1 If you've ever been to New York, you've probably seen it. I used to see it almost every day growing up on Staten Island, in New York Harbor. And even though its skin has turned green with age, it remains vibrant. I'm talking, of course, about the Statue of Liberty. This 220 tons of copper and iron is a powerful symbol of our country.

2 Now, America isn't perfect, and we sometimes fall short of our ideals, but the Statue of Liberty remains a part of our lives. We see it all the time in movies, on television, and in advertisements. The statue has become so familiar that we sometimes don't think about it. But we should. As Neil Kotler, an historian at the Smithsonian Institute, says, the statue is "a monument of breathtaking proportions."

3 I've been fascinated with the Statue of Liberty ever since I was a kid, but I never knew just how amazing it is until I started researching it for this speech. This morning, I'd like to tell you a bit about its symbolism, its history, and its architecture. By the end, I hope you'll understand why this familiar structure is a modern marvel. Let's start with its symbolism, moving from the top of the statue to the bottom.

4 At the top is the statue's most famous symbol—the torch. Ever since the statue was built, the torch has been a beacon to immigrants. It's the torch that prompted the poet Emma Lazarus to pen the famous lines that are inscribed on the pedestal of the statue: "Give me your tired, your poor, your huddled masses yearning to breathe free. . . . I lift my lamp beside the golden door!"

5 Down from the torch is the Statue of Liberty's crown. Coming out from the crown are seven rays—one for each continent. As the National Park Service explains on its Statue of Liberty website, these rays symbolize the importance of liberty around the world.

6 Less famous than the crown and the torch are the chains at the foot of the Statue of Liberty. As you can see here, the chains are broken. *National Geographic* explains that the broken chains represent the abolition of slavery and the Union's victory in the U.S. Civil War, which ended not long before the statue was built.

7 As we shall see next, the symbolism of the statue takes on added significance when we take a look at its history. Historian Edward Berenson, author of *The Statue of Liberty: A Transatlantic Story,* explains how the statue was created. At a dinner party in France in 1865, two men, Edouard de Laboulaye and Frederic Bartholdi, came up with the idea of building a statue for the United States. Laboulaye was an expert on American politics and wanted to commemorate the end of slavery. Bartholdi was a brilliant young sculptor who envisioned a colossal monument he called "Liberty Enlightening the World."

8 Construction of the statue began in 1876 and was completed 10 years later. All the building was done in France. You can see in this photo what the statue looked like with the buildings of Paris in the background. After the statue was finished, it was taken down as you can see here, put in boxes, and shipped to New York, where it was reconstructed.

9 When the statue was unveiled in New York, more than 1 million people flocked to the harbor to see it. Shown in this painting, the celebration was one of the biggest in American history. "Liberty Enlightening the World" had finally found its permanent home.

10 Today we take the Statue of Liberty for granted, but it was considered an architectural marvel when it was built. If you look at the statue from the outside, it looks solid—like it's made completely of stone. But looks can be deceiving.

11 The statue's exterior is not made of stone, but of copper. And it's only 2.4 millimeters thick—not much thicker than this penny. Yet despite its thin copper skin, the statue stands 151 feet tall and towers 305 feet above the water, if you include the pedestal. Think about the wind and the weather that have beaten against it for 130 years. The thin copper skin wouldn't be able to survive without something really strong underneath.

12 So what is underneath? As represented in this slide, there's an iron skeleton underneath the copper skin. Darcy Grigsby, author of the 2012 book *Colossal,* explains that the skeleton is made of a 92-foot-tall pylon that is stuck deep in the stone pedestal. The skeleton has flat metal bars that connect the copper skin to the pylon. These bars work like springs; they provide the strength and flexibility that allow the Statue of Liberty to survive the harsh weather of New York Harbor.

13 If the interior design of the Statue of Liberty reminds you at all of this structure, that's because it was created by the same man who would later build the Eiffel Tower. You can definitely see similarities between the open structure of the Eiffel Tower and the engineering principles employed in the interior design of the Statue of Liberty.

14 Architectural historian Yasmin Sabina Khan says in her book *Enlightening the World* that the statue's design was such a stunning technical achievement that people referred to it at the time as the eighth wonder of the world.

15 In conclusion, I hope I've shown you some of the reasons why the Statue of Liberty remains a wonder of the world. Its symbolism, history, and architecture make this 220 tons of copper and iron a modern marvel. So the next time you're in New York City, the next time you see the statue on television, in movies, in magazines, just remember—there's a lot more to it than meets the eye.

According to a recent study, half of American adults were exposed to dangerous levels of lead when they were children. Much of this exposure came from the nation's water supply, which is the subject of the following persuasive speech on a question of policy.

In arguing for federal legislation to reduce lead levels in the water supply, the speaker presents a range of high-quality supporting materials. To demonstrate the seriousness of the problem, he cites news organizations, ordinary citizens, researchers, and government agencies. To support his solution, he cites elected representatives and environmental groups. Taken together, these sources help skeptical listeners understand the need for action and the practicality of the speaker's plan.

As you can see by viewing the speech on Video A.4, the speaker also uses visual aids to clarify his points and to help the audience keep track of his ideas. Poised and confident, he has excellent energy, eye contact, and vocal variety.

connect

View "Getting the Lead Out" in the online Media Library for this appendix (Video A.4).

1 "It's crazy. It's like a third-world country." That's what Carlos Young said. "I thought I was going to die." That's what Joyce Wilson said. "Disgusting. They need to fix the problem." That's what Mitchell Gerow said.

2 These voices, from the Michigan news website *MLive,* represent only a few of the thousands of people who endured the Flint, Michigan, water crisis of 2015–2017. The crisis happened when Michigan changed the way Flint received its water. Because of this change, lead levels in the city's water supply skyrocketed. People couldn't drink the water, couldn't bathe with it, couldn't cook with it. Thousands became ill, and the full health consequences will continue for decades.

3 But the problem of lead in America's water supply goes far beyond Flint. A 2016 investigation by the news agency Reuters found 3,000 water systems across the United States with lead levels higher than Flint. Even right here in Madison, local officials recently found elevated lead in the drinking water at six public schools.

4 Before working on this speech, I hadn't realized the extent of lead in our drinking water. And according to my class survey, most of you don't consider it a major health risk. But now I'm convinced that we cannot continue to ignore this problem.

5 Today, I'll explain the extent of the problem and why it's so dangerous. Then I'll look at a plan of action that can help solve the problem. Getting the lead out of our water supply won't be easy, but it's something we have to do—for the sake of our generation and future generations. Let's start by looking at the scope of the problem.

6 Lead in our drinking water comes primarily from lead pipes that carry water into our homes, offices, schools, and dormitories. It's hard to say exactly how many lead pipes are out there. A 2016 article in the *Detroit Free Press* explains that most cities didn't track the use of lead pipes historically. However, a recent study by Joseph Ferrie, an economist at Northwestern University, shows that around 6 million homes receive water through lead pipes. Another 81 million homes receive water through pipes with lead soldering and fixtures, which can leach just as much lead into the water supply as the pipes themselves.

7 Drinking water contaminated with lead causes a number of serious, potentially deadly health problems. According to the Environmental Protection

Agency, in adults those problems include high blood pressure, joint and muscle pain, memory loss, mood disorders, problems with pregnancy, and more.

8 But the health effects are much worse in children—brain damage, learning difficulties, behavioral problems, ADHD, seizures, and more. Most troublesome is the fact that these problems are not temporary. As science writer Alexandra Ossola stated at the time of the Flint crisis, "Lead is toxic. If it makes its way into the still-developing brains of young children, many of the effects can be permanent."

9 The Environmental Protection Agency, working through its branches in every state, is supposed to test and regulate lead levels, but not enough is being done. Right now, the EPA defines excess levels of lead in water as 15 parts per billion. When lead gets that high, utility companies are supposed to enact a treatment plan and get lead levels down.

10 However, a 2016 study by CNN found that 5,300 water supply systems are currently in violation of this EPA rule, and many more systems don't test their water at all. Out of those 5,300 violations, the EPA has taken action in only 88 cases—that's fewer than 2 percent of the violations. According to Erik Olson of the Natural Resources Defense Council, far too often "neither the states nor the EPA take any formal enforcement action," leaving "millions and millions of people" at risk.

11 Now that we've seen the problem of lead pollution in our drinking water, what can be done about it? I support a plan originally proposed in Congress by Senator Ben Cardin of Maryland. Known as the TrueLEADership Act, it has three main parts:

12 First, it would provide $70 billion over 10 years to fund the removal of lead pipes by utility companies, municipalities, neighborhoods, and homeowners. This will give cities and property owners a financial incentive to start removing lead pipes now, before the problem gets worse.

13 Second, the plan would require all water utilities to regularly test and report on the amount of lead that they pump into our homes. This will provide public information that we all have a right to know about the amount of lead in our water. It will also identify the water systems most in need of immediate attention.

14 Third, the plan would provide special support for children who live in areas with elevated lead in the water supply. This will be crucial as the affected kids learn and develop.

15 This plan would be practical and effective. It has support from such public health and environmental organizations as Clean Water Action, Earth Justice, and the American Public Health Association. It also has broad support in the U.S. Senate with 30 co-sponsors, including our own Senator Tammy Baldwin. As Baldwin states, the bill will "invest in better solutions to confront water problems throughout the country by building a modern, made-in-America water infrastructure."

16 In conclusion, I hope you now understand the problem of lead in our water supply and how we can begin to solve it. There is no reason why any child or adult in America should suffer from lead poisoning caused by their drinking water.

17 The time has come to get the lead out of our water supply so we will never again have a tragedy like that in Flint, Michigan. You have a right to drink clean, healthy water, and so does everyone else in the United States.

THE LIVING-WAGE SOLUTION

Despite the existence of a federal minimum wage, millions of fully employed people in the United States do not earn enough money to rise above the poverty line. The following persuasive speech on a question of policy argues that one way to address this problem is by replacing the minimum wage with a living wage, which can be adjusted to local conditions and expenses.

The speech is organized in problem-solution order. After establishing the need for a living wage, the speaker sets forth her policy and explains how it would work. Notice how clearly she goes through her main points and supports them with high-quality, expert evidence. Knowing that some listeners were skeptical about mandating a living wage, she takes care to address their reservations and to demonstrate the practicality of her plan.

Because the speaker advances a complex argument and employs a wide range of supporting materials, she also utilizes visual aids to clarify her points and help the audience keep track of her ideas. You can view the speech on Video A.5.

connect

View "The Living-Wage Solution" in the online Media Library for this appendix (Video A.5).

1 José Morales was sleeping on cardboard boxes in a garage in Compton, California. Before the sun came up, he would walk to a nearby bus stop, where he would ride the bus for two hours to Los Angeles International Airport, where he worked as a janitor. On two occasions, he was mugged while waiting for the bus. Working 40 hours a week for minimum wage, this was the best he could do.

2 But then José's situation improved drastically. As Robert Pollin, an economist at the University of Massachusetts, reports, José received health insurance and a 36 percent raise. He had enough money to rent his own apartment and to buy a car. It all happened because José started to receive the living wage.

3 What is the living wage, you ask? Well, it's not the same as the minimum wage. The minimum wage is set by Congress and is the same in every part of the country. The living wage goes beyond the minimum wage. As the *Wall Street Journal* reported in August 2013, the living wage is tied to the local cost of living and can vary from location to location. Its purpose is to help workers and their families meet the most basic standard of living, even when that standard of living is higher than the minimum wage.

4 I first heard about the living wage last semester in my econ class. After researching it for this speech, I've come to the same conclusion as numerous economists and public-policy researchers. The living wage can help the working poor without adversely affecting businesses or the health of the economy.

5 That's why we need to pass federal legislation mandating a living wage—a wage that can help people secure the basic necessities of life. So let's first look at the difficulties faced by the working poor, and then we'll look at the living-wage solution.

6 Poverty remains a significant problem in the United States in part because wages have not kept up with the cost of living. According to a recent study by the Bureau of Labor Statistics, more than 46 million Americans live in poverty. Of these 46 million, 10 million are referred to as the "working poor"—people who are employed at least 27 weeks a year and who are still stuck in poverty. Of these 10 million people, half—5 million—are employed full time. They work 40 hours a week, 52 weeks a year, but they still can't make ends meet.

7 How can that be? It happens in part because of the federal minimum wage. Since 2009, the minimum wage has been $7.25 an hour. If you calculate that, someone working full time would earn just over $15,000 a year. For an individual, that's just above the poverty line. The problem comes when there are two-, three-, or four-person households—as with a single mother trying to squeak by. It's almost impossible to raise a family on $15,000 a year.

8 Another problem is that the federal minimum wage doesn't change until Congress changes it—and we all know how long it can take for Congress to do anything. In fact, it took Congress more than 10 years to raise the minimum wage from its previous $5.25 to its current rate of $7.25. As a result, millions of workers were still earning in 2008 what they had earned in 1998.

9 The result was "a lost decade for wage growth," according to *The State of Working America*, published in 2012 by Cornell University Press. The same book predicts another lost decade if we don't take action soon.

10 So what can we do? How can we help make sure that people who work full time earn enough money to lift themselves and their families above the poverty level? One way is to implement a federally mandated living wage.

11 The first city in America to institute a living wage was Baltimore, in 1994. Since then, the living-wage movement has spread to more than 140 jurisdictions. However, as David Neumark, Matthew Thompson, and Leslie Koyle reported in a 2012 issue of the *Journal of Labor Policy,* most living-wage laws cover only people who work for companies with government contracts. At best only 1 percent of workers in a city receive the living wage. It's time to cover everyone who works full time—and to do so with a national living-wage law.

12 Here's how such a law would work. First, we would calculate the living wage for every county in the United States. To do that, we'd use the living-wage calculator created by Amy Glasmeier, a professor of Urban Studies and Planning at MIT.

13 Based on this calculator, the living wage in Chicago, my hometown, for this year would be $10.48 per hour. In Dallas, it would be $9.29. In New York, it would be $12.75. As you can see, there is large variation in the cost of living across different parts of the country. A national living wage would account for these variations.

14 Second, we would tie the living wage to the Consumer Price Index. The Consumer Price Index tracks the price of goods and services in different parts of the country. As the Consumer Price Index increases, the living wage would increase at the same rate.

15 In Chicago, the Consumer Price Index rose by 2 percent last year. The living wage in that city would then go from $10.48 an hour to $10.69 an hour. And it would cover everyone who works full time, whether they work for the government or in the private sector. In this way, we can ensure that wages for everyone keep up with the cost of living.

16 As you might expect, there is opposition to instituting a living-wage policy. Those who oppose the living wage offer two main arguments. First, they argue that the living wage would be too costly for businesses. But that's not what Jeff Thompson and Jeff Chapman, researchers at the Economic Policy Institute, found. After surveying existing living-wage laws, they found that the increased cost of wages is offset by higher productivity and lower employee turnover. Happier workers mean stronger businesses.

17 The second argument of critics is that the living wage will lead to fewer jobs. But again the research doesn't bear this out. A 2011 study in *Economic Development Quarterly* by T. William Lester, a professor at the University of North Carolina, found that living-wage laws do not have a large negative impact on employment. In a 2012 study, Lester, who specializes in labor economics, found that living-wage laws can actually "create jobs of higher quality." In addition to being good for workers, a living-wage law can benefit businesses and the economy in general.

18 In conclusion, the time has come to pay American workers a wage that will keep up with the cost of living. We need a federally mandated living wage. In a time of massive corporate profits and skyrocketing executive pay, those at the bottom of society deserve to advance along with those at the top.

19 Those like José Morales, who I mentioned at the start of my speech, deserve a better future. "Everyone thinks that working here at the airport we must earn a lot of money," Morales says. "It's not true, but at least now with the living wage we can hold our heads up high." And that's something everyone working a full-time job should be able to say.

CHANGING LIVES THROUGH THE LITERACY NETWORK

"America's low literacy crisis," states one expert, "is largely ignored, historically under-funded and woefully under-researched, despite being one of the great solvable problems of our time." The following persuasive speech on a question of policy addresses this problem and encourages the student's classmates to join her in volunteering as literacy tutors.

Like many speeches that seek immediate action, this one follows Monroe's motivated sequence. As you read, pay attention to how the speaker develops each step in the motivated sequence—gaining attention, demonstrating a need, presenting a plan, visualizing the benefits of the plan, and calling for action. Also notice how skillfully she uses the methods of persuasion discussed in Chapter 17.

As you can see from Video A.6, the speaker's persuasiveness is further enhanced by her sincere, personable, engaging delivery.

connect

View "Changing Lives Through the Literacy Network" in the online Media Library for this appendix (Video A.6).

1 Imagine being dropped into a foreign country—a country where you can't read the street signs, can't order food from a menu, can't fill out a job application. You're surrounded by scribbles and squiggles that simply don't make sense. Now imagine that that country isn't a foreign one, but your own.

2 That's exactly what people like Dwayne MacNamara experience on a daily basis. A father of two daughters, Dwayne has struggled with reading and writing for years. These struggles made it difficult for him to find a job, to take care of his family, and to develop a positive self-image. "Not being able to read and write as well as other people," Dwayne says, "has taken a life-long toll on my confidence and my ability to make sound decisions."

3 Dwayne is far from alone in dealing with these problems. Low literacy affects millions of adults throughout the United States, including right here in Madison and Dane County.

4 For the past year, I've been volunteering at the Literacy Network—a local, Madison-based, nonprofit organization that helps adults and families with reading, writing, and speaking skills. I've seen the problems people face because of low

literacy, and I've also seen how improved literacy can change people's lives for the better. Today I'd like to encourage you to join me as a volunteer. But first let's look more closely at low adult literacy and the problems it can cause.

5 According to a report from the U.S. Department of Education and National Research Council, more than 30 million adults in the United States lack basic literacy skills. Another 60 million have only basic skills, but little beyond that.

6 When you add these two groups together, 90 million people—more than 40 percent of the adult population—have trouble reading the newspaper, understanding instructions from a doctor, registering to vote, or reading a lease for a place to live. As the National Commission on Adult Literacy states, we face an "adult education crisis that permeates every aspect of American life."

7 The problem is even worse when you consider the social consequences of low adult literacy. According to a report from the American Institutes for Research, 42 percent of people with less-than-basic literacy skills live in poverty. Adults with low literacy are less likely to participate in the workforce, to assist with their children's education, and be involved in their community.

8 Here in Madison we are not immune to these challenges. The Literacy Network estimates that 17,000 people in Dane County lack "the functional literacy skills needed to read a letter from their children's teacher, a label in a grocery store, or instructions from a doctor." Another 38,000 don't know English well enough to perform these tasks.

9 When I interviewed Jeff Burkhart, Executive Director of the Literacy Network, he told me that "even though we live in a university town, thousands of people still struggle with everyday literacy skills necessary for success."

10 So what can you and I do to help combat the problem of low adult literacy? One option is to volunteer at the Literacy Network. It offers a range of services that include basic skills of reading and writing, learning English as a second language, even math and health skills. Best of all, all these services are free. Individuals and families pay absolutely nothing to receive help.

11 But the Literacy Network can only offer its services for free if it has enough volunteers—and that's where you come in. Whatever your skill set, the Literacy Network has a way for you to help. You can join me as a tutor and help improve people's writing, speaking, and reading skills. If tutoring doesn't sound right for you, you can help with data entry, fundraising, or scheduling. There are also positions for photographers and those with computer skills.

12 If you volunteer as a tutor, you don't need prior experience, teaching certification, or fluency in another language. You'll attend a training seminar at which the staff will show you exactly what to do. I have to admit: I was a little nervous during my first training seminar. But it calmed my nerves and helped me understand exactly what I was doing. Then, when I met my adult learner for the first time, I was ready to get started.

13 But, you may be asking, how much time does it take to be a literacy tutor? The usual commitment is two hours a week. It can be before class, after class, during lunch, on the weekends—whatever works best for you. You can even pick the place. I meet my learner in a study room at Memorial Library. It's a convenient spot for both of us.

14 Whether you volunteer as a tutor or in some other capacity, you *will* change the lives of people who have suffered for far too long. Remember Dwayne MacNamara, who I mentioned in my introduction? He lives here—in Madison.

Because of the Literacy Network, he now works at a home-improvement store, where reading instructions and dealing with customers is essential.

15 Dwayne is also able for the first time to help his kids with their homework. He even reads to them every night before bed. "The Literacy Network gave me the skills I needed to succeed," Dwayne says. "I have become more confident, and I am more motivated and excited to go forward with life."

16 Dwayne's experience is matched by many others. Here are some brochures you can take a look at after my speech. They are filled with success stories from people here in Madison whose lives have been changed through literacy.

17 So I hope you will join me as a volunteer. You can help someone's life go from isolation and despair to a life of progress and promise.

18 "Improving Lives Through Literacy"—that's the motto of the Literacy Network. It's a motto I've seen come to life over the past year. And it's a motto I hope you see for yourself by becoming a volunteer. Thank you.

MAKE A WISH

The aim of a commemorative speech is to pay tribute to a person, a group of people, an institution, or an idea. The following talk commemorates the Make-A-Wish Foundation, a nonprofit organization that helps children with life-threatening medical conditions live out one of their dreams. The speaker focuses on three praiseworthy characteristics of Make-A-Wish: its generosity, its selflessness, and its ability to heal through hope. Her family connection to the organization adds an emotional dimension that is often part of commemorative speaking.

As you read the speech, notice the elegance and clarity of the speaker's language and how she begins and ends each main point in parallel fashion. If you watch the speech (Video A.7), you'll see that the speaker's delivery is sincere, confident, and hopeful—just the right tone for the subject matter.

connect

View "Make a Wish" in the online Media Library for this appendix (Video A.7).

1 It was the thrill of her life—a vacation to Walt Disney World. For any five-year-old, it would have been a dream come true. But for this particular five-year-old, it was much more.

2 It was the first time in two months she had been able to leave the children's hospital for more than a few hours. She met Mickey Mouse, who placed a crown on top of her little bald head. She rode the spinning teacups, which helped her forget the upcoming bone-marrow transplant. And she stepped inside Cinderella's castle, where she felt like a princess, if only for a day.

3 This little girl's name is Trisha, and Trisha is my little sister. She has acute lymphoblastic leukemia, a life-threatening form of cancer. Trisha was able to visit Disney World because of a remarkable organization, the Make-A-Wish Foundation. Established in 1980, its mission is to grant "the wishes of children with life-threatening medical conditions to enrich them with hope, strength, and joy." Here is an organization that deserves our recognition because of its generosity, its selflessness, and its ability to heal through hope.

4 First, generosity. The Make-A-Wish Foundation grants all wishes at no expense to the families. The trip to Disney World included Trisha, our parents, and me. The Make-A-Wish Foundation took care of everything.

5 How can it do that? Through the generosity of its donors. Seventy percent of the foundation's revenue comes from donations; the rest comes from business

partners and philanthropists. For children, for families, for those who need hope, Make-A-Wish spends $140 million a year making dreams come true. That's generosity.

6 Second, selflessness. Make-A-Wish Foundation needs people to help grant wishes as much as it needs money. It finds these people in the form of selfless volunteers. From celebrities like Taylor Swift to wrestler John Cena to presidents like Bill Clinton and Barack Obama, Make-A-Wish relies on people who have been given much and who want to give back.

7 But the volunteers aren't just politicians and superstars. They're the people behind the scenes orchestrating the visits and vacations. They're the counselors who help these kids identify their most heartfelt wishes. They're the office workers who enter data, answer phones, and finalize details. Make-A-Wish has 25,000 active volunteers who give their time to help kids like my sister. That's selflessness.

8 Finally, healing. From something as simple as lighting a Christmas tree to becoming a police officer for a day to receiving a visit from stars at Nickelodeon, Make-A-Wish finds a way to help children escape the reality of their illnesses. Not only does this put a smile on their faces, but it gives them hope, and hope can be a powerful thing. It can even pave the road to recovery.

9 Just ask my sister. Today she's sixteen years old and in her junior year of high school. Her cancer is in remission. She's on the dance team, she spends way too much time shopping, and she sends more text messages in a day than I can believe. If you ask her what her turning point was, it was her trip to Disney World. That's healing.

10 Trisha, my parents, and I will always be grateful to the Make-A-Wish Foundation for its generosity, its selflessness, and its ability to heal through hope. Make a wish, because dreams really do come true.

Index

speaking outline for, 238–239
with visual aids, 239, 260–261
Reliability of statistics, 140–141
Religion, of audience, 100
Repetition
to create rhythm, 219
in question-and-answer session, 241–242
Representative statistics, 140
Research
gathering materials through, 112–130
guidelines or tips for, 126–130
internet, 118–123
interviews for, 123–126
library, 114–118
note taking for, 124, 125, 126, 127–129
overview of, 130–131
personal knowledge and experience
for, 112–114
preliminary bibliography, 126–127
for speech topic, 77, 88–89, 112–130
starting early, 126
thinking about material during, 129–130
Residual message, 87
Ressa, Maria, 40, 219
Reverence, appeals to, 330
Rhetoric (Aristotle), 5
Rhetorical questions, 176–177
Rhythm, 218–220
alliteration, 219–220
antithesis, 220
defined, 218
parallelism, 218–219
repetition, 219
Robinson, Felicia, 28–29
Roddick, Courtney, 264
Rodgers, Hendrik, 312
Rodrigo, Olivia, 10
Roosevelt, Franklin, 4, 232

S

Sanchez, Pedro, 21
Sandberg, Sheryl, 94
Sanger, Margaret, 8
Satisfaction, in Monroe's motivated sequence,
303, 304, 305
Scale questions, 106, 107
Schenk, Jeffrey, 26
Search engines, 118
Seinfeld, Jerry, 8
Setting, for speeches, 19, 102–103, 356
Sexual orientation, of audience, 101
Shah, Saanvi, 109
Shakespeare, William, 235, 294
Shields, Alyssa, 49–50

Signposts, 168–169
Similes, 217
Sincerity, for emotional appeal, 332
Singh, Maira, 315
Situation, in speech communication
process, 19
Situational audience analysis
defined, 102
disposition toward occasion, 105
disposition toward speaker, 104–105
disposition toward topic, 103–104
physical setting, 102–103
size of audience, 102
Size
of audience, 102
of visual aids, 255
Skype, 359, 360, 362
Slippery slope fallacy, 328
Small groups
avoid interpersonal conflicts in, 376–377
benefits of, 370, 372
brainstorming in, 382
commit to goals of, 375–376
consensus in, 382, 383
defined, 372
encourage full participation in, 377
fulfill individual assignments in, 376
hidden agenda in, 376
keep discussion on track in, 378
leadership in, 372–375
listening in, 376
overview of, 386
presenting recommendations of, 384–385
problem-solving, 372, 381
reflective-thinking method in, 378–384
responsibilities in, 375–378
Smith, Margaret Chase, 219
Software. *See* Presentation technology
Solution
problem-cause-solution order, 301–302
problem-solution order, 161–162, 300–301
problem-solving small groups, 372, 381
in reflective-thinking method and,
382–384
Sotomayor, Sonia, 314
Source citations
checklist for, 149
format for, 127
for online sources, 149
oral presentation of, 148–150
for paraphrases, 38, 129
for quotations, 36–37, 129
for statistics, 142, 149
for testimony, 148, 149